NEW YORK UNIVERSITY SERIES IN
EDUCATION AND SOCIALIZATION IN AMERICAN HISTORY

General Editor: Paul H. Mattingly

THE CLASSLESS PROFESSION
American Schoolmen of the Nineteenth Century
Paul H. Mattingly

THE REVOLUTIONARY COLLEGE
American Presbyterian Higher Education, 1707–1837
Howard Miller

COLLEGIATE WOMEN
Domesticity and Career in Turn-of-the-Century America
Roberta Frankfort

SCHOOLED LAWYERS
A Study in the Clash of Professional Cultures
William R. Johnson

THE ORGANIZATION OF AMERICAN CULTURE, 1700–1900:
Private Institutions, Elites, and the Origins of American Nationality
Peter Dobkin Hall

AMERICAN COLLEGIATE POPULATIONS
A Test of the Traditional View
Colin B. Burke

OLD DARTMOUTH ON TRIAL
The Transformation of the Academic Community in
Nineteenth-Century America
Marilyn Tobias

THE ORGANIZATION OF AMERICAN CULTURE, 1700–1900:

Private Institutions, Elites, and the Origins of American Nationality

by
Peter Dobkin Hall

New York: NEW YORK UNIVERSITY PRESS: 1982

Library of Congress Cataloging in Publication Data

Hall, Peter Dobkin, 1946–
The organization of American culture, 1700–1900.

(New York University series in education and
socialization in American history)
Includes bibliographical references and index.
1. United States—Social conditions. 2. Social
institutions—United States—History. 3. Historical
sociology. I. Title. II. Series.
HN57.H253   973   81-16806
ISBN 0-8147-3415-4   AACR2

Manufactured in the United States of America

For S.H.P.H. and M.R.H.H.

Contents

CONTENTS

Acknowledgments

As is necessarily the case with a book that has been nearly a decade in the making, my debts are innumerable. First, I would like to thank Burton R. Clark, John Perry Miller, John Simon, and Charles Lindblom for including me as a participant in the Higher Education Research Group and the Program on Non-Profit Organizations at the Institution for Social and Policy Studies at Yale. I am grateful for their willingness to provide financial, secretarial, and research support for my work, for their generosity in sharing their time and insights, and for their courage in bringing together scholars from the social and policy fields to seek new understandings of pressing social problems. Second, I would like to thank James McLachlan, John Whitehead, Donald Meyer, Paul DiMaggio, Thomas Bender, James Winn and the participants in the Wesleyan University History Department Faculty Seminar for their willingness to read and comment on portions of this manuscript. I am especially grateful to William R. Taylor, Rose Laub Coser, Fred Weinstein, David Allmendinger, Paul Mattingly, and C. D. B. Bryan for their friendship, patience and encouragement over the years. I owe a special debt to Karyl Lee Kibler Hall who, in sharing both her own research and her life, has never ceased to remind me that New England is not the hub of the universe.

Stony Creek, Connecticut
1 June 1981

Introduction
The Organization of
American Culture

The title of this book indicates its theme, but not its focus or purpose. Its purpose is to examine the evolution of American nationality, the ability of Americans to conduct their economic, political, and cultural activities on a national scale, as opposed to a local or regional one. To this end, it focuses on the social groups and the institutions through which nationality was achieved. Because private for-profit and non-profit corporate organizations operating first on a local, but ultimately on a national scale replaced the family and the local community as the primary instruments for implementing the fundamental tasks of production, distribution, communication, socialization, and social control, the book concentrates specifically on the rise of social groups whose outlook was national and who were able to translate their national ideals into institutional and operational reality. It is a history of national business and cultural institutions and a national class.

The theme propounded here is that, in America, private organizations took the place of both the state, the family, and the locality in conducting fundamental economic and cultural activities. These private organizations and the groups that created and maintained them contained and redefined the centrifugal and disorderly tendencies of the political and economic marketplace. Family and locality remained as the contexts in which American lived out their lives, but private corporations, operating on a national scale, took over the tasks of coordinating production and distribution, formulating implementing social policy, and shaping the ideological framework and intellectual instruments through which reality was defined and acted on. As private institutions acquired functions hitherto carried out by the family and the locality in a democratic-capitalist marketplace, they became the most powerful institutions in American economic and cultural life, and their creators, administrators, and members became the most influential decision makers in American society. The rise of private corporate institutions brought about political, economic, and cultural nationality. And by the early twentieth century, as the conduct of the modern national state required not only national ideals, but the high levels of technical competence through which such ideals could be translated into social and economic policy, a partnership was formed between the private and public sectors. Out of this partnership came the dominant political consensus, the welfare state liberalism, and the group of policy makers and administrators known as "the Establishment."

1. American Culture Defined

This book is concerned with culture not as a set of aesthetic and intellectual formulations, but as a set of social institutions used by a people in organizing the entire range of their fundamental activities.[1] American culture as it had come to exist by the beginning of the twentieth century had two specific characteristics: it was a mass culture involving the coordination of the activities of nearly one hundred million people across a geographical area of over three and a half million square miles; and the greater part of this task of coordination was conducted by private for-profit and non-profit corporations.[2] American culture in the twentieth century is characterized by masses of individuals who produce goods and services that they do not consume and consume goods and services that they do not produce—and by institutional mechanisms that coordinate the flow of goods and services, as well as the recruitment and training of the managers of those institutions, on a national basis.

In contrast, the culture of Americans before 1850 was local and familial. Most Americans lived in towns and villages of less than 2500 inhabitants which produced the greater part of the food, clothing, shelter, and intellectual and welfare services consumed by their citizens.[3] These goods and services were produced and consumed primarily within the context of the family: of the 7.7 million Americans in the workforce in 1850, 4.9 million operated family farms; the remaining 2.8 million (with the exception of a few hundred thousand who worked on railroads and a handful of large-scale industrial establishments) worked in homes and family businesses.[4] The typical farm was the family farm. The typical business was a "small, personally owned and managed" enterprise.[5] The sources of information, identity, and ambition were local or regional: people read local newspapers and received their career training locally, usually through the family-controlled system of apprenticeship; although many were seeking their fortunes in the West and in the growing cities, most people lived out their lives in the places where they had been born.

The development of a national culture tied these communities together, linking their economies, identities, and life styles to metropolitan centers through the medium of large, privately-controlled corporate institutions. What the railroad and the telegraph did for the economies of American's localities, the rise of the national universities and professional associations did for its intellectual life, its occupational structure, and its world view. Just as the depot and the telegraph office had, by the end of the nineteenth century, become outposts of national economic coordination in nearly every American town and city, so the school, the doctor's office, the lawyer's chambers, the church, and the library became the recruiting stations and transmitters of national intellectual and professional life. Although at the outset the opportunities offered by economic and cultural nationality were ones that Americans were free to accept or reject, by the last decades of the nineteenth century their power began to be perceived in many quarters as irresistible and threatening, giving rise to an assortment of political protest movements. By the 1920s, the power of the elites had become so pervasive that they exercised undeniable influence over every aspect of American life, from child care through diet and career choice.[6]

Mass culture is paradoxical. On the one hand, it is a horizontal phenomenon characterized by equalization and standardization of opportunities and styles of life. Individuals in a modern mass culture are presented with a nearly incalculable range of choices. On the other hand, the equalization and standardization of opportunity for millions of individuals necessitates the existence of elites whose task it is to define and limit the range of choices by gauging and shaping public desires and expectations and bringing them into line with the capacities of the political, economic, and cultural system. These technical and administrative units facilitate the orderly flow of goods, services, and information. In economic life, the elites set and implement policies within and between productive and distributional entities. In intellectual life, these elites, composed of experts in fields ranging from advertising through literature and academic specialities, define the range, consequences, and meaning of individual and collective choices. Indeed, the intellectual sector—the university, the foundation, the professional organization, and the communications industry—provides the fund of information on which economic and governmental policies are based, as well as recruiting the elites themselves. The paradox of mass culture, with its coexistent equality and elite power, is compounded by institutional machinery that connects the masses and the elites. The power of the elites in America has been based not on any formal legal status, but on their ability to perform their chosen tasks competently. And their ability to perform competently has been based, in turn, on their ability to recruit their personnel meritocratically, on the basis of talent and performance, rather than on narrower criteria of ethnicity or kinship.

Thus, while fundamental sectors of social, economic, and political activity in America have, from the mid-nineteenth century, been increasingly dominated by hierarchical large-scale organizations, this domination has been accompanied by an astonishing broadening of opportunities for the masses. And the technical, policy, and managerial elites, rather than opposing or resisting the extension of opportunities for the masses, have championed them. The survival of the private corporation in America, whether as a manufacturing firm producing automobiles for the masses or as a university educating those who will lead and educate the masses, has been based on the willingness of the private sector to embrace public responsibilities and, to paraphrase James McLachlan, on the willingness of the patrician to become a social democrat.

Needless to say, the peculiar configuration of mass culture in America, which has placed so great an importance on the private sector, has exacted a price. Democratic-capitalist culture is, as Tocqueville noted, conformitarian, utilitarian, and materialistic. The creation of the range of opportunities offered by a national culture has not only compromised the survival of local, regional, and ethnic identities, it has also involved, as in the instance of the Civil War and the suppression of radicalism in the twentieth century, outright oppression. Certainly the power of the mass media and national advertising, and the nationalization of intellectual life (especially in the teaching profession), have, viewed critically, amounted to "brainwashing." But the purpose of this book is not to judge whether the national imposition of the standards, life styles, and values of eastern-based Anglo-Americans was a fair exchange for the diversity and complexity of a more heterogeneous and less unified culture. Nor is it concerned with the question of whether a viable national culture could have been developed that was less ethnocentric, more publically accountable, and less centralized and hierarchical. It is, rather, intended as an examination of the social groups and institutions that brought our privately dominated national culture into being.

2. The Problem of American Culture

Describing and analyzing the rise of a set of fundamental institutions and social groups of such immense historical and current significance provides a fascinating challenge to an historian of American culture. Because the private corporation came into being so recently, the scholar has little difficulty in ascertaining when and where the first banks, colleges, hospitals, professional societies, manufacturing and transportation companies were established. He can record with precision at what dates, in what areas, and in what ways national corporate institutions first appeared and continued to grow. And in so doing, he can document the rise of the national technical, managerial, and policy elites and record the development of the organizational forms and personality types that characterize and make possible a large-scale national mass culture. Having outlined the developmental and structural features of American culture, he can begin to suggest the effects of these contextual issues, particularly the issue of private control, on the content of the culture.

This challenge is attractive because it provides an opportunity to deal with the whole sweep of American history as a coherent developmental phenomenon rather than a chronologically arranged jumble of dates, periods, and movements. For all its significance and historical uniqueness, scholars have given little attention to nationality as anything but a political phenomenon. Efforts to view it in terms of the development of business, welfare, or intellectual institutions have been looked on as rather peripheral enterprises.[7] And attempts to examine the common social, economic, and institutional bases of nationality in any of its manifestations have been treated with defensiveness and outright hostility.

Until the 1950s, most American historians only grudgingly acknowledged the linkages between nationality as a political phenomenon and its social, economic, and ideological correlates. Preferring narrative rationalistic accounts of the past, they were repelled by the tendency of more theoretically grounded interpretations to transform what they regarded as a set of unique and non-replicable events into a deterministic set of "ideal types linked only by logical necessity." This reluctance to accept the theories and methods of the social sciences as tools of historical investigation had complex roots in the origins of the discipline itself. The study of American history as an academic enterprise had originated as an effort by spokesmen for northern industrial elites to legitimate the outcome of the Civil War.[8] Stemming as it did from a group of scholars with close personal and professional ties to institutions that were not only intimately identified with the definition of the war's purposes, but also concerned with plotting the course of post-war national development, the account of the American past that emerged was, not surprisingly, a vision of irresistible progress toward a more rational society. This commitment to rationality was reinforced by the structure of the historical profession itself. For as scholars were recruited into the profession meritocratically, they came inevitably to identify their personal achievements with the institutions in which they operated— and these, in turn, with the social groups on which the universities depended for political and economic support. For these reasons, attempts to question the rationality or disinterestedness of actors in the American past were viewed as attacks on the motives and personal accomplishments of historians as individuals, the disinterestedness of the historical profession, and the legitimacy of the social order with which historians and the discipline of history had come to so closely identify itself.

Not until after the second World War, with the emergence of broad and sustained political attacks on intellectuals and privately-controlled institutions of culture and policy-making, did American historians begin to use the social sciences. Searching for a body of ideas through which they might legitimate the achievements of twentieth-century liberalism to which they and their institutions were so closely tied, a new generation of scholars, led by men like Richard Hofstadter, turned to the sociological and psychological critiques of mass culture that had been created by European émigrés to explain the rise of fascism and communism.[9] These critiques became the basis for a comprehensive reinterpretation of American society, past and present, in which the roles of elites and elite institutions were viewed as the sources of stability and freedom in industrial society. In the pluralistic interpretation of American society, politics was seen as conflict "not among groups, but among group leaders, socialized into the dominant values and association of industrial society."[10] By channeling the interests of the masses through a meritocratically recruited and consensually unified leadership structure, social and economic problems could be rationally and disinterestedly solved and the dangers of mass politics avoided.

The pluralist reinterpretation of American society hinged, as M. P. Rogin has pointed out, on the selective application of social theory and analysis. It worked only as long as it could be shown that the pluralists were accurate in demonstrating that mass movements like populism and the "New Right" were irrational and moralistic, while establishment-fostered group politics were rational, disinterested, and, most importantly, successful. The failure of liberal domestic and international policies in the 1960s, combined with the collapse of the liberal political coalition, broke the ties between scholarship and power that had existed since the mid-nineteenth century. With that severance, it has become possible not only to use the tools of social analysis to explore the "interestedness" of the scholarly enterprise and of the national power centers to which it had attached itself, but also to connect this analysis to a reinterpretation of other sectors of social, economic, and political action. It has become possible, in other words, to view the American past holistically: chronology has become a coherent developmental process; sectors of activity that had been viewed as discrete have become interrelated manifestations of a system of collective behavior. From such a standpoint, causation becomes multifactoral and multidirectional. The study of the past, rather than being impoverished and oversimplified by such an approach (as, in fact, it was by traditional particularistic rationalism), is immensely enriched by the range of phenomena that can be legitimately considered historically (causally) significant. No longer limited by the map of rationalism, we can begin to explore the complex territory of American history.

A cultural approach to American history offers more than an intellectual challenge, however. It is a task with vital policy implications. The failure of liberalism and the liberal state in the second half of this century has stemmed less from the flaws of America's leaders or the defects in our national morality than from defects in the enterprise of knowledge on which liberal policies have been based. Because we so uncritically accepted the fragmented disciplinary map of reality as a description of reality itself, we conceived and implemented policies which, as events of the last two decades have shown were unworkable. We have built a system of mass higher education without thought for placing its graduates. We have built a vast national system of highways without contemplating either the social and political consequences of suburbanization or the ecological and economic consequences of national dependence on petroleum-fueled private motor cars. We have encouraged family planning without regard to the impact of lowered population growth on our economy and on such entities as the Social Security system. The list goes on and on. If we are to avoid catastrophe on the one hand, and the "long anguish of degeneration" on the other, we must turn towards creating a body of social scholarship which more accurately and dispassionately describes the world in which we live. Such a body of scholarship must not only abolish the false distinctions between the past and the present, but also those which separate the disciplines. For the real world in which we live in the present is the product of the past. And that past is systemic. The specialized sectors of activity are, in fact, integrally interconnected. The convergence of history and social science and of the social sciences with one another is not an academic fad. It is an urgent response to the impoverishment of social policy and political leadership.

Happily, this intellectual enterprise is well underway. Pluralist historical scholarship, whatever its faults, opened the door to expanding the subject matter of American history to include the whole range of social, economic, and political phenomena. Post-pluralistic scholarship, through the work of such synthesizers as Robert Weibe, Alfred Chandler, Burton Bledstein, and Larence Veysey, and such investigators of more particular dimensions of the past as Stephan Thernstrom, David Allmendinger, Philip Greven, George Frederickson, and Morton Horowitz, is pointing the way to an integrated view of the American past. The work of the synthesizers, by tracing out the parallel development of national systems in industrial management, public administration, the professions, and education, has demonstrated that the development of American nationality was far more than a political or intellectual phenomenon.[11] The monographic efforts have complemented this multisectoral picture of national development by examining the fundamental demographic, social structural, and institutional processes that propelled the growth of national systems and connected one sector of activity with others.[12] With their chronological sweep and implicit thematic coherence, the works of these scholars are placing history on firm ground as a legitimate social science.[13]

In the meantime, the social sciences have been moving towards an accommodation with history. Sociology, although it began as a set of general propositions based on historical analysis (the work of Max Weber is a pre-eminent example of this use in history), strayed in the course of the twentieth century into studies that required no historical dimension (such as market and opinion research) or were so general (as in those studies concerned with modernization or accounts of the "structure of social action") that they cut themselves off from any ascertainable historical referent. Only community studies, such as those done by the Lynds, W. Lloyd Warner, and others, remained committed to multisectoral approaches with a genuine dependence on historical facts. Grand theorists like Talcott Parsons, however, were aware, even if casually, that their depiction of modern society as universalistic, bureaucratic, and specialized was not entirely accurate and that the rational and functionally specific roles of modern professionals and institutions were interconnected and influenced by functionally diffuse patterns of friendship, kinship, and loyalty, and by concrete and particular historical experiences.[14] Similarly, both psychologists like David McClelland and economic historians like Thomas Cochran and William Miller were, by the early 1950s, chafing under the restraints of narrow, unisectoral, ahistorical approaches to economic phenomena.[15] The inadequacies of social and economic theory in accounting for such central issues as economic development were despairingly cited by Cochran in 1955:

> . . . a general theory of society—specifically, some sort of sociology of change—is necessary to account for economic development. The role of the entrepreneur in capital formation and other activities is shaped by a combination of factors involving personality types, cultural attitudes, technological knowledge, and available physical resources. Merely to list these factors calls attention to the intangible character of all but one of them. The personality culture complex may someday be segmented into measurable factors, but that achievement appears to be far in the future.[16]

At the time that he wrote, Cochran could hardly anticipate the methodological and theoretical advances in the field of history that would come out of the pluralists' use of the social sciences, the convergence of interest by all social disciplines on the problem of modernization, or the application of computers to social, economic, and historical data. Of course, neither the possession of an inexhaustible fund of raw information nor the development of the techniques that now enable scholars to handle such masses of data necessarily leads anywhere. The crucial element is a set of concepts that hypotesize the relative significance of bodies of data to one another. Such a set of concepts—concepts of culture—may be found in the field of anthropology. Of all the modern social sciences, anthropology has been the most effective in formulating general frameworks for the analysis of the totality of human action, a framework that encompasses not only formal ideas, but also material resources, technology, institutions, personality types, and, most important of all, an historical dimension. But anthropology was until recently an enterprise that invested the better part of its energies in studies of primitive and marginal cultures. Only when the other social disciplines' demands for an "encompassing general theory of society" became acute enough and when, in the 1970s, historians began to produce detailed accounts of previously ignored fundamental social institutions—families, communities, firms, legal systems, and institutions of socialization and social control—would cultural approaches to the American experience become possible.

3. Nationality and the Organization of Culture

To point to developments in scholarship that portend an integrated view of cultural development is easy. To create such an integrated view successfully is another matter. In attempting to meet this challenge, I have had to make some difficult choices of what to study and how to study it.

I have chosen to focus this enquiry on cultural nationality because of the inclusiveness of the concept. As an enquiry into culture, rather than into the emergence of national business, professional, political, or educational entities, this book can begin to account for the fact that these large-scale organizations developed at the same time and that their development was remarkably interconnected through their dependence on common personnel and institutions. As an enquiry into the development of nationality, such an approach permits examination of a temporally deep and geographically extensive—yet internally coherent—range of phenomena.

I cannot, needless to say, attempt to account for the whole American past. Therefore, I have introduced the limiting concept of cultural organization. This concept implies that culture, rather than merely being a mass of undifferentiated behavior, is, in fact, structured in a number of important ways. First, there is a functional hierarchy of activities in which the satisfaction of biological imperatives constitutes the foundation of a cultural system.[18] The character of higher-level institutions is related to, though not necessarily determined by, their role in facilitating the fulfillment of these lower-level imperatives. Second, there is a structural hierarchy in which historical accident, or the ability of some groups to perform certain basic tasks sooner and/or better than others, advances them to positions from which they can lead and set the pattern of activity for others.[19] In investigating the organization of American culture, I am thus limiting myself to the study of the origins of the national institutions through Americans by the twentieth century would conduct fundamental tasks of production, distribution, communication, and socialization, and to the study of the social groups that took the lead in bringing these national institutions into being.

This enquiry is divided into three parts. The first will outline the differential development of the American colonies through the seventeenth and eighteenth centuries and will attempt to identify the reasons why certain groups in New England had, by the early nineteenth century, created organizational mechanisms and ideological orientations that enabled them to set basic economic, social, and cultural patterns for other sections. The basic organizational mechanism was the private corporation. The dominant ideological orientation involved both a national outlook and a peculiar sense of responsibility for the welfare and actions of others. The second part of this study will examine the legal basis and the social and economic consequences of corporate activity. These consequences will be shown to include not only substantive changes in the means of production and socialization, but also alterations in the personality types produced by the new corporate agencies of socialization and the changes they brought about in the means and organization of production, distribution, and communication. This section will also attempt to document the interaction of new personality types and new institutional forms in generating nationally extensive communities of values on which national economic and political life would subsequently be based. The third and final part of this study will outline the emergence and coalescence, during the Civil War and in the decades following the war, of genuinely national institutions of business and education and will suggest the extent to which these institutions were dependent on the formation of a national elite. The study will conclude with some speculations on the relation between the nationalization of business and education in the nineteenth century and the nationalization of politics and the creation of a mass culture in the twentieth. It will, finally, draw some conclusions about the effect of the privately-controlled corporate organizational context on the content of American culture.

This book should not in any sense be viewed as a definitive account of either the particular institutions and social groups to which it devotes attention or of their role in the forging of American nationality. Many of the areas on which I touch, especially the history of American business, have been underexplored. Other areas have grown so rapidly that they have exceeded my ability to encompass their literatures. It is my hope that this book will be paradigmatic in a way similar to Bernard Bailyn's *Education in the Forming of American Society* (1960).[20] Just as Bailyn drew together a vast range of specialized literatures in order to suggest that education was central and intrinsic to all other sectors of social action, so I would like to suggest some aspects of the structural and functional relations between education and other sectors of activity. Any such attempt invites criticism and revision. Fortunately, scholarship, though a solitary activity, is a collective endeavor. And if the defects of this book produce creative responses rather than mere criticism, it will have justified itself.

PART I:

The Crisis of
The Old Order

CHAPTER ONE

New England and America in the 1780s: Prospect and Retrospect

The evolution of American society in the seventeenth and eighteenth centuries was not uniform. The colonies had been established by groups of settlers with different religious convictions, economic interests, and political outlooks. Material circumstances, climate, resources, and topography varied within and between areas of settlement. The influence of the Mother Country also differed from area to area, promoting a range of degrees of subjection to imperial authority and dependence on the British mercantilist comercial system. Initial differences and the subsequent interplay of institutions, resources, and externalities determined divergent courses of development among the British colonies of North America.

The common effort to achieve independence from Great Britain and the successful political unification of the former colonies in the late 1780s cannot obscure the fact that the Founding Fathers represented social and economic systems that, even before the advent of industry in the North and cotton agriculture in the South, were only superficially similar.[1] These similarities were not insignificant. All the former colonies were still predominantly agricultural, though the commercial plantation agriculture of the South was a world apart from the family farms of the North, which were still primarily subsistence operations. All were still dependent on relations with foreign commercial interests: the South needed a market for its agricultural products; the North needed a market for the output of its forests and fisheries; both needed a source of credit and manufactured goods. All the former colonies were led by members of social and economic elites that united wealth, learning, and respectability, statesmen who could count on the deference and support of their constituents. But there the similarities end.

Underlying these superficial similarities between the colonies were profound differences based not merely on their divergent historical origins or agricultural forms, but on the integrity of their fundamental social and economic institutions. In New England, the religious ideology and social origins of the Puritan settlers led to a social order based on families and corporate communities.[2] The perpetuation of these communities was based on their ability to supply their members with material resources, especially land. This occurred through the distribution of common lands and a system of partible inheritance.[3] By the first half of the eighteenth century, population pressure was placing strains on available material resources, on ideology, and on fundamental social institutions, family, church, and community. New England entered a social crisis the resolution of which benefitted some groups more than others. Most New Englanders were farmers. Tied to the land, they found themselves pushed out of subsistence agriculture into the market system as they sought to provide land or appreticeships in the crafts for their sons out of their dwindling holdings. Agriculture became diversified as farmers attempted to timber, fish, and cobble their way to solvency.[4] The population became mobile, as landless sons looked first to uninhabited portions of New England and then to lands claimed by the New England states in Pennsylvania, western New York, and the Northwest Territory.[5] And the crisis generated a steady stream of migrants to the city and into the trades and professions.[6] While some *individuals* unquestionably benefited from the disintegration of the older social and economic order, the merchants of the coastal cities succeeded both in maintaining their integrity as *groups* and in emerging in a unique position to propose and implement organizational alternatives to family and community. They presided over the developing market system. They profited from the commercialization of agriculture and the diversification of rural energies into such crafts as shoemaking and shipbuilding. And they benefitted, both politically and economically, from their positions as agents for British merchants in search of markets and raw materials.[7]

Curiously, neither the pervasive social crisis nor the ascendancy of the merchants significantly altered the apparent intergrity of traditional institutions or social groups. Family, church, community, and the alliance of merchants, magistrates, and ministers known as the "Standing Order," were still, as of the 1780s, the bases of New England society. But the crisis had profoundly altered their purposes and their relations to one another: agricultural and artisan families were decreasingly able to provide for their children; the integrity of communities was being eroded by diminishing material and human resources; the unity of the established Congregational church was being challenged by doctrinal struggles and its hegemony diluted by the growth of rival sects and the demand in many quarters for religious toleration. And the Standing Order, though still intact at the end of the eighteenth century, had experienced a major shift in its center of gravity. Where once leadership in New England had been a more or less equal alliance of "wealth, learning, and respectability," both the magistracy and the ministry were coming to depend on the power of the wealthy.[8] The admission of laymen to the governing boards of Harvard and Yale after the Revolution was a symptom of the shift that lay beneath the apparently stable surface of New England society: the ascendancy of the urban merchants who would, within fifty years, not only transform the clerically-controlled, state-supported, local colleges into wealthy, private, national universities, but also create a new economy based on corporate banking, insurance, manufacturing, and transportation enterprises. They would also create a range of new corporate institutions of welfare and education: privately funded asylums for the insane, the blind, and the deaf and dumb; hospitals, professional schools, libraries; public lecture series, scholarship funds, missionary and reform societies. And these private corporate institutions would not be merely local in their impact. They would be dramatically expansive, not only reaching out directly to build railroads, mines, and factories in the West and South, but also setting the formal institutional pattern for economic, educational, and welfare activities across the nation, as New England's emigrants colonized the nation's new territories.[9] All these achivements, of course, lay in the future. What mattered from the standpoint of the post-Revolutionary world was the extent to which New England's social crisis had altered its basic social dynamics without altering its social structure or its conceptions of social authority.[10]

The South underwent nothing comparable to New England's social crisis.[11] Because of its system of commercial plantation agriculture, the rise of commerce that so affected development in the North had no real influence on the fundamental institutions of the region. That is not to suggest that southern society was unchanging in the course of the eighteenth century. Immigration, especially of Scotch-Irish yeomen, to the back and up-country caused a measure of political ferment.[12] The Great Awakening disturbed the loose establishment of the Anglican church.[13] And economic problems involving the decline of agricultural productivity, growing indebtedness, and the uncertainties of the international market for southern goods, unsettled the region. But the South's basic social, economic, and political arrangements remained largely unaltered until the introduction of cotton agriculture in the 1790s. The integrity and stability of the South's institutions is suggested by its response to the advent of cotton cultivation: the plantation system was perpetuated and extended.[14] New organizational forms, especially the private non-profit and for-profit corporation, and new sectors of social and economic activity—transportation, banking, education, and social welfare—remained either underdeveloped until the late nineteenth century or were developed by outsiders, especially entrepreneurs and professionals from New England.[15] Although independent from Great Britain, the former colonies of the South perpetuated traditional institutions and their traditional dependency on England and, ultimately, New England for credit, manufactured goods, technology, and the higher education of its young.[16] While the southern way of life and its "peculiar institution" would prove to be geographically expansive and its political leadership unusually effective on the national level, this expansiveness and influence would be a product of the stability and integrity of older forms of organization rather than a product of organizational innovation or new groups of leaders.

Th situation in the middle colonies—New York, New Jersey, and Pennsylvania—more closely resembled New England than the South. There were, however, distinctive factors that made the region unlike either.[17] Like New England, the middle colonies underwent a commercial revolution in the eighteenth century. Fertile agriculturally and possessing broad navigable rivers—the Hudson, the Delaware, and the Schuykill—the merchants of New York and Philadelphia grew wealthy presiding over the movement and sale of farm products and manufactured goods, much as the merchants of New England, who lacked such natural bounties, prospered from the polygon of trade.[18] Like the New Englanders, New Yorkers and Philadelphians were early promoters of new corporate organizations—banks, hospitals, museums, professional societies, and colleges. But because of their religious and ethnic heterogeneity, they were unable to generate either the dominant social groups or the effective and concentrated organizational enterprise of New England.[19] Private cultural enterprises such as Columbia and the University of Pennsylvania were crippled by political and legal strictures, products of rival religious and ethnic groups that feared the influence of collectivized private wealth or were opposed on religious grounds to institutionalized charity.[20] Major economic enterprises, the building of the Erie and such as Pennsylvania canal systems, were entrusted to the state, for in this context of tumultuous heterogeneity and intense intergroup rivalry, only the state could mediate and unite the interests of factions.[21] New Yorkers and Philadelphians were unquestionably successful in building thriving metropolitan centers, but they were less

expansive and, though organizationally innovative, less organizationally effective than New Englanders. Though greatly exceeding Boston
in population and aggregate wealth, the great cities of Pennsylvania and
New York were not, as Boston would be until the 1860s, the national
centers of investment capital and literary culture.[22] The only college of
the middle states to assume national importance before the late nineteenth century was Princeton. And it was founded by New Englanders
and, through the Presbyterian Church, was part of an institutional network rooted in New England.[23]

From the standpoint of the 1780s, the newly independent states that
were shortly to perfect their union through the Constitution appeared
to possess more similarities than differences. Their economies were
predominantly agricultural. Their social and political structures and institutions closely resembled one another. Their people spoke a common
language and shared, for the most part, an adherance to the Protestant
version of Christianity. Moreover, they had fought together in a common cause to gain independence from an oppressive colonial regime.
But the Constitution, as far as nationality was concerned, was no more
than a promissory note. The nation was far from united even as to the
wisdom of national federation.[24] And the struggle to establish the power
of the federal government would rage intensely, but intermittently, from
the rebellions and resolutions of the 1790s through the middle of the
nineteenth century, when the Civil War would settle the issue. Although
the war firmly established the preeminence of national institutions of
government, it would be another half-century before political life assumed a genuinely national character.[25] The achievement of cultural
nationality through the development of national economic, social, and
intellectual institutions did not follow automatically from the actions of
the Founding Fathers. As the United States grew toward full nationhood
in the course of the nineteenth century, its regions, whatever their
similarities at the outset of the process, would contribute to it differ-
entially. The New England states, because of certain peculiarities of
ideology, demography, and social dynamics, would, I argue, exercise
more influence over the development of cultural nationality than any
other region.

CHAPTER TWO

The Institutional Crisis
Of Eigthteenth-Century New England

When the legislator has once regulated the law of inheritance, he may rest from his labor. The machine once put in motion will go on for ages, and advance, as if self guided, toward a point indicated beforehand. When framed in a particular manner, this law unites, draws together, and vests property and power in a few hands. . . . If formed on opposite principles its action is still more rapid; it divides, distributes, and disperses both property and power. Alarmed by the rapidity of its progress, those who despair of arresting its motion endeavor at least to obstruct it by difficulties and impediments. They vainly seek to counteract its effect by contrary efforts; but it shatters and reduces to powder every obstacle, until we can no longer see anything but a moving and impalpable cloud of dust, which signals the coming of Democracy.[1]

In the course of the eighteenth century, all of Britain's North American colonies underwent social crises as the populations of older settlements began to grow more rapidly than available resources. But the character and resolution of these crises varied, establishing cultural patterns and social dynamics that, as the nation took shape, exercised differential degrees on influence on the configuration of national institutions. What gave the social crisis in New England its peculiar character was not partible inheritance, which was more or less universally practiced in the colonies, but the impact of partible inheritance on institutions. In other parts of the colonies, population pressure, rather than destroying older institutions, led, as in the case of the South, to the expansion of one particular type of older institution—the plantation—at the expense of urban-mercantile and rural-subsistence forms. In the middle colonies, the swelling populations migrated either to the cities or onto the vast proprietary landholdings of urban merchants like the Penns and Allens in Pennsylvania or the Livingstons in New York. Even when family and community resources could no longer cope with problems of social control, education, and public health, and new institutions were created, the power of these new institutions was held in check by political, ethnic, and sectarian rivalries, and the power of older institutions, especially the state. But in New England, because of the peculiar pattern of settlement, the social crisis became an institutional one. New Englanders, unlike the other colonists, had organized themselves as corporate communities. In such communities the ability of families to carry out fundamental tasks of production, socialization, and social control was based on collective resources, especially undivided lands. As these resources ceased to exist, the integrity of these corporate communities and the families within them was compromised. And what resulted was more than geographical and occupational mobility. for the failure of the institutions of family and community left New Englanders in a situation of declining prosperity, public order, and social consensus. The strains on material and institutional life were, by the 1740s, undermining even the religious unity that had been at the core of the region's settlement.

While New Englanders might have turned to the state, as other colonists did, the interests of the state were peculiarly tied to the interests of a private group, the Standing Order—the ministers, merchants, and magistrates through whom the collective will was articulated both locally and translocally. And when a social crisis compelled the state to expand its functions beyond a narrow range of legal and military activities, it usually did so through private groups, not through creating new adminstrative agencies. Thus, for example, the creation of the early banks, bridges, turnpikes, canals, and hospitals—and the institutionalization of legal and medical training—were, although viewed as public functions, parcelled out to the individuals who comprised the Standing Order. As the social crisis advanced to the point at which the personal and institutional authority of the Standing Order came to be questioned, those individuals continued to control the new institutions and, to a remarkable extent, to view themselves as possessing public responsibilities. Even though the state would open up to all the right to create private corporations and would expand its functions into realms that it had previously left to chartered private entities, neither the power of the state nor the entrepreneurial and voluntaristic vitality of the newly liberated "common man" would ever seriously challenge the corporate institutions of the privatized Standing Order. The political state in the

Age of the Common Man would be too much a creature of contending interests to counter effectively the activities of the private sector. For the "common men" were not socialists. They had a vital stake in the survival of the legal and economic forms on which the power of the Standing Order was based. And as they sought to become *un*common men by using the market system and its new institutional forms, they also looked to older institutions, especially those controlled by social groups that had maintained their intactness over time, to legitimate their successes. Just as many southern small farmers looked to the day when they would own slaves and plantations, so a remarkable number of New England's small farmers and entrepreneurs aspired to send their sons to Harvard and Yale and to emulate the manners and mores of their betters. And the "Brahmins" (as they came to call themselves), because they tenaciously clung to concepts of public responsibility and because the success of their economic and eleemosynary enterprises depended on public participation and support, structured their institutions to include rather than exclude the newly successful. Eventually, by the 1860s, they would begin to make good their claim that, though privately wealthy and powerful, they had been worthy stewards of the public interests—far better, indeed, than the state itself had been.

1. The Model of Puritan Society in New England

While the Puritans were not the first group determined to remake the world into a better, purer, more Godly place, they were certainly among the first to have the opportunity to do so on a *tabula rasa*. Transplanted to the New World, they did not have to engage in warfare against an old order in order to translate their ideology into institutional reality. That they were on an "errand into the wilderness," building a new social order based on their interpretation of the Holy Scriptures, does not mean that they had freed themselves of the heritage of the Old World. They carried with them their historical experience as Englishmen of the seventeenth century. And they selected from that experience those aspects of political, economic, and cultural life most consonant with their religious doctrines.

It is no exaggeration to say that New England was founded on the corporate idea. From the Charter of the Massachusetts Bay Company (1629) through Governor Winthrop's statement of basic social philosophy, "The Model of Christian Charity," it is clear that the Puritans brought with them and consciously adhered to the notion that mankind was properly organized into corporate groups:

The definition which the Scripture gives us of love is this: love is the bond of perfection (Cor. 3:14). First, it is a bond, or ligament. Second, it makes the work perfect. There is no body that does not consist of parts, and that which knits these parts together gives the body its perfection, because it makes each part so contiguous to the others that they mutually participate with each other, both in strength and infirmity, in pleasure and in pain. To instance the most perfect of all bodies: Christ and His church make one body. The several parts of this body considered apart before they were united were as disproportionate and as much disordered as so many contrary qualities or elements, but when Christ came and by His spirit and love knit these parts to Himself and to each other, it became the most perfect and best proportioned body in the world.[2]

Although justified by scripture, the corporate idea was also fundamental to the medieval historical experience in which men were knit together by ties of mutual obligation to defend and defer to one another. Medieval Europe was organized into corporate groups both civil and ecclesiastical. Villages functioned as corporate bodies, making collective decisions about sowing and harvesting crops, dividing land, and using the commons. The basic unit of ecclesiastical organization was a corporate body, the parish, which held property, educated the young, and cared for the poor. Artisans and craftsmen were organized into corporations called guilds, which regulated the prices and quality of goods for the benefit of their members. Although the Puritans rejected many of the specific corporate organizations with which they had had experience in the Old World, the general concept of corporatism became the organizing principle of their new society.

While the Puritans recognized the individual to the extent that he was the fundamental unit in their social and religious universe, they regarded him as meaningless, if not dangerous, in their scheme of social organization. To be sure, the individual soul was the arena in which salvation was to be sought—the receptacle of grace. But it was only in the gathering of believers together as a church that the spiritual search could be carried on. The church was, for the Puritans, a corporate body composed of believers. Similarly, the state was a corporate body of freemen and their elected officers. These civil and ecclesiastical bodies were based on a more elementary social grouping, the family, which the Puritans likened to a "little Commonwealth," or a corporation in miniature.

The Puritan religious and political order depended on the family for existence. Just as the lawmaking capacity of the state depended on the gathering and consent of the freemen, its ability to enforce those edicts depended on the militia, a gathering of the men of arms-bearing age out of the family. Just as the church consisted of a gathering of believers to instruct and guide one another in their spiritual searches, so the church depended on the family to enforce its ethical injunctions and to catechize the young. Beyond this, however, the Puritans stripped the church of the educational and social welfare functions that it had borne in England, allocating those activities to families instead. In addition, the family remained the center of economic activity in farming, the crafts, and commerce.

Because the Puritans saw the family as the fundamental building block of society, they ordained in their social legislation a system of property holding and transmission that would perpetuate it. Just as lands were allocated to the heads of families of each town at their founding, providing each head of family the wherewithal to subsist and enforce his authority over his dependents, so the system of inheritance required that the paternal property be divided more or less equally between the surviving children. This not only gave female children dowries, but, more importantly, gave each male child the material basis on which to maintain his own family and, in turn, become a part of the social order.[3]

Puritan society in its ideal form was a corporate one, lacking both formal organizations and recognized individuals. The absence of formal organizations stemmed from the congregational character of both church and state.[4] Both institutions were family based, deriving both their policy-making and implementation functions from the families of the commonwealth. They possessed no means, other than the voluntary consent of the freemen, for carrying out their mandates. Similarly, because everyone was required to live under family authority in an established houshold, the individual was not a being of any social consequence in Puritan society.[5]

Given its orientation toward corporatism and toward a system of property holding and testation consonant with that ideal, the Puritan settlement of New England proceeded in a remarkably cellular fashion. When individual families wished to leave an established community, they banded together with those with similar interests and sought a grant of land from the General Court and dismission from their church. On receiving the grant, they moved as a group to the new location, distributed a part of the town lands to the heads of households (saving the rest for common uses and for later distributions as the population increased), and sent out a call for a minister.[6] By the late seventeenth century, most of what we know as Connecticut and Massachusetts had been divided up into family-based townships, each containing a church, each economically based on subsistence farming, each a self-governing unit, subservient only to the collective will of the General Courts in Boston, New Haven and Hartford. While there were certainly sharp clashes over specific political and religious questions, there was at the same time an overall social consensus. Nonetheless, stresses were beginning to emerge in the social order that would prove to be the undoing of Winthrop's "City upon a Hill."

2. The Transformation of Puritan Society: Ideology, Population, and Available Resources

Although the overwhelming majority of the inhabitants of Massachusetts and Connecticut were engaged in subsistence farming, it was, at the same time, a diversified society. The coast was dotted with good-sized towns whose primary activity was commerce. The merchants of Boston, Hartford, New Haven, Newburyport, Salem and other coastal towns were a large and influential group. Artisans flourished both in the cities and in the country, supplying both the demand for luxuries by the merchants and the daily needs of farmers for such necessities as shoes, wagons, and farm implements. There were no professionals in modern sense. Legal matters were handled by a variety of individuals, merchants and magistrates, on a part-time basis. Since the system of justice was based on arbitration of disputes, not on an adversary system, there was no need for legal advocacy.[7] Similarly, medical problems were handled by a variety of persons including midwives and clergymen.[8] The only members of a learned profession to constitute a significant group in seventeenth century New England were the ministers.[9]

The mandates of Puritan social ideology affected each major occupational group differently. It appears that the farmers adapted most easily to them; for a subsistence agriculture based on man and animal power, it was not difficult to absorb the energies of all family members in the task of day-to-day survival. Similarly, life in rural towns was traditionally collective in nature. As in England, the farmers built their homes close together in the center of town, using common lands for pasturage and wood-gathering, and sharing their labor in the building or roads and walls, harvesting, planting and other tasks.[10] For artisans too, compliance with the family-based order was consonant with the organization of the crafts in the Old World. Most of the labor in the workshop was supplied by the artisan's own family. Artisan skills were passed on through a system of apprenticeship in which a young boy (usually a relative of the master) entered the craftsman's family, remaining under his tutelage and authority until ready to establish his own family workshop.[11] The only major break with the past for the artisans was the absence of guilds. Their functions were taken over by town officials who inspected the quality of materials and workmanship and regulated prices.[12] These officials made no attempt to control the number of persons working in any given craft. For the growing society did not, at the outset, suffer from an overabundance of skilled artificers.

For the merchants and professionals the story was quite different. As Bernard Bailyn has shown in *The New England Merchants of the Seventeenth Century*, conflicts developed within the first decade of settlement between the corporatist effort to regulate prices for the general good and the entrepreneurial desire to maximize profits. The long term effect of this struggle was to forge the merchants into a distinct interest group which was often opposed to both the letter and the spirit of Puritan social legislation. Beyond limiting profits, the practice of partible inheritance limited the ability of merchants to accumulate capital transgenerationally. While an individual merchant might do very well for himself during his own lifetime, his capital was, in the end, family capital, subject to laws of distribution requiring provisions for the widow and surviving children. The results was that the merchant's capital base was kept small and his operations marginal and dependent on the good will of correspondents in the old country. Since Puritan law forbade first-cousin marriage, the only way around these strictures on capital accumulation was through partnerships between fathers, uncles, and brothers. But without effective forms of peer control and lacking the social cement of kin-marriage, partnership firms were a fairly unstable device.[13]

It seems ironic that the clergy should have found its situation in Puritan New England a difficult one. But as with the merchants, there were certain fundamental differences between their historical experience in England and the realities that they encountered in the New World.[14] In England, where most of the ministers of Massachusetts and Connecticut had begun their careers, clerics were part of a hierarchical ecclesiastical structure. They were appointed to their positions, not elected by congregations. Their income usually came from an endowment, not from their parishioners. Finally, however onerous the episcopacy may have been in England, it provided a forum for the setting forth of doctrine and a machinery for enforcing it. In New England things were very different. Ministers were elected and supported by their congregations and served at their pleasure. There was neither an episcopal nor a formal synodical organization to connect and enforce discipline among the churches. Even basic doctrinal questions were decided in the end not by the ministry, but by the communicants. Finally, ministers, unlike farmers, artisans, and merchants, could not pass their vocation on to their children. While one—or even several—sons could be trained in the ministry, there was no guarantee that they would succeed to their fathers' posts. Thus, in spite of the importance of religion and the clerical role in New England's "Bible Commonwealth," ministers were a dependent and rather unstable group.

Forces of fundamental change in the Puritan social order began to emerge towards the end of the seventeenth century. While there were proximate political causes stemming from the efforts of the British to consolidate their holdings in the northeast into a single Dominion of New England under the control of a royally appointed governor, the more compelling factor involved a tension between Puritan social ideology and the physical resources needed to perpetuate it. This tension affected the farmers—the largest occupational group in the population—most acutely. And their response, in turn, touched off a general crisis both in the occupational structure and in New England's family-based corporate institutions.

In order to perpetuate a social order based on patriarchal households, Puritan ideology mandated a system of partible inheritance in which each child, regardless of sex or birth order position, was assured of a more-or-less equal share in the paternal estate. These shares, whether transmitted *inter vivos* or on the death of the head of the household, provided the means by which sons could become patriarchs in their own right. As long as the farming communities contained enough undistributed lands to accommodate the sons and grandsons of the original inhabitants, there were no problems. While paternal estates were divided between surviving children, thereby breaking up and diminishing the family's land capital, successive distributions of the town's common land made up for this erosion in the size of individual land holdings. But when the towns began to run out of common lands towards to end of the seventeenth century, forces of basic social change began to emerge.

Fathers were faced with six strategic options in the face of this crisis. They could: 1) subdivide their estates beyond the point of meaningful agricultural productivity; 2) reduce the size of their families; 3) delay adult autonomy for their sons; 4) encourage geographical mobility by purchasing farms for their sons in other places; 5) encourage occupational mobility, sending sons into occupations that required no land capital; 6) reconsolidate their resources through marriage. All were employed to varying extents through the course of the eighteenth century.[15] Average landholdings in older settlements fell precipitously through the eighteenth century, as families divided estates no longer supplemented by distributions of common lands.[16] There was a dramatic decline in births per marriage (in Andover, from 6.0 in the late 1600s to 3.0 by the 1780s), though whether this was due to birth control techniques, continence, or later marriage ages in unknown.[17] Fathers delayed autonomy for their sons, preventing them from marrying until later in life and retaining control of family lands until their deaths.[18] In some places, multi-generational households, with married sons living with their parents, became common.[19] Unoccupied sections of New England, Maine, New Hampshire, Vermont, and northwestern and northeastern areas of Connecticut and western Massachusetts came to be populated by migrating families from older settlements, often on lands purchased by fathers for their sons.[20] And farmers, who had originally begun to engage in crafts activities to supplement farm incomes, began sending their sons into the crafts as full-time occupations.[21] And in every family, through distinctly differing patterns, marriage was used either to consolidate estates threatened with partition or to forge alliances through which labor, land, and skills might be more effectively combined.[22]

But all these strategies, however combined or varied, could only delay the erosion of the Puritan communal order. Paternal authority, the basis of public order, could not be maintained when obedience no longer carried with it the material rewards of full autonomy. Even when fathers could successfully provide for their sons by settling them on farms in other places or by setting them up in the crafts, both continuity and authority were altered in character. A son who was a shoemaker would relate more to other shoemakers and to the entrepreneurs to whom he sold the fruits of his labor than to his father. At best, authority was divided; at worst, it ceased to exist. Similarly, geographically mobile sons, while retaining significant contacts to their parents and the communities in which they had been born, were bound to be more independent and more responsive to the communities in which they had come to live than to the places and people they had left behind. And, most important, whatever strategy was followed, all pushed farmers into a market system over which they had little control.

The other major occupational groups in New England, artisans, merchants, and the clergy, faced a similar tension between ideology and resources and confronted similar strategic options in resolving it. But the tension affected each group at a different point in time. And it varied between groups, depending on the nature of their resources and the particular manner in which the strategies were pursued. Farmers were primarily concerned with land and labor as resources—and pursued courses of action that would conserve them. Artisans, on the other hand, were primarily concerned with the conservation of skills, markets, and to a greater or lesser extent, depending on the labor-intensiveness of the craft—of labor.[23] As long as New England's towns were short of craftsmen, artisans could hand down their knowledge, tools, and workshops to their sons. And if, as in the case of young Benjamin Franklin, the son found his father's trade uncongenial, or if prospects in the father's trade appeared unpromising, the boy could be apprenticed in the workship of some relative in another skill. But, lacking guilds, artisans had no control over the number of practitioners in their trades. As immigrants continued to come to the new world, as the sons of land-short farmers came into the towns and cities in search of new occupations, and as their own fertility continued at a high rate, the artisans began to confront the same difficult choices faced by the farmers. They followed similar strategies: reducing family size, encouraging occupation and geographical mobility, reconsolidating resources through marriage. As with the farmers, the results were no more satisfactory. Continuity and authority were disrupted. With the exception of such high-skill trades as printing and gold and silversmithing (in which the process took a little longer), artisans found themselves having to chose between being proletarianized or becoming entrepreneurs.[24] In either case, they became subservient to the market system in which they were beholden to merchants as sources of credit and raw materials and for access to buyers beyond the confines of the locality.

The clergy may have faced the problems posed by partible inheritance before any other group. At no point was the pulpit regarded as the sort of personal property that could be handed down from father to son. And even if sons did succeed their fathers as ministers, as was the case in some early New England communities, only one son could occupy a pulpit—and ministers, like all other fathers, usually had many sons to provide for. The collective biographies of Harvard and Yale graduates give eloquent testimony to the strategies adopted by the New England clergy as it attempted to provide for its children. Many sons did become ministers, either succeeding to their fathers' positions, or migrating to new settlements. Because clergymen held high status in the communities in which they served, and because they often came to those communities as young unmarried men, they often married the daughters of prominent families, especially those of merchants and large landowners. Accordingly, it was not uncommon for the sons of clergymen to become protegés of their maternal grandparents or uncles, becoming merchants and landowners themselves. Or they might, if their fathers possessed medical or legal knowledge, become physicians, attorneys, or magistrates. But, once again, partible inheritance placed the clergy, as it placed farmers and artisans, in a situation of dependency. To place sons as their successors, they depended on the good will of their congregations, especially that of the wealthy and prestigious members. To place their sons as merchants or heirs to landed estates, they depended on the good will of their in-laws. And this dependency became more profound over time as the social crisis, in eroding the authority of fathers and pushing all sectors of society into the market system, began to erode the doctrinal consensus and the order of deference on which the ministers and the power of the church as an institution depended. This consensus, already undermined in the late seventeenth century by controversies over the criteria for admitting church members to full communion, was further eroded by the increasing divergence of corporate ideology from competitive and individualistic reality.[25] By the early decades of the eighteenth century, clerical authority and the status of clergymen in their communities could only be maintained by actions that made churchmen dependent either on the legislature (as in the case of Connecticut, where the Saybrook Platform established a presbyterian ecclesiastical organization embracing the colony's churches) or, as in the case of Massachusetts, on powerful factions of congregations—which, in the coastal settlements, were usually mercantile. As Lyman Beecher noted,

> That was a new thing in that day for the clergy and laymen to meet on the same level and cooperate. . . . The ministers had always managed things for themselves, for in those days the ministers were all politicians. And, fact is, when they got together, they would talk over who should be governor, and who lieutenant-governor, and who in the Upper House, and their counsels would prevail.[26]

Where once clergymen, as the only highly educated translocal group, had led the colonists, forming their opinions and serving as advisors and sometimes as masters of the magistrates, by the mid-eighteenth century they were struggling for survival, assaulted by rival denominations, internal schisms, and unruly congregations. In the countryside of Connecticut and western Massachusetts, the clergy tended to muster the support of their congregations through emotional, evangelical appeals and to consolidate their positions through alliances with other New Light ministers and their lay supporters.[27] In the coastal cities, especially in eastern Massachusetts, they preached milder, more rational doctrines and forged alliances with the wealthiest and most powerful elements in their congregations, the merchants. Whichever course they chose led them towards dependency, either on the uncertain faith of the people, or on the interests of the merchant elite.

Of New England's occupational groups, the merchants were the most successful in adapting to the challenges posed by partible inheritance. This was due in part to the nature of its capital resources—money and markets—which were, unlike land, labor, or skills, intrinsically more flexible and expandable, and to the nature of the mercantile firm, which could absorb the surplus of sons, cousins, and nephews more easily than an artisan's workshop or a family farm. The mercantile firm of the eighteenth century was unspecialized, embracing a wide range of activities including transportation, wharfage, manufacturing, credit, and wholesale and retail sales.[28] With activities requiring so broad a range of competency, it was not difficult to find places for needy relatives or sons in search of careers. Captial could be increased through judicious marriages that combined business advantages with useful political and commercial alliances. And family capital and contacts that might be scattered by partition could be reconsolidated through cousin-marriages between the children of partners. Although some sons were diverted into occupations other than commerce, they tended to be sent into fields closely related to commerce, especially the law. By the mid-eighteenth century, merchants had largely managed to overcome the forces that were overwhelming other occupational groups. Partnerships that had been dissolved by death or incapacity were re-established in the next generation by children who also recombined testamentary shares through marriage. The strategic choices that faced other groups, especially mobility and delayed autonomy, were either avoided or modified in ways that reduced their destructive effects. The accommodating and diffuse nature of the mercantile firm made geographical and occupational mobility largely unnecessary, escept in instances, such as when sons became lawyers, where it furthered merchant influence and remained closely bound to commerce. Autonomy was delayed—average age at first marriage for males rose from the early twenties to the early thirties between the late seventeenth and the late eighteenth centuries. But the willingness of sons to continue their subjection to parental authority was rewarded by increasing responsibilities in the firm as young men rose from clerking in the counting house and sailing before the mast to become supercargoes, officers, and ultimately, partners or captains.

Another contributing factor to mercantile stability was British commercial policy. By limiting their markets and range of activities by statute and by rendering themselves agents and correspondents of British firms, New England merchants were freed of the necessity to raise large capital and of the risks and uncertainties of international trade. In addition, the imperial system presented them with opportunities for windfall profits as privateers and as suppliers to the British military—and with opportunities for gaining political influence as appointed officeholders and imperial agents. Thus, while other social groups were losing their integrity and material resources and failing to fulfill their responsibilities towards their children and their communities, merchants were successfully adapting their family structures and productive activities, increasing their resources, and expanding their influence and cohesiveness.

Not until the American Revolution did New England's merchants have to face the crisis of institutions that had troubled other groups for almost a century. While the war and independence presented the merchants with new challenges and opportunities for profit, it also revealed the inadequacy of the family firm as a basis for large-scale commerce. Within the British commercial system, New England merchants had been able to depend on correspondent firms overseas for credit and markets. And they, in turn, had functioned as carriers of raw materials to Britain and as markets for British manufactures. Their own firms required neither large capital nor levels of competence exceeding the resources of the family. But independence, in opening up the world to them, also taxed their ability to mobilize capital and sustain risks. Many merchants who, like Jonathan Jackson, had been conspicuously successful before and during the war, found that post-war trade was far less certain:

> Mr. J. left home in December, 1783, and visited Great Britain and Ireland, and afterwards France. In those countries he solicited consignments. At that time our home country realized the want of foreign goods, but the supplies from the old countries were at very high prices, and in our exhausted state we were unable to pay for them. On his return home Mr. Jackson must have found the same embarrassments which existed in every part of the United States.[29]

Insolvent, Jackson was forced to vacate his magnificent Newburyport mansion, auction its contents to cover his debts, and move into the house of his brother-in-law, Nathaniel Tracy, who had also failed. He made ends meet for the rest of his life by calling in political favors for appointment to salaried public positions (he was in charge of the first federal census in Massachusetts) and to corporate sinecures (he was president of the Boston Bank and Treasurer of Harvard College).[30] Jackson's experience was not unique. Many prominent merchants either failed or came very close to failure during the 1780s and 90s, either because of the collapse of markets and shortage of credit or because of the incompetence of partners and employees who had been sent overseas to drum up business.[31] Had they been able to take advantage of new opportunities through organizations other than family firms, they might have been able to deal more effectively with these problems. As it was, while merchants entered the post-war period as the most powerful and influential of all social groups, their power and influence were no longer assured.

At the same time, merchants faced another kind of challenge. The war had forced British officialdom and its American allies (including many of the colonies' most prominent merchants) into exile.[32] While the mercantile revolutionary leaders moved quickly into the vacated seats of power, they soon found, especially as they attempted to collect taxes to finance the recent war, that the animus the citizenry had once directed against the colonial oppressor was being directed against them. The post-revolutionary economic situation underlined the dependency of all social groups on a market system of which the urban merchants were the most conspicuous beneficiaries. As occupants of the top level of the political structure they were also obvious targets for popular animus. And, as the old corporate order of deference and consensus began to break apart, the merchants and their allies in the clergy and the law came under direct attack both by mobs and by more orderly political forces.[33]

3. Towards Collective Action

The fact that the merchants were able to contain the disorders of the 1780s and were, in spite of economic uncertainties, able to maintain an overall solvency, cannot conceal the fact that, by the late eighteenth century, older modes of corporate organization had failed both for them and for all other social groups in New England. The family alone could no longer carry out basic tasks of production, socialization, and social control. Communities, which had depended on families to perform these tasks and which had unwritten their ability to do so out of their corporately-held resources, no longer possessed the means for such subventions. Cities like Middletown, Connecticut, which, until the war, had seldom had more than half-a-dozen indigent or distressed persons to care for per year and which had cared for them by boarding them out with local families, found themselves overwhelmed by widows, paupers, and orphans.[34] Even local families of long standing were expecting city authorities to care for their indigent relatives. Towns and cities, despairing of their ability to take responsibility for unfortunates who had asked for public assistance, spent inordinate amounts of time and money corresponding with one another and bringing suit to recover the costs of assistance to poor and disabled persons not native to their localities. The crisis of resources had led to an institutional crisis that affected all levels of society.

Clearly some sort of collective response was called for, though what form it should take was not at all clear. There were two obvious possibilities. One involved direct action by the state to uphold credit, to underwrite public welfare, and, through deferring or repudiating payment of war debts, to reduce the tax burden that many, especially backcountry farmers, found so onerous. The other involved state action to create private, corporately chartered groups to undertake these tasks, as had been done in England since before the time of Queen Elizabeth.[35] There were also other less obvious levels at which collective response could take place. These would involve the building of alliances between individuals and groups sharing common political, religious, and economic interests. These alliances could take the form of either new kinds of formal organizations—voluntary associations, chartered corporations, fraternal societies, and political parties—or new kinds of social groupings—ranging from communistic religious communities through extended forms of family interconnection.

CHAPTER THREE

The Social Basis of Collective Action

In no country in the world has the principle of association been more successfully used or applied to a greater multitude of objects than in America. Besides the permanent associations which are established by law under the name of townships, cities, and counties, a vast number of others are formed and maintained by the agency of private individuals. . . .

In the United States associations are established to promote the public safety, commerce, industry, morality, and religion. There is no end which the human will despairs of attaining through the combined power of individuals united into a society.[1]

The New Englanders, like many other Americans in the late eighteenth century, were quick to turn to collective endeavor in responding to the vast array of social, economic, and political challenges that confronted them. Established merchants banded together to seek corporate privileges as cities, separating commercial sections of their towns from rural ones and establishing legal and administrative procedures that served their interests more effectively than the town meeting and the selectmen.[2] Younger merchants and professionals organized Masonic lodges which functioned both as mutual support societies and as bases for establishing trust, credit, and political influence.[3] Manufacturers formed associations to promote industry and to lobby for legislative and popular support of their enterprises.[4] Merchants and farmers combined their energies to organize societies to promote more scientific and productive agriculture.[5] Professionals, especially physicians, associated to exchange information, to set fees, and to regulate professional training and examination. New religious denominations were organized as factions of established congregations took advantage of the postwar atmosphere of religious tolerance to worship as voluntary gatherings of believers in doctrines that more powerfully affirmed their newfound selfhood and more accurately reflected their altered relations to the community as a whole. The older churches, attempting to counter the new sects and to combat the rising tide of "infidelity," organized Sunday schools, moral reform societies, and charitable endeavors.[6] The move towards collective organizations was both rapid and pervasive, involving virtually all social groups, from artisans, with their "Mechanics' Societies," through merchants, with their banks, insurance companies, and city councils. But as I will attempt to suggest, the effectiveness of collective action varied according to a number of factors, including the cohesiveness of an organization's constituency, its wealth (endowment or capital), and the extent to which formal oganization was complemented by informal social ties among its participants.

1. Trust, Alliances, and the Capacity for Collective Action

The most obviously necessary element in any kind of voluntary collective action is, of course, a sharing of common aims among the individuals who comprise a group. Less obvious, but equally important, is trust. For even if individuals share common goals, they are not likely to commit themselves fully to their pursuit unless they believe that their comrades are equally committed and are, in fact, pursuing those goals for their mutual benefit. In a social context lacking in formal institutions that issue credentials of trust (as modern universities, for example, grant degrees as emblems of specific competency), there are two sources from which trust can be derived. The first is experience: the ability of individuals from personal observation and long acquaintance to know whether or not other individuals will do what they promise to do. Trust on this basis assumes that the individuals involved have lived in the same locality, shared some intense common experience like war or college, or done business together over a lengthy period of time. The circumstances of life in the late eighteenth century rendered the first possibility increasingly uncommon, the second the possession of only a handful of veterans and college graduates, and the third simply unlikely—as business tended in the eighteenth century to be carried on primarily by persons who were related by blood to one another.[7] The second basis of trust, really the most important one from the standpoint of organizational innovation, is accountability: the existence of mechanisms by which promised performance can be guaranteed. Mechanisms of accountability permit the creation of trust among groups of individuals who have no long-term experience with one another. Moreover, they permit trust to be broken down into less diffuse segments. One can trust another individual to repay a loan, for example, if one holds title to his property. One does not have to know anything else about him or share any other sort of connection. Thus the voluntary bodies that came into being after 1780 could depend upon their members to participate because they made only limited claims on the resources and loyalty of those members, and because their democratic structure enabled members to hold their elected representatives accountable for their actions.

The existence of formalized mechanisms of accountability was limited before the Revolution, for such mechanisms were either products of the legal system, which was rudimentary before the end of the century, or of corporate organizations, which the colonial legislatures were neither willing nor legally able to create. Without easily formulated and legally feasible mechanisms of accountability, colonists, when they needed to enlarge their circles of trust to embrace more persons that the members of their households, turned to the corporate institutions that were available to them, the church and the town, and to marital alliances. The accountability of officials in a corporate organization like a town or a church is obvious; that resulting from marital alliances is less so unless one places it in the context of some particular context of activity. In business, for example, the relationship between partners was a particularly vulnerable one. As Joseph Story would describe it in the mid-nineteenth century,

> In virtue of this community of rights and interests in the partnership stock, funds, and effects, each partner possesses full authority to sell, pledge, or otherwise dispose of the entirety of any particular goods, wares, merchandise, or other personal effects belonging to the partnership. . . . The law . . . treats each partner, without any nicety of discrimination . . . as possessing a dominion over the entirety of the property, and not merely over his own share, and, therefore, as clothed in all the ordinary attributes of ownership.[8]

> . . . the mutual respect, confidence, and belief in the entire integrity of each partner, and his sincere devotion to the business and true interests of the partnership; good faith, reasonable skill and diligence, and the exercise of sound judgment and discretion, are naturally, if not necessarily, implied from the very nature and character of the relation of partnership.[9]

Of course, before the passage of reformed bankruptcy laws in the 1820s, there was no limitation of a businessman's liability and no distinction made between his personal property and the property of his firm. Thus, if his property proved insufficient to cover his debts, his creditors could jail him. The relation of partners in such a context means, therefore, a willingness to place one's life in the hands of others. A relationship of this degree of mutual trust could not merely be founded on a common interest in making money. It required mechanisms to ensure an ongoing accountability and a broad identity of interests. In the eighteenth century, the basis of trust underlying the relation of partners was established in two ways: through consanguinity, in which partners were brothers, fathers and sons, or uncles; and through marriage, in which two unrelated individuals cemented their commercial relationship by marrying one another's sisters—or through other more complex exchanges of relatives.

New England's major occupational groups used marriage in different ways to enlarge their circles of trust in furtherance of their particular goals. Their need to create patterned marital alliances varied according to their resources, their ambitions, and the character of their productive activities. Farmers used marriage to reconsolidate partibly divided family estates, to retain a hold on the labor of their sons, and to bring new land and labor into their families. Artisans used marital alliances to preserve skills, tools, markets, and labor. The clergy's marital alliances were directed to the consolidation and extension of influence both within and beyond the communities they served and to the solidification of bonds within their profession. And merchants used marriage to consolidate capital, commercial contacts, and political influence. These diverse needs were most effectively served by different kinds of marriage patterns. And these patterns gave rise, in turn, to alliance systems possessing varying degrees of extensiveness and cohesiveness. Such variations, inasmuch as they underlay the circles of trust that, in turn, made collective action possible, had much to do with determining which social groups in late eighteenth-century society were able to create corporate organizations and use them effectively.

Marriage in modern America is a matter of individuals and of the bonds of sentiment and mutual attraction that bring men and women together. While social background, common experiences, education, and, in some strata of society, such institutionalized rituals as the society *debut* may narrow the pool of potential marriage partners to persons of a certain status, income, or geographical origin—and while with decreasing frequency, parents may veto a marriage—, neither parents nor social institutions now exercise much influence over marital choice. This is hardly surprising given the fact that, the myth of "marrying the boss's daughter" notwithstanding, family is of small significance in the impersonal and meritocratic worlds of business, education, and the professions. Only at the margins of society, at its topmost level, where marriage still involves property relations, or at the bottom, where ethnic or religious solidarity is a consideration, can one find limitations on individual marital choice.[10]

In colonial America, where household and enterprise were identical, the marital choices of children were of enormous consequence, having important bearing on the possession of property, on the ability to do business, on the effectiveness of parental authority, and on the extent of one's influence beyond one's immediate circle of kin.[11] Because of its importance, marital choice constituted one of the most important "coping strategies" through which colonial families dealt with the problems posed by partible inheritance and the crisis of institutions. And as a strategic rather than a sentimental issue, it was a matter of parental choice—not the choice of the partners themselves.

Colonial marriage patterns have not been systematically studied. The extant evidence is scattered and the samples used have been small.[12] The situation is further complicated by intraregional variations: though not forbidden by law, certain types of marriage, especially the marriage of first cousins, were not practiced in Connecticut, while they were freely employed in Massachusetts after 1700. There were further variations according to local custom. And as has been suggested, there were variations between occupational groups. Nevertheless, the small evidence we have on marital strategies is suggestive—though far from complete or persuasive.

2. Farmers: Isolation and Dispersion

The marital choices of New England farmers were determined by a number of factors. These included the consolidation of land, labor, and authority, and the solidification of alliances within local community factions or status and income groups. There is evidence that marriages were sometimes used in attempts to overcome community factions, by joining contending groups together. Since virtually every family in a colonial New England farming community possessed land, there was, in theory at least, a basic equality among potential marriage partners. All children stood to inherit some portion of the paternal estate and to become heirs of grandparents or childless relatives. There were, nonetheless, certain factors that made some partners more desirable than others. Certainly, for example, those who possessed land contiguous to one's own more desirable than those living at a distance: since some living nearby could be kept under a father's influence, their labor would be available for such collective tasks as plowing and harvesting, and through the testamentary process or through marriage negotiations, contiguous property might come into one's family, consolidating one's holdings in a particular part of town.[13] Similarly, the threat of partible division of family land holdings might be overcome or reduced by choosing mates from one's own family, especially relatives on one's father's side, since males tended, especially after the crisis of resources began to inherit larger amounts and choicer parcels of family land.[14] There was a sentimental issue here as well, based on the desire of participants in a social system in which authority was patriarchal and identity patrilinial to preserve in the male line property that had traditionally belonged to the family.[15] Because contiguous land often, due to the testamentary process, belonged to one's brothers, the selection of mates on grounds of contiguity often also meant selection of mates on grounds of kinship in the paternal lines. Farmers, in sum, were likely to favor three basic types of marital alliances: 1) relationships in which neither contiguity nor kinship played a role but which were based on sentiment and short-term advantages, such as political alliances; 2) relationships in which either contiguity *or* kinship were factors; 3) relationships in which contiguity *and* kinship were factors.

These three types of alliances could be pursued in a number of ways. All, I would argue, led to social fragmentation and to a diminution of the capacity to act collectively. Randomized marital choices pursued within a limited pool of families would, over time, lead to local communities in which everyone was related in one way or another to everyone else. In such a situation, kinship ceases to be of any consequence: being related to someone would grant no particular advantage, unless the tie was a very close one, as between parents and children or husbands and wives. While one could imagine a situation of this sort leading to community cohesion, to a uniting of interests, anyone familiar with the history of New England towns knows that cohesion was not a characteristic that they possessed by the eighteenth century. If anything, the collectivization of kinship led to a magification of differences between families and individuals and acted as a source of conflict, not a source of consensus. In fact, such patterns promoted the destruction of communal corporatism by placing individuals in a position to decide what kinds of relationships would be most individually advantageous. And such opportunities necessarily promoted factions and differences in wealth and status, rather than eliminating them.

Relationships in which contiguity or kinship were factors would lead to more complex marriage patterns and clearer patterns of social and economic differentiation. When contiguity was a factor, farmers might, as some Connecticut families evidently did, establish a set of relationships between a group of four to six neighboring families.[16] These relationships would enable families to exchange children and solidify bonds between them without, for two generations at least, violating the strictures on first-cousin marriage.[17] The pattern of exchange could be prolonged by the introduction of outsiders. But as appears to have happened in Middletown and Middlefield, Connecticut by the late eighteenth century, these patterns could either collapse into consolidation of family groups through the marriage of cousins, uncles and nieces, and step-siblings, or generalize themselves into undifferentiated community kin-relations. Bonds between families might also be established through simpler means, sibling or cousin exchanges, in which brothers and sisters from one family married brothers and sisters in another or in which a set of cousins from one family married a set of cousins from another. These simpler means, however, like the more complex ones, when projected out over several generations led either to a disappearance of the significance of kinship or to exclusive family clustering— both of which were inimical to collective action. Finally, farmers might encourage first-cousin marriages to ensure the consolidation of contiguous land and the labor of their sons. Such marriages, because they were primarily concerned with the conservation of properties in the male line, would necessarily favor the marriages of sons to the father's brother's daughters. For when the children of brothers who also owned contiguous land and who stood to inherit shares of paternal property were joined together, not only were relations between the brothers/ fathers-in-law reinforced, but, on the ultimate testamentary division of their property, their lands would converge in the paternal line. In the meantime, their authority over their children would be unambiguous and directed to common purposes. Such cousin marriages, by concentrating land and labor within family groups, may have been an effective antidote to the partition and scattering of resources. But they also isolated families from one another and contributed to factionalization. And in the long run, it was, without the addition of new property, a losing strategy, only delaying, not preventing, the erosion of rural resources. If the grim analyses presented by Henretta, Greven, and Lockridge accurately portray the steady impoverishment and rising contentiousness of rural New England, this diminution of resources was complemented by an erosion of the structural possibilities for collective action. Wherever farmers might turn, they found their autonomy turning into dependence, their capacity for collective action breaking down into competitive individualism. This individualism, while propelling some young men into the cities to become merchant princes or industrialists, propelled more into the urban proletariat.[18] Although some farmers attempted to perpetuate older schemes of autonomy and communalism in the West, they usually found that, within a generation, the same forces of fragmentation and dependency were taking hold. For without common lands, the process of fragmentation was accelerated and compressed into one or two generations instead of three or four.

3. Artisans: Employees and Entrepreneurs

The artisans as a group present a variety of complex alliance patterns, none of which were successful in serving as a basis for effective collective action.[19] To begin with, artisans were never a coherent or unified group except insofar as they shared a common social status. Artisanship embraced a wide range of activities and required varying levels of skill and capital. A rough typology of artisans in the eighteenth century might rank them the following way:[20]

High-Skill, High Capital, Cooperative Artisans: Shipwrights, Housewrights, Millers, Tanners, Printers, Papermakers, Glassmakers, Braziers, Clockmakers, Ironmasters. (These activities required combinations of skills and capital from more than one artisan craft.)

High-Skill, Low-Capital, Individual Artisans: Blacksmiths, Silver and Gold Smiths, Tinsmiths, Joiners, Cabinetmakers, Tailors, Potters, Bakers, Hatters, Cutlers, Hornsmiths, Wheelwrights, Bookbinders, Plumbers, Gunsmiths, Locksmiths.

Low-Skill, Low Capital, Individual Artisans: Coopers, Sawyers, Fullers, Curriers, Weavers, Barbers, Peruke-makers, Shoemakers, Fisherman, Mariners, Laborers.

If artisans were fragmented by the variety of their productive activities, they were also divided by organization within the crafts, which, lacking a guild form, broke artisans within any given craft into competing individual household enterprises.[21] And within those household enterprises, craftsmen were further divided by status into masters, journeymen, and apprentices. Beyond being competitive with one another, these household enterprises, even within particular crafts, were, in addition, separated by religion (Quaker potters, for example, sought alliances only with other Quakers) by income, and by geography.[22] Finally, the absence of guilds placed artisans in an ambiguous position in relation to the economic and social system, a position that was particularly inimical to collective action. On the one hand, it was to their advantage to perpetuate craft loyalty, transmitting their skills from generation to generation, intermarrying with families in their own or in related crafts, and, when threatened, moving towards collective organization to control prices, markets, and quality. On the other hand, it was to their advantage to see themselves as entrepreneurs, using their craft to advance the economic and social interests of themselves and their families. Not only was the choice of craft loyalty socially isolating, inasmuch as it required that craftsmen form their primary alliances within small groups, but efforts towards collective organization on a narrow craft basis were likely to be frustrated both by the intrinsic fragmentation within the craft (between workers at the several levels of status, between religious and ethnic groups and between competitive household enterprises) and by legal doctrines, such as those applied in the famous Philadelphia Cordwainers case of 1806, which branded artisan combinations as conspiracies in restraint of trade.[23] In any case, even when combinations could be achieved, unless they included *all* artisans in a given craft, they merely created opportunities for entrepreneurs. When the New York bakers struck in 1802 in an attempt to force city authorities to raise the price of bread, they found their market being taken over by an industrial enterprise, the New York Bread Company, organized by Alexander Hamilton and a group of mercantile associates.[24] Entrepreneurship, while it might lead artisans towards more effective control of markets, generally led them away from artisanship itself. Men who rose from artisanship to manufacturing and marketing had a tendency, once they had accumulated some capital or prestige, to become capitalists, severing their connections with their craft origins and investing their wealth in whatever ventures seemed most advantageous. This familiar pattern was set by Benjamin Franklin, who rose from printer to publisher to statesman, and followed by many others.

In spite of the organizational divisions, internal conflicts, and external political, legal, and economic pressures that separated one craft from another and, within a craft, one enterprise from another, artisans did attempt to create alliances. Without craft-level solidarities such as guilds, the family and the set of alliances it could generate became the basis for the preservation and transmission of skills, tools, markets, and labor. These alliances varied according to the needs of the craft, depending on the level of skill required, its labor intensiveness, the local market for its products, and the extent to which production required cooperation with related crafts. Artisans might marry practitioners of their own crafts to limit competition, pool resources, and share markets. Or they might marry into families in crafts that drew on similar markets and raw materials. Practitioners of high-skill, cooperative, labor intensive enterprises such as ship-building could seek either skill-consolidating alliances, such as those found by Farber among the Becket, Rowell, Leach,

Babbige and Hawkes families of Salem; or skill-combining alliances, such as those among the Savages, who were ship-builders, and the blacksmiths, ropemakers, blockmakers, and riggers of Middletown, Connecticut; or market-consolidating alliances, such as those found in Portland, Connecticut among the shipbuilders, the sawyers (who controlled the timber supply), and the quarrymen (whose stone was the commodity carried by the ships).[25] Such alliances usually enabled families to maintain geographical stability, though they often led to the dilution of paternal authority (since a son in a craft other than his father's had less reason to obey him) and to a breakdown in intergenerational patterns of craft transmission. The loss of a familial basis for craft solidarity was important, since it left artisans in particular trades joined only by their common interests as producers.

High-skill crafts that were neither cooperative nor labor and capital intensive tended to generate geographically extensive alliance patterns.[26] Local markets for the products of such crafts as printing and silversmithing were distinctly limited. And, as a result, sons were sent off to establish workshops in communities other than those into which they had been born. Ideally, these geographically extensive patterns should have led to networks in which the new workshops in new places continued to serve as bases for training and employing relatives, thereby maintaining intergenerational continuity of craft and authority. In trades like printing, in which skills and tools were scarce and valuable, this sort of network did form and hold together for a remarkable length of time.[27] Thus, for example, Samuel Green of Cambridge, Massachusetts (1615–1702) fathered two sons who became printers in Boston, Samuel and Bartholemew. Bartholemew Green, who established the first newspaper in the colonies in 1704, fathered three sons and a daughter. One son, Jonas, left Boston to work with his brother, Timothy, in New London, Connecticut—and then moved on to Philadelphia and, finally, to Annapolis, Maryland where, in 1745, he established the second newspaper in that colony. Another son, Bartholemew Green, Jr., stayed in Boston, where he became the partner of his brother-in-law John Draper (who had married his sister), and where he produced two sons who also became printers. The third son, Timothy Green, moved to New London in 1714. He and his sons established printing businesses and newspapers in that city, in Hartford, in New Haven, and in Norwich. His greatgrandchildren included the Connecticut bookbinders and booksellers, Thomas and John Green, the Norwich printer Samuel Green, and the founder of the *Virginia Herald* (1787), an early southern newspaper. The perpetuation of printing over five generations in the Green family was an unusual achievement. Few crafts managed to perpetuate themselves within any one family for more than three. The Greens managed this feat by accompanying geographical dispersion with fairly regular exchanges of personnel, in which sons in one place were sent to learn their trade with uncles or grandparents in other places. As printers, the Greens were in an excellent position to maintain such long-term patterns of exchange and communication. Other crafts were not so fortunate. Silversmiths, for example, who were fairly stable as a group through the mid-eighteenth century, found it impossible to maintain either geographical stability or networks as the number of smiths—both their own children and apprentices and more recent immigrants—began to exceed the demand for their products.[28] What had begun as an effort to build networks ended, by the late eighteenth century, in a pattern of flight from adversity, with silversmiths either abandoning the trade entirely, allying themselves with merchants to create manufacturing firms, or using their skill with metals to create new industries, such as clockmaking (industrial pioneer Eli Terry had been trained as a silversmith).

Marriages among high-skill artisans of this sort tended to be short-term alliances of advantage, not long-term relations of exchange or consolidation among or within families. Since they were geographically mobile, such artisans often married into unrelated families in the new communities to which they had migrated—or, as in the case of the geographically stable tinsmiths of Berlin, Wallingford, and Meriden, Connecticut, they intermarried with other tinsmiths or with families in allied trades.[29] Either way, they tended to lose their identities, either being absorbed by the communities in which they had settled, or turning away from the crafts to become manufacturers or entrepreneurs.

Low-skill artisans, mariners, fishermen, shoemakers, potters, barbers, and others, having little to preserve in the way of special skills, tools, markets, or trained labor, tended to favor alliance patterns that enabled them to remain in one place. Sometimes, as in the case of the Quaker potters of Essex County, Massachusetts, these alliances resembled the multi-family sibling and cousin exchanges seen among certain farm families:[30] the first generation involved a triple sibling exchange between the Shoves and the Osborns and marriages of the three Osborn daughters into the Upton, Purinton, and Boyce families (all of whom were potters and Quakers); the next generation involved the marriages of the three children of George Shove to an Upton, a Purinton, and a Boyce—thus tying together the relations of the previous generation. In the third generation, however, the pattern began to break down. Although not forbidden by Massachusetts law to marry cousins, this Quaker group apparently discouraged it. Only one marital connection, that of Theophilus Shove, Jr. (1741–1803) to his father's brother's daughter's daughter, Lydia Purinton, took place. The Quaker potters began to marry outside their craft and outside their sect. Some became geographically mobile, setting up a short-term network in relation in western New York. Others became entrepreneurs. Nonetheless, the Quaker potters were, unlike most artisans in their own and other low-skill crafts, able to maintain four to five generations of continuity. More typical, however, was the pattern that Farber found in the Archer family of Salem. Such patterns were, basically, relations of mutual support which preserved authority, labor, and geographical stability—without leading to craft continuity or broadly effective alliances. Such patterns were brought into being through encouraging marriages of sons to their fathers' brothers' daughters (a pattern of isolation) or through connections to families in unrelated crafts (a pattern of dispersion) which could open up new trades to sons. Thus, for example, in the Archer family of Salem, Jonathan Archer (1671–1746), a cordwainer and cooper, had three sons.[31] Jonathan, the eldest, became a mariner; Samuel, a peruke-maker; and Nathaniel, the youngest, a cooper like his father. Jonathan Archer, the mariner, also had three sons. The eldest was apprenticed to his paternal uncle to learn peruke-making; the second was trained as a seaman by his father; and the third, Samuel, became a tailor, probably learning the trade from a maternal uncle. Samuel Archer's only son, like his father, became a peruke-maker. Nathaniel Archer's four sons followed a variety of occupations, none of them their father's: two became mariners, like their paternal uncle Jonathan; one, who was retarded, became a laborer; the youngest and most successful, having learned peruke-making from his paternal uncle Samuel, parlayed his craft into entrepreneurship, becoming a "trader" and inn keeper.

Artisan unity, either among artisans as a group, or within particular crafts, was undermined by the absence of guilds that could control competition and markets and by the absence of stable patterns of intermarriage that could tie craftsmen to their crafts. Competition was aggravated both by their own high birth rate and by the migration to the colonies, especially after 1750, of craftsmen from England who were fleeing the industrialization of their own crafts.[32] Competition and changing public tastes (such as the decline of demand for wigs and the growing preference for imported Staffordshire pottery over native products) pushed artisans into geographical and occupational mobility, scattering their human and technical resources. An artisan in the eighteenth century faced an impossible dilemma. He had to choose between being tied to his craft, becoming proletarianized as competition eroded his earnings and as his markets and raw materials were taken over by entrepreneurs, and becoming an entrepreneur himself, altering the process and organization of production to reduce costs and increase output, and enlarging the market for his product beyond the locality.

Either way, the pressures led to individuation, not towards collective action.

It is true that in certain trades in certain places—among the shoe-makers of Lynn and Philadelphia and the printers and bakers of New York—voluntary associations, resembling both guilds and embryonic modern labor unions, did develop. But they were local and usually did not come into being until the craftsmen had already surrendered control of their trade to entrepreneurs.[33] Even when entrepreneurs in certain crafts attempted to increase their access to credit through forming "mechanics" and other special purpose banks, they had problems en-listing sufficient support among themselves to make these ventures successful.[34] The only real recourse to collective action that artisans had was electoral politics—which they took to with a vengeance as sup-porters of Jefferson and Jackson.[35] But successful political action in America involved the creation of stable coalitions, coalitions that would not only unite the scattered interests of the artisans, but join them with those of the farmers, shop-keepers, and other social groups. As the work on politics in the early Republic uniformly shows, such coalitions were inevitably unstable and shortlived, reflecting the diversity of their constitutents.

4. The Clergy: Cohesion and Dependency

The clergy, unlike farmers or artisans, were relatively successful in developing effective local and translocal alliances which, in turn, led to patterns of collective action and to formal corporate institutions. This is not surprising, for the clergy were, by their very nature, a group with clearly defined common interests, a group whose members had been trained together at either Harvard or Yale (thus having shared an in-tensive common socialization experience), who were often sons of cler-gymen themselves (thus having kin-continuity), and who presided over a social institution, the church, whose interests they had a vital interest in preserving. The clergy, as earlier suggested, followed simultaneously two patterns of alliance-making, a bifurcation dictated by the nonin-heritable nature of the clerical office. On the one hand, they cultivated close ties with important lay families in the communities in which they served, which strengthened their power in their congregations and opened up occupational opportunities for their sons. On the other hand, they cultivated trans-local alliances with other clergymen (to consolidate professional identity) and with powerful laymen (to further the interests of the church). An example of this dual pattern of local and translocal alliances can be seen in the Hall family of Wallingford, Connecticut:[36]

the Reverend Samuel Hall (1695–1776) married Anne Law, daughter of the Governor of Connecticut, Jonathan Law (1674–1750). Law's fifth wife was Eunice Hall, sister of Samuel. (She later married the Reverend Samuel Andrew of Milford, whose aunt, Abigail Andrew, had been Governor Law's second wife; finally, she married Col. Joseph Pitkin of Hartford, a member of a powerful political family.) Hall's son, Samuel, was intended for the ministry, but died of smallpox shortly after graduating from Yale. His other children, however, perpetuated his local and translocal interests. His eldest daughter, Lucy, married Charles Whittelsey, son of the Reverend Samuel Whittelsey of Wallingford. (Hall's niece, Susannah Hall, had married Whittelsey's brother, Elisha; Hall's brother, Benjamin, had married Whittelsey's first cousin, Abigail Chauncey of Durham; another brother, Elihu Hall, had married Whittelsey's sister, Lois.) This solidified local alliances. Hall's second daughter, Anne, married the Reverend John Foot, Hall's assistant and successor to the pulpit at Cheshire. Hall's sons became prominent local farmers, large land-owners, and magistrates. One, Elisha, was sent to Yale, probably in the hope that he would follow his father into the ministry. But by the time he had completed his education, in 1764, Hall's Old Light faction of Congregationalism was in retreat and his prospects for a pulpit on acceptable doctrinal terms were poor.

The Hall pattern was not unusual. An examination of the Fellows of Yale through the eighteenth century shows a similar bifurcation of intensive local and translocal connections. The following list shows some of the connections between the ten ministers who founded Yale:[37]

James Noyes of Stonington: brother of Yale Fellow Moses Noyes; he married Dorothy Stanton, daughter of one of the leading families of that place. Noyes' son, Joseph, became a Yale Fellow in 1735.

Israel Chauncey of Stratford: the youngest son of Harvard president Charles Chauncey; his brother, Nathaniel, was minister at Windsor—and father of the Reverend Nathaniel Chauncey of Durham, who became a Yale Fellow in 1746, and of Sarah Chauncey, wife of the Reverend Samuel Whittelsey of Wallingford. Chauncey's sister, Sarah, married the Reverend Gershom Bulkeley, minister at Wethersfield. Israel Chauncey married Mary Nichols, whose sister married Yale Fellow Joseph Webb. Chauncey's children included Charles Chauncey, minister at Stratfield, and Isaac Chauncey, minister at Hadley, Massachusetts. Through the marriages of his son Charles to Sarah Burr, daughter of John Burr and Sarah Fitch, and to Sarah Wolcott, sister of Governor Roger Wolcott, Chauncey became connected to the most politically important families in the colony.

Abraham Pierson of Killingworth: son of the Reverend Abraham Pierson of Lynn, Massachusetts, Branford, Connecticut, and Newark, New Jersey; he married Abigail Clark, daughter of a wealthy Milford family whose sister, Mary, was the first wife of Governor Law. His son, John Pierson, was a founding trustee of Princeton and married Ruth Woodbridge, daughter of the Reverend Timothy Woodbridge, a Yale Fellow. Her mother, Mehitable Wyllys, was a member of the politically powerful Wyllys family. Mehitable's sister, Mary Wyllys, was the mother of Yale Fellow Jared Eliot.

Samuel Mather of Windsor: an offshoot of the famous "Mather Dynasty" of Massachusetts clergymen, he married Hannah Treat, daughter of Governor Robert Treat. His son, Azariah Mather, was minister at Saybrook.

Samuel Andrew of Milford: he married Abigail Treat, daughter of the Governor and sister of Hannah, wife of Samuel Mather. His children included the Reverend Samuel Andrew, who married Eunice, daughter of the Reverend Samuel Hall of Cheshire, and widow of Governor Law; Abigail Andrew, who married Governor Law (whose first wife was Anne Eliot of Guilford, sister of Yale Fellow Jared Eliot); and Elizabeth Andrew, wife of the Yale President, Timothy Cutler. Andrew's granddaughter, Abigail, married the Reverend William Russell of Middletown—whose mother, Mary Pierpont, was the daughter of Yale Fellow James Pierpont. Russell's father was Yale Fellow Noadiah Russell.

Timothy Woodbridge of Hartford: son of the Reverend John Woodbridge of Newbury and Andover, and Mercy, daughter of the Massachusetts Governor, Thomas Dudley. His brother John was a minister at Killingworth and husband of Abigail Leete, daughter of Governor William Leete of Guilford. John's son, the Reverend John Woodbridge, was minister at West Springfield and husband of Jemima Eliot, sister of Yale Fellow Jared Eliot and of Anne Eliot, wife of Governor Law. Woodbridge married Mehitable Wyllys, widow of his predecessor, Isaac Foster, and daughter of Samuel Wyllys of Hartford. His children included the Reverend Timothy Woodbridge, minister at Simbury; Mary Woodbridge, wife of William Pitkin of Hartford; Ruth Woodbridge, who married John Pierson, son of the Reverend Abraham Pierson; Ashbel Woodbridge, who became at Yale Fellow in 1745, and who married another Pitkin daughter; and Susannah, who married into the Treat family.

James Pierpont of New Haven: he married thrice, first to Abigail Davenport, granddaughter of founder of New Haven, John Davenport, and sister of Yale Fellow John Davenport. Her mother was the sister of Yale Fellow Abraham Pierson. Pierpont's second wife was Sarah Haynes, daughter of the Reverend Joseph Haynes. Pierpont's third wife was Mary Hooker, daughter of the Reverend Samuel Hooker and member of Hartford's founding family. His children included Abigail Pierpont, who married Yale Fellow Joseph Noyes; Samuel Pierpont, minister at Lyme; Sarah Pierpont, who married the famous Reverend Jonathan Edwards, revivalist and first president of Princeton; Mary Pierpont, who married the Reverend William Russell of Middletown, son of Yale Fellow Noadiah Russell; and James Pierpont, rector of the Hopkins Grammar School at New Haven. Pierpont's grandchildren included Pierpont Edwards, leading Connecticut politician, Esther Edwards, wife of the Reverend Aaron Burr, president of Princeton, and Mary Edwards, who married Major Timothy Dwight of Northampton and whose son, Timothy Dwight, would serve as President of Yale.

Noadiah Russell of Middletown: he married into the Hamlins, Middletown's most prominent political family. His children included Yale Fellow William Russel, minister of Middletown, who married the daughter of Yale Fellow James Pierpont; and Daniel Russell, minister at Stepney and husband of Catherine Chauncey, cousin of Yale Fellow Israel Chauncey.

Joseph Webb of Stratford: he married Elizabeth Nichols, whose sister Mary, was the wife of Yale Fellow Israel Chauncey. His children included the Reverend Joseph Webb, minister of Newark, New Jersey and New Haven; and Elizabeth Webb, who married Samuel Pomeroy. Pomeroy's mother, Abigail Strong, was the widow of the Reverend Nathaniel Chauncey of Durham and the mother of the Reverend Samuel Whittelsey of Wallingford, a Yale Fellow.

The only Yale founder not to enjoy extensive connections with his colleagues and with influential political and economic interests was Thomas Buckingham, who was also the only Fellow who had not graduated from college.

The ministry would have been in a fine position had it not been for the fact that their alliances and high positions were built on the shifting sands of popular favor. As the church began to split doctrinally over the Great Awakening and as it began to come into competition with other denominations, first the Anglicans, later the Methodists and Baptists, ties to the powerful proved insufficient to protect them from dissenters in their own congregations. The situation was complicated by the willingness of some powerful families, in spite of their connection to the Old Light establishment, to support the popular New Light side.[38] Thus, for example, the Whittelseys of Wallingford supported the New Light minister, James Dana, to succeed the Reverend Samuel Whittelsey (Dana had married a Whittelsey daughter) against the will of the older, wealthier Halls in the acrimonious Wallingford Controversy of the 1750s.[39] When the clergy, led by such men as Yale President Thomas Clap, switched over to the New Light side, it was following the popular trend rather than leading it. And this tendency to follow rather than lead was symptomatic of a growing dependency on lay power in the face of a broad erosion of ecclesiastical authority.

If the clergy had, by the second half of the eighteenth century, declined in autonomy and authority, it had, on the whole, succeeded in maintaining its identity as a group and in generating geographically extensive professional networks. Ministers had, in other words, maintained their capacity for collective action. And even though kinship was an important element in maintaining group solidarity, the clergy remained remarkably inclusive, accommodating newcomers to their ranks through the practice by which young ministers began their careers as assistants to older ministers and, upon succeeding to the pulpit, married their daughters. But the price of this cohesion was dependency—either upon evangelistic appeals to the populace or upon the good will of the wealthy and politically consequential.

A symptom of this dependency can be seen in the shifting base of financial support of New England's two clerically controlled colleges, Harvard and Yale. Grants from the colonial and state governments to Harvard had averaged over two thousand dollars a year up to 1735; for the period 1736–1750, when the controversy over the Great Awakening was at its peak, grants dropped steeply, ranging from a low of $378 to a high of $942.[40] Although the grants recovered during the Revolutionary period between 1756 and 1785, the rise of Anti-Federalism and Jeffersonianism curtailed legislative generosity. The legislature gave nothing to Harvard between 1791 and 1811. The state's last contribution to Harvard was a sum of $100,000 given to the medical school between 1811 and 1825. Based as it was on a tax on banks, this was hardly a conspicuous example of legislative generosity. Yale fared no better than Harvard.[41] Although the legislature was relatively openhanded between 1701 and 1755, the rise of the New Lights and the political opposition to the Old Light-controlled college led to a curtailment of funds between 1756 and 1760. When President Clap shifted his allegiance to the New Light side, legislative support resumed, only to be stopped again in 1775, when political opposition to the college arose again over Yale's resistance to the inclusion of laymen on its governing boards. Yale received nothing from the state between 1776 and 1792. In the early 1790s, as the conservative reaction to the French Revolution brought the clergy and the merchants together to form the basis of the Federalist Party, and as that party enjoyed a brief period of popular support, the legislature gave Yale $40,629. But after that point, government support effectively ceased, with the exception of two small bonuses from bank charters. The decline in public support for the colleges is an accurate measure of the decline in public confidence in the clergy. For the colleges were the most visible targets of clerical power. With the growing unwillingness of the public to support the clergy and its colleges, it was forced to turn elsewhere for support. Harvard turned to the wealthy merchants of Boston, including them, after 1780, on its governing boards and reaping a rich harvest of donations in return. While public donations to Harvard between 1700 and 1800 had totalled 55 percent of all contributions (the large proportion of private donations in this period had come from England), public support dropped to 33 percent between 1801 and 1825.[42] The slack was taken up by a small body of mercantile donors, most of them from Boston. Yale followed a somewhat different pattern.[43] At first, hoping for continued legislative support but, at the same time, being reluctant to lose control of the college, the clergy accepted a legislative proposal to include six members of the upper house of the legislature as *ex officio* members of the Corporation (the clergy retaining ten seats). When Federalist unity began to crumble at the beginning of the nineteenth century, the clergy turned to the population of New Haven, which had a definable interest in the college's prosperity, and to appeals to its denominational constituency. The appeals were effective: while private contributions to Yale has comprised only 29.6 percent of all donations between 1701 and 1800, between 1800 and 1825, they amounted to 84.6 percent. These funds, like the private monies donated during the eighteenth-century period of legislative parsimony, came from a remarkably broad and largely mercantile constituency. Unlike the donors to Harvard, however, the donors were not merely wealthy New Haven or Hartford magnates. They were from all over Connecticut and, by 1761, New Yorkers had begun to appear on the subscription lists. And by 1822, when Yale conducted a fund drive to create a professorship of divinity, 19 of the 49 donors were from out of state—including such prominent New York merchants as Arthur Tappan, Garrit Smith, Richard Varick, and Henry Rutgers.[44] As the clergy in Massachusetts lost public confidence, it split into Unitarian and Trinitarian factions. The Unitarians, who regained control of Harvard, turned to an urban mercantile constituency for support. The Trinitarians appealed to their dispersed fellow-believers—and founded Williams and Amherst. In Connecticut, the Congregational clergy, while remaining unified, turned to their denomination as well. And as Connecticut Congregationalists were migrating in great numbers to New York City and to new settlements in the South and West, this constituency soon became a national one. In all cases, however, the relationship of the clergy to its constituency had been transformed from an authoritative one to a dependent one. And the increasing significance of the mercantile component in the private constituencies was unmistakable.

5. Toward a Hierarchy of Relative Influence

Although subjected to the same pressures of population on ideology and available resources in the course of the eighteenth century, the major occupational groups of New England responded in different ways. All attempted to adapt their basic institutional form, the family enterprise, to changing circumstances. But the success of these adaptations varied according to the nature of the groups' occupations and the types of strategies followed. These strategies involved the creation of alliances between families. They could take a number of forms, inclusive or exclusive, geographically entensive and intensive, linking families along occupational lines, by proximity, or by kinship. The outcomes of these efforts to build alliances varied according to the character of the alliance. In most instances—those affecting the majority of the farming and artisan population—the outcome was individualism, as families proved increasingly unable to fulfill either their social or their economic functions. Individuation was not necessarily a bad thing: some individuals with luck, pluck, and a capacity for hard work could become wealthy and prominent. And in any case, the failure of older forms of family and community vastly increased an individual's options—as Milton described the situation of Adam and Eve on being expelled from the Garden of Eden:

The world was all before them, where to find their place of rest, and Providence their guide.

Of course success in this new world of individuals could not depend merely on individual exertions. Whether in pursuit of economic, political, religious, or intellectual ends, individuals had to band together in voluntary associations in order to be effective. And the new corporatism, based not on the collective will, as towns and churches had been, but on the actions of individuals in pursuit of their private interests, came into being. It took an astonishing variety of forms, from entities as small as partnerships and early corporations (which seldom counted more than a dozen employees and stockholders), through political and denominational groups embracing thousands of individuals. But while possessing the common characteristic of voluntary association between individuals, these new institutional forms varied in permanence and effectiveness, depending on, among other things, the strength of the ties between the individuals who comprised them. The strength of these ties, as this chapter has attempted to show, was determined by earlier patterns of alliance-making. The more individuated people were, the less their capacity for collective action and the less their ability to form stable corporate organizations. The course of the social crisis of the eighteenth century had led to a situation in which the majority of New England's population was both materially impoverished and organizationally incapacitated. Only the clergy and the merchants retained a significant, though impaired, capacity to form strong alliances. And this capacity, combined with the material resources of the merchants, would give these groups a marked advantage in creating effective corporate organizations.

New England at the end of the eighteenth century presents a complex cluster of institutional possibilities. On the one hand, private groups were emerging that controlled central credit, transportation, social welfare, and educational institutions. On the other hand, the bulk of the population was endeavoring to form its own private institutions while, at the same time, looking to the state both to assist them and to curtail the dominance of small but powerful urban groups. The basic question of the first half of the new century would be whether the masses of new individuals would be able to combine successfully enough to make the state the apex of the pyramid of relative institutional influence, or whether the numerically small, but materially wealthy and organizationally cohesive urban elite, and its allies in the clergy and the new professions of law and medicine, would prevail.

CHAPTER FOUR

The Merchants of New England: Strategy and Structure

Yet this intricate commercial mechanism with its many interrelated parts was not an impersonal machine existing above men's heads, outside their lives, to which they attached themselves for the purposes of trade. The New England merchants of the mid-seventeenth century had witnessed the creation of this network of trade; they knew that human relationships were the bonds that kept its parts together.

The same principle was at work in the selection of agents, factors, and correspondents in the importing trade as operated in the fishery. Being both all important and extremely fragile and unreliable, commercial ties were best secured by the cement of kinship or long friendship.[1]

It would be an error to consider the merchants of the seventeenth and eighteenth centuries in New England as a unified group.[2] Although they shared certain common economic and political interests, they were internally divided in a variety of ways. They differed in background, some having been in commerce since the founding of the colonies, while others were new to trade, being either more recent immigrants (like Thomas Amory and John Cabot) or having recently ascended from small shop-keeping and artisanship (like Stephen Codman). They differed in religion, some favoring "orthodox" Calvinist Congregationalism, some leaning to the liberal Arminian Congregationalism that would become Unitarianism and Deism; some were Anglicans, others were Quakers. They were divided politically, depending on the character of their commercial activities and the nature of their alliances with political and clerical authority, and these differences were aggravated as the Revolutionary crisis of the mid-eighteenth century separated Tory from Whig. They were further divided by geography. Although they tended to be concentrated along the coast or, as with the merchants of Middletown and Hartford, along major inland waterways, they were scattered among cities and towns of various sizes and levels of development. Finally, they were divided into a myriad of family enterprises acting in competition with one another. From the standpoint of the early eighteenth century, the merchants of New England hardly resembled the portrait drawn of them by the business historian Kenneth Wiggin Porter who, in depicting them as they had come to be by the beginning of the nineteenth century, likened them to the family groups "encountered by the early western traders among the villagers of India":

> This seems natural and proper in an oriental agricultural community; but to discover kinship groups, though of a much less highly integrated character, among individualistic western traders engaged in commerce is a little surprising.[3]

In this chapter I will examine the strategies and patterns of alliances that, within a period of little more than a century, transformed the merchants from a loose occupational group to what Porter would describe as "pretty much of a closed corporation"—the cohesive and coherent pinnacle of the late eighteenth-century hierarchy of relative influence.[4]

1. The New England Merchants in the Seventeenth Century

The pattern of mercantile alliances between the 1630s and the early nineteenth century went through several distinct phases, which appear to have been dictated by changes in the character of colonial commerce and alterations in the nature of the colonial government that affected mercantile wealth, status, and access to political power, as well as influencing the strategic considerations by which the merchants actively sought riches, office, and stability. Until the last quarter of the seventeenth century, the merchants were essentially outsiders. Although many considered themselves good Puritans, they were frequently at odds with the ministers and magistrates, who saw the merchants themselves as political rivals and who viewed their efforts to earn profits as inimical to the corporate ideology of the Puritan Commonwealth.[5]

Though undoubtedly wealthier than the bulk of the colonial population, the merchants were politically immobilized by their small numbers and by official hostility. They were not only outvoted by farmers and artisans; they were also kept in check by ministers and magistrates who sought both to regulate their activities and, through such devices as church seating and listings on college catalogues, to remind the community of their tertiary status.[6] In any case, commerce until the late seventeenth century was a marginal activity in the colonies. Most people were subsistence farmers and, as a result, only minimally dependent on markets and with little need for imported goods. Further, the colonies had little to offer England in terms of direct exports once the fur trade dwindled in the first few decades of settlement.

Although Bailyn makes much of mercantile intermarriages in the seventeenth century, I belive that he exaggerates their significance.[7] It is certainly true, as he asserts, that merchant families did intermarry and that, by the end of the century, most of the leading families were interconnected. It is equally true, however, that they looked to the ministry and magistracy for mates for their sons and daughters. If the merchants could not gain access to power and status directly, by virtue of wealth or election, they could attain these ends through marital alliances with more powerful groups. Thus, for example, the merchant John Hull (1624–1685), although himself married to the daughter of fellow merchant Edmund Quincy, Sr. (1602–1635), married off his only child, Hannah to Samuel Sewell, Chief Justice of the Colony. Similarly, Edmund Quincy, Jr. (1628–1680) married successively Joanna Hoar, daughter of the Reverend Leonard Hoar, President of Harvard College, and Elizabeth Gookin, daughter of a prominent magistrate, Daniel Gookin.[8] (There were, of course, reciprocal advantages for the magistrates and ministers, for such alliances joined economic resources to their high status.

Because commerce was a relatively marginal activity and because ministers and magistrates monopolized high status positions and political offices, merchants had far less to gain by seeking alliances among themselves than they would by the eighteenth century. Even the structure of business enterprises militated against intensive mercantile alliance-making within the group. Most merchants in the seventeenth century did business as individuals, not in partnerships. So there was little need to cement that vulnerable relationship by marital ties. In any case, the merchants in this period were not as clearly defined a group as they would later become. Many, like John Hull of Boston and Stephen Codman of Charlestown, were successful artisans—a goldsmith and a saddler, respectively—who also engaged in trade.[9] Some, like the Leveretts and Dudleys of Boston and Cambridge and the Higginsons of Salem, either came out of clerical backgrounds or had actually been ordained as ministers.[10] Others, like the Quincys and Tyngs of Boston, were torn between trade and landed proprietorship in Braintree and Tyngsborough.[11] Only with the imposition of royal authority over the Puritan state and the reorganization of Britain's international commercial interests would the merchant group begin to achieve clear definition as a social group.

The collapse of Cromwell's Commonwealth in England and the restoration of the Stuart monarchy not only brought into power a regime hostile to the self-governing Puritan governments of New England, but also an economic outlook which saw the colonies as entities to be used to the advantage of the mother country. Although the Crown was not successful in its attempts to unite the northern colonies under the Dominion of New England, it did succeed in replacing the elective government in Massachusetts with a royally appointed governor and council. Although Connecticut kept its charter and with it its ability to elect its own rulers, British threats to declare the colony's townships illegal corporations and to appropriate their commonly-owned landholdings forced its inhabitants to distribute these resources to individual owners ("proprietors").[12] This altered the corporate character of the towns, not only splitting them into pre–1670 inhabitants who shared in the distribution of previously common land resources and newcomers who did not, but also, in effect, converting land from a resource over which inhabitants enjoyed only a right of use (if they left town, it reverted to the commons) to a commodity that could be bought, sold, and speculated in by both townsmen and absentee owners. Politically and economically, the merchants benefited from the Restoration—even if they did not necessarily support it (many merchants were active in the overthrow of Andros, organizer of the Dominion of New England, in 1689).[13] In Massachusetts, where a royal government with pronounced economic interests had been imposed, merchants were no longer dependent on popular opinion to gain office. In Connecticut, although merchants remained in a subservient position politically, the increasingly commercial orientation of the farmers and the conversion of land into a commodity were beginning to create a basis for mercantile ascendancy into the political structure.

The rise of the merchants as a political group was facilitated by an alteration in the character of colonial commerce. Before the last quarter of the seventeenth century, the merchants had been little more than shopkeepers and small traders, agents of relatives in England who included among their interests some trade in American commodities. The Navigation Acts of 1660 and 1673 and the Staple Act of 1663 changed this, placing the merchants in a strategic situation in the commercial system that, while restricting the range of their activities, enabled them to earn considerably greater profits from a vastly increased volume of trade.[14] These statutes gave a monopoly on the transport and marketing of all colonial goods to British merchants and shippers (including, of course, the colonists themselves) and required that European goods, even if not British in origin, be shipped to the colonies via the British Isles. By eliminating foreign competition, especially in the shipment of commodities from the southern plantations, New Englanders increased their hold over a lucrative market. By restricting imports to goods manufactured in or transshipped through England, the colonial merchants increased their control, both directly and indirectly and as agents of British interests, over the market for foreign goods sold in the colonies. Although, as Bailyn suggests, some merchants found government policies restrictive and sought to evade them through smuggling and other questionable activities, the overall effect of mercantilism favored the growth of the merchants as a powerful and cohesive group. As Porter noted,

> . . . the Navigation Acts protected the American merchant against foreign competition, and even their annoying restrictions had compensatory effects in preventing colonial businessmen from dissipating their energies upon a multiplicity of enterprises and in causing them to confine their attentions to a few types of commerce for which they were especially suited.[15]

Finally, the merchants benefited from the struggles of England and the other European powers in the years between 1680 and 1713, which, in extending British hegemony over Acadia in the north and areas of the Caribbean in the south, created new markets and entrepots—especially a lucrative trade in West Indies goods. In addition, New Englanders profited from supplying the military and from privateering.

From the standpoint of the forging of alliances among merchants, the new commercial opportunities of the later seventeenth century exerted an especially significant influence. The triangle (or, more accurately, the polygon) of trade between New England and the mother country had been established before the 1670s. In this commercial arrangement, New England goods such as fish, lumber, and cattle were transportated to the West Indies, the Canary Islands, or Spain. There they were exchanged for goods, such as sugar and wine, for which there was a market in England. Here they were sold or exchanged for British manufactures which were, in turn, reshipped to the colonies. It was a complex trade with innumerable variations.[16] The reorganization of the Empire and the imposition of mercantilist regulations gave enormous stimulus to the development of this trade, especially to Spain and the

West Indies. Such ventures, however, increased the merchants' needs for capital and reliable manpower, leading them into partnership arrangements that they had previously found unnecessary. Such arrangements, needless to say, necessarily involved the use of marital connections.

2. The New England Merchants in the Eighteenth Century

The reorganization of colonial government and commerce in the late seventeenth century coincided with the beginnings of the crisis of resources in rural areas in the early eighteenth. Together, these not only gave the merchants direct access to political power and considerable control over commercial relations between the colonies and international markets, but also, as the rural population began to be dependent on commercial agriculture and as their demands for imported goods increased (stimulated by the later Navigation Acts), the merchants were placed in a position to preside over the operations of the colonies' internal economy. There was, however, no reason why these circumstances should have necessarily propelled them towards consolidations as a group. They might well have favored socially fragmenting competition over more cooperative responses. Although their seventeenth-century experience as social and political outsiders may have contributed to their tendency to cohere, and while this tendency may have been furthered by common political and economic interests, the increasing importance of the partnership as the basic form of commercial organization and the need to bring unrelated merchants with their abilities and capital into family firms seem to have exercised a particularly decisive influence over the process of group consolidation.

In the seventeenth century, mercantile marriage alliances had been rather diffuse, directed less at creating ties between merchants' families than to connecting them to influential families in ecclesiastical and political life. Bailyn, for example, in his "Partial Reconstruction of the Tyng-Usher Connections in the Second Generation" (Figure 1), tends to emphasize the mercantile significance of marital ties by depicting men known to have engaged in trade in bold-face type.[17] Equally significant, however, if one is to get an accurate impression of the character of merchant marriage strategies, are the marriages between the seventeenth-century merchants whom he chose to study and the clergy. As he shows, in smaller type, the clergy are ubiquitous: one daughter of William Tyng married the Reverend Thomas Shepherd; of the six children of William's brother Edward Tyng, three made marriages with significant clerical families: Eunice to the Reverend Samuel Willard, Hannah to Habijah Savage (whose grandfather, Zachariah Symmes, was

Figure 1

A PARTIAL RECONSTRUCTION OF THE TYNG-USHER CONNECTIONS IN THE SECOND GENERATION

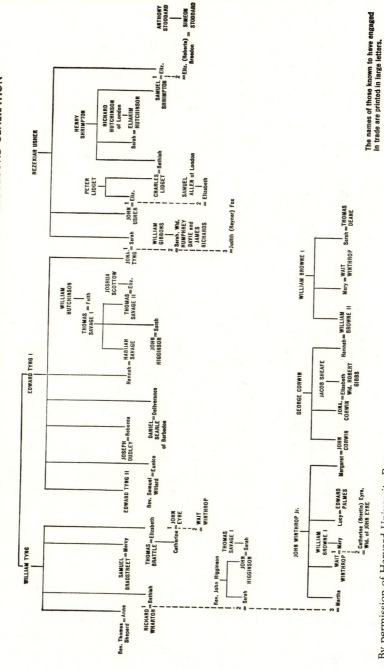

The names of those known to have engaged
in trade are printed in large letters.

By permission of Harvard University Press.

minister at Charlestown and three of whose siblings married ministers or children of ministers), and Jonathan, whose first marriage was to Sarah Usher (another granddaughter of the Reverend Symmes) and whose third was to Judith Fox, daughter of the Reverend Thomas Reyner and widow of the Reverend Jabez Fox.[18] The marriage patterns depicted by Bailyn and compiled as raw data in Savage's *Genealogical Dictionary of the First Settlers of New England* shows characteristics of *extensiveness*— the tendency to link large numbers of families together—but little *intensiveness*. There is no cousin marriage and little sibling exchange. Cousin exchanges, such as the marriages of Hannah Tyng and her brother Jonathan Tyng to Habijah Savage and Sarah Usher (Symmes grandchildren) are very rare. There appears, in the first three generations of merchant families, to be little effort to consolidate or reinforce earlier ties. The only common pattern that could be viewed as intensive is a pattern of "widow exchange," in which the widows of deceased merchants married mercantile widowers.[19] It is difficult to imagine how such connections could meaningfully solidify ties between merchants, however, since one of the males in each connection (and males, after all, were the economic actors of significance) was deceased. Rather than serving purposes of social consolidation, these alliances more likely served more immediate financial goals, for widows were entitled to a third of their husbands' estates. And in a period of acute capital shortage, in which merchants had enormous families (Thomas Savage, for example, had seventeen children by two marriages—ten of whom survived to adulthood), there was far more to be gained by marriages to wealthy widows than to the children of merchants, who were not, on the whole, especially well endowed. For after the widow took her third and the eldest son took his double portion of the remaining two thirds, there was not a great deal left for the others.[20]

With the political and commercial changes of the last decades of the seventeenth century, however, the character of the merchant group began to change. And this change was manifested not only in increasing mercantile political prominence and commercial prosperity, but also in important alterations in testamentary practice and in the structure of marital alliances. The most important of these changes in testation involved the growing tendency of widows to waive their dower rights in exchange for life estates in all or a part of their husband's property (these arrangements varied, the age of the sons often determining the widow's share).[21] At the same time, female children tended increasingly to receive types of property unrelated to the family's commercial interests (cash, jewelry, and real estate) while sons, especially those in commerce, received ships, wharves, and other properties of commercial utility.[22] This discrimination between types of property was undoubt-edly related to the increasing tendency of sons to go into business with their fathers, to the rise of the family partnership as a basic form of business enterprise, and to changes in the pattern and purposes of marital alliances.

After 1700, the merchants began to marry more among themselves. These alliances seem to have followed a bifurcated pattern: one directed at consolidation of family resources (and often using cousin marriage, which had been forbidden by the Puritans, but became legal with the suspension of the old charter in the 1690s); the other, a continuation of the older pattern, directed at creating patterns of extensive ties with other influential mercantile, clerical, and political families in their com-munities. (After 1700, the latter group came increasingly to be mercantile in character.) This shift can be seen in the Quincy family of Boston and Braintree.[23] In the first generation, Edmund Quincy, Jr. (1628–1698) married the daughters of a minister and a magistrate. Of his seven surviving children (born between 1650 and 1685), four married clergy-men or the daughters of clergymen. In the next generation, born in the first decade of the eighteenth century, all four of the surviving children of Edmund Quincy III (1671–1738) married merchants or the daughters of merchants. Two of these alliances were sibling exchanges in which Edmund Quincy IV (1703–1788) and his sister Elizabeth married John and Elizabeth Wendell, who were also brother and sister. Similarly, in the Cabot family, when John Cabot arrived in Salem from the Isle of Jersey, he married Anna Orne, daughter of another merchant.[24] Of his seven children (born between 1704 and 1720), six married merchants or the daughters of merchants; one married the daughter of a clergyman. Three of these marriages were sibling exchanges with the children of the merchant John Higginson (1675–1712) and his first wife Hannah Gardner. One was to the son of John Higginson by his second wife, Margaret Sewell. And one was to Margaret (Sewell) Higginson's brother, Mitchell Sewell. Similar intensiveness can be found among the Amorys, Holmeses, and Coffins of Boston and the Codmans, Fosters, and Rus-sells of Charlestown.

Curiously, although the partnership was beginning to be extensively used by the first quarter of the eighteenth century, these new merchant group alliances were not yet used to cement relations between partners. Partners were recruited, almost without exception, from within the im-mediate circle of blood relatives—brothers, sons, and nephews. This suggests another level to the bifurcation of mercantile alliances, in which marriages served general purposes of forming useful connections among merchants as a group, turning them, by virtue of where they found their mates, into a community within the community. At the same time, primary business alliances, such as those involving partnerships, were kept within the primary nuclear kin-group.

In the next generation, however, this too began to change. After the mid-eighteenth century, merchants were expanding the scale and scope of their activities to a point where the primary kin-group was inadequate as a source of capital and reliable manpower. As they expanded their activities, they began to draw on the previous generation's diffuse alliances as sources for partners. And these new, more inclusive, partnerships—which often included cousins and cousins-in-law—were reinforced by intensive cousin marriages and sibling exchanges. The Cabot family of Salem provides a good example of this pattern. In this first generation, John Cabot (1680–1742) did business "on his own account," but married off his children to other merchants, especially the Higginsons. Although John Cabot's eldest son graduated at Harvard and became a physician, he trained his two younger sons, Joseph (1720–1767) and Francis (1717–1786), as merchants who worked first with their father and later, after his death, in partnership with one another. In the third generation, while Francis Cabot's son, William, and Joseph Cabot's eldest son, Joseph, did business on their own, the four younger sons of Joseph perpetuated and extended the newer partnership pattern. The older boys, John and Andrew, were trained by their uncle Francis (the eldest being only 22 when their father died), and they trained their two younger brothers, George and Samuel. They proceeded, in the late 1760s, to establish a new firm, J. & A. Cabot & Company, which had as its senior partners the brothers John and Andrew and as its junior partners their younger brother George and their mother's first cousin Joseph Lee. With firms of this type one can begin to see how expanded partnerships were able to draw on a pool of men connected through earlier alliances, especially in the female line, for new capital and capability. Lee's connection to the Cabot family was not especially close; his maternal grandfather and the Cabots' paternal grandmother, Anna and Timothy Orne, were brother and sister, making Joseph and his partners second cousins through the maternal line.[25] But this distant kinship was, as he entered the partnership, cemented by two marriages; he married the Cabots' sister Elizabeth in 1769, and the eldest Cabot brother, Joseph, married Lee's first cousin Rebecca Orne in 1768. At this stage, the activities of the firm were centered on buying up local produce for sale in Spain and the West Indies and on wholesale and retail sales of imported goods to their fellow townsmen and backcountry storekeepers. When war broke out, they engaged successfully in privateering.

By the end of the war, in response to new opportunities and to the enlargement of their capital resulting from taking rich prizes and from awards of confiscated Loyalist property by the new state for their services, the Cabots began to reorder their activities, developing a galaxy of cooperative enterprises with other Salem merchants and reaching out beyond Essex County to Boston. The older brothers, John and Andrew, who had earlier married two sisters, the daughters of Beverly merchant, George Dodge, retired from the old firm, but not from commercial activity. Their younger brother George and their cousin/brother-in-law Joseph Lee established a new firm which, like the older one, carried on the West Indies trade. At the same time, John and Andrew Cabot, the firm of George Cabot and Joseph Lee, and the Beverly firm of Brown and Thorndike (Isreal Thorndike was a Cabot in-law, having married a third Dodge sister) constructed a jointly owned and operated wharf and warehouse in Salem. Another Cabot enterprise, also involving John and Andrew, was the erection of a rope walk on a strip of strategically situated real estate on the Salem waterfront across from the Beverly shore. Within two years, the three Cabot brothers, Joseph Lee, their brother-in-law Thorndike, and their father-in-law George Dodge spearheaded the incorporation of a company to build a bridge between Salem and Beverly.[26] This bridge, in shortening the distance between Boston and towns to the eastward, would funnel west-bound traffic through Salem, yielding not only direct profits from bridge tolls, but the indirect profits resulting from commerce with travellers and the overall increase in the value of real estate.

While expanding their Salem operations, taking advantage of kin-ties both to form new partnerships and new ventures beyond and between family firms, the Cabots and others were also reaching out beyond Essex County to Boston, the state's commercial and political capital. The first evidence of this appears in 1783, when the Cabot brothers attempted to obtain a charter for a bridge across the Charles River from Boston to Lechmere's Point in Cambridge.[27] The Cabots' interest in this project apparently stemmed from their having come into possession of a large parcel of Cambridge real estate—acreage that had been confiscated from the Loyalist Oliver family and awarded to the Cabots to compensate them for their losses in the disastrous Penobscot Expedition of 1779. Their petitions were unsucessful, for their efforts were opposed by an influential group of Charlestown merchants (including the Codmans and Russells) who were promoting their own project, a bridge from Boston to Charlestown. Within the year, however, the Cabots and their Essex County brethren were cooperating with their erstwhile rivals in a new venture—the incorporation of the state's first bank, the Massachusetts Bank.

In examining the first board of directors of the Massachusetts Bank, one can again see the extent to which kin-alliances both of the intensive and extensive type underlay and furthered new corporate undertakings. The bifurcated alliance patterns which first began to emerge in the late seventeenth century had over the eighteenth created both a consolidation of capital and a pool of more distantly related individuals among whom new marital and business ties could be formed. And these, in turn, could serve as a bridge between discrete family enterprises and cooperative corporate ones. Thus, for example, of the bank's twelve directors, nine were related, either by blood or marriage.[28] Some of the blood relationships, as in the case of directors George Cabot and Stephen Higginson and Isaac Smith and Oliver Wendell, went back three or four generations. Others, such as those linking director William Phillips with Jonathan Mason and Edward Payne to Thomas Russell were more recent, based on sibling and cousin-exchanges in their own generation or among their children.

The Cabot family after the mid-1780s began to move to Boston, following the new direction of its economic and political interests. Their migration was typical of those who had come to maturity during and immediately after the Revolution. In the same period, the closing decades of the eighteenth century, the Jacksons of Newburyport, the Hoopers and Sturgises of Marblehead, the Perkinses of Scituate, and many others began gravitating towards the state's center of economic and political power. A similar movement was taking place in Connecticut, although it tended to converge less on New Haven and Hartford than on New York—to which leading merchants like the Colts, Bulkeleys, Winthrops, Palmers, Griswolds, and others (along with many ambitious younger men) were beginning to gravitate.[29] In both urban centers, the newly arrived merchants both reinforced older kin-ties among themselves and formed new ties to previously unrelated families. These connections were, once more, bifurcated in character. An example of this pattern can be seen in the Cabot–Lee–Jackson alliances in Boston, in which two families like the Cabots and Lees that had been previously connected in a variety of ways formed an intensive set of marital connections with a previously unrelated family. Thus Jonathan Jackson's third son, Charles, married first Amelia Lee, daughter of Cabot partner, cousin, and in-law, Joseph Lee; and secondly, Fanny Cabot, daughter of John Cabot. Charles' younger brothers, James and Patrick Tracy Jackson, married the sisters Lydia and Elizabeth Cabot, daughters of Andrew. Jackson's daughters married Henry Lee, son of Joseph and Elizabeth (Cabot) Lee, and Francis Cabot Lowell, son of John Lowell and Susannah Cabot.[30] Similar alliances took place between the Cabots, Higginsons, and Perkinses, the Amorys, Codmans, and Lowells, and others.

The key element in these new alliance patterns was inclusion of a remarkably controlled and directed sort. Sons and daughters were not merely marrying into previously unrelated families. Rather, new relationships were being multiply reinforced by sibling and cousin exchanges. And these, in turn, served to enlarge the capital and manpower base for new enterprises. Among these new ventures was the China trade. This global activity required not only enormous capital and competent manpower, but, because of the huge distances involved, a reorganization of mercantile firms.[31] The basis of the trade was a single firm based in a city like Boston. Because it required more capital, it included many more partners than smaller earlier firms in the West Indies and European trade. At the same time, because of the enormous distances involved and the impossibility of communication between Boston-based partners and their agents in Canton and other Chinese ports, subsidiary firms were established, often involving sons and other relatives of the home firm. Kinship, once again, played an essential role in the formation of these companies—as can be seen in the interrelated activities of three major China-trading firms, J & T. H. Perkins & Company, James P. Sturgis & Company, and Russell & Sturgis. Samuel Cabot (youngest brother of John, Andrew, and George) became a partner of the brothers James and Thomas Handasyd Perkins. This commercial tie was cemented by the marriage of James Perkins to Sarah Paine, a connection of the Cabots, Higginsons, and Lees, in 1786; by the marriage of Samuel Cabot's cousin, Stephen Higginson, to Elizabeth Perkins (in 1789) and to her sister, Sarah Perkins (in 1792); by the marriage of Cabot's cousin, Barbara Cooper Higginson, to James and Thomas Perkins' brother, Samuel, in 1795; by the marriage of Cabot's cousin, Henry Higginson, to the Perkins' niece, Ann Cushing (whose brother, John, was also a Perkins partner), in 1803; and by the marriage of Samuel Cabot's eldest son, Samuel, to T.H. Perkins' daughter, Elizabeth, in 1812. The Perkinses were also multiply connected to the Sturgis family, most immediately through the marriages of James and T.H. Perkins' sisters Elizabeth and Esther to Russell and Josiah Sturgis. And the Forbses and Cushings, who also counted among their number Perkins partners, became related to the Perkins family through marriages to their children and cousins.[32]

These alliance patterns are interesting structures. First, they seem to have a triadic form in which two previously interrelated families (such as the Cabots and the Higginsons or the Cabots and the Lees) create a new set of relations with a previously unrelated family, such as the Jacksons or the Perkinses. Through the multiplicity and generational depth of older connections, the integrity and identity of the older groups was maintained while, at the same time, permitting the inclusion of new men and their money. Secondly, however, these connections vastly enlarged the pool of potential marriage and business partners, for the Cabot–Higginson–Perkins alliances, in bringing in the Perkinses, also brought in all their in-laws, the Cushings, the Forbses, and the Sturgises—families into which the other Perkins children had married. This openness in the kinship structure established the basis for a generalization of kin-relations among the members of a potentially large but nonetheless limited group. At the same time, by making ascertainable interrelations so general, it served to reduce the significance of kinship within the expanding group of families.

These patterns were not unique to Boston; they can also be found among such New York/Connecticut families as the Dwights, Hillhouses, and Woolseys, and the Palmers, Stantons, Dixons, and Williamses—and among Philadelphians of the same period. They did not, however, lead to the same social and institutional outcomes, because of legal and political obstacles that blocked the ability of the merchant families to extend their authority and influence through corporate institutions. As a result, unlike the Bostonians, the Philadelphians and New Yorkers would prove unable to extend their patterns of inclusion, which isolated them politically, economically, and socially. While Bostonians would be able to create processes through which new wealth and talent were continuously included, New Yorkers and Philadelphians would resist the newly wealthy—and Boston would maintain its pre-eminence as the nation's center of capital and intellect until after the Civil War.

3. The Ironic Ascendancy: Merchants and Institutions in the Late Eighteenth and Early Nineteenth Centuries

The rise of the merchants to social, economic, political, and intellectual leadership in the last quarter of the eighteenth century did not place them in positions of secure and stable pre-eminence. While the older forms of social authority remained intact, making the merchants the leading partners in the power alliance that constituted the Standing Order, by 1800 these forms had become largely empty ones. And within the first decade of the nineteenth century, whatever remained of the deferential, organic, corporate community institutions on which the Standing Order rested would be eradicated by the "rise of the Common Man"—the democratization of politics and economics and the replacement of tradition-based hierarchical and corporate institutions by egalitarian market relations. The ascendancy of the merchants and the rise of democratic capitalism were integrally related. The merchants rose precisely because of the erosion of older social, economic, political, and ecclesiastical institutions. But those forces, in propelling the merchants upward, also broke the population loose from older corporate forms and transformed them into a disorderly mass of competitively striving individuals.

It is difficult to place an exact date on the point at which the long-term quantitative erosion of older institutions became a qualitative alteration in the nature and type of institutions. I would place it in the late 1790s, when the economic discontent of farmers and artisans, the religious dissent of believers in new sects, and the resentment of elements of the displaced clerical and landholding elite crystalized into outright political opposition to the Standing Order.[33] With the rise of a concerted and organized opposition to civil and ecclesiastical establishments, the character of leadership was fundamentally changed. The adherents of the Standing Order could only assert claims to leadership; they could no longer possess it without engaging in the kind of political "electioneering" that rendered the political process an analogue of the economic marketplace. The development of political parties was far more than a political phenomenon—as the Federalists themselves well knew. The bitterness with which the elections of the first decade of the nineteenth century were fought, the seemingly paranoid rhetoric about Jeffersonian schemes to "revolutionize" New England, and the fears about the rise of "Infidelity" were not as far-fetched as they might seem. For the Jeffersonian challenge represented a fundamental change in the character of authority and the institutions through which it would be wielded. After 1800, wealth, learning, and respectability were no longer necessarily equivalent to political power. And for those who had inherited leadership in the older institutions of power, there was no reason to belive that the newly liberated populace would constitute anything but a mob.

But the merchants faced more than external challenges to their achievement of pre-eminence. Just as important was a set of internal challenges bearing on their ability to define themselves successfully as a group and to operate effectively in the new world of post-Revolutionary commerce. These challenges went beyond the need to elaborate on older forms of partnership to broaden the capital and manpower bases of business. They went beyond the need to expand patterns of human alliances through partnership and marriage. They even went beyond the use of the corporation as a legal device, for the early corporations were little more than expanded family firms. They posed a fundamental question about the relation between family, capital, and accountability.

New forms of economic enterprise—banking, manufacturing, insurance, and transportation—, beyond being facilitated by a new kind of organization, the private corporation, also required, if they were to become genuinely effective, levels of competence and specialized training and amounts of capital that could not easily be found within any single family. And even if they could, because these enterprises were innovative, and hence risky and uncertain in their prospects of success, it would not have been prudent for any single family to invest too great a portion of its resources in any single corporate venture. In any case, as investors in such early large enterprises as the Middlesex Canal discovered, ownership of stock did not merely mean ownership in a proportion of potential earnings of a corporation, but also made one vulnerable to assessments, payments beyond the original cost of the shares, as the corporation attempted to fulfill the promises made by its charter.[34] Limitation of liability was granted to stockholders of corporations only in rare instances before the late 1820s.[35] Before that point, participating in a joint stock company was potentially as risky as participating in a partnership.

In this context, it was obviously to the advantage of mercantile promoters of new corporate ventures to reduce risks by spreading stock ownership as broadly as possible. Diversifying ownership, however, posed other problems. On the one hand, it diluted the ability of the officers of an enterprise to act boldly—for there was always in such a situation the possiblitity that the stockholders would replace them. On the other hand, if large numbers of people were to be induced to invest in corporations, they had to have some assurance that their monies would be competently and honestly used. In either case, the expanded use of the corporation required a divorce of family, capital, and manpower that was unprecedented. For a century and a half, the merchant families had done business with and through human networks in which kinship, friendship, and marriage had been the bases for accountability and the guarantors of reliability. Suddenly their survival as an economic force was coming to depend on their ability to separate their diffuse and particular private interests from their specialized and more formally institutionalized public ones.

Effecting such a separation involved changes not only in how business could be done, but also, because businesses had been so closely tied to how families trained their young, selected their mates, and bequeathed their property, changes in the family itself. Although I have not been able to find any explicit discussions by merchants of this period bearing on the relation between new business organizations and changes in the family, their behavior suggests that they were consciously and intentionally altering the one to suit the other. Figure 2 is an attempt to suggest the strategic character of occupational, marital, educational, family size, and partnership choices in nine eastern Massachusetts mer-

Figure 2

Occupation, Marriage, Family Size, Education, and Partnership among Males (Cohort of Fathers) in the Amory, Cabot, Codman, Higginson, Jackson, Lawrence, Lee, Lowell, and Peabody Families, by Birth Cohort, 1740–1799.

Birth Cohorts	N	Merchants	Married	Married Kin	Average Age at 1st Marriage	Average Number of Children	Partnerships		% college Att.
							Primary Kin	Secondary or Non Kin	
1740–59	18	15 (83%)	15 (83%)	8 (53%)	24.3	7.7	13 (68.4%)	6 (31.6%)	22%
1760–79	31	27 (90%)	24 (80%)	7 (29%)	27.3	5.0	16 (48.5%)	17 (51.5%)	43%
1780–99	43	28 (65%)	29 (67%)	11 (38%)	28.4	5.2	13 (44.8%)	16 (55.2%)	33%

Occupation, Marriage, Family Size, Education, and Partnership among Sons of Fathers in the Amory, Cabot, Codman, Higginson, Jackson, Lawrence, Lee, Lowell, and Peabody Families, by Birth Cohort, of Fathers, 1740–99.

Birth Cohorts	N	Merchants	Married	Married Kin	Average Age at 1st Marriage	Average Number of Children	Partnerships		% college Att.
							Primary Kin	Secondary or Non Kin	
1740–59	48	36 (75%)	33 (69%)	17 (52%)	30.4	5.9	39 (60.0%)	26 (40.0%)	27%
1760–79	38	24 (63%)	27 (71%)	9 (33%)	24.3	4.7	13 (40.6%)	19 (59.4%)	50%
1780–99	47	31 (66%)	34 (72%)	13 (38%)	30.2	4.3	16 (50.0%)	16 (50.0%)	49%

chant families.[36] It shows decline in the tendency to marry kin, a decrease in family size, and a shift in educational choices towards attendance at college. These patterns, even if not motivated by economic considerations, certainly served them. Sons who did not become businessmen, but who became lawyers, physicians, or members of other non-business occupations (up to and including invalidism) did not make the same demands on family capital as sons who became merchants. For mercantile capital was financial, while a professional's "capital" involved a far less costly course of training. Similarly, smaller families reduced the number of partible divisions of estates and reduced the number of sons for whom training and careers had to be found. Both, along with the increasing use of the college as a training institution, reduced familial demands on capital, freeing it for more rational investment of a more purely economic type.

These shifts in patterns of family behavior were accompanied by shifts in testamentary practice and patterns of charitable benevolence, both of which also served to divorce capital from family claims. From the 1780s on, Boston merchants increasingly resorted to the testamentary trust as a means of circumventing the partible division of estates.[37] Through the trust it became possible to keep family capital intact by leaving it to a trustee, who would invest it to the maximum benefit of the beneficiaries—who shared in the income of such investments. Another kind of trust, the endowment, came to be the financial basis of charitable and educational institutions. By making gifts and bequests to charitable endowments, it became possible for merchants not only to underwrite the professional success of sons who had become academics or physicians instead, but also of entering commerce to increase the pool of capital available for investment in the larger economy. For it was from such investments that endowments earned the income that enabled them to serve the purposes for which they had been created.

By the 1820s, the outlines of a new institutional system were beginning to emerge clearly; families had, in effect, collectivized their capital resources through endowment and testamentary trusts. Eleemosynary and testamentary trustees were often the same persons. And they, in turn, combined the trusteeship of such charitable and educational institutions as Harvard College, the Athenaeum, and the Massachusetts General Hospital with directorships in the city's leading banks, insurance companies, transportation enterprises, and manufactures.[38] At the same time, the merchant families appear to have collectivized their human capital through settling in compact mercantile neighborhoods in which they could exercise oversight over one another's children and through the use of certain schools (especially the Boston Latin School) and Harvard College as common socializing institutions.[39] This collectivization of resources, while separating capital and manpower from family concerns, did not in any sense mean the elimination of the significance of family identity. Nor did it mean that older forms of commercial enterprise such as the partnership disappeared. Family remained the primary unit of early socialization, kinship largely determined residential patterns within mercantile neighborhoods, and family firms continued to operate in such specialized areas as stock and commodity brokerage and, by the 1840s, investment banking. But the broader institutional hierarchy through which family interests were united and differentiated from the interests of society at large selected out of these families only those most competent to oversee its interests. As Henry Lee would write to Sarah Orne Jewett,

> In Boston in my boyhood the houses were for the most part detached garden houses; there was no quarter for the rich; they and the poor, successful and unsucessful members of the same family, perhaps,—at least of the same stock,—dwelt in the same quarter; there were only enough foreigners to exercise benevolence on, not to intrude; families and friends built courts (no thoroughfares) to dwell in together, and there was a personal recognition and cooperation in all affairs,—social, municipal, ecclesiastical, educational,—which was wholesome. We all lived in this little world; all our work and all our play were there.[40]

Lee of course did not mean literally to suggest that there was "no quarter for the rich" in all of Boston. What he meant was that the proto-Brahmin families, regardless of wealth or poverty, clustered together, as a distinct body of persons related by blood and marriage who shared common interests and pursued them collectively through corporate institutions.

If the mercantile institutions served private purposes facilitating the divorce of capital from familial concerns and accomplishing the training and recruitment of competent manpower, they were also, of necessity, public institutions to a large extent. Their public character derived from a number of factors. First, because this group continued to see itself as being entrusted with public responsibilities long after electoral realities had displaced them, they continued to attempt to demonstrate their utility to the public as centers of scholarship, healing, and credit. Secondly, the identity of the merchant group was not yet fixed: the self-made men of the Revolutionary era would live on into the 1820s and 30s; their sons, born in the 1760s and 70s, were also products of a world in which social and economic boundaries were much less clearly defined. The intrinsic diversity of the merchant group, its inclusion on grounds of kinship and marriage of the not-yet-successful sons, cousins, and in-laws, and its opportunism in bringing in ambitious younger men of obscure origins like the Lawrence brothers, who had come to Boston as shopkeepers from rural Middlesex County in the teens and, by the 1820s, parlayed their earnings into prestigious marriages and proprietorships in the largest textile mills in New England, ensured that the group did not prematurely crystalize into a narrow and exclusive caste. Thirdly, in facing political and economic challenges from more newly wealthy entrepreneurs, the older group, perhaps because of its kinbased cohesiveness, perhaps because of the formally institutionalized character of its central economic and intellectual enterprises, was remarkably accomodating. After the diminution of the Jeffersonian and Jacksonian challenges of the first and fourth decades of the nineteenth century, one finds the leaders of the Boston Athenaeum, an organization in which possession of a share is, according to some social historians, the equivalent of a patent of nobility, enlarging the number of shares and selling them to persons who were only recently their avowed enemies.[41] Similarly, the sons of such leading Jeffersonian families as the Grays, Crowninshields, and Silsbees were, by the 1820s, not only attending Harvard College, but also being taken into its most prestigious undergraduate club, the Porcellian.[42] Such openness was an essential component of the group's survival, for it enabled it to gain the legal talents of men like Joseph Story, who began his public career as an outspoken Jeffersonian member of the legislature, but became within a decade the most eloquent of all legal spokesmen for the rights of private corporations and the intellectual successor to the arch-Federalist Theophilus Parsons.[43] By the same process, men of obscure origins like Nathaniel Bowditch, son of an impecunious and alcoholic Salem mariner, and Joseph Peabody, son of a rural Essex County farmer, became founding fathers of families whose names are now inevitably identified with Brahminism.[44]

It has been arranged that the Bostonians, following their loss of national political influence in 1800 and their loss of control of their own state in the teens, became an exclusive elite in decline. Their economic leadership through the course of the nineteenth century belies this characterization—even though certain scions of old Boston families were the most eloquent spokesmen for this viewpoint.[44] If writers like Dana, Henry Adams, and Charles Eliot Norton felt overwhelmed and impotent, their kinsmen busied themselves in building up the textile industry, pioneering western railroads, and creating the investment banking industry. More sophisticated commentators, while granting the economic and political activism of the merchants, suggest that, in concentrating at such institutions as Harvard the scions of old and new wealth, the Brahmin "aristocracy" was becoming exclusive.[46] While it is undoubt-

edly true that a Harvard education was beyond the means of more
young men in the nineteenth century than in the preceding century, it
is also true that money had become a kind of solvent, erasing the significance of lineage and other particularistic criteria of status and replacing them with the more democratic criteria of wealth and ambition,
the acquisition of which were within the grasp of large numbers. One
need only read Oliver Wendell Holmes's descriptions of the prevalence
in Boston's social life of millionaires who "were sweeping stores and
carrying parcels" when the "now decayed gentry were driving their
chariots" and "eating their venison over silver chafing dishes," and of
the ubiquitous presence among his students at Harvard of "the common
country boy, whose race has been bred to bodily labor" and whose
"hands and feet by constant use have got more than their share of
development" to know that Harvard's and Boston's exclusivity was of
a very inclusive sort.[47] Nor is Holmes any less frank about the extent
to which Boston's eminence was due to its ability to attract the "promising young author," the "rising lawyer," the "large capitalist," and the
"prettiest girl" away from lesser centers;[48] Boston was, as he wrote in
the *Autocrat of the Breakfast Table*, a city which "drains a large watershed
of intellect, and will not itself be drained."[49] And its ability to do this
involved more than the intrinsic attractions of the "big city." It rested
on the willingness of the city's leading institutions and families to include the talented. But as with the triadic patterns through which the
previously unrelated merchant families became consolidated at the end
of the eighteenth century, such inclusion had to be orderly and structured so that the continuing influx would not weaken the core groups's
identity. As it happened, the privately funded and controlled corporate
institutions of business, education, and charity came to function as a
kind of permeable barrier; through simultaneously socializing both the
young and older families and the sons of newer ones, they acted to
expand the merchant group's constituency while, at the same time,
preserving its form and its claims to historical and social legitimacy
intact.

PART II

The Reorganization of American Culture

CHAPTER FIVE

Beyond Tradition: Order and Authority in the New Republic

In America, the citizens who form the minority associate in order, first, to show their numerical strength and so to diminish the moral power of the majority; and, secondly, to stimulate competition and thus to discover those arguments that are most fitted to act upon the majority; for they always entertain hopes of drawing over the majority to their own side, and then controlling the supreme power in its name.[1]

The authority which public men possess in America is so brief and they are so soon commingled with the ever changing population of the country that the acts of a community frequently leave fewer traces than events in a private family.[2]

The former colonists emerged from the struggle for independence with a euphoric sense that, in having gotten rid of the "bad king" and his tyrannical institutions, they had ended all their troubles. Reason and common sense, available to everyone, would not only lead them to restore the social harmony of their forefathers, but also lead, almost automatically, towards a new and more reasonable order.[3] The hard experiences of the 1780s, with their economic dislocation, political conflict, and social disorder, revealed the extent to which the old order was a Humpty-Dumpty that neither reason, liberty, nor revolutionary optimism could put together again. It became clear to both liberals and conservatives that the Revolution would have to be "secured" institutionally lest the result be either anarchy or absolutism. These dire possibilities were underlined in the 1790s, with the collapse of the French Revolution into bloody chaos and, ultimately, military dictatorship.

Those with vested interests in the hierarchical and institutional aspects of the old order—the church, the colleges, and the state—proceeded energetically to secure what they regarded as the desirable outcomes of the Revolution. In Massachusetts, a new constitution was written in 1780 to replace the royal government and its provisional successor.[4] This document reflected the commercial character of the state and the mercantile nature of its political leadership. It required that all voters possess "a freehold estate within the Commonwealth, of the annual income of three pounds, or any estate with the value of sixty pounds."[5] Although the qualification for the franchise was not unduly restrictive, the qualifications for holding office were: members of the upper house were required to have a freehold estate of at least three hundred pounds or a personal estate of at least six hundred; members of the lower house were required to possess a freehold estate of not less than one hundred pounds or combined personal and real estate amounting to two hundred pounds; the governor was required to possess an estate valued at not less than one thousand pounds.[6] In practical terms, the constitution, while extending the franchise to over ninety percent of the property owners in a city like Boston, limited candidacy for the lower house to the top fifty percent of taxpayers, for the upper house to the top twenty percent of taxpayers, and for the governorship and lieutenant-governorship, to the top three percent.[7] This restriction of officeholding to the wealthy was complemented by the creation of new corporations. Since such entities could only be created by special legislative action, and since it took extraordinary political influence to procure such special legislation, the early corporations tended to be the creatures of the wealthy and influential and to act as a means of extending their influence into new sectors of activity.

Connecticut was able to secure the Revolution on the side of the old order not by writing a new constitution, but by resisting radical demands for such a document.[8] Never having been subjected to royal government and having evolved a set of formal and informal mechanisms that ensured elite control of the electoral process, especially through control of the nominating process, the state government remained based on the Fundamental Orders of 1639 and the Royal Charter of 1662. The old order's response to demands for reform in the 1780s and 90s consisted of efforts to raise the property restriction on the franchise, to dilute the secrecy of the ballot, and to impose moral and political tests on those seeking admission to the body of freemen.[9] As in Massachusetts, the corporations, the first of which were chartered in 1792, were organizations reserved for the wealthy, learned, and respectable, acting in what they defined as the public interest.

The securing of the Revolution in states to the west and south of New England took a profoundly different course. Rather than reaffirming the privileges of urban commercial wealth and ecclesiastical establishments, the post-Revolutionary constitutions of New York, Pennsylvania, and the southern states liberalized the franchise, diluted executive power, and provided for more equitable and proportionate representation in the legislatures.[10] In Pennsylvania, Georgia, and Vermont, the upper house was entirely disregarded. While several states later reformed these early constitutions, moving towards the creation of stronger executive branches, more independent judiciaries, and less representative assemblies, politics remained, on the whole, more under popular control in the middle, southern and new western states than in New England. The popularization of the political structure in these areas was paralleled by a complementary weakness of corporate organizations and legal structures supporting such entities. While all the states permitted the creation of corporations, the success of corporate promoters varied with the extent to which legislatures were popularly controlled. As Figure 3 suggests, Connecticut and Massachusetts led the nation in 1800 in the number of corporations per capita.[11] Further, some states, most notably New York and Virginia, placed severe restrictions on the creation of educational and charitable corporations, especially those that hoped to draw their strength from endowments.[12]

However extensively leaders of the several states may have disagreed on particular issues, such as ecclesiastical establishments and the utility of corporations, by the late 1780s there was a growing recognition that a more stable set of relations had to be created between the states. The Federal Constitution of 1787 emerged from a painfully wrought consensus which balanced the interests of the large states against the small, the commercial against the agricultural, and the populace against the elites. The Constitution left the institutional peculiarities of the states unmolested: the right of the southerners to own slaves and of the New Englanders to maintain established churches were matters left to the states. Similarly, divergent attitudes about corporations, private charities, and the nature and extent of court jurisdictions within the states were not explicitly touched upon by the new national institutional framework. Nevertheless, in creating a national context for the determination of political and legal policies, the framers of the Constitution, perhaps unwittingly, set in motion a dynamic that would undo the political hold of the Standing Order in New England, force the proponents of that order to transform the corporation into an alternative to political power, and create conditions favorable for the national expansion of private

THE ORGANIZATION OF AMERICAN CULTURE

Figure 3

Comparison of States with Respect to Population, 1800, and Number of Eighteenth-Century Charters to Business Corporations

Sources of charters	No. of charters granted	No. of charters per 100,000 population, 1800	Per cent of total charters granted	Per cent of total population, 1800	Rank with respect to no. of charters granted	Rank with respect to population, 1800
United States	2		.6			
Maine	23	15.2	6.9	2.8	5–6	14
New Hampshire	32	17.4	9.5	3.5	3	11
Vermont	20	12.3	6.0	2.9	9–10	13
Massachusetts	60	14.2	17.9	7.9	1	5
Rhode Island	20	28.9	6.0	1.3	9–10	16
Connecticut	45	18.0	13.4	4.7	2	8
New England	200	16.3	59.7	23.2	1	3
New York	28	4.8	8.4	11.1	4	3
New Jersey	13	6.2	3.9	4.0	11	10
Pennsylvania	23	3.8	6.9	11.3	5–6	2
Delaware	3	4.6	.9	1.2	14	17
Middle States	67	4.6	20.0	27.6	2	2
Maryland	21	6.1	6.3	6.4	8	7
Virginia	22	2.4	6.6	16.6	7	1
North Carolina	11	2.3	3.3	9.0	12	4
South Carolina	10	2.0	3.0	6.5	13	6
Georgia	1	.6	.3	3.1	15–16	12
Other southern states				.5		
Southern states	65	2.9	19.4	42.0	3	1
Kentucky	1	.4	.3	4.2	15–16	14
Othern western states	1			3.0		
Western States	1	.3	.3	7.2	4	4

By permission of Harvard University Press.

corporate power under the guidance of a numerically small, but organizationally innovative minority.

1. Republicanism and the Fragmentation of Authority

With the election of Thomas Jefferson as President of the United States in the fall of 1800, the days of the Standing Order of New England were numbered. The federal system, which had been devised as an effort to limit and contain the popular will, became an instrument of the popular will. It no longer really mattered that the Federalists had managed to maintain control of their state offices and their congressional delegations—or that they had, through restrictions on voting and officeholding and through the use of political and religious tests for entrance into the professions, been able to minimize the effectiveness of political opposition. For Republican control of the apparatus of national government enabled the new president to reward his supporters with appointments to a variety of highly visible public offices, ranging from postmasterships and customs collectorships through the federal bench and bar. Men who had, through the 1790s, been forced to keep their opinions to themselves, fearing persecution under state laws, the federal sedition statutes, and a myriad of less formal petty harassments, could now look beyond local power structures for aid and assistance. Jefferson's victory legitimated dissent. And though Republican party organization would remain for some years a secretive and largely underground activity in the New England states, it would increase the tempo of its organizing efforts as victories over ecclesiastical and civil establishments became real and proximate possibilities. The Federalists might rail against the new regime, but they could no longer convincingly portray it in vague and threatening terms. The infidel mob had become a legitimate political counterforce.

But Republicanism was more than a political opposition as we in the late twentieth century have come to understand it. It involved more than sets of persons with essentially the same values and beliefs competing for office.[13] The very existence of an organized political opposition challenged fundamental Federalist concepts of political, economic, and cultural authority. The Standing Order, which for nearly two centuries had seen itself as the steward of the common good—as the guardian of the church, of learning, of the state, and of the world of commerce—found itself faced with an opposition that wanted not merely to occupy the seats of power, but to alter the institutions of power. Although both the Federalists and their Republican challengers had partaken of the "Spirit of the Enlightenment," they had partaken of it in very different ways. While both had come by the mid-eighteenth century to agree on the rational and law-like character of the universe and on man's possession of reasonable faculties that enabled him to discover the laws of nature and act according to them, the Republicans and the Federalists differed in their views of the ease with which men could achieve rational understanding of the universe and the likelihood of their acting reasonably on those insights. For those who would become Jeffersonians, political, social, and economic truths were viewed as self-evident and available to everyone. Accordingly, the locus of authority lay not with institutions, civil or ecclesiastical, but with the people. For them, the motto *vox populi, vox dei* was a fundamental article of faith. And the institutional frameworks that they favored were representative, flexible, and tolerant. For those who would become Federalists, the universe was viewed in Manichean terms: however available truth might be to man, both his perception of it and his ability to act reasonably on that perception were impeded by his passionate nature. Just as the Massachusetts Puritans of the early seventeenth century had acted to contain the anarchic possibilities of antinomianism by setting forth the congregation, the spiritual community, as the arena for the pursuit of salvation, so the Standing Order of the eighteenth century sought to contain the political and economic correlates of antinomianism, democracy, and capitalism within a larger framework that could reconcile the actions of individuals with the needs of the community. They sought to do this not only through institutions, formal and informal, in which individuals were subordinated to larger collective groups—congregation, community, and family—, but also through the process of socialization, which emphasized habits and discipline. For the proto-Federalists, men might be permitted to think, vote, trade, or worship freely, but that freedom was always to be tempered by internal and external constraints imposed by the community.

The struggle between these ideologies can be traced not only to intellectual sources in the religious and political writings of the late seventeenth and early eighteenth centuries, but also to specific religious and political struggles in the various states in the pre-Revolutionary and Revolutionary periods—most notably the efforts of the new states to write their constitutions and the contest over the ratification of the federal Constitution.[14] Only in the last quarter of the eighteenth century, however, when Americans became free to translate their ideas into institutions, did these ideological differences begin to cohere into a political and metapolitical struggle. Accompanying the explicitly political contests over the form of state constitutions in the 1770s and early 1780s were other less well known struggles over such issues as the nature of legal systems and jurisdictions, the character of corporations, and the legal standing of charitable trusts. Just as the proto-Jeffersonians favored democratic unicameral legislatures, they opposed institutions of any sort that favored the private interest over the public and insulated private power from public control. Thus they tended to oppose the creation of equity jurisdiction, which enabled judges to act as lawmakers by enforcing future acts; they restricted or curtailed the creation of privately controlled charitable and testamentary endowments as instruments of the dead hand of the past over the living; and they created private corporations with the greatest reluctance, hedging their activities with an assortment of restrictions including time-limited charters, public representatives on boards of directors, and other mechanisms of public accountability.[15] The proto-Federalists, at least until political power began to slip from their grasp in the 1790s, also took a circumspect attitude towards non-accountable private power. As descendants of Puritan revolutionaries, they well knew of the oppressive possibilities of equity courts—which in England had been agencies of the Church of England.[16] They also knew, both from the seventeenth century and from the more recent experience of the activities of the East India Company (against whose monopoly powers the Boston Tea Party was directed) of the dangers inherent in grants of exclusive privilege to private corporations. Because of radical opposition, because of their own doubts and uncertainties about non-accountable private power, and because of their confidence in their ability to maintain political, economic, and cultural leadership, they were circumspect about creating broad equity jurisdictions, trusts, and corporations. And their essential ideological differences with the dissenters would not take the form of contests over these issues until the last years of the eighteenth century.

Nevertheless, the outlines of the struggle over institutions can be seen as early as the 1770s, not only in the controversies over state constitutions, but also in those over such issues as ecclesiastical establishment, religious toleration, and the control of colleges. As early as 1779, Jefferson himself sought to amend the charter of William and Mary, a private Anglican institution, in order to turn it into a state institution— an effort which continued into the 1790s, when John Marshall finally settled the matter in favor of the trustees of the college.[17] In the 1780s, radicals influenced by Jefferson made similar efforts to secularize and impose public control over Maryland's two sectarian institutions, Washington and St. John's College.[18] These efforts found their counterparts in virtually every state, including Connecticut and Massachusetts. And even though the matter would appear to have been settled by the Dartmouth College Case in 1819, it continued in several places, including Delaware, where the state legislature attempted to take over Presbyterian-controlled Delaware College, and Massachusetts, where every attempt by the merchants to amend the charter of Harvard was met by legislative efforts to reassert control over that once-public institution.[19] Where the Jeffersonians could not take over existing institutions, they created new ones. And these new institutions, such as South Carolina College (1802) and the University of Virginia (1819) were distinctly publicly controlled and funded, in sharp contrast to the trend towards private funding and governance that was already evident in New England by the first decade of the nineteenth century.[20] This contest over the colleges was paralleled by struggles over the control of the professions. The Jeffersonians favored professional autonomy, which would have rendered physicians and attorneys accountable to the public through the medium of the marketplace. The Federalists promoted the connection of the professions to the colleges, which would have located professional authority with powerful laymen rather than the public. Underlying the transformation of older institutions and the creation of new ones were acute ideological and, ultimately, explicitly political differences. The difference carried through even to pedagogical methods, in the split between those who saw the primary purpose of education as the formation of character and values and those who favored education for "utility," and in the split between those who favored the utilitarian-individualistic emphasis of Pestalozzi and those who favored the individualism tempered by character and discipline promoted by Timothy Dwight and his followers.[21]

The alternatives posed to the men of the late eighteenth century by the conservative and liberal possibilities of the Enlightenment were not ones that could be settled either intellectually or institutionally. Although we can retrospectively discern the clear differences between the two sides and track them backwards through particular conflicts and organizations to their intellectual roots, these differences were by no means clearly visible to their contemporaries, whose responses were often dictated not by ideology, but by particular events. Thus, for example, the Standing Order in Massachusetts and Connecticut might begin the post-Revolutionary period by sharing with the radicals a distrust of non-accountable legal and organizational mechanisms such as endowment trusts, equity jurisdiction, and the corporation. They might even have insisted on public influence over such entities; many non-radicals insisted on public representation on the Yale Corporation, and in Massachusetts, they advocated vastly enlarging *ex officio* representation on the Harvard Board of Overseers through the inclusion of the entire state Senate. However, as political factions began to transform themselves into parties, and as parties, based on conflicting ideologies, began to struggle for dominance, the patterns of institutional innovation in the several states came to be determined by local factors. In places like the South and West, where the Jeffersonians became politically dominant and where the older colonial elites remained strong, not only was the level of institutional innovation much lower, but the new institutions tended to be publicly rather than privately controlled and funded. In New England, where the elite rapidly lost its control of politics after 1800, the level of institutional innovation was much higher and took on a private and non-accountable character. In the middle states, especially in New York and Pennsylvania, while many new private institutions were created, they tended to be constrained by legislatures that sought to limit the extent of their influence. In New Jersey, where New Englanders and Presbyterians had settled in large numbers, the institutions more closely resembled the private and non-accountable organizations of New England.[22]

To state that the conflict was not resolved in any clear fashion and that different patterns were followed in different areas according to the political proclivities of their inhabitants is not to suggest that the alternate institutional models were equal in terms of their dynamic potentials. When Tocqueville, discussing the principle of association, stated that associations stemmed from efforts of a minority to "entertain hopes of drawing over the majority to their own side, and then controlling the supreme power in the state," he was doing more than simply describing the motives of those who form voluntary organizations. He was also making a powerful statement about the dynamic and expansive character of such organizations. If we view what he wrote in more concrete historical terms, the differential dynamic capacities of the Jeffersonian and Federalist institutional models becomes clear. The Jeffersonians, as a majority, would naturally be less inclined to create associations once they had either risen to political power or broken the hold of ecclesiastical and civil establishments. For in placing a political or religious faction on a competitive footing in "the marketplace of ideas," they would have achieved their basic goal of making the will of the citizen, believer, or consumer the delimiter of the power of the state, church, and capitalist. Having done this, they did not need to go any further—except, perhaps, in creating utilitarian and responsive institutions such as public schools and state universities which might facilitate the ability of men to make informed choices. But the Federalists, because they were believing Christians and because their conceptions of civic virtue and intellectual standards were closely tied to the extension of Congregationalism and its organic and corporate correlates of social and economic organization, had powerful motives to go beyond both older institutional forms and the confines of New England. Fueled by political and religious convictions, and further impelled by the expansive character of their economic interests, the Federalists could not be content with being merely equal contenders for public favor. From 1800 on, as they lost political power both nationally and locally, they compensated by becoming more active institutionally—by mounting an evangelical counter-offensive to political and religious infidelity that led them through the second Great Awakening, through the creation of education societies to train new ministers and teachers, to the founding of missionary societies that placed those new professionals throughout the West and South. And these religious moves were, once again, paralleled by the diffusion of land-hungry New Englanders to the frontier and to the older settlements of the West and South, by the expansion of New England's economic interests, and by the growth of secular correlates to the religious organizations, the lyceums and the abolitionist network.[23] While one might be inclined to see this expansion as accidental, there can be no doubting the intentions of those who sponsored and underwrote it. As Lyman Beecher would write in 1820 in an address to the Charitable Society for the Education of Indigent Pious Young Men for the Ministry of the Gospel,

> The integrity of the Union demands special exertions to produce in the nation a more homogeneous character and bind us together with firmer bonds. . . . The prevalence of pious, intelligent, enterprising ministers through the nation, at the ratio of one of a thousand, would establish schools, and academies, and colleges, and habits, and institutions of homogeneous influence. These would produce a sameness of views, and feelings, and interests, which would lay the foundation of our empire upon a rock. Religion is the central attraction which must supply the deficiency of political affinity and interest.[24]

The issue at stake after 1800 was not merely who should occupy political offices or what sorts of institutions people might create to pursue their interests. It was, in the view of the Federalists, a much more profound struggle, a contest between good and evil that was merely reflected in the struggle between civil order and disorder, between Jeffersonian and Federalist. The essence of the problem was stated by Gardiner Spring, a Yale graduate and leading Presbyterian clergyman of New York:

> Liberty without godliness, is but another name for anarchy or despotism. Let philosophers and statesmen argue as they please—the religion of the gospel is the rock on which civil liberty rests. You have never known a people free without the Bible; with it, they cannot long be slave.[25]

To the Federalists, authority—intellectual, political, or economic—was, if founded upon the sands of public favor, no authority at all. And without heroic measures, the new republic would collapse into the anarchy of the French Revolution.

2. Character, Justifications, and the Impasse of Virtue

Needless to say, the new republic did not collapse into revolutionary anarchy with the election of Jefferson. Nevertheless, the Federalist vision of the dangers posed by democracy and popularly defined authority, the threat of society's collapsing into either chaos or dictatorship, remained a basic theme of their rhetoric until the Civil War. Events constantly kept the theme alive: the association of Jeffersonianism with slavery, the virtual dictatorship of Andrew Jackson, and the restive agitations of laborers and urban mobs. But real root of the problem was not intellectual alone. Rather, it lay in the failure of the political struggles of the first decades of the nineteenth century to resolve fully the issue of authority. Once political, economic, and intellectual authority became separated after the Jeffersonian victory of 1800, with the political sphere controlled by the people and, in New England, the economic and intellectual sphere controlled by private corporations, a fundamental conflict developed over the sources of order and authority that could not be easily resolved—for the conflict was institutionalized in the separation of spheres of authrity. The Federalists and their descendants could amass wealth and knowledge, but had no way of translating that knowledge into political power. The Jeffersonians and their followers could amass political power, but had no way of translating it into broader economic and cultural authority.

This impasse came to be resolved in three ways. First, the Federalists, having no hope of recapturing political power, turned to the marketplace itself to vindicate their claims to power. Not only did they become economic overachievers, but perhaps more importantly, they opened up their institutions to the masses, actively seeking to resocialize them, both through religion and through its secular correlate, the development of character. Character became the functional equivalent of piety by the 1820s, not only because the conservatives had to downplay denominationalism to overcome their own internal differences (as between Congregationalists, Unitarians, and Episcopalians who might differ theologically but share similar social and political views), but also because, if they wished to attract the broadest and most talented possible constituencies for their colleges and their corporations, they had to dilute those aspects of their enterprises that might alienate prospective participants. Character by the 1820s had come to mean those aspects of personality that rendered an individual dependable and predictable, disciplined and internally controlled. The Federalists came to understand that if they could not impose their political will on the populace, establishing authority and order externally, they could do it through the educational system, by habituating individuals to certain standards of behavior and modes of self-control. Character education was essentially a compromise between unidenominational piety and regional dominance—which were unsalable species of particularism—and the demands of the marketplace, in which individuals would have to find their places according to their abilities. Because character eeucation was specifically associated with particular institutions and particular pedagogic modes, credentials from these institutions came to serve as emblems of trustworthiness and dependability. This was an essential component of a growing national economy in which, if businessmen wished to operate beyond their immediate localities, they had to have some means of assessing the reliability of the men in other places with whom they dealt and with whom they had had no previous personal contact.[26] At the same time, because the character-forming institutions both reached out to embrace new constituencies and sent their graduates out beyond their native places, they served as means of creating new kinds of personal contacts and patterns of loyalty that went beyond kinship and community. Similarly, character and collegiate associations proved to be the basis not only for establishing translocal networks, but also for the inclusion of talented outsiders in growing corporations that needed a reliable supply of dependable men. Character, in other words, was the basis for the creation of modern, large-scale organizations. And such organizations could not develop, as Chandler suggests they began to by the 1850s, without a broad constituency of individuals socialized to modes of dependable autonomy and internal control.

The second means by which the impasse between political, economic, and cultural authority came to be resolved was the extension of the machinery of character formation beyond New England. This extension involved not only the remarkable tendency of southerners and westerners, not all of them transplanted New Englanders, to send their sons to New England colleges, but also the role of transplanted New Englanders in establishing and dominating the cultural institutions of the West and South. While the Jeffersonians might have established such publicly controlled institutions as the University of North Carolina and the College of South Carolina, graduates of New England institutions almost without exception dominated their teaching staffs. The early professors at the College of South Carolina were graduates of Yale,

Brown, Dartmouth, and Princeton; the University of North Carolina
was founded and extensively staffed by Princetonians; the University
of Georgia was headed by Augustus Longstreet, who went on to be the
first president of the University of Mississippi (the second was another
Yale graduate, F. A. P. Barnard); later, Longstreet presided over the
University of Michigan.[27] Even if the administrative structures of these
institutions were formed along Jeffersonian lines of public control, their
internal structures and pedagogy followed the New England model.
Even the United States Military Academy at West Point, which went
into operation during the administration of Jefferson, was formed by
its New England-educated faculty (Yale and Dartmouth men) into an
institution whose modes of discipline were directed to character formation and derived from the model established at Yale by Timothy
Dwight.[28]

This national penetration of educational institutions by New Englanders was paralleled and reinforced by the extraordinary effectiveness
of New Englanders and the New England educated as economic and
political operators. As Lee Soltow has pointed out in his study of wealth
distribution in the United States in the period 1850–1870, "natives born
in certain New England states seemed to excel in wealth aggrandizement
no matter where they lived in the United States."[29] He goes on to show
that persons born in New England, even when living in the South or
the Northwest, were more likely to be owners of significant real and
personal property than natives of those regions.[30] This remarkable level
of economic success was echoed by comparable levels of political success. As Tocqueville observed of the composition of the Congress:

> We were assured in 1830 that thirty-six of the members of Congress
> were born in the little state of Connecticut. The population of Con-
> necticut, which constitutes only one-forty-third part of that of the
> United States, thus furnished one-eighth of the whole body of rep-
> resentatives. The state of Connecticut of itself, however, sends only
> five delegates to Congress; and the thirty-one others sit for the new
> Western states.[31]

Were one to add to these figures the southern and western natives who
were educated at New England institutions, the New England influence
would appear even more impressive—for between a quarter and a third
of the students at Yale and Harvard between 1800 and 1860 were southerners, and they were so dominant at Princeton that they set the character of the institution.[32]

The prominence of New Englanders in regions beyond New England
and the virtual colonial dependence of southerners and westerners on

New England institutions points to an important aspect of the formation of early American culture that is easily overlooked in the fruitless debates over elite power. The expansion of New England through the migration of its population and the extension of its influence through its role in educating non-New England economic, political, and intellectual leadership did not in any sense mean that New Englanders, individually or collectively, were in a position to dominate or coerce other regions. Southerners or westerners educated at New England schools continued to think of themselves as southerners or westerners if they returned to their native environs. Similarly, most New Englanders who settled in the South or West came to think of themselves as residents of those areas, adapting easily to their peculiar institutions. New England did not influence nationality by making the nation the subject of New England powercenters or even by making it adhere to political causes favored by New Englanders. Although character education might have come into being under the auspices of men with particularistic religious and political goals, it produced men who, while retaining the universalistic forms of self-discipline and self-control, easily shed the Federalist and Congregationalist associations of character if it proved convenient for them to do so. Indeed, the character educators, in concentrating so exclusively in supplying their students with "the discipline and furniture of the mind," while denying them the utilitarian particulars that might have indoctrinated them as New England loyalists, had resocialized men to behave in certain ways without providing them with the concrete information that would have made them Congregationalists and Whigs. This failing was, at the same time, the greatest strength of character education, for it made it a mode of organizing behavior that was sufficiently universal in character to be useful, applicable, and acceptable in virtually any setting. At the same time, by giving the resocialized both the immediate experience of corporate institutions and the personality traits essential for large-scale corporate enterprise, the character educators established a cultural basis for nationality: a cadre of men in all sectors of activity, widely dispersed and strategically placed, who saw the utility of large-scale corporate organizations and possessed the personality traits without which such endeavors could not succeed—in sum, a culture of organization.

Finally, in considering the expansiveness and influence of New England institutions, one should not restrict one's attention to elites. The most compellingly powerful dimension of the New England influence lay in its ability to penetrate all levels of society. Not only were New England-educated men conspicuous occupants of high judicial, legislative, and business positions—and hence, objects of emulation at a time when everyone was looking for the way to wealth; more importantly, by the strategic placement of such men as teachers and ministers, they were able to expand the loci of character education beyond New England to the common schools and churches and to the most humble settlements and their lowliest inhabitants. Thus, after the first decade of the nineteenth century, it hardly mattered whether an individual had ever been East or attended college. For if he went to school at all, the odds were very good that he would be taught the lessons of character and self-control. And in any case, thanks to the prominence of men of character and New England origins in his community, he would be reminded of the usefulness of the lessons learned at school. Thus it was, for example, that the ambitious young man Abraham Lincoln, whose family had emigrated from Massachusetts via Pennsylvania, Virginia, and Kentucky, after receiving rudimentary schooling at the hands of Azel Dorsey, an academy-trained teacher, was inspired to enter the law by watching the Princeton graduate John A. Brackenridge and the Litchfield Law School graduate John Pitcher pleading cases in the county courts of southern Indiana.[33] Successful Yankees were ubiquitous and active in the areas of southern Illinois and Indiana. And it is hardly surprising that, humble as his origins may have been, this "gawky country jake" (as Attorney Pitcher described him) should, when he began to act on his ambitions, have modelled himself on the learned and prominent Yankees of his locality, seeking their advice and loans of books from their libraries.[34] Nor is it surprising that he should have echoed their Whiggish politics and shown his willingness to participate in such Yankee institutions as the Springfield Lyceum.[35] Finally, it is hardly surprising, given the fact that he adopted accomplished Yankees as his reference group, that he should have, in the most serious crisis of the Civil War, turned to such men as Stanton and Halleck, both college men and lawyers with broad corporate experience, to reorganize the war effort. Common men like Lincoln who wanted to become uncommon men faced two alternative models of emulation in the first half of the nineteenth century: one political and individualistically entrepreneurial in the Jeffersonian and Jacksonian mold, the other cultural, character-based, and corporate, in the Federalist-Whig mold. By following the former, a young ambitious man might become wealthy and prominent, but his sphere of influence would be likely to be local and confined to the particular vocation he had chosen. By following the latter, through the process of character-formation and the institutional network, a man could, as Lincoln did, rise rapidly to national prominence.

But neither the use of character-forming institutions, expansive and pervasive as they were, nor the concrete successes of Yankees and the Yankee-educated could bring about the final resolution of the conflict between the fragments of authority—the political, the economic, and the intellectual. Only a major national event like the Civil War, in which the learned could demonstrate to the public their virtue and daring, could retrieve the broad public esteem and deference once freely granted to the wealthy, learned, and respectable. And even then, a philosophical accommodation between institutional elitism, which restricted access to truth to the learned, and the Enlightenment's belief in the imminence of truth would have to be forged. This would only come with social Darwinism, which, in relocating authority from scripture to the world of matter and observable phenomena, also articulated the relationship between unity and diversity, between individuals and collective processes, and between elites and the masses. Finally, even with the re-legitimation of wealth and learning as bases for leadership, both historically and philosophically, the difficult task of "fighting the wilderness, physical and moral" and "struggling to work out the awful problem of self-government" had only begun.[36] For as Charles W. Eliot, the young post-Civil War president of Harvard noted, to accomplish these tasks, Americans needed to be "trained and armed."

3. The Tortuous Path

Although the process of reintegrating authority and leadership would take little more than half a century and a good many persons living at the end of the old order in the 1790s would still be living when the foundations were finally laid for the new in the 1870s, the process was hardly automatic, and the rapidity of the achievement belies its difficulty. In the following chapters I will attempt to trace out some of the specific institutional developments of the period 1780–1860 in order to indicate with greater specificity the complex transformation of culture and personality that led, after the Civil War, to the reorganization of society, politics, and intellectual life. Chapter Six will consider the legal and juridical foundations of private authority in the development of the corporation and the endowment trust. Chapter Seven will consider the origins and progress of the medical profession in New England, the struggle to establish professional authority and a basis for professional claims, in which physicians looked to the marketplace, to the state, and ultimately to the private colleges for support and legitimacy. Chapter Eight will examine the development of character education at Yale, Yale's influence on education nationally, and the role of Yale and institutions dominated by Yale graduates in forming national networks of organizations and individuals who formed the cultural nuclei of new settlements in the South and West and were woven together into a coherent national group. Chapter Nine will examine the development of character education for an urban elite that would provide the model for urban elites and elite institutions in other cities.

CHAPTER SIX

Corporations, Equity, and Trusts: Legal Instruments and the Foundations of Private Authority

But although corporations were found to be very beneficial in the earlier periods of modern European history, in keeping alive the spirit of liberty, and in sustaining and encouraging the efforts for social and intellectual improvement, their exclusive privileges have too frequently served as monopolies, checking the free circulation of labour, and enhancing the price of the fruits of industry. Dr. Smith does not scruple to consider them, throughout Europe, as generally injurious to the freedom of trade, and the progress of improvement. The propensity, in modern times, has, however, been to multiply civil corporations, especially in these United States, where they have increased in a rapid manner, and to a most astonishing extent. The demand for charters of incorporation is not merely for municipal purposes, but usually for the more private and special object of assisting individuals in their joint stock operations and enterprising efforts, directed to the business of commerce, manufactures, and the various details of internal improvement. This branch of jurisprudence becomes, therefore, an object of curious as well as of deeply interesting research. The multiplication of corporations, and the avidity with which they are sought, have arisen in consequence of the power which a large and consolidated capital gives them over business of every kind; and the facility which the incorporation gives to the management of that capital, and the security which it affords to the persons of the members, and to their property not vested in the corporate stock.[1]

The development of the basic instrument of private collective action, the corporation, is usually treated by historians as a problem in intellectual history—specifically, as a matter in the evolution of legal doctrine. The standard accounts assert that corporations become private entities when, in the second decade of the nineteenth century, the grant of the corporate charter by the state came to be viewed as a contract and, as such, inviolable as long as its purposes and activities were lawful. The intellectual history of corporate privatism, however, describes only one part of the process the corporation was transformed from by which an instrument of the state into an instrument of private action. Inextricably tied to the evolution of doctrine are more concrete issues, particularly the composition of governing boards and the ability of corporations freely to hold and dispose of property. For even with fully developed doctrines affirming the inviolability of charters, corporations did not become genuinely private until they possessed full control over the succession of their officers. And without the ability to hold and dispose of property freely, formal inviolability and the composition of governing boards were only partial barriers to state interference. Thus, the development of the private corporation as an instrument for the accomplishment of the purposes of the Standing Order as it retreated from political power after 1800 involved not only the evolution of legal doctrines that considered the corporation an inviolable contract, but also the development of machinery of governance and the clarification of equity doctrine and equity jurisdiction that permitted private persons to transfer property freely to corporations, and permitted the corporations themselves to deal with property with the full rights of legal personhood.

There was nothing about the corporation as the device was used in the American colonies in the eighteenth century that rendered it peculiarly suitable as an instrument for the perpetuation of private power and authority. To be sure, the reluctance of the colonists in the seventeenth century to create certain types of corporations, especially guilds and business companies that granted monopoly privileges to private groups, was based on their experience in England with the oppressive power of such entities. But the fact that some corporations were oppressive did not prevent the colonists from making extensive use of corporations to promote public purposes.[2] Indeed, a century and a half of experience with corporations had led the colonists, especially in the North, to view the device as a mechanism of peculiarly public character, whether civil (as the legal basis for townships), charitable (as in the Boston Overseers of the Poor), educational (as in Harvard and Yale College and the grammar schools), or ecclesiastical (as in the churches and "ecclesiastical societies"). Even when, immediately after the Revolution, such business corporations as the Bank of North America (1781), the Massachusetts Bank (1784), and the early bridge, turnpike, and canal companies began to be chartered, they were conceived of as public enterprises. The fact that they were capitalized entirely or in part by private funds and governed to a greater or lesser extent by private persons, their stockholders, was not seen as necessarily giving them a private character. For especially under American law in the late eighteenth century, incorporation was not necessarily viewed as granting monopoly privileges, the right of perpetual succession, or immunity from legislative accountability.[3]

Colonial attitudes toward trusts, whether testamentary or charitable, resembled those regarding corporations. Trusts and the use of equity courts to enforce them had been well known by the early colonists as instruments of ecclesiastical tyranny and as methods by which private parties could avoid the mandates of public authority, but this did not prevent the establishment of endowments for public purposes (in the form of poor funds, lands set aside for the support of ministers, and funds for the support of learning in the colleges and grammar schools) or the use of trust-like devices, especially guardianships for minors and life-estates for widows in exchange for waivers of dower rights. Although the colonists did not as a rule establish special courts of equity, they did, as in the case of Connecticut, grant their law courts certain circumscribed equity powers—although carefully ruling out the powers of such courts to sustain equitable ownership of property (uses) as equal or superior to legal ownership.[4] In other words, trusts and equity were used in the colonies, but only to the extent that they were consonant with public purposes.

With the separation of political, economic, and intellectual authority after 1800, however, the public character of corporations and trusts became less clear. The Standing Order, as long as it unified authority in a single group which could credibly assert that its private interests were identical with those of the public, did not have to use incorporation as a means of insulating private interests from public interference. Nor did it have to develop legal or juridical doctrines that set corporate organizations distinctly apart from the broad range of public activities in which they were engaged. If corporations after 1780 served the private purpose of assisting in the separation of capital from familial interests and giving it a personhood of its own, distinct from the particular control of those who contributed to it, this collectivization was viewed as no more inimical to the public interest that the collectivization of resources that occurred in the formation of a congregation or township.

The rise of a unified political opposition to the Standing Order in the 1790s and its subsequent victory on the national, state, and local levels after 1800 compelled a resolution of the status of corporations. For if the individuals who had earlier acted in the capacity of "natural leaders" of church, state, and commerce were no longer viewed as such, what then of the privileges granted them by the states in the previous two decades? Should they be compelled to be formally accountable to the state through legislative reviews and amendments of charters, legislative rights of inspection and visitation of corporate activities, and the placement of public officials in *ex officio* capacities on corporate boards of directors and trustees? Would such legislative impositions constitute unwarranted and illegal interference with the rights of private property, especially the right of individuals to associate freely and make contracts for legal purposes? The political revolution of 1800 posed a host of difficult questions, and as the courts and legislatures groped for answers in their fragmentary knowledge of British law, their historical fears of private aggrandisement, and their ambiguous attachment to Enlightenment-derived philsophies of natural law, their decisions came to reflect the power configurations of the localities in which legal doctrines were formed rather than any overarching and widely accepted theories.

Interestingly, for all of the rhetorical force of opposition to certain early acts of incorporation immediately after the Revolution, the Jeffersonian-Republicans did not, after 1800, oppose corporations *per se*.[5] Given their commitment to political and ecclesiastical voluntarism and the involvement of prominent Jeffersonians in commerce and manufacturing, they could hardly do so.[6] They merely wanted to ensure a continuation of early traditions of public accountability, the abolition of incorporation as a special privilege, and the prevention of monopolies. Thus, for example, the Jeffersonians who established the College of South Carolina in 1801 and Jefferson himself, when he promoted the chartering of the University of Virginia in 1819, formed those institutions as corporations. Both, however, ensured public accountability by limiting terms of trustees and making them appointive positions, subject to the will of the governor and the legislature.[7] Further, even though these institutions were permitted to receive donations and bequests from private persons, their utility as instruments of private interest was limited by provisions that enabled the trustees to decline donations and made the state treasurer, not the institution's trustees, the holder and manager of such funds. In any case, the state was always envisioned as the primary base of financial support, not only because of the absence of an historical tradition of private charity, but also because of specific legislative strictures placed on charitable giving in the South after 1819.

If the Republicans accepted the corporation as an instrument both for pursuing public purposes and, within guidelines of public accountability, for pursuing private ones, the Federalists, while embracing the corporation as an essential device for organizing all kinds of activity, faced the more difficult task of protecting their vested corporate interests in church, state, and commerce while, at the same time, having to create legal doctrines that justified the protection of private interests from public interference. This was not a simple task, for it flew in the face of colonial legal traditions and of the rhetorical justifications that the Federalists themselves had used after the Revolution in persuading the public and the legislatures to create new kinds of corporations, especially in the business sector. Further, evolving credible doctrines to support the corporation as a private entity in the courts and legislatures was only half the battle. For if corporations were to be successfully justified as non-accountable private arrangements, could their promoters reasonably expect the public to support them financially through direct grants, lottery privileges, and other devices? If not, how were they to be supported? The obvious answer—obvious at least insofar as there was some historical precedent for it in New England and abundant precedent in the old world—was through charitable trusts. But once again, charitable trusts established by private benefactors raised long-established fears of the oppressive feudal civil and ecclesiastical establishments abolished by Henry the Eighth and their revival in Stuart times. It would not be an easy task for a group which, even after it lost public favor, continued to assert its role as the steward of property and virtue in the public interest, to do so through legal and juridical mechanisms that had such specific historical associations with Europe's "tattered Gothic garment." In encouraging private institutional support and the establishment of endowments, the Federalists also faced concrete technical and administrative problems; it was difficult to ensure that these private entities, even if insulated from public control, did not become too independent of their creators and donors. And this would require not only new kinds of structural and administrative arrangements within the corporations, but also the expansion of the limited equity powers of the state courts to include the administration of trusts and endowments.

Finally, even if the Federalists could bring about a redefinition of legal and equitable doctrines to sanction the private character of corporate entities, this in no way answered their larger purpose of establishing an encompassing hierarchy of order and authority in the state. Mere privatization meant acceptance of an open and uncontrollable marketplace of ideas and interests in which the device of incorporation merely aggregated the will of citizens, believers, consumers, and producers into competing corporate entities, no less conducive to disorder and no more productive of virtue than a tumultuous pre-corporate democracy. The question of privatization, therefore, was inextricably connected to another issue: the composition of corporate boards of directors and trustees not only as it affected the connection between corporations and the state, but also as it mitigated the tendency of private corporations to act only in pursuit of their own interests. In the non-profit sector, the rein on the tendency of institutions to go their own way would be the lay board of trustees—either self-perpetuating or elected by "proprietors," individuals who were considered a part of the corporation but were not directly involved in its operations, and by the strict separation between the membership of governing boards and those directly concerned with implementing corporate purposes. In the for-profit sector, the danger of institutional autonomy would be avoided through separating boards of directors for those who carried out the productive tasks of companies. In addition, there quickly developed a third level of accountability through the interlocking of corporate directorships and trusteeships. These interlocks not only promoted a coordination of purposes, but also diluted the credibility of charges that private institutions were merely pursuing their own special interests. Thus, for example, lay-controlled colleges or medical societies could not credibly be accused of merely promoting the interests of clergymen or physicians, since, through their boards of governance, they were clearly accountable to broader interests. Although the interconnected institutions could be and were accused of representing the interests of the wealthy, the wealthy could and did reply, by pointing to the broadly useful work of their corporate institutions, that they were merely acting as stewards in the public interest.

That the New England Federalists could not hope through political means to reestablish a larger order or reinstitute traditional forms of authority did not mean that they simply bided their time until, by some magical process, they were called back to past positions of broad public authority. The rise of the public interest in such forms as the breaking up of the Standing Order's monopoly on banking, education, and professional activity presented concrete problems that had to be innovatively faced. About some of these, such as the loss of educational and professional monopolies, nothing could be done. Others, especially economic challenges, required responses, since they produced not only competition, but, more importantly, economic turbulence of such violence that it threatened the stability of the Federalists' own institutions. Because they could not respond to such challenges through formal inter-institutional arrangements that democratized legislatures would have invariably viewed as monopolistic, the Federalists did so through informal ones, which not only produced models of integrative and cooperative business activity that would, in subsequent decades, provide models for establishing economic stability outside of New England, but which also promoted patterns of collective activity on the social and intellectual level that would counteract the centrifugal tendencies of the competitive and individuated world of the early nineteenth century. Through such arrangements, which combined universally available organizational entities, such as the corporation and the trust, with informal relationships between corporations or commerce and culture, the Bostonians would succeed in creating an "aristocracy of manufactures." This "aristocracy," mythically exclusive but functionally inclusive, would make Boston, by the 1850s, the nation's center of culture and capital. Boston, in other words, would succeed institutionally where other urban areas with greater resources, most notably New York and Philadelphia, would be only partially successful, their efforts at privatization frustrated by internal dissensions and political interference. And Boston would succeed where other places, such as Connecticut, with similar social interests and legal environments, would fail institutionally because of inadequate resources or an insufficiently strong social-structural basis for collective action. Nevertheless, Boston's success did not, of itself, point to nationality, even if Bostonians were powerful in the nation. Only when Boston's intensive patterns of institutional integration could combine with with those of other urban elites and, in turn, with nationally extensive networks of local elites could the half-century of impasse between private and public authority begin to resolve itself and the outlines of a larger economic, political, and intellectual order be discerned. And this would not occur until after the Civil War.

1. The Privatization of the Corporation

The colonists, as has been suggested, shared, in the seventeenth and eighteenth centuries, a universal suspicion of corporations based on painful first-hand experiences of oppression, racketeering, and monopoly in royal and ecclesiastical corporations in England. They did not, however, entirely reject the English corporate heritage, any more than they rejected the whole of English models of ecclesiastical and political organization. Just as they selected out of their historical experience those aspects of the English order that were compatible with their material needs and their assorted religious convictions, so they used the corporation selectively, almost universally rejecting uses of the device that smacked of private power and accepting those that were consonant with the generality of social and economic interests. Thus, for example, the southern colonial assemblies, while reluctantly assenting to such public corporations as parishes and, in a few instances, of municipalities (such as Charleston), created no business corporations before 1781 and, even then, did so much more slowly and with much more heated debate than assemblies in states to the northward.[8] When certain influential Virginians sought a corporate charter for the College of William and Mary in the 1680s, they did not risk arousing opposition in the colony's assembly, but went directly to the King for a royal grant.[9] The middle colonies, New York, Pennsylvania, Delaware, and New Jersey, were only slightly more bold than their southern brethren, setting up a good many public corporations, especially for charitable and educational purposes, but only one business corporation.[10] New England legislators followed the general pattern, regarding their townships as common law corporations, not requiring special grants to carry on their collective business (though their lands were granted by the colonial legislatures), regarding their ecclesiastical societies in much the same light, and differing from their colonial neighbors only slightly, in showing a somewhat greater willingness to establish colleges and schools and a scattering of business corporations.

If the Federalists were to find credible precedents for the immunity of corporations to public interference, they would have to look for it in the scanty heritage of colonial corporate activities. Most of that heritage, even in New England, emphasized the public purpose of corporations. Only in the historical development of the colleges, Harvard and Yale, could anything be found on which to base claims to special private authority. And these claims were derived not only from legal doctrine but also from practical experience in governing the colleges and defining their relations to the state, to their staffs, and to their several constituencies. Doctrine, in other words, owed a great deal to experience.

While New Englanders were aware of the form that corporations had taken in England, they were apparently unwilling to grant either Harvard or Yale the degree of institutional autonomy that English corporations enjoyed. The structure of governance at Harvard was a compromise between the English tradition of institutional autonomy and Puritan fears about the oppressive potential of corporate organizations. Rather than giving the college a single self-perpetuating board of trustees (or, as in the English universities, Fellows), they set up two boards. One, the Corporation, consisted of the President, the Treasurer, and five Fellows. Although constituted as the "body politic and corporate" of the college, their election and policies were made subject to review by a second board, the Overseers, which consisted of "the Governor, Deputy Governor, and all the magistrates of this jurisdiction, together with the teaching elders of the six next adjoining towns."[11] While the charter stated that the five Fellows need only be "inhabitants of the Bay"—that is, inhabitants of the colony—they were, with very few exceptions, tutors, the teaching staff of the institution. This was in line with the British university tradition of institutional self-determination.

But the dangers of autonomy were offset by the Overseers who, in representing the public interests of church and state, were in a position to ensure corporate accountability.

The two boards coexisted fairly well as long as the various interests in Massachusetts were able to maintain an overall social and religious consensus. But as the colony grew more prosperous, dividing into religious factions that reflected the divergent economic interests of particular occupational and regional groups, these structures of accountability began to break down. By the early eighteenth century, the always uneasy relationship between the urban merchants and the rest of the colony's agrarian and artisan population began to develop towards open conflict. The ministry was split into liberal and conservative factions.[12] The liberal faction, composed of the ministers of predominantly mercantile congregations, espoused doctrines that favored rationalism, toleration, and a loose ecclesiastical structure. The conservatives represented agrarian and artisan congregations, preached traditional Calvinism, and favored both ministerial authority over congregations and closer relations between churches. The disintegration of the religious and social consensus coincided with a crisis in Harvard's affairs. The suspension of the colony's charter in 1686 had invalidated the college's own corporate status.[13] Harvard's governing boards, however, continued to operate as they always had, while attempts were made to secure a royal charter. Without legitimate operating authority, however, the college quickly became an object of contention between the various factions. The conservatives, led by Increase and Cotton Mather, wanted to keep Harvard under the control of the Congregational Church. The liberals, led by the merchants John Leverett and Thomas Brattle and their ecclesiastical allies, were not averse to the inclusion of either representatives of the Crown or members of other denominations on the governing boards, a change that would clearly be necessary if the college wished to receive a charter from the King. Between 1692 and 1707, Harvard operated under the government of a variety of boards, as the several factions contended for control. Finally, in the summer of 1707, the *de facto* Corporation, consisting of the merchant-oriented Reverend Samuel Willard, two tutors, and twelve other persons, most of whom were liberal Congregational ministers, elected John Leverett President of Harvard. To placate the enraged conservatives, Leverett, with the consent of the royal governor, restored the Charter of 1650 with its two governing boards. With the college firmly in their hands, the liberals could afford to be magnanimous.

But the restoration of the old charter did not quiet contention over control of Harvard for long. In 1717, Leverett, hoping to strengthen the power of the liberals in setting the basic policies of the institution, abandoned the tradition of appointing tutors as Fellows of the Corporation. When deaths created three vacancies on the board, he appointed three settled ministers of liberal congregations as Fellows. Only one tutor, Henry Flynt, remained on the board. The other two tutors in the college, Nicholas Sever and Thomas Robie, became mere employees of the institution. The tutors, led by Sever, went immediately to the conservative-dominated Board of Overseers, urging them to overrule Leverett. While the Overseers could veto the Fellows, in the case of a deadlock between the two bodies, the General Court was forced to intervene. In the end, the royal governor used his influence to uphold Leverett and the liberals, and control of the institution came to rest in the hands of a body of nonresident Fellows who, because they were accountable to no one but themselves, could perpetuate the merchant-sponsored rationalism of the coastal cities. Samuel Eliot Morison, the preeminent historian of Harvard's affairs, credits Leverett with rescuing the college from provincial sectarianism and, thereby, founding the "liberal tradition of Harvard University."[14] This identification of the liberal tradition with institutional structures that were free from public accountability (but implicitly accountable to benevolent and enlightened merchants) is a theme to which we will return.

The founders of Yale were conservatives. Having no experience in the English universities, they had no need to accommodate academic traditions of institutional self-determination. And with the example of Massachusetts before them, they were not about to make any concessions to public authority. Founded in an era in which orthodox ministers were attempting to suppress the influence of rationalism and independent congregations, the new "Collegiate School" was placed from the outset under the government of an external board of ministers. Because of their preoccupation with preserving and perpetuating the rigid Calvinism that Harvard had abandoned, the founders of Yale knew that they could never hope to obtain a royal charter. So the language of the "charter" of 1701 carefully avoided any reference to the school as a corporation. The ten ministers to whom the government of the college was entrusted were referred to as

. . . Trustees, Partners, or Undertakers for the said Society . . . (with) full Liberty, Right, and Previlege to Erect, Form, Direct, Order, Establish, Improve, and at all Times in all suitable Ways to Encourage the said School in some convenient Place in this Colony and granted sundry Powers and Previleges for the Attaining the End aforesaid.[15]

Legally, the group was constituted as an unincorporated charitable trust—a perfectly unassailable form of organization should any of the college's enemies chose to challenge their authority in the Privy Council in England. Having named the Reverend Abraham Pierson of Killingworth as Rector of the "Collegiate School," the Yale trustees seemed off to an auspicious, if modest, future.

With the death of Rector Pierson in 1707, however, the lack of a corporate charter began to present very concrete problems—especially as the school was beginning to attract both public and private contributions.[16] With property at stake, the location of the school became a matter of great public concern.[17] The Hartford members of the Corporation wanted the school to be located there. New Haven and Saybrook urged their own claims. At one point, the school completely disintegrated, the Hartford, Saybrook and New Haven trustees each gathering students and each claiming to be the true Collegiate School. Finally, the matter was placed before the General Assembly, which in 1718 directed the trustees to locate the institution in New Haven. Uncertainties would prevail, however, as to the powers of the trustees, and these interfered with the school's attempts to find a permanent president. In the fall of 1723, the trustees sent a list of questions to the Assembly, asking them to clarify various aspects of the charter of 1701. The response of the legislature was the passage of an act which, without formally constituting Yale as a corporation, required the trustees to act as a body;

> first, the trustees could choose another person to replace an incapacitated or inactive trustee; second, the trustee could make decisions by a majority vote of those attending a meeting; third, a meeting could be called by any three trustees, with seven making a quorum; fourth, the minimum age for a trustee was reduced from forty to thirty; and fifth, anyone chosen rector of the college "shall by Vertue thereof become a Trustee of the same" for his term of office.[18]

The Corporation, still deeply factionalized, was far from delighted with the legislature's action. It took Yale five years to accept the amendment of its charter. But, once it did, it was ready to begin functioning as a corporation.

In placing Yale under the direct control of a self-perpetuating board of non-resident ministers, the founders of the college were seeking to avoid the conflicts over accountability that had plagued Harvard between 1692 and 1723. The ministers were, under the Saybrook Platform of 1708, accountable only to one another and the elders of their churches. This policy, however, only shifted the focus of accountability. Connecticut was, by the early eighteenth century, being torn by the same kinds of conflicts between farmers and merchants and liberal and conservative theology that had plagued Massachusetts.[19] When the founders of Yale eliminated public representation by refusing to create a board of overseers comparable to Harvard's, they shifted the struggle for control of the institution into the political realm. The increasingly ascendant merchants would, as a result, have to attempt to exert their influence over the college through local battles over the election of ministers to the pulpits of particular churches and by partisan efforts in the General Assembly to influence the policies of the institution through granting or withholding state contributions.

Through the turmoil of the Great Awakening, Yale's accountable corporation not only retained its original form, but was confirmed in it by a formal (though illegal) grant of incorporation from the General Assembly in 1745. When the college began to side with the New Lights (proponents of the Awakening) in the 1750s, the Old Lights in the Assembly attempted to assert a right of visitation and oversight of Yale's affairs, but the school successfully defended itself from political interference.[20] Not until 1792, when the clergy saw the advantages of strengthening the ties between the church, the state, and the political and economic interests of the merchants in a common defense of Federalism, did the Corporation permit public representatives to sit with it. And even then, they sat as a minority. As President Stiles noted in his *Literary Diary*:

> Mr. Hillhouse presented me with copies of the Report of Committee & Act of Assembly . . . In which the Assembly give(s) to Yale Coll certain arears of Taxes . . . on condition the Corporation associate 8 civilians, viz. Gov., Lt., G., 6 Senior Councillers. . . . This is a grant and liberal dona(tion) & a Noble Condescention, beyond all expectation! Especially that the Civilians should acquiesce in being a Minority in the Corporation. . . .The College will hereby always have a Majority of the Upper House in their friendship, & six members as a Court of Appeal in College Cases. *The clergy will have a particular and special reason now to preach up for & recommend the Election of religious & undeistical Counsellors; and tho' now & then an unprincipled Character may get into the Council, he may be hunted down in a future Election. It may be mutually beneficial by preserving a religious magistracy & a more catholic clergy.*[21]

As far as he was concerned, the admission of laymen was merely a stratagem to perpetuate Yale's essentially private and non-accountable character.

From a practical standpoint, therefore, the Federalists could depend on their experience in insulating Harvard and Yale both from public interference and from too much internal autonomy in seeing their way out of the dilemma posed by the ambiguous nature of the corporation. Both colleges had, by altering the mode of succession of trustees and by differentiating the constituencies to which they were accountable from the public and its representatives, managed to establish precedents for private control. And both charters had withstood a century of political attack. The practical experience of the colleges, however, was not their only guide. They were also assisted by the development of contract law, which, by the late eighteenth century, was tending to regard agreements between private parties as absolute and not amenable to equitable interference. As the Handlins suggest in their discussion of the evolution of the law of private rights in Massachusetts, the idea of the inviolability of contracts had been advanced during the Revolution and had been written into both the state and the federal constitutions.[22] The matter had been a subject of lengthy debate during the 1780s, as the states had wrangled over their liability for war debts. While a definitive legal opinion linking the experience of the colleges to the emerging doctrine of the inviolability of contracts would not be enunciated until the United States Supreme Court's decision in 1819 in the Dartmouth College Case, it is clear that, as early as the first decade of the nineteenth century, such arguments were being made and their applicability was seen as going far beyond the realm of the eleemonsynary corporation.[23] As early as 1809, William Tudor argued in the *Monthly Anthology* (which would soon give rise to the Boston Atheneum), that corporate charters were contracts and, hence, immune from legislative interference.[24]

In Massachusetts the effort to insulate corporate institutions from political control in the face of the Jeffersonian challenge took its most pronounced form in a renewal of the battle over the corporate status of Harvard. By the charter revision of 1780, Harvard's Board of Overseers included substantial political representation. To the old Board on which sat the Governor, Deputy Governor, certain magistrates, and the teaching elders of the churches of the towns adjoining Boston, were added the members of the Governor's council and the entire Senate of the Commonwealth.[25] In 1810, realizing the likelihood of Jeffersonian interference in the affairs of the college, the Federalists undertook a further revision of the Board:

By eliminating the State Senate, the *ex officio* members were reduced to eleven, and the clerical members were limited to fifteen, keeping existing ministers (all "men of correct principles") in office until death or removal; fifteen new laymen were to be elected by the Board itself; and the new Board, thus constituted, would fill future vacancies by cooptation. The first lay members elected by the Board were all Federalists, of the same type as the Fellows—indeed it would seem that one purpose of this Act was to make the Overseers a sort of "waiting club" for the Corporation.[26]

The Act of 1810 introduced a contractual element by specifying that it could not be repealed by the legislature alone—unless such a repeal was accepted by the Governing Board of the Corporation (thus granting the college a degree of institutional autonomy unknown heretofore and, for all practical purposes, transforming it into a private corporation in the modern sense).[27] It was highly unlikely that the Federalist-dominated Boards would accept any Jeffersonian revisions. Nonetheless, when the Federalists were routed in the elections of 1811, the Jeffersonians immediately acted to return the college to public control. In February of 1812, the legislature suspended the Act of 1810, and proposed to restore the Overseers to the form specified under the revision of 1780—with the now thoroughly "Jacobin" State Senate as the dominant group. The Corporation, of course, denied the validity of the Act. A court battle loomed. But before the Jeffersonians could take their places as *ex officio* Overseers, the Federalists had regained control of the government. Harvard, no longer fearing a Jacobin Board, thereupon accepted the Act of 1812—until it could be improved by a subsequent compromise statute passed in March of 1814. This act counterbalanced the numerical strength of the *ex officio* members of the Council and Senate with the laymen originally admitted by the charter revision of 1810.

While both Harvard and Yale retained ties to the state after 1810, they were, nonetheless, taking on an increasingly private character. The disestablishment of the Congregational Church—in Connecticut in 1818, in Massachusetts in 1833—meant that the clerical members of the college's governing boards no longer enjoyed any official status. They became mere representatives of privately supported, voluntarily gathered congregations. Disestablishment had the effect of cutting the colleges off from an important source of popular influence and financial support. In addition, the legislatures in Connecticut and Massachusetts were becoming increasingly unwilling to grant financial aid to institutions that remained under sectarian control. While the state had provided fifty-five percent of the donations received by Harvard in the period 1700–1800, it contributed only thirty-three percent in the period 1801–1825—and nothing at all after 1825.[28] At Yale, public contributions had constituted seventy percent of total donations between 1701 and 1800, fifteen percent between 1801 and 1825—and nothing at all after 1825.[29] Although the Federalist and their clerical allies continued to seek state support, they were becoming increasingly aware that such aid would necessarily require greater public accountability. By the late 1820s, with the specter of Jacksonianism looming, both Harvard and Yale had turned away from the state in favor of the cultivation of private sources of support.

By the 1820s, the Standing Order had been thoroughly transformed. Its power was no longer based on public authority, formal or informal. The disestablishment of the churches, the abolition of the property qualification for voting and officeholding, and the disintegration of traditional patterns of deference voting, had broken its hold on religion and government. Successful legislative attacks on the exclusive privileges of the professions had opened both law and medicine to the general public.[30] And the monopoly of the old colleges on higher education had been dismantled by the establishment of such institutions as Williams, Amherst and Trinity. By the second decade of the nineteenth century, the Standing Order's alliance between merchants, ministers, and magistrates was no longer an entity whose power was upheld by law, religion, and social consensus. Instead, its power now derived explicitly from its possession of wealthy and, more importantly, its control of incorporated cultural, economic, and social welfare institutions. It had become a merchant-centered group around which orbited the institutionally-oriented elements of the clergy and the medical and legal professions—each held in its path by the financial and prestige rewards of allegiance to merchant-funded organizations. It was defined less by a direct descent from the old Standing Order than by a shared ideological conviction that men of wealth and education had a special responsibility for the common weal.

Students of philanthropy are familiar with the Pauline and Calvinist doctrines of the stewardship of wealth, in which a man's riches were to be regarded not as his own, but as goods entrusted to him by God for doing God's work in the world. New England Puritanism had broadened this notion of stewardship from a simple injunction to be charitable to a broader responsibility by the wealthy for the spiritual and economic well-being of society. As the Standing Order was transformed from an official elite to an economically based class, this concept of public responsibility did not disappear. Economic success continued to carry with it public responsibilities. But those responsibilities were to be exercised neither through political officeholding nor through idiosyncratic individual acts of benevolence. Rather, they were to be discharged through donations and bequests to privately-controlled corporate institutions.

The pattern of charitable benevolence in New England shows clearly the reorientation of the old Standing Order from an elite with public responsibilities to a group whose influence was mediated through private institutions. First, it is important to recognize that there was very little private benevolence before 1800. While it is true that private donations comprised nearly half the gifts to Harvard and about a quarter of the gifts to Yale in the period before 1800, endowment income did not constitute an important part of institutional resources until the nineteenth century, when public support had disappeared.[31] It was supplanted by gifts and bequests from individuals on an astoundingly large scale. Secondly, the phenomenon of large-scale benevolence developed only after 1800, when the Standing Order was forced from public power by an upsurgent Jeffersonian democracy. It was at this point that Harvard was transformed into a private institution and a host of other private charitable organizations were established by the merchants and their allies. Thirdly, the pattern of benevolence was definitely in the direction of private charitable enterprises: of the $9,886,329 given for charitable purposes in Boston between 1800 and 1860, only twelve percent went to publicly-controlled organizations.[32] Fourthly, the pattern of participation in fund-raising for charitable purposes shifted decidedly in the direction of large donations from a small group of contributors. Of the $142,000 raised by Harvard in eight subscription drives between 1805 and 1846, ninety-five percent of the funds came from twenty-nine individuals, most of whom were closely related by blood and marriage.[33] While donations to Yale were somewhat less concentrated, five percent of the subscribers to the 1832 fund drive gave forty percent of the total sum raised.[34] Finally, the largest donations to charitable institutions came from individuals whose families directly benefited from the services of those institutions, usually as officers of governance or staff.[35]

The increasingly private character of institutional support was paralleled by the development of an ideology of benevolence in which the responsibility of the privately wealthy for cultural and educational enterprises became increasingly explicit. It was stated in its simplest form by Daniel Webster in his argument in the Dartmouth College Case in 1819:

The corporation in question is not a civil, although it is a lay corporation. It is an eleemosynary corporation. It is a private charity, originally founded and endowed by an individual, with a charter obtained at his request, for the better administration of his charity. . . . Eleemosynary corporations are for the management of private property, according to the will of the donors. They are private corporations. . . .

If the view which has been taken of this question be at all correct this was an eleemosynary corporation; a private charity. The property was private property. The trustees were visitors, and their right to hold the charter, administer the funds, and visit and govern the college, was a franchise and privilege, solemnly granted to them. The use being public, in no way diminishes their legal estate in the property, or their title to the franchise. There is no principle, nor any case, which declares that a gift to such a corporation is a gift to the public.[36]

Webster's assertion of the absolute immunity of the incorporated charitable institutions from state efforts to control them was based not only on strict construction of the laws of property, contract, and the Constitution. He also evoked much more immediate public policy concerns in language that would have been perfectly understandable to the Federalist merchants whom he so often represented in both court and Congress:

The case before the court is not of ordinary importance, nor of every-day occurence. It affects not this college only, but every college, and all the literary institutions of the country. They have flourished, hitherto, and have become in a high degree respectable and useful to the community. They have all a common principle of existence—the inviolability of their charters. It will be dangerous, a most dangerous experiment, to hold these institutions subject to the rise and fall of popular parties, and the fluctuations of political opinions. If the franchise may be at any time taken away, or impaired, the property may also be taken away, or its use perverted. Benefactors will have no certainty of effecting the object of their bounty; and learned men will be deterred from devoting themselves to the service of such institutions, from the precarious title of their officers. Colleges and halls will be deserted by better spirits, and become a theatre for the contention of politics. Party and faction will be cherished in the places consecrated to piety and learning. The consequences are neither remote nor possible only. They are certain and immediate.[37]

It was clear to Webster, as it was to the court that sustained his argument, that the willingness of private persons to support objects of charity depended upon the insulation of charitable organizations from public control. Even though these charities might be devoted to public ends, their government and property were to be regarded as the private property of their officers and benefactors.

The Dartmouth College case, though largely settling the doctrinal issues regarding the private character of the corporation as a legal instrument, left the status of such older corporations as Harvard and Yale uncertain. The final resolution of their character as wholly private institutions would take decades. Harvard, already a creature of the liberal and rationalist theology of the urban merchants, would, by 1780, begin electing laymen as Fellows. By the 1820s, both governing boards would be dominated by lawyers and businessmen. In 1852, the Congregational ministers and most of the political representatives were dropped from the Board of Overseers.[38] Finally, in 1866, the Overseers came to be elected by the graduates of the College. It took Harvard over two hundred years to evolve into a wholly private institution! Yale retained its ties to both church and state longer than Harvard, although technically, it became a private institution somewhat earlier. The college was a firm bulwark of the Standing Order until 1818, when the new state constitution disestablished the Congregational church. From that point on, the majority of the members of the Corporation, while all clergymen, were no more than a self-perpetuating body of trustees with no official standing in the state. By 1870, the government of the College, still in the hands of a group of clergymen from largely rural areas, had gotten seriously out of phase with Yale's increasingly urban, wealthy, and business-oriented alumni. At the alumni dinner during commencement week of 1870, W. W. Phelps attacked the clerically-dominated Corporation:

"The younger alumni are not satisfied with the management of the college. They do not think that in anything, except scholarship, does it keep progress with the age. They find no fault with the *men*; they find much fault with the spirit of the management. It is too conservative and narrow." Yale, he said, was out of touch with the world; it needed an addition of active intelligent alumni on its governing board so that it could have "a knowledge of what is wanted in the scenes for which Yale educates her children." No longer should the college be ruled by "Rev. Mr. Pickering of Squashville, who is exhausted with keeping a few sheep in the wilderness, or Hon. Mr. Domuch, of Oldport, who seeks to annul the charter on the only railway that benefits his constituency."[39]

Phelps' speech was only a part of a broader attack on Yale's old order. Led by influential and wealthy men, the Young Yale movement persuaded the legislature to amend the college charter, replacing the six senior councillors from the State Senate with six persons to be elected by the alumni. Not until 1906, however, would laymen obtain a majority on the Corporations.

The inclusion of graduates as a body in the governance of the colleges represented a major symbolic and structural alteration in Yale and Harvard as corporations. Structurally, it formalized a new kind of accountability. The elimination of public officials and ministers from the governing board was not a simple turning over of institutional affairs to those with the means to finance their operations. For the alumni were not, either legally or symbolically, stockholders of the institutions. Rather, while including in the body of potential trustees those with large means, it also included a wider group whose collective wisdom and oversight would prevent the school from becoming merely private—like the pet charities of the emerging plutocracy. Both Harvard and Yale had, since the late eighteenth century, graduated students who not only entered a variety of occupations, but settled all over the country. If the colleges hoped to continue to be institutions of national consequence, they had to devise structural means of reflecting their national constituencies. Thus, while turning away from sectarian and political control, the major private institutions were careful to avoid the pitfall of total privatization. Both Harvard and Yale could have, in the 1860s and 1870s, decided to eliminate clerical and political representation and make their governing boards entirely self-perpetuating. That they did not do so suggests a concern with the broader issue of accountability. And indeed, this final structural transformation would coincide with the final evolution in the ideology of cultural stewardship enunciated by men like Charles W. Eliot. The private universities would see their primary function not merely as servitors of the wealthy, but as generators of a new elite in which wealth and knowledge were made subservient to "a virtuous will," and the public interest was defined and dealt with by a nationally based technical, cultural, and administrative elite trained in elite-controlled private institutions.

If the clarification of the private status of corporations in New England was a tortuous process, the clarification of that status elsewhere, where the Jeffersonians and their successors were even more influential, was even more difficult. Even though all states after 1820 had to accept the Supreme Court's doctrine regarding the inviolable status of corporations, that did not prevent them from compromising the effectiveness of private corporations, especially educational and charitable organizations, through other means, especially in restricting the ability of individuals to give property to such corporations and the ability of such corporations to hold and manage property without interference. The evolution of the law of corporations in favor of private authority, in other words, was but one part of a more complex struggle to erect a rock-like legal foundation to save wealth, learning, and respectability from the shifting sands of public favor. Without the ability to receive and manage property freely, the application of the doctrine of private rights to the corporation was little more than an empty gesture.

2. Equity and the Endowment Trust

It has been a question of grave import, and difficult solution, whether a corporation, instituted as a charity, could be permitted to become the *cestui que trust* of lands devised for charitable uses. Corporations are excepted out of the statute of wills, and it has been decided, that they cannot be directly devisees at law. But, in England, by the statute of 43 *Eliz.* ch. 4., commonly called the statute of charitable uses, lands may be devised to a corporation for a charitable use, and the court of chancery will support and enforce the charitable donation. The various charitable purposes which will be sustained are enumerated in the statute; and the administration of justice, in this or in any other country, would be extremely defective, if there was no power to uphold such dispositions. The statute of Elizabeth has not been re-enacted in New-York, New-Jersey, Pennsylvania, or Maryland, and probably not in any of the United States; and the inquiry then is, whether a court of equity has power to execute and enforce such trusts as charities, independent of any statute, and when no statute declares them unlawful.[40]

Although the development of doctrines that defended the corporation as an inviolable private contract and the perfection of mechanisms of lay control were key elements in creating an organizational basis for the exercise of broad private authority, they were not, in themselves, sufficient to complete such entities. For as long as institutions lacked means of funding their operations free of state interference on the one hand, and remained dependent on the will of consumers of institutional services on the other, they would remain, as the Republicans well knew, dependent on changing on public favor.

The basic mechanism for giving institutions freedom from the uncertainties of state support and consumer demand was as well known to Americans of the early nineteenth century as the corporation itself. Like the private corporation, the endowment trust and the juridical apparatus that regulated it, the formal court of equity, had been largely rejected by the colonists for a number of reasons. The foremost one was the association of trusts and courts of equity with the oppressive power of the Church of England and of the Crown. This association was not remote, a dim memory from the seventeenth century.[41] In the proprietary colonies, particularly New York, courts of chancery were imposed by royal governors as instruments of executive power. They sat without juries and were immune from public opinion. They were used for a variety of purposes, particularly as devices for circumventing the common law courts and for enforcing unpopular government measures such as the collection of quitrents.[42] If equity conjured up visions of ecclesiastical and executive tyranny, trusts and uses, modes of ownership of property enforceable under equity, suggested more concrete and disturbing possibilities involving the ability of individuals and institutions to accumulate vast amounts of property and to do so immune from the mandates of common law courts and normal testamentary practice. This possibility was particularly repugnant to New Englanders, who had predicated their social system on a largely equal distribution of property in order to ensure the perpetuation of mutually interdependent corporate communities.

But equity, like the corporation, was a legal device that worked two ways. While it might be used as an instrument of oppression and as a means of insulating officials and institutions from popular pressure, it was also a means, as Zephaniah Swift put it, of

> . . . acting according to the dictates of conscience, and aiming at the attainment of abstract right, and perfect justice, [having the power] to abate the rigor, correct the injustice, and supply the deficiency of positive law where such rigor, injustice, or deficiency result as an indirect and collateral consequence, and in operation of law; and where it is apparent, that such effect was not the design and intent of the law; but if the legislator had foreseen it, he would have made provision for relief.[43]

Equity, in other words, was a means of applying higher standards of justice to situations which, if treated under the common or statute law, would have resulted in unjust consequences. The colonists, while hostile to those aspects of equity that protected privilege, freely resorted to equitable remedies for problems stemming from the strict enforcement of contracts and wills. Under equity, heirs who had been unfairly treated by a parental will could bring actions in equity to circumvent specific testamentary provisions. Similarly, merchants and artisans used equity to extricate themselves from contracts in which buyers, through strict legal enforcement, took advantage of their necessity. An example of this was pondered by John Adams as he considered the value of equity:

It is a natural, immutable Law that the Buyer ought not to take Advantage of the sellers Necessity, to purchase at too low a price. Suppose Money was very scarce, and a Man was under a Necessity of procuring £100 within two hours to satisfy an Executive, or else go to Gaol. He has a quantity of goods worth £500 that he would sell. He finds a buyer who would give him £100 for them all, and no more. The poor man is constrained to sell £500s worth for £100.[44]

In this sort of situation, equity would be applied. Indeed, it was on precisely this basis that the seventeenth-century efforts to limit the profit-making proclivities of merchants were applied. Equity was the concept underlying the doctrine of "fair price."

For a group like the Federalists, equity posed a problem. On the one hand, it was ideally suited as a juridical basis on which to set up the financial independence of new corporate institutions, and the most efficacious means of rendering such institutions as Harvard and Yale free of public and state support. On the other hand, equity, especially as applied to the enforcement of contracts, was inimical to the doctrines of contract inviolability on which the Federalists were basing the legal immunity of corporate institutions from state interference. The Republicans, needless to say, favored the equitable aspects of contract enforcement, especially as it affected such issues as bankruptcy and mitigated the independence of corporations, but opposed it as a means of insulating private property from public control.

As the colonies achieved independence from Britain, their attitudes towards equity were determined by their dual experience with it as both an instrument of justice and an instrument of oppression. All of them, with the exceptions of Pennsylvania and Georgia, either granted their common law courts equity powers or set up special courts of chancery.[45] But all of them, including Connecticut and Massachusetts, denied them the power to administer or enforce trusts. Indeed, from the confident standpoint of the years immediately following the Revolution, when the old Standing Order still held sway, even conservatives like Zephaniah Swift viewed trusts as unnecessary:

But as in this state, none of the reasons exist that did in England, for their introduction, and as no advantages can be derived from them it is not probable that they will ever be adopted. The recording of our deeds, precludes the possibility of a secret mode of conveying estates, by which the legal estate can be concealed or rendered uncetain, and a provision for prodigal children may as well be made by giving them the use of the estate during life, or to another in trust for him—as in both instances, the estate will be equally at his control and equally liable for his debts. The truth is, our general law has given the proprietors of land, every honest privilege that can be derived from uses, and trusts; that is, exemption from forfeiture and the feudal incidents, and the power of devising, and has deprived them of every unjust privilege, that was acquired by the cestui que trust, that is, exemption from liability to be taken for debts, and the power of secret conveyances, tho there be no necessity of a formal public delivery of possession.[46]

From the standpoint of the early 1790s, when the Standing Order had no particular need of protection from popular pressure, such assertions were easy to make. But as testators began to attempt to protect the integrity of their capital from the force of partible inheritance, and as institutions began to attempt to establish financial autonomy, the issues of trusts and uses that seemed so uncomplicated to Swift and his contemporaries became very complex indeed. For if the beneficiary of a trust, whether testamentary or charitable, enjoyed the equivalent of legal ownership of trust property, "taking it as tho the estate had been directly granted to him," trusts could not be used as means of insulating institutions from public or beneficiary demands.[47]

The political revolution of 1800 set off, as it did in the case of corporations, an extensive review of past practices and of legal doctrine by both Federalists and Republicans in order to advance or block efforts to broaden the power of equity courts, which, in turn, would have established a juridical basis for the employment of trusts for dynastic as well as for charitable and educational purposes. As in the case of the Federalist search for historical precedents for privatization of the corporation, this enterprise involved reviewing colonial laws of charity and testation in order to find past usages that could both be transformed in formal doctrine and used as justifications for and legitimations of new practices. The focus of the search really revolved around four issues: 1) the distinction between legal and equitable ownership; 2) the determination of accountability for the enforcement of trusts; 3) the binding force of the wishes of charitable donors and testators; 4) the nature of trust principal. The resolution of these depended on the establishment of equity jurisdiction over trusts and uses. For without such jurisdiction, all sorts of peculiar and inconsistent rulings, based on readings of the common law, might result. In Connecticut, for example, a court might decide, as it did in the 1790s in the case of *Bacon vs. Taylor*, that the "equitable owner shall take the estate in the same manner, as tho it had been granted to him."[48] In Massachusetts, on the other hand, a court might award possession to the trustee, since equitable ownership had no standing under the law of the Commonwealth.[49] The law might be further tortured by the application of common law doctrines that had nothing to do with trusts or equity, as when the Massachusetts Supreme Judicial Court in 1810 awarded a life interest to a widow, even though her deceased husband has specified that she should only get an annuity during the duration of her widowhood.[50] The judge based his decision on the common law doctrines regarding restraints on marriage. Such inconsistencies, particularly as they affected the ability of testators to determine the disposition of their property, were intolerable in a society attempting to establish a rational legal order. Even the most ardent Jeffersonian, while he might approve of obstacles to the creation of trust-based mercantile dynasties, could reasonably resent the intrusion of the state into his ability to insure the intact transmission of his farm to his grandchildren. Common law was showing itself to be insufficient to govern the increasingly complex uses of property in the new nation. And its inadequacy became even more apparent when applied to the matter of charitable and educational trusts. For if, as was the rule in Connecticut, the equitable owner took title to a trust estate "as if it had been granted to him," who then was the equitable owner of a charitable or educational trust? Did the beneficiaries of the Yale scholarship established by Bishop Berkeley in the 1740s own it? Or, because they were a general class of persons, did the public, through its representative, the state, really own it? It was all very well for Swift to state confidently that

> The original right to property is founded in the nature of things. It consists in the power of using and disposing of it without control. But in a state of society, it became necessary for the mutual convenience of mankind, that this natural right should be laid under certain restrictions and limitations. . . . But that property should be laid upon a certain, permanent foundation, there have been certain positive rules adopted by mankind, which govern the acquisition, the use, and the disposition of it. These are calculated to give the possessors a more perfect enjoyment, than can be derived from natural law, and thereby compensate for those rights which are resigned, upon entering into society.[51]

But how perfect could a citizen's enjoyment of his property be if the state interfered with his right to dispose of it for public rather than merely private purposes? Clearly charitable and educational benefactions were consistent with public policy, but without courts capable of dealing with the peculiarly equitable issues that arose from such benefaction, how could benefactors be sure that their gifts and bequests would be used as they intended—that is, how could the courts ensure their private property rights? And how, without equity jurisdiction over trusts, could the public ensure that such bequests were being made and managed in the public interest.

The resolution of these questions varied with the political proclivities of the areas in which they were debated. In the New England states, the legislatures were, after years of confusion, willing to enlarge the courts' equity powers by the end of the second decade of the nineteenth century. Those courts acted quickly to adopt English equity doctrines that protected the rights of testators to dispose of their estates, sanctioned the right of benefactors to create charitable and educational trusts, and clarified the relation between the trustee and the trust beneficiary in favor of the latter.[52] They further freed trustees from accountability to the state and to beneficiaries by adopting the "Prudent Man Rule" which stated that the only guide to "safe and discrete investment" of trust funds was the "sound discretion" of men of prudence and intelligence in the management of their own affairs, not the will of the state, or even state securities.[53] The courts tempered their protection of private rights by adopting the Rule Against Perpetuities, which limited the life of trust estates (excepting charitable and educational trusts), and by adopting the doctrine of *Cy Pres*, which ensured that trust funds established for purposes that were no longer consistent with public policy or possible of performance would be applied to the next most reasonable use. Needless to say, the liberal attitudes of New England judges served the interests of those who sought to establish a legally defensible basis for the financial stability of private institutions. For under the doctrines they established, both the state and the public were effectively barred from interfering with the ability of private groups to fund non-profit corporations and from interfering in their investment activities. The legal shell of corporate privatism was given substance by doctrines of equity and trust that made it possible to "permit the translation of the philanthropy of the past into current or future activity, activity which may or may not encourage further public or private support."[54] This was fundamental if the Standing Order were to exercise influence independent of public favor.

But the acceptance of equity, trusts, and endowed institutions was not paralleled elsewhere in the new nation, at least not to the same extent. The polar opposite of New England's liberalization of private rights developed in the form of the "Virginia Doctrine" enunciated by the United States Supreme Court in 1819.[55] In this case, Silas Hart, a resident of Virginia, had drawn up a will which devised his estate to the Baptist Association of Philadelphia for the purpose of educating Baptist youths for the ministry. Hart died in 1795. His executors, knowing that such bequests were illegal in Virginia, the state having abolished the Elizabethan *Statute of Charitable Uses* which permitted the establishment of charitable trusts, refused to deliver the funds to the Baptists. The Baptists brought suit, arguing that even if Virginia's equity courts did not possess jurisdiction over charitable trusts, the federal court could, through exercise of its own powers in equity, sustain the bequest. The executors, on the other hand, argued that even with the illegality of the devise because of the suspension of the statute of Elizabeth, such a grant to so general a class of persons as the "ill-defined and everchanging membership" of the Baptist Association was illegal because, under Virginia law, unincorporated associations could not take title to property. The court decided in favor of Hart's executors. And even though its decision did not directly affect charitable trusts already in existence under state laws, a very real threat to their existence was given a firm legal footing. Had the doctrines applied in the Hart case been extended to the states, the entire legal basis for private benevolence would have been swept away and private institutions would have become mere conduits for donations and grants to cover current expenditures.

The hostility to endowment trusts found its most pronounced expression in New York in the 1820s. Although the state had, under its 1777 constitution, permitted the liberal application of the Statute of Charitable Uses, this favorable attitude began to reverse itself in the 1780s. In 1788, the assembly voted to repeal the statute, invalidating all charitable trusts in the state save those authorized by the legislature by the granting of charters to charitable corporations.[56] In 1828, with Jacksonianism at its peak, the legislature revised the laws even more dramatically.[57] It restricted the amount of property an endowed institution could hold to an amount specifically authorized by the legislature. No testamentary bequest that increased an institution's endowment over its legislatively set limit would be upheld in a state court.[58] Further, it restricted the proportion of a descendant's estate that could be left for charitable purposes.[59] The crippling effect of such statutes would be evident in the failure of New York's institutions to grow as rapidly as their counterparts in New England and in New Jersey, which had adopted doctrines similar to those of Connecticut and Massachusetts. Between 1800 and 1859, Harvard would receive over a million and a half dollars in private donations, Yale nearly a million, and Princeton nearly a quarter million.[60] But Columbia would receive no more than thirty thousand dollars from private donors and only a little more than twenty thousand from the state.[61] And while class sizes at Harvard would swell from an average size of 44 in the first decade of the century to 89 by the decade of the 1850s, as class sizes at Yale grew comparably from an average of 52 in the years 1800–1809 to 99 in the fifties, and as those at Princeton grew from 33 to 69, Columbia's average classes would increase only from 21 to 26.[62] A similar malaise would affect the state's other charitable institutions. While the Massachusetts General Hospital, the Perkins Institution for the Blind, the Hartford Retreat for the Insane, and Hartford's American Asylum for the Deaf and Dumb would become major innovators in treatment, attracting patients and students from all over the country, New York's institutions would languish, their ability to grow hampered by the legislature's restrictions.[63] New York's charitable leadership would come in the realm of public institutions, most notably the Utica Asylum for the Insane and the state's reformed prison system.[64] But its young men and its charitable dollars would flow out of the state, to places where they would be better educated and more effectively deployed.[65]

The situation in Pennsylvania was mixed. Although the state accepted the Statute of Elizabeth, it failed to establish equity courts, thereby making the enforcement of charitable trusts difficult.[66] This situation was dramatically revealed in the famous case of *Vidal vs. Girard's Executors* in which the relatives of the Philadelphia merchant Stephen Girard attempted, in the 1830s, to block his bequest of the bulk of his estate for the establishment of an institution for the education of poor white orphans. Knowing that the Pennsylvania courts might either uphold the Girard bequest on the common law ground that enabled either the trustee the beneficiary to take the property "as if it were his own" or decline jurisdiction in the case, the heirs took the case directly to the federal courts in 1843, hoping for an application of the Virginia Doctrine. Such a decision in so important a case, bearing on the disposition of the seven-million dollar estate of one of the richest men in America, would have surely, as one jurist remarked, "prostrated almost all the property belonging to the religious and charitable associations of the country."[67] The heirs hired Daniel Webster to argue their case; the defense, Horace Binney, the foremost member of the Philadelphia Bar. Binney mounted a scholarly argument that not only demolished the plaintiff's claim that unincorporated societies could not take property by devise in Pennsylvania, but, more importantly, reviewed the dependence of the law of charities on the Statute of Elizabeth. As he made clear, charitable trusts had been in existence and enforced by English courts long before the 1601 statute, so that the legal foundation of private philanthropy could not be abolished merely by voiding that statute. Webster's argument was largely specious and was based primarily on the contrary effects of courts in permitting the establishment of institutions which, like Gir-

ard's proposed college, barred ministers of the Gospel from their premises. The court found in favor of Girard's estate, overturned the Virginia
Doctrine and finally, after a half-century of debate, affirming the legal
basis of private charitable endowments.

3. Eleemosynary Corporations: A National Perspective

The long struggle by advocates of charitable trusts did not end in
1844. For the ruling by the Supreme Court in the Girard Will case did
not affect New York, Pennsylvania, Maryland, and Virginia, states that
had repealed the statute of Elizabeth, limited the scope of equity, and
specified in their own laws the purposes for which trusts could be
established. As a result, through the course of the nineteenth century,
the development of endowed non-profit corporations—colleges, libraries, hospitals, and museums—was highly selective. States like Massachusetts, Connecticut, and Pennsylvania, which minimized legal strictures on the charitably inclined and on beneficiary institutions, became
the centers of official culture. However wealthy New York might be, it
had no universities or other cultural institutions comparable to Harvard
and Yale, the Massachusetts General and Pennsylvania Hospitals, or
the Boston Atheneum. Wealthy New Yorkers, lacking trustworthy institutions in their own state, sent many of their sons and much of their
charity elsewhere—to Yale, Harvard, and Princeton. As a result, the
development of a national culture became the peculiar task of a small
set of privately funded institutions in states in which public interference
in the affairs of private corporations was minimal.

It is no coincidence that two of these states, Pennsylvania and Massachusetts, were also centers for the development of a national economic
culture. Indeed, there was a direct functional connection between the
ability of entrepreneurial communities to accumulate capital for large
scale investment and the friendliness of courts and legislatures in those
places towards trusts and corporations of both the for-profit and non-
profit type. This connection stemmed from the efforts of entrepreneurs
in the late eighteenth century to separate family from business concerns.
As was suggested earlier, this effort took the form of a comprehensive
reorganization of business and social welfare activities, in which basic
social and economic activities were reallocated to functionally specific
organizations of the corporate type. At the same time, merchant families
were able to continue to fulfill traditional social mandates to provide
both career training and estate divisions for their children by the use
of testamentary and eleemosynary trusts, which reduced the demands
of children on family capital, enabling entrepreneurs to redirect it into

corporate investment, and also provided new mechanisms for the accumulation of capital. Endowments and trusts involved more than setting funds aside for particular purposes. Such funds had to be profitably invested. In the chronically capital-short economy of the early Republic, trust and endowment funds contributed major capital pools, often exceeding in size the capital funds of major banks. In light of these facts, it is hardly surprising that we find the charitably inclined merchants of Boston and Philadelphia taking a very direct interest in the management of trust and endowment funds. Nor is it surprising that, as Gerald White has shown in his history of the Massachusetts Hospital Life Insurance Company, the pooling of trust and endowment funds should have served as the basis for Boston's preeminence in the field of investment banking. New York may have been a wealthier city; New York State may have been, via the Erie Canal, the gateway to the west. But when it came to the mobilization of capital for large-scale enterprises, Philadelphia and Boston took the lead. It is no accident that the most important national economic enterprises of the late nineteenth and early twentieth centuries—the Transcontinental Railroad, the American Telephone and Telegraph Company, General Electric, and General Motors—were all the creations of Boston investment bankers.

But the real issue, as the Federalists of the early nineteenth century well knew, was not merely one of economic preeminence, but a more significant one of order and authority. Once they had lost control of the state, the establishment of stable economic relationships and, through the law, the protection of their rights as a religious and political minority became essential. More importantly, once they realized, as they apparently did by the end of the second decade of the century, that they needed to stabilize their organizational bases and insulate them from public intrusion if they were ever successfully to reassert their claims as guardians of the common weal, a struggle to redefine the character of the corporation and its financial base was inevitable.

The outcome of the struggle was uneven. New England remained the center of corporate privatism and charitable and testamentary endowments. New York, as late as the 1880s, still held to its restrictive doctrines—a policy almost unnoticed until the courts overturned the efforts of Samuel Tilden to leave his five-million dollar estate for the establishment of a public library in New York City.[68] Then, in a shocked recognition of the extent to which it had been by-passed by large-scale cultural and educational enterprise, it finally, in 1893, succeeded in changing its statutes. The effects were dramatic. Between 1893 and 1900, Columbia University received almost eight million dollars in private gifts, and the city's hospitals, museums, and libraries grew rapidly to national stature.[69] Pennsylvania, although a major industrial state with, by the 1870s, full equity jurisdiction and permissive charity laws, never developed as fully as Boston did. E. Digby Baltzell attributes this failure to the peculiar character of the Philadelphia elite's attitudes towards the institutionalization of authority and leadership, and to the failure of its elite to include the talented and the newly wealthy as readily as Boston's.[70] It could equally well be attributed to the uncertain legal basis for private institutions and to the ethnic and religious heterogeneity that prevented a concentration of institutional resources comparable to New England's. And the South, whose premier state gave its name to the definitive doctrine of hostility to private charity, and whose premier political leaders, Thomas Jefferson and Andrew Jackson, epitomized hostility to the private definition of public responsibility, would take no significant role in the cultural development of the New Republic.

The unevenness of the resolution of this legal and institutional struggle would have crucial bearing on the configuration of American nationality. It would ensure New England a disproportionate share of influence in educating and defining the interests of the nation. And by the Civil War, more than the question of national political integrity would be posed, but also the question of what sorts of institutions, what sort of social order, and what sort of authority could lead the American people to effective economic and cultural unity.

CHAPTER SEVEN

The Standing Order as the Guardian of Science: The Foundations of Professional Authority in Connecticut and Massachusetts, 1700–1830

> Let us show the world that a difference of opinion upon medical subjects is not incompatible with medical friendships; and in so doing, let us throw the whole odium of the hostility of physicians to each other upon their competition for business and money. Alas! while merchants, mechanics, lawyers, and the clergy live in a friendly intercourse with each other . . . physicians in all ages and countries, riot upon each other's characters.[1]

The Federalist effort to constitute a new basis for authority involved more than the fostering of doctrines of private rights and the perfection of methods of institutional control. In addition, it encompassed the extension of authority over new areas of endeavor, most notably the profession of medicine. This chapter will attempt to suggest the complexity of that process by showing how the Federalist attempt to extend the influence of the Standing Order was complemented by the efforts of autonomous professional groups to pursue their own purposes. In the case of the medical profession, as I shall show, the level of technical competence was insufficient to justify claims for legislatively enforced special privileges—the power to license and to possess a monopoly of medical treatment—so that doctors were forced to base their claims on social authority by linking them to the interests and institutions of the Standing Order. The fact that this linkage of professional training with the colleges eventually established a scientific foundation for medicine's claims for special privilege that would be broadly acknowledged by the second half of the nineteenth century should not obscure the fact that the original motives for the linkage of the profession and the college were political.

To practice medicine in modern America involves more than acting as a healer. One can heal without being a professional. The professional character of medical activity comes not from the activity itself, but from patterns of institutional participation by the healer that grant him credibility. In our own time, this credibility is reinforced by law and by the dominant pro-scientific ideology. Were this credibility or authority simply a product of the miraculous successes of medical technology, there would be no need to question it; the pre-eminence of the modern professional specialist would explain itself. But historically, the authority of the modern professional role and the cluster of institutions that support and define it emerges long before there is any substantial technical justification for it.

It is easy to overlook how recent most modern medical miracles are. Anesthetics date only from the 1840s. Abdominal surgery, although performed as early as the mid-nineteenth century, did not become a common procedure until the twentieth. Asepsis, the germ theory of disease, antibiotics, and the understanding of basic metabolic processes are all achievements of the last century. But the establishment of the institutions of professional authority, the legal monopoly of "regular" physicians, the university-affiliated medical school, the teaching hospital, the professional society, the medical library, journal, and research laboratory, have been with us for nearly two centuries. The authority of the profession as gauged by the willingness of legislatures, philanthropists, physicians, and the general public to support and patronize medical institutions, was established long before the content of medical practice could justify it.

The early establishment of professional authority in medicine is, however, more than a problem in institutional development. What makes these institutions particularly interesting historically is their remarkable success. Although a host of training alternatives existed in New England in the early nineteenth century, the aspiring physicians flocked to the college-affiliated medical schools, rejecting both the apprenticeship system and the proprietary medical schools. Similarly, patients, regardless of social or economic status, were quick to forsake the possibilities of self-treatment and the ministrations of midwives and folk-practitioners in order to place themselves under the care of certified physicians.[2] That is not to say the "regular medicine" and its institutions did not encounter concerted opposition. Physicians had to fight every step of the way to incorporate their societies, to bring those societies to support university-affiliated medical schools, to counter the claims of rival modes of treatment (ranging from self-medication to homeopathy and chiropractic), and to win the patronage of the general public. Indeed, these battles are still being fought. The existence of this opposition, however, merely heightens the significance of the question of how, given the absence of a medical technology to justify its exclusive claims to public approval and legal monopoly, and to counter the energetic assertions of its rivals and detractors, the regular physicians, as early as the 1820s, were able to establish successfully the institutional clusters characteristic of modern medicine and generate a substantial and steadily growing public and political support for their activities.

1. Conditions Favoring the Growth of Medicine as an Occupation

There was no medical profession during the first century of settlement in New England. While the colonies harbored a handful of individuals who had been trained as physicians in Europe, most healing was done either by the patients themselves, by such para-professionals as midwives, or, most frequently, by clergymen who supplemented their incomes by tending the sick. Fortunately, there was little need for an organized medical profession. Life in seventeenth-century New England was remarkably healthy, far more so than in Europe. All major studies of early New England society agree in stating that infant mortality was far lower and overall life expectancy far higher than in the Old World.[3] The great epidemics of smalllpox, typhoid, yellow fever, and cholera that would terrorize the populations of the eighteenth and nineteenth centuries had yet to appear.

As long as New Englanders lived in small, isolated agricultural settlements, they could lead lives that were longer and healthier than those of their forebears. But a lower death rate combined with higher fertility (due to lower ages at marriage) produced conditions that both brought this happy state of affairs to an end and, at the same time, lay the social basis for the development of a medical profession. Increasing populations meant increasing population density in older settlements. Higher populations also encouraged geographical mobility both to new settlements and to urban centers. The rise of trade in the cities and the elevated significance of commercial farming led to greater and more regular communication between villages, towns, and cities. And with these came a rapid deterioration of public health. In Andover, Massachusetts, for example, two-thirds of the men born before 1700 who survived to age twenty could expect to live beyond the age of sixty; of those born after 1700, less than half the twenty-year-olds had the same life expectancy.[4] Infant mortality jumped from 225 per thousand for those born between 1670 and 1690 to 534 per thousand for those born between 1730 and 1759.[5] And smallpox, the first epidemics of which appeared in Boston in the 1660s, by the 1690s was beginning to ravage previously isolated interior settlements.[6] Against the historical experience of the preceding fifty to seventy years, the deterioration of public health after 1700 brought about a demand for a higher level of medical skills.

The second level of the crisis involved the occupational structure itself. The rapidly growing population, in spite of increasing mortality and morbidity, was placing strains on the ability of fathers to provide for their sons. The perpetuation of the Puritan social order had been based on the existence of sufficient family and community resources to ensure that every head of family possessed the means to set up his sons as farmers in trade, or as artisans.[7] Inasmuch as New England's population was primarily composed of farmers, the "sufficient resource" consisted of land within particular towns. The common lands of most towns had been distributed by 1700. After that, farmers could provide for their sons either by subdividing their own properties, engaging in commercial agriculture to an extent sufficient to purchase land for sons either in their own towns or in new ones, or by encouraging their sons to leave farming for trade, the crafts, or the clergy. These strategies might have succeeded had the other occupational groups not been suffering from the same problems of providing for their sons. A town, even with a growing population, could only support a finite number of shoemakers, blacksmiths, and carpenters. The sons of artisans, like the sons of farmers in the eighteenth century, were facing diminishing prospects in their fathers' occupations and were being forced either to move on or to look for new occupational alternatives.[8] Even the merchants, whose financial capital was theoretically more elastic than the land or skill capital of farmers and artisans, were finding that establishing large numbers of sons in business was eroding their own ability to concentrate and mobilize the capital needed for commerce.[9]

The clergy, the only established profession up to the end of the seventeenth century, was encountering the most difficult situation of any occupational group. A pulpit, unlike a farm or a workshop, could not be handed on to one's children. And the number of pulpits in New England, though growing with the foundation of new towns and parishes, remained severely limited. Because ministers had cultivated their abilities as healers, it is not surprising that, as it became more and more difficult fo find places for their sons in the occupational structure, they should have begun training their sons as physicians.[10] Nor is it surprising that these early physicians should have seen themselves as more than medical artisans of the "barber-surgeon" variety. For many had been trained by university graduates, sharing in both the status aspirations and networks of communication that tied their fathers to the rising European Enlightenment. By the 1720s, the number of physicians practicing in Connecticut and Massachusetts had increased from two or three in the 1690s to a dozen in each colony. Regular patterns of medical training were established, based on the apprenticeship system. As medical practice came to be recognized as a distinct occupation, it was not long before the crisis of numbers that had affected the older occupational sectors began to affect both medicine and its fellow newcomer to the occupational structure, law.

2. The Crisis in the Medical Profession

Viewed quantitatively, the rapid deterioration in the situation of physicians in eighteenth century is remarkable. The number of physicians rose far more quickly than the population. In New Haven and Middlesex Counties in Connecticut, for example, while the population increased only fifty-five and seventy percent in each county between 1756 and 1790, the number of physicians increased by three hundred and five hundred percent:[11] These figures are particularly telling when compared to the ratio of physicians to population in the nineteenth and twentieth centuries. In 1850, there was one physician to every 5600 persons in the United States, in 1900, 1:6400, and in 1950, 1:7500.[12] Clearly, for a new and unorganized profession, the struggle for economic survival among its practitioners must have been fierce.

The increase in the number of physicians qualitatively affected the course of medical careers. Of the seventeen physicians in practice in the two Connecticut counties before 1756, all spent their lives as physicians and remained in the towns where they had begun practice.[13] But of the sixty-five physicians practicing in the two counties between 1766 and 1790, thirty percent either abandoned medicine for other occupations or left Connecticut for places where practice might be more profitable. Many more aspiring healers never even attempted to establish practices in New England. They went directly from college or from medical apprenticeships to the West and South.[14] For those who stayed, life was not easy, as suggested by this letter from a young physician in Middle-

Figure 4

Ratio of Physicians to Population in Middlesex County, Connecticut, 1756–1820, by Census Year

Census Years	Physicians in Practice	Population	Ratio of Physicians to Population
1756	9	13,017	1:1452
1774	16	17,569	1:1097
1782	18	17,712	1: 983
1790	24	20,217	1: 842
1800	16	19,847	1:1240
1810	17	20,723	1:1219
1820	16	22,405	1:1400

Ratio of Physicians to Population in New Haven County, Connecticut, 1756–1820, by Census Year

Census Years	Physicians in Practice	Population	Ratio of Physicians to Population
1756	8	18,181	1:2273
1774	22	26,819	1:1219
1782	—	—	—
1790	41	30,830	1: 752
1800	32	32,162	1:1005
1810	24	37,064	1:1554
1820	16	39,616	1:2476

town, Connecticut to his former teacher, Mason Fitch Cogswell of Hartford:

You know, my dear sir, that my prospects here are confined—confined indeed!—The place is small and I am surrounded by physicians on all sides and at no great distances; so that there is little chance for me to extend my practice even so far as the "village apothecary"—"whose fame full *six miles* around the country ran." . . . *Invention* has been sufficiently *tortured* already and ought to be permitted to repose a little after such a severe sweating as she has undergone of late—besides, there is not enough *gold* in North Carolina to purchase all the infallible remedies which are already offered for sale.—how then can a new one find encouragement?—In short, Friend Morgan, you must be content to move in a narrow sphere, for if you do not succeed by *"honest merit"* you will continue in the *vales of obscurity*, if you continue here—and if you will not be satisfied with this, you must repair to Louisiana—the modern *land* of *promise & try your fortune* among the adventurers who expect a *"better country"* there, "where Spaniards and Frenchmen & Negroes & Jacobins *dance the carmageole* together . . ." You see, sir, that at times I attempt to make merry, with what I, in the sober hours of reflection, regard in a serious light. I can, I believe, support myself here, at present by the profits of my employment—but we are a class of beings who are eternally tearing ourselves about the future—& I am tempted to think that injunction—"take no thought for the morrow"—was designed only for those who have learned to control the feelings of human nature. In regard to my practice— during the months of December and January I was seldom called on to prescribe for the sick, as few of that description were to be found—since that time however there have been a variety of complaints which at times have kept me very busy.[15]

The flood of aspiring healers and the resultant increase in professional competition presented physicians with three possible courses of action:

1. diversification of activity *beyond* the professional role, supplementing professional income by farming, shop-keeping, schoolteaching, and other non-medical activities;
2. expansion of activity *within* the professional role, supplementing income derived from clinical practice with medical teaching, dentistry, midwifery, the invention and promotion of proprietary medications, pharmacy, and the operation of private hospitals;
3. professional organization: restricting entry to the profession through the establishment of standards and competence, the rationalization of training, and the creation of a licensing system.

To have taken the first option would have been a step backward. As it was, many physicians were forced by narrow cirumstances to tend store, farm, and teach in order to get by. And for a new professional group that was attempting to define its own boundaries, raise its status, and make claims on the public as a science rather than an artisan craft, such a move would have been less than satisfactory. The second and third options appear to have been the most attractive to the majority of physicians in Massachusetts and Connecticut after 1760. And the movements to expand the range of medical practice and to organize physicians into a profession appear to have proceeded in parallel fashion.

At the outset, the efforts to expand the functions of physicians and to organize them as a profession appeared to be complementary, for the increasing level of medical technology, especially in the fields of inoculation and obstetrics, made requests by physicians for public patronage and legislative protection seem more legitimate. But political opposition to the incorporation of medical societies not only pointed out the dangers of establishing monopolies and grants of special privilege, but also, and more importantly, pointed out the contradiction between physicians' claims that they were disinterested men of science and the very real financial benefits they would accrue from state grants of incorporation to medical societies.[16] Although doctors in Massachusetts and Connecticut were petitioning their legislatures for grants of incorporation as early as the 1760s, no such grants would be made until after 1780, when the physicians began to separate their interests as entrepreneurs from their interests as men of science and when they began to form alliances with power groups beyond the realm of medicine.

Medicine was unique among the professions in that, as of the mid-eighteenth century, it had neither an agreed upon body of knowledge for aspiring professionals to master, nor any means of controlling the numbers or actions of those claiming to be physicians. To enter the clergy, a candidate had to be a college graduate, undergo an apprenticeship under the guidance of an established minister, be examined and ordained by a body of ministers, and, finally, make himself acceptable to a theologically knowledgeable congregation.[17] Although entrance into the legal profession was less formalized, it was still a far more rigorous procedure than that prevailing in medicine: although it was not a firm requirement, most attorneys required that their students be holders of college degrees, and candidates had to perform well enough as apprentices to receive their teacher's personal endorsement as to the state of their learning and character before being examined and approved by the sitting judges themselves.[18]

But medicine had no formal standards of competence or training; and the economic circumstances of physicians after 1760 undermined what efforts were made by such groups as the "Medical Society in Boston" and the Connecticut doctors of Norwich and Litchfield to establish standards.[19] Medical teaching was an important source of income for straitened doctors. And although teaching unlimited numbers of apprentices as quickly as possible worked against their own long-range interests, physicians had neither the collective will nor the legal ability to bring the situation under control. The number of physicians grew rapidly under such conditions: between 1700 and 1750, the number of doctors doubled, from six to twelve, in New Haven and Middlesex Counties in Connecticut; between 1750 and 1800, it increased almost five-fold, from twelve to fifty-eight. And in larger cities like Boston and New Haven, physicians were in competition not only with apprentices that they themselves had trained, but with numerous druggists, folk-practitioners, and outright quacks.[20] To complicate the situation, many of the druggists (such as the notorious S. H. P. Lee of New London) and quacks (including the mesmerist, Elisha Perkins) were men who had been trained as physicians and who, in viewing the unprofitable prospects of clinical practice, had strayed into medical entrepreneurship.[21] Clearly some action had to be taken to stabilize both the status and the incomes of physicians—or they would be swallowed up in the mass of artisans and small traders, abandoning whatever claims to respectability their clerical origins and scientific rhetoric might have entitled them to.

Massachusetts doctors attempted to organize a medical society as early as the 1730s.[22] This organization, however, like the Philadelphia Medical Society organized by John Morgan in 1765, was more akin to the European royal academies than to modern professional societies. Its primary purpose was the exchange of information through regular meetings and communications to the public through the newspapers. It made no effort to introduce order into the training of physicians, nor is it known to have sought special legal privileges of any sort. Not until the 1760s, when the competitive position of doctors began to deteriorate seriously, would physicians begin to move towards professional organization.

In the spring of 1765, however, Cotton Tufts, a physician of Weymouth and a Harvard graduate in the class of 1749, addressed a circular letter to a group of eastern Massachusetts colleagues. He wrote:

> There has been some time on foot a proposal forming medical societies of Associations of Doctors analogous to those of the Clergy for the more speedy Improvement of our young Physicians; as by communicating to each other any Discoveries in any of the Branches of Physick, especially Botany, for which this Country is an ample Field. To get the Profession upon a more respectable footing in the Country by suppressing this Herd of Empiricks who have bro't such intolerable contempt on the Epithet *Country Practitioner*. And to increase Charity and good Will amongst the lawful Members of the Profession that they may avoid condemning & calumnating each other before the Plebians as it is too common for the last that's call'd in a difficult Case to do by those that preceded him which we apprehend to be highly detrimental to the Profession and the chief Root from whence these very Empiricks spring.[23]

Tufts' first concern was one shared with the older society: the exchange of medical intelligence. But he added to it an urgent preoccupation with economics and professional prestige. Although making no formal proposals for regulating the practice of medicine, he seems to have been well aware of the controversial nature of his suggestion that "lawful Members of the Profession" meet to discuss regulation. For he warned the twenty-four doctors to whom the letter was addressed to be discreet:

> Presuming upon your Concurrence we desire you to promote the Design by circulating this Paper thro' the Hands of all the under mentioned Physicians, or others beyond their Limits, but we must be careful that it falls not into the hands of any but orthodox Physicians, and to prevent it you should deliver it yourself or send it by a trusty Person carefully seald & superscribed lest a teltale Wife or Child divulge that which must be as secret as Masonry till some Societies are established.[24]

The physicians met in March of 1766 in Boston and drew up a set of regulations. They agreed to meet thrice yearly, to communicate new discoveries through the clerk of the society, to invite qualified colleagues to join the organization, and to "endeavor to support the characters of its members and discountenance quacks and pretenders in physick."[25] In addition, members promised to discountenance "nostrums, arcanums, & uromancy as practic'd to deceive and filch ye populace." The society met three times—and then disbanded. Whether the organization's failure was due to disinterest on the part of its members, public opposition, or a recognition that the hard economic issues could neither be dealt with informally nor, because of the political obstacles, brought before the legislature, is unknown. Certainly the experience of the New Jersey Medical Society in the same period suggests the importance of political opposition. For, when that society attempted to include a fee schedule in its articles of association, the public revolted. As one commentator wrote,

> Some evil-minded persons had thrown odium on the proceedings of this Society, tending to prejudice the minds of the inhabitants against so laudable an Institution. . . . It was reported to the Board, that the principal clamour of the inhabitants was owing to some improper expressions having escaped some member of this Society, in regard to visiting fees and other charges which had brought the Society into disrepute with many persons who esteem it an unjust scheme invented by the Society to bring the inhabitants to terms.[26]

The New Jersey Society was unsuccessful in obtaining a corporate charter, in spite of repeated attempts.

Connecticut physicians were more bold than their confreres in other colonies in their frank and open acknowledgement of their economic motives. As early as 1763, Norwich doctors associated themselves and petitioned the General Assembly for a grant of incorporation. While employing the usual rhetoric about the utility of such a society in "promoting medical knowledge" and protecting the public against "Quacks and Pretenders," their petition proposed at its core that the members of the society be given permission to examine and license aspiring healers and, in order to enforce their authority, that:

> . . . no Person or Persons that are not already deemed Physicians who shall pretend to Practice Physic without such Approbation . . . be Allowed to Bring or Maintain any Action against any Person or Persons to Recover any Debt, Demand, or other thing for any service he or they shall Pretend to have done or Presumed to have done as a physician.[27]

While getting around the tricky question of fee-schedules, the Norwich doctors proposed a stratagem that had the advantage of suppressing the irregular practioner without inconveniencing or making explicit economic demands upon the public. They and they alone would have the right to examine and certify physicians. And only those possessing such certification would have been permitted to use the courts for the recovery of fees owed for the performance of medical services. While not barring non-certified healers from practice, this provision would have made it very difficult for them to survive in an economy in which few transactions involved cash exchanges, in which most bills were paid over time, and in which payments from the estates of deceased persons necessarily involved court action.[28]

The Connecticut General Assembly rejected the petition of the Norwich physicians in 1763 and 1774—and similar ones from Litchfield doctors in 1766, and from New Haven in 1787. Up to 1780, no legislature was willing to risk the wrath of the public by giving physicians a statutory foundation on which to erect their claims as men of science. While a part of this resistance can be attributed to a general and pervasive hostility to the creation of any type of incorporated body, and to the uncertain legality of corporate charters granted by colonial legislatures, one cannot ignore the importance of the public perception of physicians as something other than disinterested professionals.[29] After all, the Connecticut Assembly had, by accepting the Saybrook Platform in 1708, given legislative approval to a professional structure of authority in the Congregational Church.[30] And it had granted a corporate charter in 1744 to Yale College.[31] Similarly, in reorganizing its court system, it had enabled the legal profession to develop along hierarchical lines.[32] The legislatures were clearly willing to grant special privileges to bodies with unquestionable public utility. But they balked at the claims of physicians, who could authoritatively claim neither the specialized competence of lawyers and ministers, nor the structure of accountability to the public possessed by the other professions. Ministers were accountable to their congregations and, in Connecticut, to Associations and Consociations composed of other ministers and church elders. Lawyers were accountable to the bench. But physicians, at least as they conceived of themselves—and as they were perceived until after the American Revolution, were accountable only to their own colleagues. The contradiction between claims of disinterestedness and the unquestionable signs of interestedness was all too evident.

The events of the period 1776–1792 brought about changes in the political climate that enabled physicians finally to achieve collective organization with legislative sanction. Although the incorporation of the medical societies in Massachusetts and Connecticut was gained through somewhat different means, their overall paths were similar. Both depended on recruiting powerful non-medical allies: in Massachusetts, the support of the merchants: in Connecticut, the support of the Federalist clergy. There were other similarities as well. Certainly the military service of many doctors in the Revolutionary War enhanced not only their clinical abilities, but also their political connections with other officers.[33] The number of physicians serving in the legislatures of Connecticut and Massachusetts during this period is remarkable. The service of physicians in the military context also undoubtedly gave them an opportunity to alter the ways in which they had been perceived by the public. Rather than being seen as contentious, competitive, and excessively concerned with fees, they were suddenly placed on a par with chaplains as disinterested helpers of the wounded. Finally, physicians benefited from a change in the public attitude towards incorporation itself. Massachusetts doctors were able to take advantage of the atmosphere of the Revolutionary optimism of the early 1780s to succeed in obtaining a charter. Connecticut doctors, who did not move to incorporate a statewide society until 1792, were able to take advantage of the conservative reaction to the French Revolution to advance their collective interests. By the last decades of the eighteenth century, the long struggle of physicians to gain recognition as a profession on a par with the clergy and the law seemed to be moving towards a successful conclusion.

3. Medicine, Politics, and Higher Education in Connecticut and Massachusetts

As they stood in the 1790s, the medical societies of Connecticut and Massachusetts bore little resemblance to the medical associations of today. They were far more autonomous: medical education, examining, and licensing were totally under the control of the physicians themselves. Indeed, they bore more resemblance to medieval guilds than to the bureaucratized structures of our own time. The question of how they moved from autonomy to professional integration into a bureaucratic structure of university-controlled medical schools and lay-supported hospitals is a matter of considerable importance.

The folklore of medical history suggests that the convergence of the professions and the university was inevitable that physicians were eager to sacrifice their autonomy in exchange for the greater prestige and scientific possibilities inherent in university affiliation. Similarly, the folklore of university history, citing such things as Ezra Stiles' 1777 "Plan of a University," suggests that the clerically-controlled universities were eager to expand their functions beyond undergraduate education. The real forces that brought universities and the professions together are far more complex and have far more to do with politics and religion than with medicine or science.

While the successful organization of medical societies in Connecticut and Massachusetts during the 1780s and 1790s would seem to indicate a high degree of professional unity and consensus, in fact the medical profession in both states was deeply fissured. It is true that there was general agreement on the desirability of raising the status of the profession and excluding from it dangerous quacks. There was also general agreement on the utility of presenting and exchanging communications on scientific matters. Underlying this very general consensus, however, were several irreconcilable conflicts. The first involved a split between urban and rural doctors. City doctors in places like Boston, Salem, Hartford, and New Haven were, for the most part, moving towards the functional specificity that we associate with modern practitioners: they were able to support themselves by full-time medical practice. Country doctors, working in areas of lesser population density and among patients of small means, found it very difficult to support themselves by exclusive medical practice. To make ends meet they farmed, ran stores and taverns, compounded drugs, and took on as many apprentices as they could handle. They could not, in other words, afford to move towards functionally specific professional roles. The conflict between the rural and urban doctors took somewhat different courses in the two states. In Massachusetts, when urban physicians like John Warren turned to Harvard College in 1782, persuading its new president, Joseph Willard, to establish a medical school, only minor irritation was expressed by the profession. Doctors like Isaac Rand complained to their colleagues that:

. . . Warren is an artful man, and will get to the windward of us all. He has made a proposition to the club that, as there are nearly a dozen pupils studying in town, there should be an incipient medical school instituted here for their benefit, and has nominated Danforth to read on materia medica and chemistry; proposed that I should read on the theory and practice of physic, and some suitable person on anatomy and surgery. He was at once put up for the latter branches; and after a little maiden coyness, agreed to commence a course.[34]

The following year, in 1783, the medical society voted to appoint a committee to "consider Whither the Doings of any of the literary Societies in this Commonwealth, interfere with the Charter Rights of the Medical Society."[35] This early conflict was quickly smoothed over by a conference between representatives of the society and the secretary of the Overseers of the College in which it was agreed that no conflict of rights existed between the two "Literary Societies."[36] That no serious friction developed between the medical society and Harvard in the early years is hardly surprising. For the society at its founding in 1781 was dominated by city doctors and Harvard graduates (of the 31 incorporators of the society, 18 were from Boston, Salem or Newburyport; 18 of the 31 were Harvard graduates, 13 from the city and 5 from the country).[37] But between 1781 and 1793, while the city doctors were carefully limiting entrance into the profession, their country brethren were training, examining, and admitting a large number of young physicians. In the eleven-year period between 1782 and 1793, only four fellows were admitted to the society from Boston, Salem, or Newburyport, while twenty-five were admitted from rural areas. Of the new members, all four from the city held Harvard degrees, while only half of the new country members did. By 1793, the society was dominated by rural physicians, many of whom had never attended college. In that year, it addressed an angry remonstrance to the legislature protesting Harvard's involvement in teaching and examining aspiring physicians:

Not long after the Establishment of the Medical Society The University at Cambridge founded Medical Professorships, voted in 1782, and proceeded at length to confer the Degree of Bachelder of Physic on such as had gone through Two Courses of Lectures been examined by their Professors and to give the Person graduaded a Diploma constituting him a qualified Practitioner—and it appears in one or more Instances that had undergone an Examination by the Censors of this Society and had been rejected as unqualified for the Practice of Physic and Surgery.

This Interference of the University has already produced Uneasiness and Jealousy and will further tend to produce animosities and Disputes destructive of the Peace & Harmony of both Societies and will in its operation tend also to retard the Progress of Medical Knowledge.[38]

Evidently, the society's protest must have fallen on deaf ears in the Boston merchant-dominated General Court, for nothing was ever heard of the matter again. The merchants by this point controlled Harvard and were unlikely to engage in any activities that would dilute its power. The doctors, on the other hand, seem to have been content to share what rights they possessed with the University.

The second major source of conflict within the medical societies was political in nature, and directly related to efforts by certain factions within the societies to link them to the colleges. While these conflicts followed somewhat different courses in Massachusetts and Connecticut, the organizational issue involved, the autonomy of the medical profession, was basically the same. In both states the evidence for the outlines of the conflict is fragmentary: neither of the medical societies kept detailed records of its debates, nor did they record on a member-by-member basis votes on crucial issues. Futher, none of the combatants left any substantial body of papers describing the issue and personalities involved. Nonetheless, one can piece together the broad dimensions of the conflicts within the medical societies of Connecticut and Massachusetts over the issue of university affiliation.

From the standpoint of our own time it is difficult to imagine the linkage of medical training to universities as having any great political content. Harvard and Yale, after all, are private institutions. And if private institutions wish to make arrangements with the professions to improve the quality of medical training, so be it—as long as it neither involves public expenditure nor impairs the common good. In the late eighteenth and nineteenth centuries, however, issues were not so clear-cut. Neither Harvard nor Yale could be considered a private institution: while both possessed corporate charters and were nominally autonomous, both were also sustained by public subsidy and closely tied to the established churches of Connecticut and Massachusetts. But their public nature consisted of more than financial and ecclesiastical ties. They were, in fact, central institutions of the "Standing Order."

Because both Harvard and Yale were, by the last quarter of the eighteenth century, completely identified with a certain type of civil and religious orthodoxy, the seemingly innocent linkage of college to profession was a matter of enormous political consequence—at least for members of the professions whose political and religious views differed from those of the Standing Order. To place the training, examining, and credentialling of professional aspirants in the hands of these institutions was to link them explicitly to the propagation of those orthodoxies. Needless to say, significant factions in both the Connecticut and Massachusetts medical societies were bound to oppose any such connection vehemently.

Inasmuch as the Massachusetts Medical Society and the Harvard Medical School were established at almost the same time (the Society in 1781, the Medical School in 1782), the conflict between proponents and opponents of the Standing Order and the linkage of the professions to it did not break out in the acute form that would characterize the attempts to link Yale to the Connecticut Medical Society. In the early 1780s, the general political consensus that had sustained the Revolution was still intact, and the sharp political differences over the Federal Constitution of 1789 and Federalist political activity had yet to emerge. So the creation of the Medical School at Harvard was greeted with only token resistance by the Society, most of it based on personal animosity among its members.

But Harvard was not content merely to share the right to grant credentials with the Medical Society. Through the 1780s it aggressively moved forward in an attempt to expand its influence:

> In 1784 the College Corporation tried to induce the General Court to establish a public infirmary in Cambridge, or to let the professors and their pupils practise in the Boston Almshouse; these proposals were defeated by a peppery memorial of the Massachusetts Medical Society, charged with animus against Warren.[39]

Obviously the Corporation was attempting to supplement the courses of lectures that it offered its students with a course of clinical training mwhich would have otherwise been available only through apprenticeship to members of the Medical Society. By 1795, resorting to mercantile benevolence, the College-oriented physicians were able to establish the Boston Dispensary, an infirmary for the Boston poor, and, by 1811, the Massachusetts General Hospital. The College outflanked the Medical Society by relying on the private resources of its mercantile constituency. Still, with the exception of the outburst of 1793, relations between the College and the Medical Society remained superficially cordial. Harvard President Joseph Willard diplomatically invited the President and officers of the Medical Society to attend examinations of candidates for medical degrees. And he granted honorary degrees to the leaders of the Society.

But as political tensions between Jeffersonians and Federalists rose in Massachusetts in the late 1790s, the political factionalization of the Society and Harvard became evident. In 1812, a group of physicians presented a petition to the general Court requesting a charter for an organization that would rival both the Medical Society and Harvard. It was to be called the Massachusetts College of Physicians. The partisan character of the proposed college was underlined not merely by the fact that it challenged the medical hegemony of the Federalist-dominated Medical Society and Harvard, but by the presence of several notorious Jeffersonians among its incorporators.[40] The best known of these men was Benjamin Waterhouse, who would, by 1812, be discharged from his professorship in the Harvard Medical School for his political sympathies.

> The proponents of the rival medical school had undoubtedly offered Waterhouse a chair in that institution, in return for support which he lent in a not very tactful manner. He inserted in a Boston newspaper an anonymous squib about the town's wanting a new fire company, and being opposed by "Captain Squirt" of the old fire company who declared that the new one would reduce the efficiency of the old; and that even if he grew too old to run for fires, his son "young Squirt" would carry on. Lest anyone miss the point of the satire, Dr. Waterhouse rang Dr. Warren's doorbell on Park Street with the paper in his hand the morning it appeared. Dr. Warren appeared at the door long enough to remark, "You damned rascal, get off my steps or I'll throw you off!" Dr. Waterhouse then walked down State Street, stopping every acquaintance he met to point out the articles, relate what Dr. Warren had said, and exclaim, Now, *what* do you suppose Dr. Warren meant by *that?*"[41]

"Old Squirt" and young Squirt were, of course, Dr. John Warren, president of the Massachusetts Medical Society and Hersey Professor of Anatomy and Surgery in the Harvard Medical School, and his son, Dr. John Collins Warren, Recording Secretary of the Medical Society, who would shortly succeed to his father's post at Harvard. The Warrens were the chief proponents of the linkage of Harvard and the Medical Society and the Massachusetts General Hospital. They were, of course, Federalists, and closely linked to the merchant group through ties of friendship and marriage. The transparency of Waterhouse's fire-engine satire is revealed by the extent to which its language paralleled the proposals and remonstrances written in connection with the chartering of the new medical institution.

The Federalists, describing themselves as "the guardians of science" and the "patrons of the healing art," quickly rallied to prevent the effort to create an autonomous medical institution. Harvard President John Thornton Kirkland, who had married into the premier merchant family, the Cabots, and John Lowell, the chief lawyer of the merchant group, appeared before the legislature to argue against the rival school.[42] The Harvard Medical School was represented by Dr. James Jackson, son of a leading merchant and a relative of Lowell and Kirkland. The Massachusetts Medical Society appointed a committee led by John Warren, Aaron Dexter, and Benjamin Shurtleff, all of whom were connected to the merchant group. Although control of the legislature had shifted from the Federalists to the Jeffersonians (Republicans) in the fall elections of 1811, and prospects looked good for the new medical school— in spite of the power of the opposition to it—, the petition was narrowly defeated. While the Senate decided by one vote to grant the charter, it was defeated in the lower house.[43]

The reasons for the failure of the Jeffersonians to gain a charter for their medical school are not at all clear. Certainly the effort has to be viewed against the broader background of the efforts of the legislature to take control of Harvard itself by revising its charter in 1812.[44] They may well have hoped that by supporting Harvard's medical monopoly, and then taking over control of the whole institution, they would have more to gain than simply a new autonomous medical school. The effort to take over Harvard was stymied, however, by a provision of the Federalist-sponsored 1810 charter revision which required that any future alterations in the charter had first to be approved by the College's governing boards.[45] Since these boards had been turned into Federalist strongholds by the Act of 1810, which had eliminated all but five of the popularly elected ex-officio Overseers (there had been forty-six), they were unlikely to approve the Jeffersonian proposal. Although a court contest over this issue seemed inevitable, the Federalists regained control of the state in 1814 and rendered it a moot point.[46]

The effort to link the medical profession in Connecticut to the Federalist-dominated Yale College was both more protracted and more overtly political than the struggle in Massachusetts, although the issues were basically the same. The first indication of Yale's interest in medicine can be found in Ezra Stiles' "Plan of a University," a memorandum written in 1777 while Stiles was negotiating the terms of his appointment as president of the college.[47] While historians have suggested that Stiles' "Plan" was a blueprint for the future of the college, the facts suggest otherwise. Although Yale possessed the means to create medical professorships, especially after the state grant of 1792, neither Stiles nor any other college official made any effort to do so until 1806, when Nathan Strong, a Fellow of the Corporation, proposed the creation of a medical professorship at Yale. This proposal was political in its motivation.

Like its counterpart in Massachusetts, the Connecticut Medical Society was split both between country and city physicians and, by the late 1790s, between Federalists and Jeffersonians. Whereas in Massachusetts the conflicts between the factions were separated by almost two decades, in Connecticut the urban/rural, functionally specific/functionally diffuse split was meshed and contemporaneous with the partisan conflict over the linkage of Yale and the medical profession. A happy general consensus prevailed within the Connecticut Medical Society until 1796, when city doctors, led by Mason Fitch Cogswell of Hartford, attempted to centralize control of the society in the hands of city doctors. First, Cogswell proposed to lengthen the terms of officers of the society, insulating them from popular control.[48] The following year, he proposed to remove the power of granting licenses to practice from county societies, concentrating it instead in the hands of a central state-wide licensing board.[49] These measures, had they been adopted, would have given the Hartford and New Haven Federalists who dominated the medical society control over the medical profession comparable to Yale's control over candidates for the ministry. Having failed to gain their ends through administrative measures, the Federalists tried another tack. In 1799, they proposed the appointment of a committee to "take into consideration and digest some regular system of education to be pursued by candidates for the practice of physick and surgery."[50] In making this proposal, the Federalists undoubtedly hoped to broaden their base of support within the society. While country doctors were bound to oppose efforts to centralize control of the society in the hands of their city brethren, concerns about the status and economic situation of the profession were shared by both urban and rural physicians. In addition, enough country doctors were Yale graduates to guarantee the success of proposals to formalize medical training and link it, even in a tentative manner, to their alma mater. In May of 1800, the committee, chaired by New Haven Federalist Eneas Munson, delivered its report. It was brief and to the point.

That no candidate for the practice of Physic and Surgery in this State shall be admitted to examination until he shall have attained the age of twenty-one, is of good reputation, and shall have had a collegiate education, and shall have studied at least two years with some reputable Physician or Surgeon; or if he has not had such a preparatory education, shall have studied at least three years with such a practitioner, and shall not be licensed to practice unless found qualified as follows, viz.: A general knowledge of Natural Philosophy, Chemistry and Botony, and a thorough knowledge of Materia Medica, Pharmacy, Anatomy and Physiology, Theory and Practice of Physic and Surgery.[51]

The report was clearly a compromise. The Federalists would have preferred standards for admission to candidacy that would have made a college education mandatory, thus restricting entry into the profession to the well-to-do and politically sound. The country physicians, many of them Jeffersonians and religious dissenters, would naturally have been opposed to such a requirement. So the committee provided that candidates for examination who had not attended college would be eligible, as long as they studied under a physician who had been college educated. This latter provision, with the fact that medical training itself would remain in the hands of the profession, made the proposal acceptable to the majority of members.

Although this reform of medical education was accepted by the Fellows of the Connecticut Medical Society in May of 1800, the struggle seems to have crystalized the anti-Federalist opposition. By the fall of 1801, the two most vocal Federalists in the society, President Eneas Munson and Treasurer Mason Fitch Cogswell, had been voted out of office and replaced by a slate of Jeffersonians.[52] While Munson's response to this "conspiracy" was to resign from the organization, Cogswell, who was also one of the Hartford Wits, took up his pen and wrote an intemperate and partisan attack on the Jeffersonian leadership of the medical society and its ideas about medical education.[53] Cogswell's barbs were particularly directed at Samuel Woodward, Secretary of the Society, and William Brenton Hall, its Treasurer. Both Woodward and Hall were outspoken Jeffersonians and supporters of the idea that the society should function as a teaching medical faculty. After assaulting Woodward as a fomenter of faction and as an adulterer and patron of brothels, Cogswell turned his attention to Woodward's ideas on medical education:

Hail sons of learning! raise your wondering sight!
Behold what wonders Woodward brings to light!
Wonders, which come not of ancient lore;
Wonders, which learning never knew before;
Wonders, which neither Greece, nor Rome would boast,
Nor ever flourished on Europa's coast,
Nor medic schools, nor College's have heard,
Nor only in Connecticut appeared.
Strange, wond'rous strange—Distemper new and rare!

Calling aloud for Aesculapian care.
By Potter gender'd in Convention-wall,
The brat's conceived, & sworn on Doctor Hall,
Fathered by Gander—time being now full sped,
In Babcock's press the Strumpet's brought to bed,
While men of science wond'ring, stood to see
Of such an offspring what the sire should be.[54]

The offspring was the compromise plan on medical education. "Gander" (Woodward), Potter, and Hall were the Jeffersonian leaders of the society. "Babcock's Press" was the *American Mercury*, the main Jeffersonian newspaper in Connecticut. There was clearly no doubt in Cogswell's mind that the resistance to turning the society towards Yale was political in character. Having dealt with Woodward, Cogswell turned to Hall, one of the most prolific private medical educators in the state:

See next arise and puff across the stage,
The learned puppet of this learned age.
This *pious* child in Middletown appears,
With tongue much more supplied, than brains, or ears. . . .
With him, to make young Doctors rules are vain,
"Blair's Lectures" only, make the business plain,
With those in hand, he turns them out as fast
As tramping tinkers pewter buttons cast.
Strange, very strange, that in one soul we find
Such great & numerous offices combined;
Surgeon, Demagogue, Preceptor, Preacher,
Dentist, Physician, Midwife, Rhetoric-teacher,
Moral Philosopher, Schoolmaster, *all*
Unite, & harmonize in Doctor Hall.

For all of Cogswell's fulminations, the Medical Society was firmly in the hands of his political and professional enemies. This situation was particularly frustrating because medical education in the hands of men like Hall was not really debased and unscientific. Hall was a Yale graduate (1786) and had studied medicine at the medical school of the University of Pennsylvania.[55] He was one of the first Connecticut physicians to have formal training in obstetrics and is credited with having introduced smallpox vaccination into the state. A broadside circulated by Hall in 1802, advertising his willingness to take on students, promised both clinical and theoretical training and elements of a classical education.[56] The threat presented to Cogswell and his Federalist allies was not the destruction of professionalism by Hall and the Jeffersonians, but the success of an autonomous guild-organized profession.

Having failed in their attempts to take over the profession from within during the period 1796–1801, the Federalists began to put pressure on Yale to get involved in medical education. Once again, Mason Fitch Cogswell was the leader. He was both a relative and close friend of Yale President Timothy Dwight and of Corporation Fellow Nathan Strong.[57] Strong's proposal that Yale should establish a medical professorship was based not only on Cogswell's promptings, but on the fact that Strong's son and Timothy Dwight's younger brother were studying medicine under Cogswell's direction. If the Medical Society could not be returned to Federalist control, then the only course of action was to create a rival organization that they could dominate.

As it happened, both courses of action were followed. Even if Yale did create a medical school, the Federalists must have realized that the Medical Society possessed a legal monopoly in medical licensing through the provisions of its 1792 charter. It appears that the Federalists were preparing to attempt to oust the Jeffersonians at the convention scheduled for May 1807. The society convened twice a year, and the spring meeting was, because of the difficulty of travelling in springtime over Connecticut's muddy roads, usually sparsely attended. If the Federalists could ensure a high turnout of their own faction in May, they had a good chance of regaining control. Fate, however, intervened. In October of 1806, just after returning from the general convention of the Medical Society at New Haven, Jeremiah West, President of the Medical Society, collapsed and died. Normally, the society would have permitted its Vice-President to perform the duties of the deceased President until the next general meeting in October. The Federalists, however, appear to have recognized that they had an opportunity to strike. The charter of the Connecticut Medical Society provided that only twelve of the organization's thirty-six Fellows were necessary as a quorum to transact business. Accordingly, they took the unprecedented step of calling a special meeting in January 1807 to convene at Hartford for the purpose of choosing a President, "in consequence of the death of their late President, Dr. West."[58] It was a rump meeting. Exactly twelve Fellows attended. Since the Federalists only needed seven votes to control the session, they proceeded in short order to elect Federalists John R. Watrous and Mason Fitch Cogswell as President and Vice-President. At the next regular meeting in May 1807, they consolidated their control still further, replacing the Jeffersonians who had served as Secretary and Treasurer of the organization with loyal Federalists.[59]

With the Federalists back in control of the Medical Society, the stage was set for entertaining Yale's proposal to establish medical professorships. At the May 1807 meeting, a committee was appointed to consider the idea, consisting of Federalists Watrous, Cogswell, Eli Ives and John Barker—and a lone Jeffersonian, Joseph Foot.[60] By the fall of 1808, they had reported in favor of the idea, and a new committee was created to meet with representatives of Yale to discuss the proposed medical institution.[61] This committee, although dominated by Federalists, contained several outspoken Jeffersonians. It met with representatives of the Yale faculty under the chairmanship of Dwight through the fall and winter of 1807 and 1808. While the Federalists might control the Medical Society, they could not entirely silence its Jeffersonian members. Benjamin Silliman, a member of the joint committee, in describing the negotiations between the Medical Society and Yale reported that "at first there was jealousy of the College and it was necessary to conciliate." Unfortunately Silliman did not report the specific issues upon which the jealousy centered; he merely reported that after they were "removed" the only obstacle blocking agreement was the fear expressed by certain physicians on the committee that "indigent but meritorious young men should be excluded from the proposed Institution on account of inability to pay the fees of the professors." This objection was satisfied by a promise on the part of Yale to accept, gratis, one student from each county selected by the Medical Society for his "intelligence, worth, and poverty."

The final plan of union between the Medical Society and Yale was clearly a compromise designed to satisfy most of the political and professional factions.[62] For the Federalists, the plan required that candidates for examination be college graduates and have attended the Medical Institution. In addition, the granting of degrees was to be concentrated in the hands of a joint committee of Yale and the Medical Society. For the Jeffersonians and other advocates of professional autonomy, the plan provided that non-college graduates could be considered for examination if they had studied with a licensed physician for three years and attended a course of lectures in the Medical Institution, thus guaranteeing teaching incomes to physicians through the apprenticeship system. In the end, of course, it was a Federalist triumph. The compromise had bought off the Jeffersonian coalition, satisfying each of its elements, and succeeded in placing control of the profession in the hands of Yale College.

4. The Significance of Early Professional Organization

The rapidity with which eighteenth-century physicians moved from being an unorganized and low-status group to a tightly institutionalized learned profession is striking. Only half a century had elapsed between the unsuccessful efforts of Connecticut and Massachusetts doctors to obtain corporate charters for their medical societies and the establishment, by the 1820s, not only of those societies, but also of a cluster of powerful and heavily endowed incorporated medical institutions. In Massachusetts, these included the Boston Dispensary (1795), the Massachusetts General Hospital and the McLean Asylum (1811), the Massachusetts Eye and Ear Infirmary (1820) and the Perkins Institution for the Blind (1832)—institutions whose endowment comprised the largest single category of benevolence of the $2.9 million given by Bostonians for charitable purposes between 1800 and 1845.[63] Connecticut medical institutions included the Hartford Retreat (1823), the American Asylum for the Deaf and Dumb (1825), the New Haven Hospital (1826), and the Hartford Hospital (1825). These institutions were also generously supported. The Hartford Retreat, for example, raised almost twenty thousand dollars from donors all over the state in its original subscription drive, an amount equal to nearly half of Yale's endowment.[64] By some means, physicians had managed to alter dramatically their status and public estimation within a very short time.

How did they do it? Certainly not by demonstrating to the public any remarkable increase in technical competence. While it cannot be denied that the performance of the profession was improved by such innovations as vaccination and the formal knowledge of anatomy, physiology, and pharmacology that came from institutionalized medical training, these innovations wer hardly of the sort that could lead to the reversal in public attitudes that one encounters in the period 1760–1830. Far more unlikely as a transforming force was the association of medicine with the institutions and social groups in which political, financial, and cultural power resided—the Standing Order. By becoming gentlemen, physicians became socially credible. And from this social credibility came professional authority.

Politicized struggles over the direction of the medical profession were not unique to New England. Comparable battles were waged in New York between Columbia's School of Medicine and the New York College of Physicians and Surgeons, and in Pennsylvania between the proponents of the Medical School at the University of Pennsylvania, the medical lecturers at the Pennsylvania Hospital, and the founders of the autonomous Jefferson Medical College.[65] They had a variety of outcomes. In New York, Columbia essentially surrendered its prerogatives to the physicians. Although there was an official merger, the college's preeminence over medical training would not be reasserted until 1860, when the College of Physicians and Surgeons again became the Medical Department of Columbia University.[66] In Philadelphia, the medical profession would split, some physicians maintaining their allegiance to the University, others to the more proprietary Hospital and Jefferson Medical College.[67] In Maryland, curiously, a proprietary institution, the Maryland College of Medicine, would, by associating with similarly minded lawyers and clergymen, lead to the creation of the University of Maryland in 1812.[68] This institution was built along purely Jeffersonian lines, enjoying faculty self-government and sharing its profits among its faculty members.[69] By the 1820s, it would be taken over by the state and organized along more conventional, New England-based lines.[70] Even where Jeffersonians had a free hand, medicine had to reach beyond itself in order to justify its claims.

The organization of the medical profession in the late eighteenth century and its linkage to the colleges in the early nineteenth was a transitory phase in the history of the professions in America. As with the Standing Order itself, medicine lost its claims to broad public support in the 1820s, with the repeal of licensing laws in most of the states that had passed them in the Federal Period. While large numbers of Americans enthusiastically resorted to self-treatment and availed themselves of the numerous health-fads of the ante-bellum period, "regular" physicians, like the Whig descendants of the Federalists, bided their time in a medical analogue of Henry Clay's preference for rectitude over the presidency. In the meantime, however, they established an institutional basis, backed by mercantile wealth, for real scientific progress. Thus, while "irregulars" and "empiricks" (as well as homeopaths, Thompsonians, Phrenologists, and a host of others) hawked their miracle cures, real medical miracles began to be performed in the hospitals and medical schools of Boston, New Haven, and Philadelphia. However, as the tumultuous course of medical reform in the late nineteenth and early twentieth centuries shows, even major technical advances were insufficient to bring about the final establishment of orthodox, university-affiliated, research-based medicine as authoritative. Millions of Americans continued to use patent nostrums and to patronize quacks,[71] and many physicians opposed the reform of medical schools and the upgrading of their research components. As in the Federal period, changes came only when reform-minded physicians were able to generate the financial and political backing of magnates like J. P. Morgan and immensely wealthy foundations like the General Education Board.[72]

The development of medicine as a profession and the evolution of the structures of authority through which it both controls its own members and gains public credibility cannot be viewed as an irresistible progress based on the intrinsic value of medical services. As western-trained physicians in the Third World have learned in attempting to impose modern medicine in traditional contexts, the traditional healer and his clients abandon their old ways, however ineffective, with the greatest reluctance. Credibility is a product of the symmetry between description and prediction only in a culture in which that material relationship is embraced as valid by fundamental social groups. "Science" is of no value to social groups whose power structure and internal equilibrium are based on other criteria. Even in our own culture, the authority of science, as mediated through the authority of a specific professional group, was established extrinsically, through the institutions of politics, economics, and culture, and through the patronage of powerful groups, rather than intrinsically, on the basis of its own merits. And it was only in the Progressive Era of the early twentieth century that a new ideological and institutional consensus was formed that enabled the final victory of "science" over "superstition."

CHAPTER EIGHT

Institutions, Autonomy, and National Networks: The Resocialization of the American People

. . . if we do fail in our great experiment of self-government, our destruction will be as signal as the birthright abandoned, the mercies abused and the provocation offered to beneficent Heaven. . . . No spasms are like the spasms of expiring liberty, and no wailings such as her convulsions extort. It took Rome three hundred years to die; and our death, if we perish, will be as much more terrific as our intelligence and free institutions have given us more bone, and sinew, and vitality. May God hide me from the day when the dying agonies of my country shall begin![1]

The issue of order and authority was not perceived by the Standing Order as merely political, a matter of preserving New England's influence over national affairs or protecting New England's economic interests. The Federalists approached it with a millennial urgency, recognizing that the task involved the redemption of the nation and the realization of America's special mission in the world. If their initial response to the problem of national redemption was coercive and narrowly joined to New England's sectarian and commercial interests, after 1800, with Jefferson's national victory, and even more after 1818, with the failure of the Hartford Convention and the defeat of the establishment in Connecticut, the proponents of order were forced to alter their approach. It was all very well for Federalist politicians like Fisher Ames to wallow in impotent rage or for George Cabot to become "in every sense so abstracted from the political world that he learned of the selection of the man who replaced him in the United States Senate only by reading about it in the newspapers."[2] But the threat posed by Jeffersonian individualism was inescapable. And if the Jeffersonian revolution of 1800 had made the marketplace and the will of the individual consumer, believer, and citizen the ultimate arbiter of authority, the Standing Order would, if it seriously sought to pursue what it viewed as America's mission in the world, have to engage the marketplace and act on the individuals within it. Lacking the instruments of coercion possessed by its European counterpart, the American Holy Alliance would have to proceed "by voluntary association working through free institutions."[3]

The Standing Order, in retreat from political power after 1800, had only two organizational bases from which to proceed in its effort to reestablish order and authority: institutions of religion and institutions of education. Although religion was threatened by post-Revolutionary toleration acts that permitted dissident sects to operate freely and by Jeffersonian efforts to disestablish churches, the Federalist faith in the utility of religion as a means of providing the moral core viewed as essential to democracy and to civic virtue remained unimpaired. Indeed, because the corporate status of the churches was, unlike their formal establishment, unchallenged by the Jeffersonians, the Standing Order was able to proceed through religious organizations to launch a concerted effort to extend its influence beyond the realm of politics. This effort took the form of what one historian has called the "evangelical united front."[4] The "united front" involved more than mere evangelism, although religious revivalism, in the form of the Second Great Awakening, provided the fuel for the "evangelical machinery," the network of organizations that the Federalist sponsors of the revival proceeded to erect. This machinery, through the education societies, provided funds for the hundreds of young men who were moved by the revival to forsake their plows and workshops, and enabled them to attend college, where they were to be trained as ministers and teachers.[5] (Actually, some of them became merchants, physicians and lawyers.) Following graduation, many were placed in strategic positions as teachers and preachers in new settlements in the West and South through the domestic missionary societies. And their contact with the "mother country" of New England was maintained through a wide assortment of religious newspapers, and through eastern-based temperance, Bible, tract, and Sunday-school societies.[6] Because of the peculiarly expansive and implicitly political character of these organizations, and because their spread was closely tied to the migration of New Englanders to the

South and West, their impact was not confined to religion. As Paul Johnson points out in his study of the Second Great Awakening in Rochester, New York, the basic support for the revival of religion came from transplanted New Englanders and was closely tied to their efforts to wrest political and economic control of the city away from the older local elite.[7] As such, evangelical religion came to be closely tied in some places to the nationalist political party, the Whigs, to the anti-Masonic movement, and to a broad range of social reform efforts including, ultimately, abolitionism and support for the Republican Party.[8] Most importantly, however, the machinery of the evangelical united front resulted in the establishment of distinctive privately-supported and controlled corporate institutions, usually staffed by New Englanders, as the cultural core of the new settlements. These institutions, when combined with the unusual acquisitiveness and high level of economic success among New Englanders wherever they went, ensured that New Englanders, even if vastly outnumbered, as was the case in southern Illinois, Indiana, Kentucky, and in the South itself, managed to set the tone of the local culture. Thus, for example, young men as diverse as the sons of the First Families of Virginia who poured into Harvard, Princeton, and Yale after 1810, and the young and gawky Abraham Lincoln in rural Illinois, looked to New England, New Englanders, and New England-institutional patterns of corporate voluntarism as models for emulation. Even when political differences over such issues as slavery and the tariff began to separate northerners and southerners into different national political factions, the common institutional core, the disposition to organize activity through private corporations and the recognition of a moral core that made possible effective individual and collective action, remained intact.

The Jeffersonians had no organizations comparable to those created by the Federalists. To be sure, the Jeffersonian political enterprise was set up along bureaucratic lines. But its impact went little further than politics. For in specifically separating political authority from economic, intellectual, and religious authority, and in concentrating their efforts in the realm of politics, the Jeffersonians had cut themselves off from a major source of influence. In the end, by the 1830s, this would have serious effects. For the religious dissidents who had supported the party because of its stand on religious toleration would move away from the secular and anti-clerical elements in the Democratic party and find common cause with the moral reformers and their national organizational machinery. Thus, even when Jacksonians and non-New Englanders were predominant numerically and consistently able to outvote their conservative opponents, New Englanders were able to exert their influence in other more important and less easily perceptible ways.

The institutions on which Americans in the new republic centered their attention as they looked for alternatives to politics as a source of order and authority were the school and the college. This concern with education, which was shared by both Jeffersonians and Federalists, stemmed from their common heritage of Protestant Christianity, which emphasized the importance of the believer's direct access to the Word, and from their common grounding in the political thought of the Enlightenment, which stressed the importance of an educated electorate in a Republic. If the Federalists and the Jeffersonians agreed on the importance of education, they differed violently on the kinds of institutions through which it should be carried out and on the forms of pedagogy, curriculum, and discipline appropriate to educational institutions in a new republic. The Jeffersonians favored publicly and locally controlled schools and colleges and, because they believed in the immanence of truth and the preeminence of man's rational faculties, advocated systems of pedagogy that emphasized the practical and utilitarian over abstract morality, and systems of discipline in which students exercised control over one another. Jeffersonian education in its purest form was based on the educational thought of the French Enlightenment, particularly on the writings of Rousseau and Pestalozzi:

> The Pestalozzian theory of education could not have been more dramatically at odds with conventional theories of education in the Western world. Pestalozzi had been inspired by reading Rousseau's old pedagogical fantasy, *Emile*, and he had resolved to implement the principles which it—and the whole thrust of Enlightenment humanism—implied. Rote-learning from books, and the kinds of false conceits that books taught, were eschewed as an inadequate, indeed a perilous base, on which to set the early education of a healthy, courageous, happy, and creative human being. Men should live according to the laws of nature, and nature herself should be the teacher, both the extrinsic nature that surrounded the child and the child's own nature within. The teacher was not to be an authority but rather a kind of friendly Socratic elucidator, who put the child in the way of knowledge and, depending on his natural curiosity and enjoyment of learning, encouraged him to *discover*, in himself and the world, the elementary principles on which all knowledge was based. The child learned the mental reckoning of numbers, arithmetic, and geometry by manipulating objects; morality and ethics from inner contemplation; geography, geology, biology, astronomy, and the other natural sciences in excursions and observations. The child was never to be punished; but his natural sociability would readily inspire him to follow his teacher

in the disciplined marches, gymnastic exercises, use of firearms, and military drill which Pestalozzian educators believed were necessary to a free people.[9]

As actually implemented, however, Jeffersonian education in the local schools took the form of a curriculum of "basics" and a system of discipline based on the Lancastrian model in which

> one master instructed a number of older pupils, who, in turn, taught younger ones carefully prescribed lessons. Discipline was strict, based often on shame and the use of humiliating punishments. Competition among students was keenly promoted.[10]

Linking Pestalozzianism with Lancastrianism may seem at first glance to be an exercise in likening the progressive educational philosophy of John Dewey to the authoritarian life-adjustment educational practices of some of his followers. But just as the variants of progressive education are derived from a common body of assumptions about the relation of the individual to the collectivity which emphasize subordination, so the Pestallozian and Lancastrian systems are linked by common assumptions about the immanence of truth in "the facts," and by the democratization of discipline.

The Federalist response to the educational challenges of the early republic, especially as they lost control of the political system and, hence, of public education, was to form their own schools, private incorporated academies, in which pedagogy, curriculum, and discipline reflected their distinctive views of education and the roles they envisioned for individuals in the world of democratic capitalism.[11]

The most influential of the Federalist educational reformers was Timothy Dwight.[12] Born to a wealthy mercantile family in western Massachusetts, Dwight was the grandson of Jonathan Edwards, the leader of the Great Awakening. He graduated from Yale in 1769. A tutor there until the outbreak of the Revolution, in 1776, he joined the army as a chaplain, serving until his father's death two years later forced him to return to Northampton to care for his mother and his younger brothers and sisters. After four years as a farmer, schoolmaster, and politician (he served two terms in the General Court), Dwight was called to the pulpit of the Congregational church at Greenfield (now Southport), Connecticut. Here he began his work as an educational reformer, work that he would later carry on to Yale.

In order to supplement his clerical income, Dwight, like many of his fellow ministers, was the master of the village school. As in many of the small rural schools of the time, students ranged in age from five through twenty and included both males and females. The usual methods of discipline in these institutions were brutal, ranging from fines through fists and whips. Shaming and degradation were also frequently resorted to. But Dwight proceeded very differently:

> [Dwight] believed that persuasion could accomplish better results than coercion; that fines were more a penalty upon the parent than the pupil. Experience led him to the conclusion that the rod was effective only with children in their earliest years and failed to accomplish its purpose when they were older. . . . He preferred "earnest and affectionate reproof," confinement, or "neglect."

> When a child slipped into some error of conduct, Dwight took him aside and in kindly manner discussed it with him, explaining clearly and persuasively why such behavior was wrong. This he found best to do in private. Public rebuke, he decided, aroused in the child too keen a sense of disgrace, and injured his pride too deeply. It had the effect of driving him to conceal his guilt by "arts," equivocation, and lies; and made him so resentful that, brooding sullenly, he tended to seek revenge either by combining with his fellows against the instructor or by committing the sin again. This . . . defeated the purpose of discipline. On the other hand, when a youth faced a respected, fatherly adviser in private, he found himself at war only with his own conscience. Once convinced of his error, he would more willingly admit his guilt and turn from sin, grateful for the guidance of one who, he knew, acted from genuine affection.[13]

Dwight's radical attitudes about discipline were more than mere products of a kindly spirit. They were, rather, part of an exhaustive analysis of society itself, most of which is contained in his poetic epic, *Greenfield Hill*. He was well aware of the relation between child rearing and the development of personality. And his recognition of the importance of internal control, self control, in securing both individual success and social order was based in his theory of social personality:

> Vain hope! by reason's power alone,
> From guilt no heart was ever won.
> Decent, not good, may reason make him;
> By reason, crimes will ne'er forsake him.
> As weeds, self-sown, demand no toil,
> But flourish in their native soil,

Root deep, grow high, with vigor bloom,
And send forth poison, for perfume;
So faults, inborn, spontaneous rise,
And daily wax in strength, and size,
Ripen, with neither toil, nor care,
And choke each germ of virtue there.

Virtues, like plants of nobler kind,
Transferred from regions more refined,
The gardner's careful hand must sow;
His culturing hand must bid them grow;
Rains gently shower skies softly shine,
And blessings fall, from realms divine.

Much time, and pain, and toil, and care,
Must virtue's habits plant, and rear:
Habits alone thro' life endure,
Habits alone your child secure;
To these be all your labors given;
To these, your fervent prayers to HEAVEN.[14]

Complementing Dwight's belief in internal control, guilt, and habit—as opposed to shame, conformity, and punishment—was a new notion of pedagogy. It was not enough, in Dwight's view, to discourage students from sloth and misbehavior. They as individuals had to be encouraged to want to excel. The traditional pedagogy had depended on "emulation" to encourage scholarly performance. Dwight objected to this because emulation stimulated envy and pride and, like shame in discipline, was more geared to external conformity than to internal reform. As a good New Light Calvinist, Dwight wanted his students "to be actuated by a desire to do their best for the glory of the Creator"—not merely because they would be admired by their peers. Dwight's solution to this problem was twofold. First, he attempted to give his students a great deal of individual attention, praising them when they were excelling and criticizing them for their failures. Secondly, he distributed to them "little prizes" based not on their absolute attainments, but on their progress. By doing this, Dwight was able not only to nurture excellence, but also to refocus the objective of achievement from a student's behavior to a student's attitude, from product to process. This was exactly analogous to refocusing discipline from shame to guilt. The final product, ideally, would be an individual who was self-motivated to do well and be good. Such an individual would not be only the perfect product of New Light Calvinism, but also a good and enterprising citizen in a republic.

The Standing Order's religious and educational efforts were limited at the outset by their tendencies to particularism, which limited their influence to Congregationalists, Presbyterians, and New Englanders. Broadening these efforts into movements of national consequence required two things: first, a willingness to accept Protestants who were neither Congregationalists nor Presbyterians—the Baptists, Methodists, and Episcopalians—as equal partners in the evangelical united front, which they appear to have done by the 1820s, and secondly, the devising of organizational mechanisms whose reach went beyond those who attended private academies.[15] The latter effort would take place in two phases, first through a reform of the colleges, and secondly, in the mid-nineteenth century, through a reform of the public lower schools by college graduates.

1. Timothy Dwight and the Reform of Religion and Learning at Yale

The traditional system of college discipline was hierarchical and organic in character.[16] Students were organized into four classes—Senior, Junior, Sophomore, and Freshman—each of which by seniority exercised authority over the other through a fagging system. Within the classes, discipline was maintained through peer pressure. The behavior of individuals reflected on the honor of their class as a group and, as a result, each class endeavored to maintain a standard of honorable conforming behavior among its members. The president and the tutors were remote figures. At Yale, for example, students were expected to remove their hats at least ten rods from the president and five yards from a tutor. While the president and tutors were the ultimate sources of authority and dispensers of justice, daily order was maintained through the hierarchy of classes.

Complementing this hierarchical and organic system of discipline was a system of pedagogy based not on individual achievement but on group experience. Classes recited their lessons as a group before the president and tutors. There were no written examinations and no systematic attempts to assess individual progress. Emulation of one's superiors was viewed as the key to excellence. Ambition and competition were behaviors inimical to the collective conformist values by which the colleges, and society, were governed.

When Timothy Dwight was called to the presidency of Yale in 1795, he had spent nearly two decades refining his educational philosophy, a set of ideas and practices based on his practical experience as an educator, his Congregationalist religious beliefs, and perhaps most importantly, his political awareness and activism as one of the leaders of

Connecticut Federalism. He immediately put his ideas into action. Fagging, the system in which discipline was administered by upperclassmen to those behind them, was abolished. The ancient system of fining and shaming was replaced by what came to be known as the "parental system," which Dwight exercised "by lectures to the classes and private conversations with the wayward."[17] Another element in his effort to put the "parental system" into practice was his effort to supplement the tutors, most of who were only a year or two older than the upperclassmen, with older men with professorial rank. Even though most of the professors who joined the Yale faculty during Dwight's presidency did so as instructors in the professional schools, their very presence on campus altered the face of authority at Yale. Suddenly, the arbiters of justice were not just the president, the professor of divinity, a few young tutors, and the upperclassmen. They were joined by learned physicians, attorneys, and professors of chemistry, mathematics, and natural philosophy.[18] Accompanying these changes were the first outbursts of a new religious movement, the Second Great Awakening, which Dwight fostered first among his undergraduates and subsequently as a national movement.

Dwight's reforms did not come to an end at his death in 1816. He was succeeded at Yale by his protegé, Jeremiah Day, who had gone from his tutorship at Yale to take over Dwight's academy at Greenfield and, by 1801, had become professor of mathematics at his alma mater. Day did not merely imitate Dwight's reforms; he carried them further than Dwight would have imagined possible. It was during Day's administration that the famous *Yale Report of 1828* was written. While this document is best known for defending the classical tradition against demands for "relevant" vocationalism, it is, in fact, far more than that. Its defense of the classics is based less on a clinging to the traditional for its own sake than on a very Dwight-like understanding of what training for autonomy in a republican government was all about. The Report begins by posing the question: "What then is the appropriate object of a college?" It replies:

its object is to *lay the foundation of a superior education*; and this is to be done, at a period of life when a substitute must be provided for parental *superintendence.* . . .

The two great points to be gained in intellectual culture, are the *discipline* and *furniture* of the mind; expanding its powers, and storing it with knowledge. The former of these is, perhaps, the more important of the two. A commanding object, therefore, in a collegiate course, should be, to call into daily and vigorous exercise the

faculties of the student. Those branches of study should be prescribed, and those modes of instruction adopted, which are best
calculated to teach the art of fixing the attention, directing the train
of thought, analyzing a subject proposed for investigation; following, with accurate discrimination, the course of argument; balancing
nicely the evidence presented to judgement; awakening, elevating,
and controlling the imagination; arranging, with skill, the treasures
which memory gathers; rousing and guiding the powers of genius.
All this is not to be effected by a light and hasty course of study;
by reading a few books, hearing a few lectures, and spending some
months at a literary institution. The habits of thinking are to be
formed, by long continued and close application. . . .

No one feature in a system of intellectual education, is of greater
moment than such an arrangement of duties and motives, as will
most effectually throw the student upon the *resources of his own
mind*. Without this, the whole apparatus of libraries, and instruments, and specimens, and lectures, and teachers, will be insufficient to secure distinguished excellence.[19]

This was Dwight's doctrine of habit in prose form. It was also a remarkable peroration on the subject of how to educate people for autonomy. The object of education for Dwight's followers was not to gain
information, but to acquire the ability to think independently. They too,
like Dwight, were keenly aware of its utility to a republic:

Our republican form of government renders it highly important
that great numbers should enjoy the advantage of a thorough education. On the Eastern continent, the *few* who are destined to
particular departments in political life, may be educated to the purpose; while the mass of people are left in comparative ignorance.
But in this country, where offices are acceptable to all who are
qualified for them, superior intellectual attainments ought not be
confined to any description of persons. *Merchants, manufacturers,
and farmers*, as well as professional gentlemen, take their places in
our public councils. A thorough education ought therefore to be
extended to all these classes. It is not sufficient that they be men
of sound judgement, who can decide correctly, and give a silent
vote, on great national questions. Their influence upon the minds
of others is needed; an influence to be produced by extent of knowledge, and the force of eloquence. . . . If it is knowledge, which
gives us command of physical agents and instruments, much more
is it that which enables us to control the combinations of moral and
political machinery.[20]

2. Yale as a National Institution

It is important to note that by 1828, Yale was in a very different situation than it was when Dwight assumed the presidency in 1795. By 1828, the church had been disestablished, and the college no longer received any public support. It subsisted on tuitions and fees and a meager income from its small endowment. One of the objects that the faculty had in mind in drafting the *Yale Report* was attracting private support, and two years later it would initiate its first fund drive among its alumni and friends scattered across the country. Yale was, moreover, in a highly competitive situation. It no longer had a monopoly on higher education in Connecticut: Trinity had received a charter in 1823, and Wesleyan would be granted one by 1831. Improved transportation and the founding of new schools placed it in competition not only with older schools like Harvard, Brown, Princeton, and Columbia, but also with newer colleges like Williams, Middlebury, Colby, Amherst, and Bowdoin. It was therefore imperative, in the minds of Yale's professors, to make the college's philosophy of education and the advantages that flowed from it as explicit as possible.

It is also important to note that Yale' student body had changed considerably since the last decades of the eighteenth century, and that this change made Yale's commitment to the classics and to character-building all the more important. After 1800, the students entering Yale were older, poorer, and from a far greater range of geographical origins than their predecessors.[21] While Yale continued to attract the sons of Connecticut merchants and professionals, ever-increasing numbers of boys from poor backgrounds, inspired by the Second Great Awakening to study for the ministry or sent out into the world to seek their fortunes, were gaining admission to the college. The increasing range of geographical origins was due in part to the wholesale migration of Connecticut merchants, professionals and farmers to New York and points west and south. In 1789, ninety-six percent of the graduating class of Yale had been born in Connecticut; by 1800, the proportion of Connecticut-born graduates was eighty-eight percent; by 1830, it amounted to only forty-four percent.[22]

The increasing diversity in the backgrounds of students was accompanied by a pronounced shift in students' vocational and residential choices. Up to 1780, nearly half of every graduating class at Yale went into the ministry. Beginning in 1780, there was a pronounced shift away from religion. By 1800, only nine percent of the students became ministers. While the exertions of Dwight and Day made the ministry more popular to the extent that, by 1820, nearly a quarter of the graduates were becoming clergymen, the church never regained its former attraction. The prime beneficiaries of the decline of interest in the church were law and teaching. Law, which had only engaged the interest of sixteen percent of the graduates before 1780, boomed. By 1800, over half the graduates became lawyers, a proportion that, in succeeding years, would stabilize at about a third of every graduating class.[23]

This shift in the vocational choices and geographical and social origins of Yale graduates was accompanied by a remarkable surge of geographical mobility.[24] Yale was not merely attracting students from all over the country and sending them back to their native places. Something much more complex was happening: students from New York were either going west or staying in New England; New England students were going south and west; westerners were ending up in New York. While the overall movement was from east to south and west, there were many subpatterns of movement in which graduates who ended up spending most of their careers in New England also spent time in New York or in the west and south. Yale appears to have become by 1820 an important entrepôt not only for New Englanders seeking greater opportunities but also for Southerners and Westerners moving towards eastern commercial and cultural centers. Yale's curriculum, with its meritocratic and universalistic emphasis, was ideally suited to socializing this wildly diverse student body.

But Yale's significance as a national institution went well beyond its ability to attract students from outside Connecticut. Just as important was its role, and the role of its graduates, in promoting the establishment of private schools and colleges in the West and South. While the expansive tendency was already evident in the mid-eighteenth century, when Yale graduates were instrumental in establishing Dartmouth, Princeton, and Columbia, it became even more evident after 1790, when Yale graduates acted as the dominant figures in establishing, governing, and teaching at Williams, Middlebury, and Trinity in New England; New York University, Hamilton, the United States Military Academy (West Point), Rutgers, and Lafayette in the middle states; Kenyon, Western Reserve, Transylvania, Oberlin, and the universities of Illinois, Wisconsin, Michigan, Missouri, and California, in the West; and the United States Naval Academy, St. John's, The College of Charleston, and the universities of Maryland, Missouri, North Carolina, South Carolina, Georgia, Louisiana, Alabama, and Mississippi in the South. Yale, of course, was not alone in this enterprise of collegiate imperialism; it was assisted in this task by Princeton and Dartmouth, the officers of which shared in the political, pedagogical, and theological outlooks of Timothy Dwight and Jeremiah Day, and were their allies in the evangelical united front. And Dwight's doctrines were carried out into the lower schools by men like Henry Barnard, William Woodbridge, and other early promoters of the professionalization of teaching.

3. The Centum Milia Fund and the Origins of a National Alumni Constituency

There can be no doubting that Dwight, Day, and their Federalist and Congregationalist friends would have preferred that Yale, while attracting students from all over the country, should remain in their own hands. They had good reasons to believe that New England was, if not the hub of the universe, then certainly the hub of culture and civic virtue. But having lost control of Connecticut politics and, thereby, state support, the college was placed in a difficult situation. For without the support of the state and the established church, the college could not hope to carry out its public mission unaided.

No sooner had the citizens of Connecticut voted in the party of ecclesiastical disestablishment than Yale made its first moves to create a private basis of financial support. The Tolerationist victory came in the September elections of 1817; by March of 1818, the college issued its first general appeal for funds:

> BEING insufficient to found and support Professorships, and enlarge the Library, to the extent which the advanced state of science demands, many respectable citizens, in different parts of the State, friends of the College, have advised that an appeal be made to the liberality of the public, in aid of the Institution—And the President and Fellows having concurred in the proposition, the undersigned, a Committee, appointed to carry the same into effect, cherish the hope that, when the wants of the College are known, the public will not suffer its interests to languish.[25]

The simple broadside was signed by a committee consisting of three members of the faculty, one lawyer, and three New Haven merchants who were largely interested in the government of the College. The appeal did not generate much attention. 1818 was a year not only of political crisis, but also of financial depression. Futher, the College's understated appeal was unlikely to stimulate the interest either of non-Congregationalists, who had turned their backs on Yale, or of Yale's Congregationalist partisans. For the college did not state its case with any particular urgency.

The officers of the college reacted to the failure of their plea for funds by proceeding along two lines. First, they came to recognize that if they were to be successful, they could not simply appeal to the public. Rather, it was clearly necessary to appeal to that segment of the public which sympathized with the school's political and sectarian goals. Secondly, they became aware, probably by casting an eye at Harvard's rapidly increasing endowment, tha the college's funds, once acquired, could yield considerably more as investments in commerce than as investments in land and mortgages.

The appeal of 1818 was, within four years, revised as a much more sectarian document.[26] The college needed, it stated, not only new dormitories, by also a new chapel. It was also necessary, given the impulses unleashed by the Second Great Awakening, to ensure that the services of Yale remained available to the pious but impoverished young men of New England. This appeal was somewhat more successful: between 1821 and 1825, Yale took in almost $75,000 in donations, most of them to support the Dwight Professorship of Sacred Theology. Religion was not the only sentiment on which the officers of the college played in seeking a more stable economic foundation.[27] Both local pride and the American fascination with science were the banners waved in 1825, when Benjamin Silliman wanted to raise $20,000 for the purchase of a collection of minerals deemed vital to the continued study of geology at Yale.

But the most promising scheme, both for increasing the college's old resources and multiplying those that the officers expected from the friends of science and religion, was a banking operation. The Eagle Bank was organized in 1812 by James Hillhouse, the treasurer of Yale, and his associates, Eli Whitney and William Woolsey. All three were part of a complex genealogical relationship between the Woolsey and Dwight families. Eli Whitney was married to President Dwight's first cousin, Henrietta Edwards; President Dwight was married to Woolsey's sister; Dwight's sister, Elizabeth, was married to Woolsey; and Treasurer Hillhouse had married successively two first cousins of banker Woolsey.[28] Placed in charge of the bank as president was a young lawyer named George Hoadley, who was married to the daughter of William Woolsey and Elizabeth Dwight (Mrs. Hoadley was also President Dwight's niece). As far as it went, there was nothing unusual about this intersection of family and business. Many early corporations were family-dominated. What made the Eagle Bank exceptional was its heavy dependence on Yale's "permanent funds."

The college's initial investment in the Eagle Bank was modest, in accordance with its modest means. As of 1820, Yale's endowed funds (exclusive of land) consisted of one hundred and thirty-eight shares in the Phoenix Bank of Hartford (worth $8,223.51) that had been granted by the legislature in support of the Medical Institution, twenty-eight mortgages and notes worth $12,400, and fifty-eight shares of Eagle Bank stock worth $5,800.[29] While this amount constituted only ten percent of the bank's total capital, it represented nearly a quarter of Yale's endowment. As the college's appeals for funds began to attract attention after 1823, rather than diversifying its investments, Yale poured everything into Eagle Bank stock. Although state law forbade any "college, school, or Ecclesiastical Society" from investing more than $5000 in any one bank, the influential Hillhouse was able to persuade the legislature to grant Yale a special exemption.[30] Accordingly, half of the fund gathered for the Dwight Professorship of Theology was put into Eagle Bank stock. By 1824, investment in the Eagle Bank constituted almost half of Yale's endowment. Yale itself began acting as a bank. Beginning in 1823 it started soliciting funds from churches all over the state, not for Yale's benefit, but for profitable investment in the Eagle Bank.[31]

Had the New Haven entrepreneurs been better bankers, Yale might have been a very wealthy institution. Unfortunately, New Haven was not Boston. The Elm City's bankers had neither the experience nor the organizational expertise to protect their pet bank from the turbulence of the early American money market. While the Bostonians had liberally used charitable endowments to capitalize their corporate ventures, they had also devised a system under the aegis of the Suffolk Bank to ensure liquidity in times of financial panic. This system required that non-Boston banks deposit specie (hard money) equal to the amount of paper and banknotes that they had in circulation. This guaranteed that, should a panic develop, no more specie could be withdrawn from the Boston banks than the "foreign" banks had on deposit. New Haven had no such buffer. And when a ripple of fear rolled up through the New England financial community in September of 1825 and people rushed to the Eagle bank to exchange their notes for specie, the bank was forced to close its doors. When the dust had settled and the College began to tote up its losses, it was found that not only was most of its endowment wiped out, but it was entangled in lawsuits brought by churches that had entrusted their funds for investment to Yale.[32] Yale had not only gone broke; it had alienated many of its most ardent religious partisans.

Yale's first gesture was to turn to the state for help, but the legislature wanted nothing to do with the college. Next, it tried to organize an alumni group called the "Society of Alumni of Yale College," which sold memberships at two dollars apiece. It was a good idea, but with the school's alumni so scattered, it was unreasonable to expect any great income from that source without particular exertions. The affairs of the college seemed to have suffered a permanent setback, and no one knew what to do about it.

In February of 1831, President Day received a letter from one Wyllys Warner, a graduate of the class of 1826, who was living in New Orleans, tutoring the children of a wealthy Yale alumnus. As Warner had been at Yale both as a student and tutor during the Eagle Bank debacle and had some experience in fund-raising as an agent for the Dwight Professorship, he not unnaturally began making contacts with other alumni in the New Orleans area and acquainting them with the situation of their alma mater. Warner made the following proposal to President Day:

> . . . My principal object in writing at this time, and to the President, is to request of him, *a general commission as agent of the College,* with any facts relative to its condition, its prospects, or plans of effort, which may not be in my possession. The President will probably recollect that the Commission which he wrote me was confined to the Theological Department. I think it would be well to time the date of the commission back at the time of the appointment, and enclose the same in a letter. . . . It might be well to forward a copy of the resolution of the Society of Alumni passed at their last meeting, perhaps also a word from some member of the society to Alfred Herman, Esq., and a line from Mr. Olmstead to L. C. Duncan, Esq. might be of some consequence. . . . An acquaintance here and conversation with a few gentlemen of wealth and influence may be productive of something either now or hereafter.[33]

Warner's suggestion found eager hearers. By the spring of 1831, he had returned to New Haven to consult with Day and the other officers of the college. In July, while Warner began privately gathering contributions in Connecticut and western New York, Professor Goodrich composed and sent out a "circular letter" announcing the agreed-on plan of action:

> I wish now to mention a subject of deep interest to every friend of Yale College. It has been obvious for years that their venerable institution cannot long continue to discharge her duties to the public without efficient pecuniary patronage. While Cambridge has an income of $25,000 a year from permanent funds that of Yale College is scarcely $2500. While Cambridge with a library of from thirty to forty thousand volumes expends $1000 a year on the purchase of books, Yale College with a library of only nine thousand volumes can with difficulty appropriate $400 a year to this important object. . . .

Under the circumstances some spirited friends of the College at the south have proposed the plan of making one great and final effort on the broad scale of our whole country to raise $100,000 by subscription, and to place the institution *at once* on a safe and honorable foundation. Extensive consultations have been held with friends of the College on the subject and the result has been universal approbation of the plan. A full conviction that it can be accomplished and a tender of large subscription on condition that the business can be taken up on a broad scale. Members of a number of classes which have graduated within the last ten years have expressed their fullest confidence that $2500 or $3000 would be contributed as a class donation by their respective classes. It is thought that one quarter of the sum might be raised by the classes which had graduated since 1820. Some individuals who are earning their subsistance by the instruction of schools have voluntarily tendered subscriptions of $100 if such a plan should be adopted. The senior class for the present year have already resolved to take the lead. A general meeting of the alumni on this subject will be held on the day before commencement, Tuesday, September 13, at four o'clock p.m. It will probably be the fullest ever assembled. A representation will be present from New Orleans and other remote places.[34]

As Goodrich's circular suggests, the spring discussions between Day, Warner, and others interested in the welfare of Yale must have been wide-ranging. They appear to have recognized that Yale's importance as a national institution was not merely a rhetorical assertion. It was a reality that had to be dealt with. With students drawn from all over the country and graduates nationally dispersed, the college had to make its fund raising effort on the "broad scale" of the whole country. Further, the leaders appear to have recognized the significance of class organization as a basis for soliciting funds. Students and alumni did not, they realized, relate to Yale as an abstraction. They related to it as a set of concrete ties of friendship, kinship, and common experiences in a class context (a very Dwightian notion).

Of course, they did not abandon hope of Yale's traditional constituencies, as Wyllys Warner's travels during the late spring and summer of 1831 show. He paid as much attention to non-alumnus village nabobs in backcountry Connecticut as he did to wealthy alumni and prominent Congregationalists in New York. Efforts were even made to prod the college's friends in the legislature to renewed action in favor of Yale. What comes through most clearly from Warner's almost daily reports to President Day is the importance of personal contact between agents of the college and potential benefactors, combined with emphatic assertions of Yale's national importance. By the end of July 1831, letters like the following were beginning to arrive in New Haven:

> It has been my determination for two or three years past that whenever it should be in my power I would make a donation to Yale College, having always considered that institution as the most influential and useful in the country, not only in a literary and scientific, but in a moral and religious point of view, and moreover being much impressed with the conviction that it had been overlooked and neglected among the great objects of benevolence of the present day—My determination was much strengthened by a conversation had with you at Farmington a few months since in which you mentioned to me many particulars in relation to your wants and having recently learned from the Reverend Mr Warner who called on me with a letter from Professor Silliman that an effort was to be made at the next commencement to relieve the wants of the College. . . .
>
> The amount I intend to give is Five Thousand Dollars. . . .[35]

The great meeting of the friends and alumni of Yale on the question of the proposed fund drive in September of 1831 was resounding success, and a remarkable testament both to Wyllys Warner's talents as an organizer and to Yale's national character. Chairing the meeting was James Kent, the leading judicial intellect of New York State, a graduate of the class of 1781. Also there was Stephen Van Rensselaer, the immensely rich Patroon of Albany, a former Lieutenant-Governor and Member of Congress from New York. With him were his three sons, all recent Yale alumni. The meeting not only acclaimed the need for a nation-wide fund drive, but also repeated in the strongest terms the college's importance as a national institution:

> . . . the state of society is greatly changed. The standard of education is very greatly elevated among all classes, and in all the departments of learning. The comforts of life are multiplied. The inventions in the arts, and the changes in the habits of the community are numberless, and have imposed upon Colleges the necessity of a somewhat more liberal system of expenditure. The early plan of conducting the affairs of Yale College, in respect to the conveniences of living and study, and especially to the course of instruction, would at the present day be deemed unworthy of the Institution, and would doubtless result in its ultimate ruin. Neither institutions nor men can long remain stationary in our country, without sustaining a loss of rank and character; and Yale College,

aware of this fact, has pushed onward, striving to keep pace with
the progress of society; and in doing this, she is rapidly exhausting
her powers. Without more aid therefore, she must soon come to
a final stand. Nor should it be forgotten, that Yale College has had,
for many years, a greater number of students than any American
College. But she has no warrent that such will be the case in the
future—certainly she has not, if deprived of her character, or which
is the same thing, the means of preserving it. Other Colleges are
springing up in every quarter of the country, and in this fact, all
should change. In these circumstances however, if Yale fails to
maintain her rank as a primary Institution, her students are reduced
and her last resources are gone.[36]

But Yale was doing more than trying to part rich men from their
money by appealing to their desire to maintain Yale as an institution
of national importance. In a period in which Harvard was being increasingly criticized as a seminary for the rich and an enemy of democracy, Yale was willing to make a surprisingly Jacksonian assertion:

The College is also in want of funds for the relief of necessitous
students. Individuals of this class, have not unfrequently risen to
the highest stations of influence and authority in the nation. The
welfare of our republic requires, that such men be educated. Other
Colleges very generally offer education to them at a reduced price.
Yale must therefore do the same, both to promote the interest of
the community and to secure her own prosperity.[37]

The final results of the 1832 fund drive were gratifying: $108,733 was
pledged to Yale.[38] Most importantly, especially for the future direction
of the college, a number of interesting trends became apparent that
spelled a clear departure from traditional bases of support. First, the
alumni constituency emerged as the most significant contributing group;
over sixty percent of the subscriptions came from graduates. Secondly,
while Connecticut subscribers donated the largest amount of the total,
subscriptions from outside Connecticut constituted almost half (44 percent) of the total fund. Thirdly, and perhaps most important of all, the
largest average subscriptions came from out-of-state alumni. While the
average pledge from Connecticut was $146, the average pledge from
New York was $385, and from Massachusetts, $220. Not only were
subscriptions from out-of-state alumni higher on the average than those
gathered in Connecticut, but out-of-state alumni participated on a much
higher basis.

The significance of the out-of-state alumni as the emerging primary
constituency of the college must have been greeted by Yale's officers

with a certain amount of ambivalence. On the one hand, it supported their contention that Yale was an institution of national significance. On the other hand, it contained an implicit threat to the school's ability to remain a citadel of Connecticut-dominated Congregationalism and Federalism (which, by the 1830s, had become Whiggery). The officers of the College were not unmindful of the threat. In the course of his travels, Wyllys Warner more than once found himself in situations in which potential donors balked at supporting an institution over which they could not exert any significant influence. In New York, for example, in conversing with the Reverend Gardiner Spring, a leading Presbyterian clergyman and a graduate of the class of 1805, the following scene ensued:

> I have seen Doctor Spring, find him more alarmed at the Theology of Yale than ever—he says he will not oppose me, but I fear his negative influence. He is much pleased with your sermon, expresses a high regard for the Academical Department, but fears it must be swept away with the tide of censure. The fact that Doctor Taylor does not reply to Dr. Wood leads him, and he says, others to believe that Dr. Taylor intends to keep his views to himself and propagate them silently through his students.[39]

And religion was not the only ground on which potential donors reined in their impulses to support Yale. Warner arrived in Washington, D. C., in mid-February of 1832, during the great debate on the "Tariff of Abominations," a strong protective tariff that would have distinctly favored New England manufacturers over southern planters. Here Warner found that, because of feelings over the bill, doors that had once been open to Yale, like that of John Calhoun, who had given one hundred dollars for the Dwight Professorship some years before, were now closed. He wrote dispairingly to President Day, who tried to reassure him:

> South Carolina is chafed with the hearings of the tariff upon her interests; and if she finds no relief from the measures of the present session, I think she will not be very ready to send money to the north. You are, however, in a better position than I am, to form an opinion of our prospects in that quarter. If the south does not help us, we must be ready for a resolute charge upon the cities, and upon Connecticut.[40]

Although the subscription was successfully accomplished without major assistance from the south, Warner's reports about political and religious differences between the alumni and the officers of the College, coupled with Yale's obvious dependence on the good will of out-of-state alumni, must have been disquieting. When the college next attempted to raise funds, in 1854, it proceeded much less indiscriminately than it had two decades before, confining its appeals to a small number of wealthy Connecticut and New York alumni. The time would come, however, when the college would have to face the uncomfortable fact that an institution which drew both its students and its financial support from persons outside of Connecticut would have to concede the alumni some degree of control.

Yale's resistance to the involvement of alumni and other laymen in its governance was atypical of the other agencies of the evangelical united front. The colleges founded by Yale graduates, most notably Dartmouth, Princeton, and Williams, included sympathetic laymen on their governing boards from their inception. The reasons for this inclusiveness were diverse. In part, it stemmed from a recognition of the political opposition that tight clerical control had aroused against Yale from the 1740s on. In part, it was a product of the distinctively New Light origins of the newer colleges, particularly the fact that New Light theology and organization were much more predicated on voluntarism than on Old Light coercion. Certainly the fact that the newer institutions were not state-supported played a role, for it meant that, from the beginning, they would have to seek financial assistance from wealthy laymen. Indeed, some, like Williams, went so far as to nominate as trustees men like H. Van Schaak,

in the hope and expectation, as he had no children, that he would bestow a portion of his property on the college.[41]

But it was seldom necessary to take on men like Van Schaak, merely because they were wealthy and might leave bequests in favor of the college (as Van Schaak, in fact, did not). For there were plenty of laymen who were willing to contribute their money and their energies to colleges and related enterprises. Even before the mounting of the united front, in the mid-eighteenth century when the New Lights were still doing battle with theological conservatives, the founders of Princeton found it to their advantage to include as trustees such powerful laymen as William Smith, Attorney General of New York, Peter Van Brugh Livingston, a New York political leader and Treasurer of the State, and Edward Shippen, scion of a prominent Philadelphia family and an important Pennsylvania jurist.[42] And even Yale had made significant concessions to the laity through the Act of Union of 1792, permitting them broad informal influence, especially in governing the College's financial affairs.

Beyond the realm of the colleges, in the tract, moral, temperence, missionary, and education societies, the influence of laymen was decisive. Such enterprises simply could not be carried out on a narrow clerical basis. And although clergymen like Lyman Beecher took the lead in establishing the organizations and in articulating their purposes, laymen like the Tappans, Gerrit Smith, Richard Varick, and the Van Rensselaers in New York; and the Hubbards, Evarts, and Greenes in Boston provided the basic financial and administrative support for the enterprise.[43] Yale's effort in the Centum Milia Fund merely underlined what was already obvious by the late 1820s to most participants in the evangelical united front: that the effort of national redemption, the restoration of order, authority, and virtue in the republic, could not rest on narrow sectarian and geographical bases. The aristocracy of virtue would have to be inclusive if it hoped to be effective.

4. Alumni, Student Societies, and the Development of National Networks

The outcome of the revolution that had taken place at Yale and the other institutions that sympathized with its goals involved far more than a set of changes in pedagogy, curriculum, and discipline. Internally, the revolution in teaching and the suppositions about character formation that lay behind it brought about major changes in how students related to one another. The devaluation of the college class as a corporate group with major responsibilities for collective discipline, combined with the increasing size of college classes, which impeded the highly personal relationships that made peer discipline effective, had resulted in the formation of social clusters within college classes based on mutual interests in morality, politics, or special subjects. These student societies came, by the 1830s, to play a major, if not definitive role in the organization of student life and were, especially given the classical focus of the curriculum, an important part of the utilitarian component of the college education. For in these societies students not only gained access to specialized bodies of knowledge that they were denied by the prescribed curriculum, but, perhaps more importantly, they gained practical experience in political skills—debating, writing, and defending their ideas before their peers.[44] Student societies rapidly took on a hierarchical form, as some, especially those with a broader political or social focus, came to contain the most talented, influential, and articulate members of the student body. They became settings for the display of the colleges' primary product, character. For only men of character, those who were intelligent, honest, dependable, and poised, could attract the attention of the upperclassmen who selected their successors for the societies, and of their classmates, whose opinion was decisive in determining class leadership, to be elevated to the most prestigious societies. In some places, as at Harvard, the student societies favored the wealthy and socially prestigious. But at the majority of colleges, particularly Yale, Dartmouth, Amherst, Williams, and Princeton, election seems to have been remarkably meritocratic: geographically and occupationally balanced.[45]

The increasing diversity of students' geographical and economic backgrounds heightened the importance of the student societies as a part of the college experience. By the 1820s, when the student society movement began to be a distinctive characteristic of the colleges, over half of the students at Yale, Princeton, Williams, Amherst, and the other collegiate centers of the evangelical united front had been born outside of the states in which the colleges were situated. More and more students came from the South and the Middle and Far West. And fewer and fewer of these students were expecting to follow their fathers' careers, to enter family businesses, or to pursue careers in the places where they had been born. For students cut off from traditional sources of values and control, excluded from the communities and kin-based support systems available to earlier generations, the college experience as a whole and, in particular, the process of mutual socialization fostered by the student societies assumed inordinate importance. For the college and the friendships formed in college became the basis of community and continuity that had largely ceased to exist in society itself. An indication of the importance placed by alumni on such ties is suggested by such encounters as this one, involving William Patrick, a Williams graduate of the Class of 1798:

> In 1869 Dana and Hutchins, then members of the college, met him at Concord, N. H., and knowing that he was an early graduate of the college, introduced themselves to him. His first question was, "Gentlemen, are you Philologians or Philotechnicians?"[46]

College administrators favored the formation of student societies. Not only did men like Dwight and Day encourage the activities at Yale of the older eighteenth-century societies—Linonia, Brother-in-Unity, and Phi Beta Kappa—they also promoted new ones.[47] The Moral Society at Yale was viewed by Dwight as particularly useful in combating infidelity and misbehavior among students. And under Day the Calliope, the Benevolent, and the Society of Alumni were formed. The pace of student organization increased in the 1820s, as the increasingly diverse student bodies strove to enunciate common values and to articulate a viable sense of community, and as the colleges themselves came to recognize the utility of such organizations in maintaining ties between alumni that were useful in fundraising efforts. In this period, student societies changed in character. They ceased to be merely class organizations and, with the emergence of the "secret societies" at Yale and other institutions, became graduate organizations that published catalogues of their members and, through various activities, kept graduates abreast of changes in the colleges and interested in the activities of their undergraduate members. By the mid-1830s, many student societies had ceased to be merely local affairs and were, like Alpha Delta Phi, organizing on a national basis and meeting in annual conventions.[48] For those not fortunate enough to be selected by the societies and fraternities, and for the purpose of tying the interests of the society men to those of the institutions as a whole, the graduating classes themselves became formal organizations by the 1840s, electing officers, publishing regular class-books, holding reunions, and gathering funds.

By the mid-nineteenth century, Yale and the other evangelical institutions had become, through the student societies, the hubs of nationally extensive networks of graduates who maintained regular communication with one another. This worked not only to the advantage of the colleges—twenty of the thirty-eight organizers of the Yale fund drive of 1871 were society men—but to the mutual advantage of the graduates, who came to regard collegiate affiliation and society membership as important indicators of character and trustworthiness and, hence, credit-worthiness and employability. Through such contacts, for example, the Yale graduate Charles Miner Runk, an attorney and real estate speculator in Allentown, Pennsylvania, gained access, in the 1870s, to the capital resources of the Penn Mutual Life Insurance Company, a coup that enabled him to buy up and develop the whole west end of the city in which he lived.[49] Similarly Charles S. Hall, a Yale graduate of 1848, an attorney in Binghamton, New York, represented the interests of the New England Insurance Company in its litigations in the courts of Broome County.[50] Certain firms, like the New York Central Railroad and the United States Trust Company, came to be known as Yale firms, just as the American Telephone and Telegraph Company, the Chicago, Burlington, and Quincy Railroad, and the House of Morgan would, by the second half of the century, be known as Harvard firms because of their preference for the graduates of that institution.[51]

Because the enterprise of character education was centered in the colleges, and because the society system and the organization of alumni into a functioning communication network on a national scale stemmed from the colleges, character, the possession of certain traits of personality in which individuals were rendered peculiarly trustworthy by their willingness to subordinate personal ambition to higher purposes, came to be associated with the credentials issued by the colleges. The possession of a degree and membership in certain student societies came to signify more than the mastery of a body of knowledge; it was a credential of a more general kind of trustworthiness and breadth of purpose which, as the nineteenth-century economy and its political and social activities became more diverse and tumultuous, assumed particular importance, both in the view of the college men themselves and, by the end of the Civil War, in the eyes of society itself.

But it would be a grave error to suggest that the significance of character education and national networks was restricted to a nationally dispersed group of a few thousand college graduates. Its real significance lay in the extent to which the college influence permeated every community in the country. Through the evangelical institutions, college graduates dominated the pulpits and taught in the common schools of the West and South; college men set the tone of professional life, not only by their polished manners, but by their ability to draw on the resources of the great world beyond their localities for capital, clientage, and knowledge. It was no accident that young men like Abraham Lincoln found their inspiration, and their access to the best law books, in the transplanted New Englanders and graduates of New England schools who practiced in the rural counties of southern Illinois. For who else at the time participated systematically in a larger world, maintaining communication with persons beyond the locality? Nor is it any accident that young men like Jonas King should have presented themselves to men like the Williams graduate William H. Maynard in his school room at Plainfield, Massachusetts:

One cold morning, as he entered the school room, he observed a boy whom he had not before seen. The lad soon made known his errand. He was fifteen years old; his parents lived seven miles distant; he wanted to obtain an education, and had come from home that morning to consult Mr. Maynard on the subject. Mr. Maynard asked him if he had any acquaintance in the place who would assist him. "No." "Well, how do you expect to obtain an education?" "I don't know; but I thought I would come and consult you on the subject." He discovered that young King possessed good sense, but no uncommon brilliancy. He was impressed with the cool and resolute manner in which the young man was willing to encounter difficulties which would intimidate common minds. Mr. Maynard made provision for having him board in the family with himself, the lad paying his way by manual labor.[52]

King went on to graduate from Williams in 1815, to study theology at Andover, whence he "labored as a missionary in the Southern States."

After a brief stint as Professor of Oriental Languages at Amherst, he went to Greece as a missionary, where he died in 1869. If tying oneself into the collegiate network was not an essential condition for mobility of this sort, it certainly facilitated the process. And King's story was not unusual; it was typical.

Not only did the colleges reach out to the masses through evangelism, moral reform, and the schools, they also did so through such enterprises as the lyceums and other mutual improvement and education societies, which were first developed in New England and later spread across the nation with the migration of New England's population. Originally proposed by Josiah Holbrook in an article in the *American Journal of Education*, a publication begun by Yale graduates Henry Barnard and William Woodbridge, the lyceum became a national network that brought to rural communities in and beyond New England the wisdom of such men as Bronson Alcott, Lyman Beecher, Orestes Bronson, George William Curtis, Ralph Waldo Emerson, Oliver Wendell Holmes, Theodore Parker, Wendell Phillips, and many others.[53] The lyceum, the mechanics' libraries, the temperance societies, and the Young Men's Christian Associations were in many ways organizational parallels to the collegiate networks. And their parallelism was not accidental, for college men played important roles both in their formation and in determining through journalism, through speakers' bureaus, and through financial support, the direction of their interests.[54]

By the 1850s, the movement which had begun as a religiously-based evangelical counteroffensive to the ideas of Thomas Jefferson and the French Revolution had cast a very wide net over the nation as a whole. It had undergone important changes, becoming secularized and geographically and denominationally particularistic. Politically, from the standpoint of its founders, it had failed, or so it appeared as the nation moved inexorably towards civil war. The hope of the Dwights and the Lyman Beechers had been for a much more rapid and direct national influence:

> When all the colleges are under our control it will establish our sentiments and influence, so that we can manage the civil government as we please.[55]

The Federalist Party had failed. The Whig Party had been still-born. And the reintegration of cultural, economic and political authority seemed either a lost cause, or a goal whose achievement lay far in the future. To others, however, especially those for whom the discontinuity of moral and political authority seemed most intolerable, the coming national crisis, which they exerted themselves to bring on through antislavery agitation, seemed a great opportunity to carry the war of words and institutions into the political arena. And among these were not only radical clergymen, merchants, professionals and others who partici- pated in the collegiate networks, but also, and perhaps more impor- tantly, obscure men, men like John Brown and Abraham Lincoln, who had been profoundly influenced by the cultural activities of the evan- gelical united front and its agents.

CHAPTER NINE

Class and Character in Boston: A Pattern of Regional Integration

As the conditions of men constituting the nation become more and more equal, the demand for manufactured commodities becomes more general and extensive, and the cheapness that places these objects within the reach of slender fortunes becomes a great element of success. Hence there are every day more men of great opulence who devote their wealth and knowledge to manufactures and who seek, by opening large establishments and by strict division of labor, to meet fresh demands which are made on all sides. Thus, in proportion as the mass of the nation turns to democracy, that particular class which is engaged in manufactures becomes more aristocratic. Men grow more alike in one, more different in the other; and inequality increases in the less numerous class in the same ratio in which it decreases in the community.

But this kind of aristocracy by no means resembles those kinds which preceded it. It will be observed at once that, as it applies exclusively to manufactures and to some manufacturing callings, it is a monsterious exception in the general aspect of society. The small aristocratic societies that are formed by some manufacturers in the midst of the immense democracy of our age contain, like the great aristocratic societies of former ages, some men who are very opulent and a multitude who are wretchedly poor. The poor have few means of escaping from their condition and becoming rich, but the rich are constantly becoming poor, or they give up business when they have realized a fortune. Thus the elements of which the class of the poor is composed are fixed, but the elements of which the class of the rich is composed are not so. To tell the truth, the class of rich men does not exist; for these rich individuals have no feelings or purposes, no traditions or hopes, in common; there are individuals, therefore, but no definite class.[1]

. . . the millioncracy, considered in a large way, is not at all an affair of persons and families, but a perpetual fact of money with a variable human element. . . . this trivial and fugitive fact of wealth does not create a permanent class unless some special means are taken to arrest the process of disintegration in the third generation.[2]

If the net cast by Yale and the other institutions of the evangelical united front over the nation was a broad and loose one, which caught many sorts of men in many different ways, the net cast by Boston lay in a smaller sea and was woven of a finer, more discriminating mesh. If Yale and the other evangelicals were concerned about redeeming the nation, Bostonians were, on the whole, concerned only with perpetuating their preeminent position in the affairs of Boston and its environs. Although the merchants' economic interests grew steadily more wide-ranging as Boston capital became the basis for the China trade, the exploitation of Pennsylvania iron and Michigan copper, and the construction of the western railroads, their cultural, religious, and political interests failed, until the 1850s, to reflect the dynamic nationalism of their economic interests. Through the 1820s and 1830s, as Yale, Princeton, Williams, Dartmouth, and other denominational institutions raised funds and recruited students from all over the country, Harvard was, its southern students notwithstanding, becoming to a significant extent the preserve of a small group of wealthy eastern Massachusetts mercantile and professional families.

The reasons for this difference are fairly obvious. Where the evangelical organizations of the Standing Order served and reflected the interests of a primarily rural or recently urbanized constituency whose common interests were largely defined by religion, politics, and geographical origin, the privately-controlled institutions of Boston, including its hospitals, professional schools, and libraries, were closely tied to the commercial interests of the merchants who funded them and whose children comprised a significant proportion of their staffs and their clientele. For the evangelical ministry of Connecticut and western Massachusetts, the desideratum of organizational activity was converts; for the merchants of Boston, the desideratum was the enlargement of capital and of the body of potential consumers. Enlarging capital, which in turn made it possible to reach larger markets, was the merchants' primary task. And inasmuch as enlarging capital required the creation of the mutual trust and common values essential to effective collective economic action, it is not surprising to find them de-emphasizing the importance of religion and politics. For such issues served only to create conflicts that interfered with economic rationality and the combination of capital.

But the divergence between Boston's tight, local, seemingly exclusive institutional pattern and the evangelicals' loose, decentralized network was not as great as it might appear. Both had stemmed from a common set of assumptions about the corporate nature of society and the relation between the wealthy, learned, and respectable and the masses. Both struggled to promulgate common values, to overcome the centrifugality and tumult of the political, economic, and intellectual marketplace. Underlying the divergent scope of their activities was a common concern about character education and the necessity for training Americans for autonomy. Ultimately, by the 1850s, as the evangelical impulse became secularized and as Boston's economic interests became more national, the two patterns would converge and become the basis for an operational national culture and economy.

1. The Problem of Boston

Probably no city in the United States conveys an impression of long-term stability and continuity as well as Boston. The Cabots and the Lowells, Harvard College and Beacon Hill, and the golden dome of the Statehouse are folkloric emblems of a deeply-founded social and economic order. That order is, in fact, by no means as old as it appears to be. The Boston Brahmin, the institutions of proper Boston, and the folklore of permanence and continuity were very much the creations of a nineteenth-century, merchant-dominated elite.[3]

While it is certainly true that mercantile hegemony had become fairly well established in Massachusetts by the early eighteenth century, it is important to recognize that the commercial magnates of the pre-Revolutionary period were not the founders of the new post-Revolutionary economic and cultural order. Most of the families whose names we instantly identify as bastions of proper Boston were, until the 1780s, not in Boston at all.[4] The Cabots were in Salem; the Lowells, in Newburyport; the Adamses, in Braintree. While certain families can trace themselves to pre-Revolutionary Boston origins, the vast majority came to the city after the war to fill the political and commercial vacuum left by the Tory exodus.

While Boston in the 1780s was certainly dominated by the merchants, they were not by any stretch of the imagination an integrated or coherent group. Their merchant fathers were daring, ambitious, and successful men who had come to the city with their capital, gained by privateering, supplying the Revolutionary armies, and through the confiscation of Loyalist property, to establish political reputations and to take advantage of the commercial opportunities that Boston and its great harbor offered. Undoubtedly they expected to be able to do business in traditional ways, through family firms, using family capital and family members as employees. The only difference, they thought, would be one of scale.

A number of compelling forces altered their plans. First, it quickly became apparent that traditional forms of business organization were unsuited to new conditions of commerce. The pre-Revolutionary sedentary merchant, trading with reliable commercial correspondents in the trans-Atlantic and West Indies trades, operated under very different circumstances than the entrepreneur who hoped to take advantage of the great and unexploited markets of the Far East and Latin America. Even in European trade, Boston merchants no longer enjoyed the protected position that British mercantilism had made possible. Risks increased with the growing scale and scope of trading enterprises. Europe was becoming an armed camp, filled with hazards for New England's ships and cargoes.

These changes in the conditions of commerce were complemented by the dramatic rise in domestic disorders during the 1780s. Armed mobs closed the courts in the counties of Western Massachusetts. Boston was teeming with prostitutes and beggars. The political unity that the Revolution seemed to promise collapsed as the politically ambitious sought to exploit popular discontent for private purposes. Even religion became a battleground for contending economic and social interests as earlier conflicts within the established Congregational Church intensified toward a schism between the Calvinists and the rationalist Arminians.

Risk, disorder, and diversity pushed the leading merchant families toward cooperation rather than competition. They had far more to gain by working together in political and commercial enterprises than by working at cross purposes. By the 1790s, merchant families, both old Bostonians and newer arrivals, began intermarrying, forming political alliances, and engaging in jointly-funded corporate enterprises. The decision to collectivize manpower and capital was powerfully manifested in the creation of new and closely interrelated commercial and cultural institutions. These became the means not only for extending their hegemony over larger areas, but also for structuring and mediating their new relations with one another.

2. Character and Commerce

Late eighteenth-century Boston's merchant fathers were following a common pattern in encouraging vocational diversity among their sons.

Unlike the farmers and artisans, however, they retained a vested interest in their sons who followed non-commercial pursuits. New to Boston, these mercantile strangers in a strange land clung together, taking residences close to one another, visiting together, and taking refuge in the familiar and comfortable world of family sentimentality.[5] There was, of course, more than sentiment involved in the efforts of fathers to retain ties to their sons. For children, regardless of their vocations, were still the building blocks of commercial and political alliances that were, in turn, the basic elements of certainty and trustworthiness underlying the new corporate enterprises.

In their willingness to promote vocational diversity, Boston's merchant fathers were not willing simply to let their sons go. They complemented their sacrifice of control over their sons' career choices by reallocating authority and oversight to collectively controlled institutions. These institutions would, in turn, delinate norms of behavior deemed necessary for fulfilling positions of trust and responsibility in collective enterprises. It is precisely at this point, the early decades of the nineteenth century in which the children of the mercantile elite were being liberated from direct paternal control, that the term "character" came into frequent use in American parlance—and became an obsession in the literature and conversation of Bostonians.[6]

Character took on new and specific connotations in the context of autonomy. It ceased to mean simply the particular traits that distinguished one individual from another and took on a meaning which suggested the degree to which an individual was the possessor of behavior traits that the community had established as praiseworthy and socially desirable. In the new definition of the term an individual possessed character to the extent to which he could be counted on to act correctly and responsibly of his own accord in situations in which he would have been free to act otherwise. The possession of character, internalized authority, was the factor that transformed autonomy from being a potential source of anarchy to being an essential component of the emerging corporate order.

Because personal autonomy was made possible for merchant children by the collectivization of resources in institutions, it is hardly surprising that institutions should have been the primary vehicles for the formation and transmission of character. There were a number of institutional means for fostering the development of character in the young. Some were the mere by-products of common experience; others were intentionally directed to that end.

Certainly the most powerful force leading to the formation of character among merchant group children was the simple factor of common upbringing. They lived in the same neighborhoods, went to the same schools, played together, and expected to marry one another and do business together. In the premetropolitan Boston of the early nineteenth century, these children could enjoy an intense commonality of experience that would, fifty years later, be possible only in the exclusive boarding schools. Whether in the classroom together or in battles with boys from other neighborhoods on Boston Common, the moral and intellectual qualities of individuals soon became apparent not only to their fellows, but to their teachers and parents. The next regular step in this "accidental" process of character formation is described by Henry Adams in the *Education*:

> For generation after generation, Adamses and Brookses and Boylstons and Gorhams had gone to Harvard College, and although none of them, as far as known, had ever done any good there, or throught himself the better for it, custom, social ties, convenience, and, above all, economy, kept each generation on the track. Any other education would have required serious effort, but no one took Harvard College seriously. All went there because their friends went there, and the College was their ideal of social self-respect.
>
> Harvard College, as far as it educated at all, was a mild and liberal school, which sent young men into the world with all they needed to make respectable citizens, and something of what they needed to make useful ones. Leaders of men it never tried to make. Its ideals were altogether different. The Unitarian clergy had given to the College a character of moderation, balance, of what the French called *Mesure*; excellent traits, which the college attained with singular success, so that its graduates could be commonly recognized by the stamp, but such a type of character rarely lent itself to autobiography. In effect, the school created a type but not a will. Four years of Harvard College, if successful, resulted in a autobiographaical blank on which only a watermark had been stamped.[7]

Adams' description of Harvard is remarkably perceptive once one has penetrated his facetious manner and his acceptance of the folklore of his own social class. In fact, none of the families mentioned by Adams had long traditions of Harvard attendance: Henry's great grandfather was the first of his family to attend the college; only one Boylston and four Gorhams had graduated from Harvard during the eighteenth century; the Brookses were all descendants of the parvenu insurance magnate Peter Chardon Brooks.[8] As with most of the merchant families who comprised the Brahmin group, attendance at Harvard did not become a norm for these people until the nineteenth century. Nor should one take seriously Adams' assertion that economy was an important motive in directing mercantile sons toward Cambridge. For Harvard was, especially after 1800, an institution whose expenses placed it well beyond the means of the average citizen.[9] These statements aside, however, Henry Adams' description of Harvard and its social function is astoundingly accurate: "All went there because their friends went there"; the College was their ideal of social self-respect"; "The school created a type but not a will." Clearly, in Adams' view, Harvard was a seminary for the production of respectable, useful, and dependable men. Such men were exactly what an orderly capitalist economy would require. And in spite of their wealth and opportunities, the young Bostonians who would attend Harvard were being subjected to many of the same experiences and expectations enunciated in the *Yale Report of 1828*—for was not "mesure," moderation and balance, very similar to the "discipline and furniture of the mind" that Yale's faculty hoped would underlie and govern the acquisition of mere knowledge?

2. Reforms at Harvard

Harvard as it existed in 1780 was no more suited to the task of resocializing the leaders of the new order than Yale or Princeton had been. It was still very much an institution of the early eighteenth century, and its students were still disciplined by fagging, fines, and rustication; it had only recently abandoned the practice of listing its students in order of social status; there was no individualized grading system; and the faculty consisted only of the President, the tutors, and three professors. While the college faced many of the same problems as Yale during the post-Revolutionary period—the need for new forms of discipline, the obligation to educate a republican elite, the necessity to create alternatives to church and state as primary support groups—Harvard's solutions differed from those devised in New Haven. These differences stemmed less from ideology (for Harvard and Yale were both staunchly Federalist) than from the composition of their support groups. Where Yale's new clientele was geographically dispersed, and defined by its allegiance to a particular set of religious doctrines, an ideal that would "travel well" wherever its possessors might end up in the great world (and where they might end up was, for Yale graduates after 1780, highly uncertain), Harvard's post-Revolutionary patrons had very specific social concerns as well. They knew that they were a monied elite; their sons would be the richest and most powerful men in the Commonwealth. At the same time, both their Calvinist religion and their classical education made clear to them the dangers, temptations, and possibilities for decadence that hereditary wealth and power presented to its possessors. A Harvard education would have to do more than socialize "sound men." It would have to suit them for autonomous dependability in the concrete context of Boston's emerging corporate institutions. And it would have to be a means of bridging the differences that obstructed the full development of collective activity and class consciousness among the members of Boston's elite.

To state the problem this way is, of course, to distort it. The merchants and lawyers who began to dominate Harvard in 1780 still thought of themselves as part of an intact traditional Standing Order, and saw their primary task as one of adapting that order to new conditions. They could hardly foresee the changes that their own economic activities would unleash, especially as they affected the composition of their own social group. They could not anticipate that railroads, banking, and manufacturing would eventually relegate shipping to a minor role in the economy. Nor could they have imagined the role that new productive forces would play in elevating scores of new men to positions of great importance in the corporate world. Yale could recognize and deal with the difficulties presented by infidelity and the possibility of disestablishment in a single decade. Harvard, as an institution whose primary constitutency was defined by wealth and power, had to confront a series of challenges as the rapid economic growth of the ante-bellum period altered the composition and self-consciousness of its patrons. As a result, while the primary reforms at Yale were made in the 1790s and persisted without significant alteration until 1871, reforms at Harvard would come in phases, reflecting the changing interests and composition of its patronage group.

The first phase of reform at Harvard came during the presidency of Joseph Willard, who was inducted into office in 1781. A creature of the Enlightenment, Willard fostered the sciences. The medical school was established, and the faculty of the college grew from three to five. His reform of discipline was by no means as clearcut as the "parental system of government" introduced by Timothy Dwight at Yale. While fagging was abolished in 1798, collegiate authority remained remote:

President Willard's notion of maintaining authority was quasi-military. One thinks of him as young Washington Allston caricatured him in 1798: strong, rugged features peering out from an enormous white wig; black small-clothes and black gown. Every student's or tutor's hat must come off when the President entered the Yard, or woe betide! To delinquents his attitude was austere and forbidding. 'Stiff and unbending,' he 'feared to treat his most exemplary pupils with the least familiarity lest it engender contempt.' Undergraduates who entered his study were greeted with 'Well, child, what do you wish?'[10]

If discipline under Willard was parental, it was parental in the older, more patriarchal sense. There was nothing in his manner, or in the regulations of the college, to encourage the exercise of internal control. Students, rather than feeling guilty about their misdeeds, devoted their energies to evading the oversight of the officers of governance, cheerfully paying for their offenses with fines and rustication. Not surprisingly, the tide of disorder rose during Willard's administration.

A complete reorientation of the college towards new ideals would not occur until the regime of John Thornton Kirkland, who held sway from 1810 to 1828. Although no self-conscious pedagogical reformer in the Dwightian mold, Kirkland seems to have possessed an intuitive understanding of the kind of authority that was needed in the new world that his students faced. Like Dwight, he was a model for what he hope his students would become. And he related to them on the human level.

> His manners were marked by dignity and benignity; they invited confidence and repelled familiarity. . . . With severe reproofs of misconduct, he mingled so much humaneness and so easy and natural appeals to the better elements of character in those whom he was obliged to censure, that his reproof acted like a benediction, and they who received it left his presence abashed, penitent, grateful, and attached.[11]

Nor surprisingly, student societies flourished under Kirkland, though they would never assume at Harvard the importance that they enjoyed at Yale. Older organizations like the Speaking Club (1770), the Institute of 1770, Phi Beta Kappa (1781), the Hasty Pudding (1795), and Porcellian (1798) were joined by a host of literary, religious, scientific, and social clubs, some of them lasting only a year or two, others becoming permanent features of undergraduate life.[12] Class spirit rose too: the Class of 1822 was the first to issue a printed report, and graduates began to return to Cambridge at Commencement time to meet and celebrate with their former classmates.

Although Kirkland humanized the old regime and reoriented its spirit in the direction of character education, he was too much of an eighteenth-century gentlemen to make substantive reforms in the organization of discipline and in the curriculum. Although major reforms in these areas came about during his administration, they were not of his making, but were forced upon him and a largely reluctant faculty be the governing boards. Kirkland, like his predecessor Joseph Willard, was a protegé of the geniuses of seaborne commerce whose privateers had made them fortunes during the Revolution and who had pioneered the great China Trade. These merchants, while pioneering New England's first significant corporate ventures into banking, transportation, and manufacturing, still placed a premium on kinship, friendship, and loyalty. Like Mr. Fezziwig in Dickens' *Christmas Carol*, they did well by doing good. But their children and the newer men whose fortunes were derived from new technologies and forms of organization were tougher and less sentimental. Having neither the assurance of a remembered past in which the Standing Order had been preeminent, nor the comfort of doing business in the comfortable precincts of a Salem, Newburyport, or Revolutionary Boston, where risks were controlled and one's fellow businessmen were known quantitites, these young veterans of the early corporate world were not about to leave either discipline or pedagogy to chance or to force of personality. Unhappy with the state of Harvard's curriculum and finances, they undertook a complete review of the situation, beginning in 1823.

This review produced a series of recommendations that would finally accomplish for Harvard the modernized structure and curriculum that Yale had achieved decades before. In the area of discipline, the "parental" influence of the President was supplemented by the abolition of fines and rustication as primary means of social control. In their place there would develop a gradual equalization of relations between faculty and students, the faculty addressing their charges as "Mister," treating them and expecting them to act like gentlemen.[13] Punishment was to be reserved for great offenses; minor student idiosyncracies were to be increasingly tolerated. In the area of curriculum the large recitations that had characterized American colleges since their foundation were replaced by small classes based on student proficiency. Student academic progress was to be strictly monitored, and every one placed on a "scale of merit." The virtues of emulation were to be encouraged not only through the personality of the President, but also by the addition of distinguished members of the Boston community on the faculties of the new professional schools in law and divinity. Finally (a feature that would not come to Yale until much later), students were given far greater latitude in what they studied. Although far from a full-blown elective system, Harvard's willingness to trust its students to make intelligent choices with regard to their intellectual interests was remarkable. Under pressure from George Ticknor, Edward Everett, and other graduates who had studied abroad, modern literature, languages, and history had, by the late 1820s, found a place in Harvard's curriculum.

3. Harvard and the Boston Mercantile Community

If the reforms of discipline and curriculum that were introduced to Harvard at the end of the Kirkland regime were consonant with the merchants' ideas about character and internal control, the man chosen to succeed Kirkland was the ideal individual to preside over their implementation. Rather than placing a clergyman in charge of the college, the Fellows, for the first time since the election of John Leverret in 1708, chose a merchant as president. This choice, while a departure from tradition, was perfectly in line with the reforms of the preceding decades: it was not only a token of the mercantile interest in the institution, and of the Dwightian notion that the president should be an object of emulation, but also signified the functional ties that were developing between Boston's incipient ruling class and its institutions of culture.

Josiah Quincy was no ordinary merchant.[14] He was an exemplar of the ideals of the Standing Order in a capitalist context. He was a man of family in the Holmesian sense, the descendant of a line of prominent public servants going back to the foundation of the colony. He was a man of learning, a Harvard graduate, holder of honorary degrees from Yale and Princeton, scion of four generations of graduates, a man who had grown up with books. He had, in addition, been trained as a lawyer and admitted to the bar. Quincy possessed more, however, than a noble liniage. Although he came from a well-to-do family, he did not start out in life as a wealthy man. However, his extensive speculations in Boston real estate and his involvement with major corporations in the city—including the Provident Institution for Savings, the Massachusetts Hospital Life Insurance Company, the Massachusetts Fire and Marine Insurance Company, and others—made him a very wealthy man. His estate was valued at $700,000 at his death in 1864. He was a political leader, serving as a member of Congress, in the Massachusetts State Senate, and as Mayor of Boston. Quincy, in sum, combined the ascriptive characteristics which the newly rich merchants envied with the personal accomplishments of political and mercantile success which, they well knew, could only be won through hard work. No better man could have presided over and exemplified the ideals of Harvard's efforts to foster character in its students.

Although Quincy was originally chosen as Harvard's president because the Fellows hoped that he would place the affairs of the college, its finances and goverance, on a businesslike basis, he carried his preoccupation with rationality and order into the reform of undergraduate life. Undoubtedly his desire to "make the College a nursery of high-minded, high-principled, well-taught, well-conducted, well-bred gentlemen, fit to take their share, gracefully and honorable in private and public life" was the shared goal of every president since Harvard's foundation.[15] But his method of accomplishing that end was a radical departure from past practices, for autonomy restrained by character was his explicit model of the gentlemen. Accordingly, he began to put into effect what he called his "philosophy of prevention."

The pervading principle of his treatment of the undergraduates was to make them a law unto themselves, by the development of a sense of honor and self-respect, which should make the severity of discipline unnecessary. . . . In his intercourse with them he always took it for granted that they were gentlemen and men of honor. He never questioned the truth of any story any of them told him, when in academic difficulties, however improbable it might be. That statement was accepted as the truth until it was overthrown by implacable facts and inexorable evidence. Then, beyond a doubt, the unhappy youth was made to know the value of a good character by the inconvenience attending the loss of it. Still, even in such cases, every kindly encouragement was extended to the offender to rehabilitate himself in his own self-respect and in the good opinion of his superiors.[16]

Quincy's philosophy of discipline, while it retained some of the rhetoric of the traditional system—particularly the concept of honor—had redefined and refocused the locus of authority. "Honor" no longer involved how one appeared to one's peers; for Quincy it had become bound up with the notion of self-respect and the "good opinion of one's superiors." The locus of authority, in other words, had been shifted from an individual's relations with his peers as a group on whose honor one's behavior reflected and to whom one was most immediately accountable, to an individual's relation with himself and, in particular, with that part of himself which knew well the expectations of his superiors. Guilt, the ability to anticipate the consequences of one's actions, was the essence of Quincy's "Philosophy of Prevention."

But Josiah Quincy did not restrict his efforts to transform his charges into gentlemen to the system of discipline. He made strenuous efforts to give positive incentives to students, to expose them to models of correct and polite behavior, and to place them in situations in which they could display themselves to best advantage. He treated the undergraduates as responsible individuals, addressing them as "Mister"—an honor that, until his presidency, had been reserved for holders of the master's degree. He opened his house once a week to students, giving them an opportunity to socialize with his family (including his four unmarried young daughters) and distinguished visitors from Boston. He replaced crude implements used in commons with Liverpool china and silver engraved with the college seal. In sum, he treated the students as gentlemen and expected them to behave as such.

Unfortunately, he may have expected too much of his unruly charges.[17] In the spring of 1834, the undergraduates, feeling their oats, began making bonfires in Harvard Yard. In the course of their frolics an altercation occurred between some students and a member of the faculty. The tenuousness and optimism of the philosophy of prevention became apparent. Quincy decided to "make an example" of certain students, and their classmates protested, first by petition, ultimately by a rampage of destruction. Quincy's response was impolitic: he ordered the dismissal and rustication of the entire sophomore class and then instituted grand jury proceedings against the probable offenders. While no criminal charges were ever lodged, Quincy lost his popularity among the students.

But the loss of popularity in no way involved a loss of influence. Quincy's shift in the modality of discipline was a permanent change in the course of the college. It wedded the college's modes of acceptable behavior to those of the commercial and professional worlds of Boston. And under Quincy the college ceased to be merely a means of diverting sons from business careers into the professions and became a common means of socialization for all sons of the merchant group. Before Quincy's presidency, no more than thirteen percent of the graduates had gone into business; by the end of his regime, the proportion would begin to ascend steadily, until it reached the level of thirty percent, where it remained until the beginning of the twentieth century.[18] By the 1860s a Bostonian could write, of Harvard as Henry Adams did in his *Education*, "Everyone went there . . . ."

4. Networks and Classes: Harvard and the Formation of an Urban Ruling Class

Yale was founded on the rock of Calvinism and sustained by a clerically dominated and state-supported ecclesiastical structure. When it lost state support, it fostered the development of a national network of strategically placed professionals and businessmen who had benefited from their years at Yale and who, in turn, were willing to send their money and their sons to it. Harvard, however, was founded on the shifting sands of wealth and politics, and as a result its future, especially through the tumultuous years of the early nineteenth century, depended on the extent to which those sands could be stabilized.

It was a difficult situation, one having less to do with Harvard itself than with the patronage group on which it had come to depend, the leading commercial and professional families of Boston. These families, many of whom were newly prominent, were fully cognizant of their lack of coherence as a group and of the intrinsic ambiguities of introducing a supportive social stability. Insufficient attention to wealth and power could lead to decadence, to a debilitating rigidity and timidity— as Prescott's histories of the Spanish empire reminded them.[19] Too much attention to acquistiveness could, on the other hand, lead to an equally dangerous and self-defeating amorality. These concerns were largely implicit in the opening decades of the century, when the makers of the great fortunes were still alive and actively guiding and sustaining not only their own affairs, but also those of their children and grandchildren. But as wealth began to be institutionalized, taken out of partnerships and family firms and put into diversified portfolios and trust funds, and as the sources of wealth themselves became overwhelmingly corporate, anxieties about the future came to be more openly expressed. Needless to say, these worries were futher stimulated by the arrival in Boston of thousands of impoverished Irish immigrants.

From the earliest decades of the nineteenth century, a certain degree of social stability had been gained through the close ties between Harvard and Boston's cultural and commercial corporations. Just as a boy who acquitted himself well at the college could, especially after the presidency of Josiah Quincy, expect to find a good place in a Boston bank, brokerage firm, or textile mill, so an aspiring professional could, if he proved himself, find himself on the board of trustees of a major charity, serving as the guardian of a family trust, or enjoying a professorship in the medical school or a post at the Massachusetts General Hospital. To a very significant extent, in trading off primary functions to institutions, Boston's merchant families had given their institutions a rather exclusive and family-like character.

The familial character of Boston enterprises was, by the 1850s, presenting genuine difficulties to the city's financial community. There was a growing tendency to exclude newer entrepreneurs from certain central financial institutions like the Suffolk System, and their response to it was not to attack it politically, but simply to ignore it and circumvent it by organizing another central bank. More seriously, charges were being made from responsible quarters against the quality of the merchant group's management of its enterprises. These charges, because they underlined the connection between Brahmin management of corporations and control of endowed institutions, raised very troubling questions about whether the inheritors of the mantle of the Standing Order were, in fact, placing their own private interests ahead of the public's. J. S. Ayer, a Lowell physician and large stockholder in the textile industry, began his 1863 attack on the mill managers by giving a capsule hstory of the transformation of economic management in Massachusetts during the preceeding thirty years:

> The capital and labor employed in the Manufacturing Corporations constitute one of the great interests of the State, which profits by their prosperity, and suffers with any adversity that befalls them.

These institutions were originally organized by a few men, who united their capital like co-partners, and obtained such charters as they desired from the State Government. Under charters thus granted, which were well suited to their early condition, our manufacturing companies, so long as that condition continued, were well managed and very prosperous. The small number of owners, by devoting their personal attention, and by bringing all their shrewdness, energy, and perserverance to bear for the welfare of their enterprises, as other partners do in the management of their property, were so far successful as to afford a generous employment to industry and a profitable investment to capital.

But a generation has passed away. Time has changed the relations of owners and managers, until only traces of their original condition remain. The originators—large stockholders, or principal owners, as they were called—of these institutions have died (three or four only of them are now left, and they feeble old men); their estates have been distributed to their heirs, and sold out to the public.[20]

The diffusion of the original proprietors' large stockholdings did not, according to Ayer, result in a diffusion of power over corporate affairs. Because most stockholdings were small and were in the hands of a numerous and geographically dispersed body of owners, the descendants of the old proprietors were able to perpetuate themselves in control. These descendants often owned no stock in the corporations on whose boards they sat, but voted proxies and the stockholdings of trusts and charitable endowments. Because they had little if any direct interest in such corporation, Ayer charged that they set policies which, while personally advantageous, were disastrous to the companies over which they presided.

Nepotism was, according to Ayer, at the center of the problem. Again and again he iterated the ruinous consequences of employing the relatives of mill management in responsible positions:

At a stockholders' meeting of the Hamilton Manufacturing Company, it was charged by one of the owners resident at the mills, that the Treasurer had sent his son (an inexperienced youth) to buy cotton at the South; that, although paying for good cotton, the venders had taken advantage of him, and put off a quantity of miserable trash filled with sand, stone, etc., which was piled up in a heap by the side of the picker-house at the mill; and that the Company must lost not less than fifty thousand dollars by this piece of nepotism.[21]

This was not an isolated instance:

> The stockholders of the Boott Company, finding their property depressed by mismanagement, desired to select some able and practical man for a Treasurer, who could restore the Corporation to a prosperous condition. Attempting to move for this purpose, they were met with the assertion that the Company was largely in debt; that one of the Directors, a wealthy man, would furnish it with money and credit, if his son-in-law were elected Treasurer, and without such aid the Corporation must fall. . . . It was not claimed that their candidate had any especial fitness or qualifications for the post except having married one of the Director's daughters.[22]

These charges raised difficult problems for those concerned about the future of the merchant group. For Ayer had all too accurately described the situation that was coming to prevail not only in the for-profit sector, but also in the management of cultural institutions: the founders of the group, while they may have cemented their alliances with marriages and common associations, had direct and immediate stakes in the prosperity of their ventures. Underlying the ties of kinship and acquaintance were explicit understandings between hard-nosed, uncompromising entrepreneurs. For their descendants, those who were coming to maturity in a world of corporate institutions, the secondary ties were beginning to take precedence. These second and third generation magnates were caught in a dilemma: on the one hand, continued economic pre-eminence depended on universalistic inclusion of new men in their enterprises according to criteria of competence; on the other hand, such inclusion undermined the ability of these families to define themselves and to function successfully as a coherent social group.

It was, by the late 1850s, becoming increasingly clear that Boston stood at a crossroads. Enterprises were becoming ever larger, and their success was increasingly determined by their ability to tap national sources of capital and national markets—and to control sources of raw industrial materials. Equally important was the city's ability to attract first-rate men, men whose intellect knowledge, and ambition were as basic a resource as coal or cotton. Although Boston bankers and manufacturers were operating in New York, Philadelphia, and points west as early as the 1830s, their sojourns away from "the Hub" tended to be temporary. They nearly always returned to Boston without establishing any long-term alliances with financial communities in other cities. While their operations certainly enriched both themselves and their native city, their failure to establish permanent ties or organizations outside of Boston suggests not only an ultimately limited vision of the United States as an economic entity, but also the role that Boston would play in its development.

Boston at mid-century, while prosperous and growing, was troubled. For the interface between merchant families, Harvard, and the city's cultural and commercial institutions was only a partial solution to the problem of social stability. As the likelihood of a Civil War became increasingly apparent, the city's financial success provided little comfort to its aspiring patricians. For its thoughtful citizens knew that nothing underlay their claims to be the cultural and economic stewardship tradition of the old Standing Order but their possession of wealth.

This apparent failure of the wealthy Bostonians to live up to their responsibilities was particularly troubling to Samuel Atkins Eliot who, in a series of articles and pamphlets beginning in the 1840s, attempted to reconcile the possession of wealth with the broader claims of stewardship. Eliot, unlike many Bostonians of his time, felt this conflict acutely. For in his own person, he united the old anti-commercial ministerial elite and the newer aristocracy of trade and manufacturing: generations of Eliots had served as officers of Harvard College and as ministers of churches in Massachusetts and Connecticut; but he owed his own position of eminence as Treasurer of Harvard and trustee and director of a host of corporations and charities to the commercial successes of his father and to his marriage to the Lyman family, whose very new fortune had come from textiles and other manufacturing enterprises.[23]

Eliot appears to have been preoccupied with defining the responsibilities of the privately wealthy in public life and, in particular, with clarifying the character of institutions like Harvard which had, until the Dartmouth College case and the disestablishment of the Congregational Church, been deemed in the public sector. His pamphlet, *Harvard College and Its Benefactors* (1845), undertook a rewriting of the history of the college in order to demonstrate two propositions:[24] first, that Harvard had, in spite of state aid, always been a private institution; second, that the private contributions for Harvard's support had always exceeded those of the public. Although more recent commentators have pointed out the fallaciousness of many of Eliot's conclusions, especially his calculations of the proportions of public to private support, they have tended to overlook the motives that caused men like Eliot suddenly to begin inquiring into the history of institutions like Harvard in the 1840s.[25] By that point it had become apparent that Jacksonianism would not disappear with the retirement of the General, and that the attacks on private power and, in particular, on its institutional manifestations, be they banks or colleges, would not cease. Further, the wealthy themselves were having to confront the fact that however sentimentally they might be inclined to view themselves as part of a continuum of wealth, learning and respectability stretching back to the founding of the colony, they were, in fact, something quite different—a group whose power was based in wealth, not in virtue.

Eliot was trying in his writings from the 1840s on to reestablish the linkage between wealth and virtue not only by revising history in order to demonstrate the public-spiritedness of the wealthy in the past (thereby validating their claims as stewards), but also by clarifying the nature of stewardship in the new context of private corporate institutions. As essential component of this effort was effectively answering the charges of the Jacksonians that the benevolence of the privately wealthy was contaminated by interested motives:

> . . . persons who are farmers or mechanics in this country often use a language and exhibit a tone of feeling which are inconsistent with the state of things here, and are applicable only to what is found in Europe. They talk of the oppression of the rich; when there is not a rich man in America that can, and perhaps not one that wishes, to oppress them. They talk of others being held in more respect, and of themselves as being despised; when there are as many mechanics and farmers in town, city, county, and state offices, both legislative and executive, as of all other sort of persons put together; they take as decided a lead in all measures, public or private, as they are personally qualified to do; and very frequently they throw others completely into the shade. Now if this be contemptuous treatment, what would be respectful? If this be oppression, who is free?[26]

Eliot's emphasis the ascendancy of mechanics and farmers to positions of political power once monopolized by the Standing Order makes it possible for him to argue that the rich are, if anything, politically disadvantaged:

> Riches alone do not enable a man to be much of an oppressor anywhere, and in this country the rich man can make no figure at all in that line. There must be position and privilege superadded to wealth to make it possible to oppress, and in New England neither that position nor that privilege can be attained by any body. So far is the rich man from having attained them, that he is, in truth, farther from them than other persons. He is jealously watched, constantly suspected, and is very commonly regarded as a fair subject for that covert system of attack, which, though in a different way to be sure, is as great a favorite with the Yankee as with his predecessor, the Indian. The language and conduct of

public bodies, especially the legislatures, show pretty accurately the tendency of feeling and though among the mass whom they represent.[27]

Because they are objects of suspicion, driven from situations of political power, Eliot can argue that their benevolence is disinterested and not a means of self-aggrandisement.

It is curious that Eliot, in his 1845 essay on Boston charities, fails to address the main issue: the Jeffersonian-Jacksonian charge that control of private corporations rendered political power irrelevant, since such corporations were immune from legislative interference. When he finally did address the point, in an 1860 essay on the same subject, his argument had become much more refined. Rather than denying that the control of private institutions was a basis for power, he confronted the issue head-on, asserting not only that it was, but also that it was only proper that it should be so:

> When it is seen, as one would think it must be seen sooner or later, that political advancement, in this country, does not imply, as it did in other times and nations, great power over the relations of society, the exclusive ambition for political distinction, which is a sort of contagious mania among us, must subside; and other objects, such as science, theology, and law, much share, at least to a greater extent than heretofore, the devotion of aspiring minds. Power, we know, will always be the object of ambition; but, we trust, not necessarily nor exclusively political power. In this country already, the possession of political power means a very different thing from what it means on the Continent of Europe, or even in England.[28]

To assert the preeminence of cultural over political power was not, however, to assert the power of an aristocracy or ruling class in society. Rather, Eliot suggested that the primary function of institutions of culture was to increase the ability of individuals to master themselves, an ability which, in turn, would make them more effective in the world:

> In the absence of external control, which constitutes what is commonly understood by freedom, self-control becomes more and more important; and self-control is one of the last and best results of the highest religious, moral, and intellectual cultivation. Upon the extension of personal self-control, as a principle to guide our public and private conduct, depends the success not only of individuals, but of nations, in the career of humanity; and whoever desires to see the institutions and liberty of the country preserved must desire

the progress of education in every department, until all the powers of the human mind shall be so appropriately and adequately cultivated, as to make them subservient to a virtuous will.[29]

In Eliot's mind, apparently, the openness of privately controlled institutions to the talented and the ability of such institutions to render such people more useful as citizens and entrepreneurs was sufficient justification for their existence. It mattered little that the "virtuous will" to which the "cultivated" and self-controlled became subservient was funded, administered, and articulated by private persons.

For Samuel Atkins Eliot, the relation between power and charitable benevolence was unclear. Wealth and charity did not imply any stewardship over morality, religion, or the intellect that the public was willing to acknowledge. This ambiguity was not merely a rhetorical strategem designed to divert attention from the self-serving aspects of benevolence. It was, rather, a product of the confused state of ante-bellum culture in America. Harvard and Yale had no monopoly on higher education. And higher education appeared to be, until after the Civil War, an opportunity to which a diminishing number of young men resorted. The privately-supported hospitals and asylums had their state-funded counterparts. Religion and literature had become matters of individual preference. The benefactors of private institutions did not even have a monopoly on wealth. Thousands of entrepreneurs grew rich unhampered by any desire to share their fortunes with institutions of charity and culture. The benevolently wealthy could make no special claims on the public. They were merely another group of individuals competing in the great American marketplace for the esteem of their fellow citizens. Samuel Atkins Eliot labored under the difficult task of reformulating traditional notions of cultural stewardship in the face of political attacks and in the context of new and unfamiliar institutional forms. And in so doing, he found himself in a position similar to that of the promoters of the evangelical united front in the same period. Both had made converts and accumulated capital; both had striven to promote virtue through the organization of charity and reform. But the ultimate goal towards which they had worked, the achievement of political power, seemed as far away as it ever had. Indeed, for the Bostonians, it may have seemed even more distant, tied as they were to regionalism and to the needs of a particular cluster of families. Unable to legitimate the linkage between economic power, benevolence, and politics, Eliot and other Bostonians of his era questioned not only their ability to make their possession of wealth permanent, but also their ability to be worthy of possessing it.

5. New Money and Old Families: Oliver Wendell Holmes and the Origins of Brahminism

Certainly the most articulate spokesman of these anxieties was Doctor Oliver Wendell Holmes. A brilliant physician and professor in the Harvard Medical School, Holmes had written essays and doggerel since his undergraduate days. Suddenly, in the late 1850s, he began to write more sustained and more serious literary works. His first long work, *The Autocrat of the Breakfast Table*, is filled with anxious and ambivalent statements about the problem of class formation. The first chapter of the *Autocrat* seems to favor the idea of class cohesion, the erection of formal barriers to exclude the newly rich:

—Self-made men?—Well, yes. Of course everybody likes and respects self-made men. It is a great deal better to be made in that way than not to be made at all. . . .

Your self-made man, whittled into shape with his own jack-knife, deserves more credit, if that is all, than the regular engine-turned article, shaped by the most approved pattern, and French polished by society and travel. But as to saying that one is every way the equal of the other, that is another matter. The right of strict social discrimination of all things and persons, according to their merits, native or acquired, is one of the most precious republican privileges. I take the liberty to exercise it, when I say, that, *other things being equal*, in most relations of life I prefer a man of family.

What do I mean by a man of family?—O, I'll give you a general idea of what I mean. . . .

Four or five generations of gentlemen and gentlewomen; among them a member of his Majesty's Council for the Province, a Governor or so, one or two Doctors of Divinity, a member of Congress, not later than the time of top-boots with tassels.

Family portraits. The member of the Council, by Smibert. The great merchant-uncle, by Copley, full length, sitting in his arm-chair, in a velvet cap and flowered robe, with a globe by him, to show the range of his commercial transactions. . . .

Books, too, with the names of old college-students in them,—family names;—you will find them at the head of their respective classes in the days when students took their rank on the catalogue from their parent's condition. . . .

No, my friends, I go (always all other things being equal) for the man who inherits family traditions and the cumulative humanities of at least four or five generations. Above all things, as a child, he should have tumbled about in a library. All men are afraid of books who have not handled them in infancy. . . . One may, it is true, have all the antecedents I have spoken of, and yet be a boor and a shabby fellow. One may have none of them and yet be fit for councils and courts. Then let them change places. Our social arrangement has this great beauty, that its strata shift up and down as they change specific gravity, without being colgged by layers of prescription. But still I insist on my democratic liberty of choice, and I go for the man with the gallery of family portraits against the man with the twenty-five daguerreotypes, unless I find out that the last is the better of the two.[30]

This is a profoundly ambivalent statement. One wonders why Holmes resolved his preference in favor of the man of the family, and why he constantly repeats the refrain "all other things being equal." The sources of his ambivalence seem fairly clear. Holmes himself, like most of the "proper Bostonians" of his generation, had mixed origins: his father, although a learned man and a protegé of Ezra Stiles, was from back-country Connecticut and could boast no Smiberts or Copleys in his family gallery; his mother, on the other hand, was from the ancient and very distinguished Wendell family of Boston and Portsmouth.[31] Holmes, while nominally the possessor of the attributes of a man of family, must have been uneasy in his possession of them, knowing as he did that he owed his social status to a fortunate marriage. He could no more repudiate the virtues of the self-made man than he could repudiate his own paternity. But at the same time, he clearly wished to be able to draw out some sort of valid boundary between his social group and the world at large.

In a later essay in the *Autocrat*, Holmes resolves the problem in the other direction, suggesting that Boston's strength as a city depends upon its ability to tap the talent of the provinces, drawing the ambitious into its commercial, cultural, and social life:

Boston is just like other places of its size;—only perhaps, considering its excellent fish-market, paid fire department, superior monthly publications, and correct habit of spelling the English language, it has some right to look down on the mob of cities. I'll tell you, though, if you want to know it, what is the real offense of Boston. It drains a large watershed of intellect, and will not itself be drained. If it would only send away its first-rate men, instead of its second-rate ones, (no offence to the well-known exceptions,

of which we are always proud,) we should be spared such epi-
grammatic remarks as that which the gentleman has quoted [that
Boston State-House is the hub of the solar system]. There can never
be a real metropolis in the country, until the biggest centre can
drain the lesser ones of their talent and wealth.—I have observed,
by the way, that the people who really live in two great cities are
by no means so jealous of each other, as are those of smaller cities
situated within the intellectual basin, or *suction-range*, of the large
one, of the pretensions of any other. Don't you see why? Because
their promising young author and rising lawyer and large capitalist
have been drained off to the neighboring big city,—their prettiest
girl has been exported to the same market; all their ambition points
there, and all their thin gliding or glory comes from there. I hate
little toad-eating cities.[32]

If, on the one hand, the "man of family" is to be preferred (for what,
Holmes never tell us), the greatness of Boston, or any other city, depends
on its ability to gather the intellectual and economic harvest of the
regions surrounding it. The problem of how to accommodate the rising
and ambitious to the "cumulative humanities" of traditional status is,
once again, unanswered.

In the next-to-last essay in the *Autocrat*, Holmes propounds the problem of class in its most troublesome form. Stepping away from the
merely ascriptive aspects of long-term possession of wealth (portraits,
distinguished ancestors, and the like), he asserts, as a physician, the
concrete benefits that wealth confers on its possessors:

We are forming an aristocracy, as you may observe, in this country,—not a *gratia-Dei*, nor a *jure-divino* one,—but a *de-facto* upper
stratum of being, which floats over the turbid waves of common
life like the iridescent film you may have seen spreading over the
water about our wharves,—very splendid, though its origin may
have been tar, tallow, train-oil, or other such unctuous commodities. I say, then, we are forming an aristocracy; and, transitory as
its individual life often is, it maintains itself tolerably, as a whole.
Of course, money is its corner-stone. But now observe this. Money
kept for two or three generations transforms a race,—I don't mean
merely in manners and hereditary culture, but in blood and bone.
Money buys air and sunshine, in which children grow up more
kindly, of course, than in close, back streets; it buys country places
to give them happy and healthy summers, good nursing, good
doctoring, and the best cuts of beef and mutton. . . . As the young
females of each successive season come on, the finest specimens

among them, other things being equal, are apt to attract those who can afford the expensive luxury of beauty. The physical character of the next generation rises in consequence. It is plain that certain families have in this way acquired an elevated type of face and figure, and that in a small circle of city connections one may sometimes find models of both sexes which one of the rural counties would find hard to match from all its townships put together. Because there is a good deal of running down, of degeneration and waste of life, among the richer classes, you must not overlook the equally obvious fact I just spoke of,—which in one or two generations more will be, I think, more patent than just now.[33]

Beginning in commerce, the fact of wealth transforms lives, establishes more healthy conditions, institutionalizes a life style that is defined not only by good doctoring and good eating, but also by education, occupation, and marriage. Holmes is clearly unfolding for his readers the progressive elaboration of class institutions and behavioral patterns over time. With the passage of each generation, the characteristics and, implicitly, the institutions, of the class become more clearly defined. There arises the problem, as Holmes, the father of adolescent sons, well knew:

The weak point in our chryso-aristocracy is the same I have alluded to in connection with cheap dandyism. Its thorough manhood, its high-caste gallantry, are not so manifest as the plate glass of its windows and the more or less legitimate heraldry of its coach-panels. It is very curious to observe of how small account military folds are held among our Northern people. Our young men must gild their spurs, but they need not win them. The equal division of property keeps the younger sons above the necessity of military service. Thus the army loses an element of refinement, and the moneyed upper class forgets what it is to count heroism among its virtues. Still I don't believe in any aristocracy without pluck as its backbone. Ours may show it when the time comes, if ever it does come.[34]

Holmes wrote these words during the spring of 1858. His young men would very soon have a chance to "earn their spurs."

Doctor Holmes' meditations on the problem of stabilizing the wealthy and educated families of Boston into a class did not end with *The Autocrat of the Breakfast Table*. He continued to dwell on the subject in his first novel, *Elsie Venner*, which was serialized in the *Atlantic Monthly* in 1859 and 1860. Although he was still unable to resolve his ambivalence about the relation between ambition and tradition, he managed to define the problem more clearly and analytically. The first chapter of the novel is entitled "The Brahmin Caste of New England." In it he attempts to draw distinctions between the aristocracies of the old world, modern classes as defined by the possession of wealth, and the "Brahmin Caste of New England," which constituted the pool of education and breeding that occasionally overlapped with wealth and power.

Holmes dealt with aristocracy in a few words. "There is nothing in New England," he wrote, "corresponding at all to the feudal aristocracies of the Old World."[35] What is called an aristocracy in this country is, in Holmes' view, "merely the richest part of the community," some of whom were well-bred, others "only purse-proud and assuming." They are not an aristocracy, wrote Holmes, but a class. Class, for Holmes, was a very impermanent thing—the embodiment of the social problem with which he was attempting to grapple:

> It is in the nature of large fortunes to diminish rapidly, when sub-divided and distributed. A million is the unit of wealth, now and here in America. It splits into four handsome properties; each of these into four good inheritances; these, again, into scanty com-petences for four ancient maidens,—with whom it is best that the family should die out, unless it can begin again as its great-grand-father did. Now a million is kind of golden cheese, which represents in a compendious form the summer's growth of a far meadow of craft or commerce; and as this kind of meadow rarely bears more than one crop, it is pretty certain that sons and grandsons will not get another golden cheese out of it, whether they milk the same cows or turn in new ones. In other words, the millioncracy, con-sidered in a large way, is not at all an affair of persons and families, but a perpetual fact of money with a variable human element. . . . Of course this trivial and fugitive fact of personal wealth does not create a permanent class, unless some special means are taken to arrest to process of disintegration in the third generation. This is so rarely done, at least successfully, that one need not live a very long life to see most of the rich families he knew in childhood more or less reduced, and the millions shifted into the hands of the country-boys who were sweeping stores and carrying parcels when the now decayed gentry were driving their chariots, eating their venison over silver chafing-dishes, drinking Madeira chilled in em-bossed coolers, wearing their hair in powder, and casing their legs in long boots with silken tassels.[36]

Holmes, in pondering the problem of social stability, must have been reading de Tocqueville. For like the Doctor, the author of *Democracy in*

America had traced the variability of wealth-holding to the law of inheritance:

> When the equal partition of property is established by law, the intimate connection is destroyed between family feeling and the preservation of the paternal estate; the property ceases to represent the family; for, as it must inevitably be divided after one or two generations, it has evidently a constant tendency to diminish and must in the end be completely dispersed.[37]

But where Tocqueville foresaw an absolute domination of the law of the marketplace over both property and culture, "a middling standard . . . fixed in America for human knowledge," Holmes saw something else. He agreed with the Frenchman that

> There is no class . . . in America, in which the taste for intellectual pleasures is transmitted with hereditary fortune and leisure and by which the labors of the intellect are held in honor.[38]

That is, he recognized that the "taste for intellectual pleasures" was not necessarily transmitted with "hereditary fortune and leisure." But he was unwilling to concede that the guardianship of culture had to be joined to wealth and power. Instead, he referred implicitly to Tocqueville's discussion of the situation of culture during New England's earliest years. "I have stated in the preceding chapter," wrote de Tocqueville,

> that great quality existed among the immigrants who settled on the shores of New England. Even the germs of aristocracy were never planted in that part of the Union. The only influence which obtained there was that of the intellect; the people became accustomed to revere certain names as representatives of knowledge and virtue. Some of their fellow citizens acquired a power over the others that might truly have been called aristocratic if it had been capable of transmission from father to son.[39]

Holmes believed that the "influence of the intellect" was both a characteristic of certain families and existed more or less independently of the possession of power and wealth. Indeed, its independence from power was, to a significant extent, the cause of its survival. This was the "Brahmin Caste of New England:"

> There is . . . in New England, an aristocracy, if you choose to call it so, which has a far greater character of permanence. It has grown

to be a *caste*,—not in any odious sense,—but, by the repetition of the same influences, generation after generation, it has acquired a distinct organization and physiognomy. . . .

If you look carefully at any class of students in one of our colleges, you will have no difficulty in selecting specimens of two different aspects of youthful manhood. . . . In the first, the figure perhaps is robust, but often otherwise,—inelegant, partly from careless attitudes, partly from ill-dressing,—the face is uncouth in feature, or at least,—the mouth is coarse and unformed,—the eye unsympathetic, even if bright,— . . . —, the voice is unmusical,—and the enunciation as if the words were coarse castings, instead of fine carvings. The youth of the other aspect is commonly slender,—his face is smooth, and apt to be pallid,— . . . ,—his lips play over the thought he utters as a pianist's fingers dance over the music,—and his whole air, though it may be timid, has nothing clownish.

The first youth is the common country-boy, whose race had been bred to bodily labor. Nature has adapted the family organization to the kind of life it has lived. . . . You must not expect too much of any such. Many of them have force of will and character, and become great scholars. A scholar is, in a large proportion of cases, the son of scholars or scholarly persons.

That is exactly what the other young man is. He comes of the *Brahmin Caste of New England*. This is the harmless, inoffensive, untitled aristocracy referred to, and which many readers will at once acknowledge. There are races of scholars among us, in which aptitude for learning . . . [is] congenital and hereditary. Their names are always on some college catalogue or other. They break out every generation or two in some learned labor which calls them up after they seem to have died out. At last some newer name takes their place, it may be,—but you enquire a little and you find it is the blood of the Edwardses or the Chauncys or the Ellerys or some of the old historic scholars, disguised under the altered name of a female descendant.[40]

Having provided his readers with a definition of his Brahmin protagonist as a social type, Holmes proceeded to introduce him as a concrete individual. His name was Bernard Langdon, a college graduate and medical student, scion of an ancient but poor Brahmin family from one of the old ports north of Boston. As the story opens, Langdon is shown asking his professor, the narrator, for a certificate of character that will allow him to teach at a backcountry academy. His family, it appears, is no longer able to support his studies and he hopes, like many young men of his generation, to earn enough money be teaching to complete his degree. The professor, while happy to recommend Langdon, worries about him, worried that, because he will be teaching in a girl's school, he may make a matrimonial misalliance

[with some] fresh-faced, half-bred country girl, no more fit to be mated with him than her father's horse to go in double harness with Flora Temple.[41]

"I would not," the Professor continue,

have a man marry above his level, so as to become the appendage of a powerful family connection; but I would not have him marry until he knew his level. . . . But remember that a young man, using large endowments wisely and fortunately, may put himself on a level with the highest in the land in ten years of brilliant unflagging labor. And to stand at the very top of your calling in a great city is something in itself,—that is, if you like money, and influence.[42]

Through his narrative of Langdon's activities, and through his expression of his own anxieties about Langdon, the Professor (Holmes) sketched out his model of the proper relation between intellect and commerce, between the permanent Brahmin Caste and the "trivial and fugitive fact of personal wealth." That model consisted of a set of institutions—colleges, hospitals, professions—that mediated relations between new money and old culture. Through them, in Holmes' view, new money became civilized and old culture monied. Essential, however, was the necessity for the two to meet on the common ground of accomplishment. And so they did for Holmes' protagonist: after receiving his degree and practicing for a short time, Bernard is offered a professorship in a medical school "in an ancient and distinguished university." This enable him to marry Miss Letita Forrester, "daughter . . . of the great banking firm . . . of Bilyuns Brothers & Forrester."[43] Having fulfilled the requirements of the Professor's model, they live happily ever after.

Oliver Wendell Holmes' ambivalent dilations on on the subject of caste and class, like those of Samuel Atkins Eliot on charity, could state but not solve the problem of order and authority. While individuals within the sphere of private institutions, whether in Boston, New Haven, or the towns and villages of the South and West, might improve themselves and their environs through reform and character, the larger political and economic reality remained unaffected. The fragmentation of authority was an irrefutable fact of American life. It was also an unbearable fact. For, unless authority could be reintegrated, the Brahmins, their institutions, and the American mission as they perceived it would be swept away, if not in an historical cataclysm, than by the collapse of the Brahmins' ability to maintain an adequate sense of personal and group identity. For it was the sense of higher purpose that made Bostonians benevolent. And that sense of higher purpose had been sustained by the hope of its ultimate translation into political leadership. If that hope disappeared, so too would benevolence. And, lacking any sense of mission, the class and the men who comprised it would become indistinguishable from the striving masses, governed only by self-interest and passion.

PART III

The Reintegration of Authority and the Organizational Foundation of the National Order

CHAPTER TEN

The Ante-Bellum Period
Prospect and Retrospect

I understand you are preparing to celebrate the "Fourth," tomorrow week. What for? The doings of that day had no reference to the present; and quite half of you are not even descendants of those who were referred to at that day. But I suppose you will celebrate, and will even go so far as to read the Declaration. Suppose, after you read it once in the old-fashioned way, you read it once more with Judge Douglas' version. It will then run thus: "We hold these truths to be self-evident, that all British subjects who were on this continent eight-one years ago, were created equal to all British subjects born and then residing in Great Britain."

And now I appeal to all—to Democrats as well as others—are you really willing that the Declaration shall thus be frittered away?— thus left no more, at most, than an interesting memorial of the dead past?—thus shorn of its vitality and practical value, and left without the germ or even the suggestion of the individual rights of man in it?[1]

Throughout his public life, from his campaign speeches to the people of Sangamon, Illinois in the early 1830s, through his addresses to the Young Men's Lyceum in Springfield in 1837 and to that city's Washingtonian Temperance Society in 1842, to his later exchanges with Stephen Douglas and his statements as President of the United States, Abraham Lincoln's spoken and written works reveal a central theme. This theme focused on the necessity for men to submit themselves to a higher moral law, a moral law that stemmed from more than their immediate interests. And for Lincoln this higher moral law, while generally identified with reason and the need for reason to prevail over "interest, fixed habits, or burning appetites," was more specifically identified with historical progress, and in turn, with the ability of Americans to fulfill the promises made by their Revolutionary forefathers:

> Of our political revolution of '76 we are all justly proud. It has given us a degree of political freedom far exceeding that of any other nation of the earth. In it the world has found a solution of the long-mooted problem as to the capability of man to govern himself. In it was the germ which has vegetated, and is still to grow into the universal liberty of mankind. But, with all these glorious results, past, present, and to come, it had its evils too. It breathed forth famine, swam in blood, and rode in fire; and long, long after, the orphan's cry and the widow's wail continued to break the silence that ensued. These were the price, the inevitable price, paid for the blessings it bought.

> Turn now to the temperance revolution . . . what a noble ally this to the cause of political freedom; with such an aid its march cannot fail to be on and on, till every son of earth shall drink in rich fruition the sorrow-quenching draughts of perfect liberty. Happy day when—all appetites controlled, all poisons subdued, all matter subjected—mind, all conquering mind, shall live and move, the monarch of the world. Glorious consummation! Hail, fall of fury! Reign of reason, all hail![2]

For Lincoln, as for the New Englanders who influenced him and who would, twenty years later, join him in the task of national redemption, political liberty was, in itself, meaningless unless subordinated to a higher moral authority. And he, like them, looked forward to the fulfillment of the nation's moral commitment:

> And when the victory shall be complete,—when there shall be neither a slave nor a drunkard on the earth,—how proud the title of that land which may truly claim to be the birthplace and the cradle of both those revolutions that shall have ended in that victory. How nobly distinguished that people who shall have planted and nurtured to maturity both the political and the moral freedom of their species.[3]

Morality for Lincoln, and for his New England mentors, was not merely the subordination of passion and self-interest to reason. It was grounded,

in his view, in a concept of duty defined not individually, but institutionally. And he specifically identified it with institutions in the private
sector. As he stated in an 1839 speech on Van Buren's proposed subtreasury system, a substitute for the private Bank of the United States:

> We, then, do not say—nor need we say to maintain our proposi-
> tion—that bank officers are more honest than government officers
> selected by the same rule. What we do say is that the interest of
> the sub-treasurer is against his duty, while the interest of the bank
> is on the side of its duty. Take instances. A subtreasurer has in his
> hands one hundred thousand dollars of public money; his duty
> says, "You ought to pay this money over," but his interest says,
> "You ought to run away with this sum, and be a nabob the balance
> of your life." And who that knows anything of human nature
> doubts that in many instances interest will prevail over duty, and
> that the subtreasurer will prefer opulent knavery in a foreign land
> to opulent poverty at home? But how different is it with a bank.
> Besides the government money deposited with it, it is doing busi-
> ness upon a large capital of its own. If it proves faithful to the
> government, it continues its business; if unfaithful, it forfeits its
> charter, breaks up its business, and thereby loses more than it can
> make by seizing upon the government funds in its possession. Its
> interest, therefore, is on the side of duty—is to be faithful to the
> government, and consequently even the dishonest among its man-
> agers have no temptation to be faithless to it. . . . It is because of
> that admirable feature in the bank system which places the interest
> and duty of the depository both on one side; whereas that feature
> can never enter into the subtreasury system. By the latter the in-
> terest of the individuals keeping the public money will wage an
> eternal war with their duty, and in very many instances must be
> victorious.[4]

For Lincoln, morality was more than the subordination of passion and
interest to reason. It also involved the participation of individuals in
institutional structures that normalized such subordination by placing
duty and self-interest on the same side. Lincoln's concept of morality
was utilitarian, but not utilitarian in the sense of considering morality
a rationalization for self-interest. Rather, the utility of morality was
derived from its relation to nature and to a conception of nature as a
revelation of higher purposes. Thus morality was a product of reason,
and reason was revealed by men's effectiveness in pursuing their particular purposes in the material world. Government, from this viewpoint, set interest and duty at cross purposes because the purpose of

the agents of government was to stay in office. Whatever their private morality, they would tend to do whatever they could, however immoral, to be re-elected. The purpose of private corporations and of individuals engaged in productive labor was to earn profits. They could only do so, in the long run, by doing whatever they did—farming, trading, banking, manufacturing—in consonance with nature's laws, by improving their methods and organization and making themselves more perfect instruments for pursuing their particular purposes. They were accountable, in other words, to nature. And by following nature, by observing and understanding natural processes and effectively transforming them into goods and services, private enterprises, both individual and collective, put duty and self-interest on the same side. While actors in the private sector were accountable to the passions of the populace in the sense that the limit of their actions was the will of the consumer, the will of the consumer was governed, ultimately, by his ability to satisfy his passion most fully for the lowest price. Thus by virtue of competition, those producers who satisfied those passions most effectively would be the most successful. And their ability to satisfy needs successfully would be dictated not by popular passion, but by accountability to nature, the understanding of which enabled producers to most effectively serve the public. Accountability to nature, to higher principle, was ensured through competition and through a framework of government and law maximized freedom, and hence competition, in the private sector. This accountability to nature and its higher laws was linked to historical progress and to the fulfillment of America's historic mission by a conception of the Founding Fathers as a group who had, in carrying out and securing the Revolution, established a legal and constitutional framework that maximized the possibilities of individual action, engendered competition, and thereby progressively brought men into greater understanding of and participation in natural law. The violation of nature by the expansion of the power of government into the sphere of private action impeded competition and man's ability to act according to higher principle.

Lincoln's equation of morality and private accountability was a remarkable echo of the viewpoint set forth by Samuel Putnam in his decision in the case of *Harvard College and Massachusetts General Hospital versus Armory* in 1830, the decision which enunciated the Prudent Man Rule:

> . . . it may well be doubted, if more confidence should be reposed in the engagements of the public, than in the promises and conduct of private corporations which are managed by substantial and prudent directors. There is one consideration much in favor of investing

in the stock of private corporations. They are amenable to the law. The holder may pursue his legal remedy and compel them or their officers to do justice. But the government can only be supplicated.[5]

In Putnam's opinion, "substantial and prudent" individuals were far more reliable fiduciaries than public officials, both because their wealth was an indicator of their prudence and because they were accountable, in a way that government and its officials were not, to the public. Putnam repeated this point in considering what constituted a "safe" investment of funds entrusted to a fiduciary:

> Do what you will, the capital is at hazard. If the public funds are resorted to, what becomes of the capital when the credit of the government shall be so much impaired as it was at the close of the late war?

> Investments on mortgage of real estate are not always safe. Its value fluctuates more, perhaps, than the capital of insurance stock.

> Again, the title to real estate, after the most careful investigation, may be involved, and ultimately fail, and so the capital, which was originally supposed to be as firm as the earth itself, will be dissolved.

> All that can be required of a trustee to invest, is, that he shall conduct himself faithfully and exercise a sound discretion. He is to observe how men of prudence, discretion, and intelligence manage their own affairs, not in regard to speculation, but in regard to the permanent disposition of their funds, considering the probable income, as well as the probable safety of the capital to be invested.[6]

For Putnam, as for Lincoln, prudence, duty, and efficiency lay in the private sector, which rendered men accountable to one another, to law, and to nature for their actions. The state, whether through a subtreasury scheme, or through tying the hands of trustees in the investment of funds, could only diminish accountability, and hence morality, rather than increasing it. By the same reasoning, slavery was an evil not because it violated the rights of blacks, but because, through the Fugitive Slave Law and other enactments by the federal government, it had transformed the government into a mechanism for the perpetuation of a "private pecuniary interest" not merely in the states where slavery was legal, but everywhere in the nation. In attempting to make the bondage of the Negro "universal and eternal," the South and its Democratic allies in the North had forced the government into areas of private action. The only answer lay in restoring the state to its proper role.

Lincoln's opposition to slavery was based on the same grounds as his opposition, twenty years earlier, to the Jacksonian Subtreasury scheme:

> A favorite argument in behalf of this scheme is, that it is a divorce of Bank and State, and the creation of an Independent Treasury.

> To this you the committee answer that it will divorce bank and State only to cement a union still more dangerous—the union of political influence with the influence of money—the Executive patronage with the control of the public purse. It will create a treasury, independent (it is true) of the people, and of their representatives, but dependent upon the President, the Secretary of the Treasury, and thousands of subordinate officers, who hold their appointments at the discretion of the President; among whom are to be included numerous secret agents who, under color of examining the accounts of collecting and disbursing officers, may be sent into every part of the Union to operate upon elections. . . .

> In considering their safety, it should be constantly recollected that the owners and managers of banks, when properly regulated by legislative provisions in their charters, like other individuals, interested to transact business securely, are desirous of making and not losing money, and that these circumstances . . . render them, in point of safety, generally, much superior to the Individual agents of the United States.[7]

In Lincoln's mind, the national crisis of the mid-nineteenth century was only incidentally a matter of slavery. Slavery was emblematic of a set of more profound evils that had beset the republic when its political revolution was not accompanied by a moral one. The problem for Lincoln—as it had been for Timothy Dwight, Jeremiah Day, Samuel Atkins Eliot, Oliver Wendell Holmes, and many other Americans since the first decade of the century—was that the promise of American Life had not been realized, that the moral revolution had not taken place. And because it had not, by the 1850s, political liberty itself was endangered.

The challenge posed to Americans by the election of 1800 had not been adequately met. Political authority had, decade after decade, diverged even farther from moral authority. And although the wealthy, learned, and respectable, and those like Lincoln who had come to share their outlook, had managed to associate themselves in the hope of "drawing over the majority to their own side, and then controlling the supreme power in its name," the mass of the American people, a universe of social, economic, and political particles in bewilderingly constant motion, went their own infinitely diverse ways. Attempts to bridge the gap, to articulate the relation between the moral elite and the masses, whether through evangelism, education, benevolent institutions, or moral reform, had been only partially successful. The nation was deeply divided.

Lincoln himself recognized that the divisions were more profound than the obvious sectional, political, or occupational ones. The issue was not whether one favored the South over the North, slavery over freedom, farming over manufacturing, or the city over the country. As he pointed out in his 1856 "Fragment on Sectionalism," the battle over the extension of slavery was only superficially a sectional conflict. Northern Democrats had, in fact, led the efforts of southerners to extend slavery. The fundamental issue was the relation of morality to "immediate, palpable, and immensely great pecuniary interest."[8] And the willingness of individuals to place morality over interests, whether in the sphere of temperance, tariff and banking policy, or the building of railroads—the willingness of individuals to subsume themselves to the collective achievement of nationality in moral terms—was what divided Americans. Lincoln's opposition to slavery was not based on the extent to which it denied Blacks their rights, but on the extent to which the advocates of slavery and popular sovereignty denied the moral principles that made political liberty possible:

> I hate it because it deprives our republican example of its just influence in the world; enables the enemies of free institutions with plausibility to taunt us as hypocrites; causes the real friends of freedom to doubt our sincerity; and especially because it forces so many good men among ourselves into an open war with the very fundamental principles of civil liberty, criticizing the Declaration of Independence, and insisting that there is no right principle of action but self-interest.[9]

As Lincoln took great pains to make clear, in this speech and in many others, the issue was not slavery, or drunkenness, or the national bank. The issue was the relation between "right principle" and "self-interest." And "right principle" was not merely an abstraction, but a matter of fulfilling the nation's historical mission, the achievement of nationality, and, on the individual level, the subsuming of passion to reason in the form of self-control. For Lincoln, as for the Standing Order of the late eighteenth century, the voice of the people was not the voice of God. And the nation, as it moved towards the Civil War, was divided over this question. Where was the voice of God? What constituted true authority?

By the 1850s, the answer to the question was far less simple than it had been in 1800. By the middle of the century, religion had become a babel of creeds; economic life, even in Boston, competitive and tumultuous; politics, a matter of pandering to the lowest common denominator. Assertions of moral superiority, even on the part of a powerful and wealthy minority, were hopeless. For cultural and professional elites, even if largely meritocratic in character, were, by the very fact that they were elites, condemned to political ineffectiveness. A half-century of failure and the dying off of the older generation of Revolutionary and Federal worthies was, moreover, bringing about a crisis of faith among the descendants of the Standing Order and those who had been caught up in their broad-ranging organizational efforts to redeem the nation. This crisis of faith not only involved the efficacy of institutions, as seen in the troubled meditations of Eliot and Holmes, but also involved doubts about the theological and political doctrines on which the Standing Order and Federalism had been founded. Holmes, the grandson of Ezra Stiles, satirized the failure of Puritanism in "The Deacon's One Hoss Shay" and Harriet Beecher Stowe, daughter of the Reverend Lyman Beecher, began to criticize the "horror of an autocratic God who had punished the whole of humanity for Adam's sin and whom meither good works nor piety could hope to dissuade from His sentence."[10] If authority did not lie in religion or politics, where did it reside? If there were principles higher than self-interest, how could one ascertain them? The first fifty years of the nineteenth century had created an unbearable tension between the guardians of "higher principle" and the hard realities of American society and politics. The failure of Puritan theology and Puritan social forms demanded more than an intellectual response. For far more was at stake than the survival of a body of ideas. Rather, as Lincoln had pointed out in his speeches, the survival of the American mission and American institutions was on the line. The validity of higher principles could only be demonstrated in the world. And yet how could it, when the world, at least as defined politically, rejected them?

These questions could not be answered by ideas alone. They could only be answered by events. The Civil War would give those who adhered to higher principles an opportunity to do their work in the world, to reestablish their connection to the masses in a way that the masses would recognize. And the War would be accompanied by a body of ideas, social readings of the work of English naturalist Charles Darwin, that would articulate the relation between individual actions and collective processes on the commonly respected rhetorical ground of science. Although some would read Darwin as a justification of unrestrained individualism of the Jeffersonian and Jacksonian variety, others, particularly the proponents of higher principles as defined by a particular class of persons and a particular set of institutions, could credibly point out that science and history justified private authority, as represented by the benevolently wealthy, over public authority.

The Civil War would change everything. It would give the old Federalist class an opportunity to demonstrate its capacity for heroic leadership in the national interest. The heroism of men like Robert Gould Shaw, the "College Colonel" and the "Slain Collegians" whom Melville celebrated in his war poems, would be emblematic not only of the new public regard for "men of family," but also of that class's reinvigorated self-confidence. Wealth was the goal for which most American strove. The rich would be admired rather than suspected. The corporation, as a means to wealth, would become an unquestioned part of American life. Learning, too, would be admired as a way to wealth, for the war, more than anything else, would demonstrate the very practical virtues of high technology.

By 1874, when Harvard's young president, Charles W. Eliot was asked to justify the private institution, he was able to assert ringingly the ideal of cultural stewardship in a way that his father could not. He began his defense of the tax exemption enjoyed by private eleemosynary institutions by rhetorically turning Daniel Webster's Dartmouth College argument on its head:

> The property which has been set apart for religious, educational, and charitable uses is not to be thought of or dealt with as if it were private property; for it is completely unavailable for all the ordinary uses of property, so long as the trusts endure. It is like the work of the city or state, and so cannot be reckoned among the public assets; it is irrecoverable and completely unproductive.[11]

In asserting that the public use of private institutions rendered them something other than private property, Eliot was by no means suggesting that the state had a right to interfere with them. For such interference would not only discourage private benevolence by removing the certainty that benefactions would be applied to objects designated by the donors; it would also, as a result, add materially to the public expenditure. For without private institutions of charity, the state would have to pay in full for services which heretofore had cost it no more than a tax examption.

But the real justification for these institutions was not financial; it stemmed from their special character. They were different from both the state and private economic enterprise, but essential to both:

> The reason for treating these institutions in an exceptional manner

is, that having no selfish object in view, or purpose of personal gain, they contribute to the welfare of the State. Their function is largely a public function; their work is done, primarily indeed, for individuals, but ultimately for the public good. It is not enough to say of churches and colleges that they contribute to the welfare of a State; they are necessary to the existence of a free State. They form and mold the public character; and that public character is the foundation of everything which is precious in the State, including even its material prosperity.[12]

Eliot's introduction of the role of institutions in forming character was an elaboration of his father's discussion of their role in cultivating self-control. But in the post-war period, Eliot, with the heroism of the slain collegians resonating through the public consciousness, was able to give the term a far greater degree of social specificity. While character, like self-control and wealth itself, was available to any one who chose to strive to develop it, it tended to be most effectively cultivated by certain people in certain organizational contexts:

> To develop noble human character is the end for which States themselves exist, and civil liberty is not a good in itself, but only a means to that good end. The work of churches and institutions of education is a direct work upon the human character. The material prosperity of every improving community is a fruit of character; for it is energetic, honest, and sensible men that make prosperous business, and not prosperous business that makes men. Who have built up the manufactures and trade of this bleak and sterile Massachusetts? A few men of singular sagacity, integrity, and courage, backed by hundreds of thousands of men and women of common intelligence, courage, and honesty. The roots of the prosperity are in the intelligence, courage, and honesty. Massachusetts today owes its mental and moral characteristics, and its wealth, to eight generations of people who have loved and cherished Church, School, and College.[13]

Eliot had brought the ideology of benevolence full-circle and had devised a means of recombining private charity and public stewardship. For he succeeded in adding to the traditional argument that character was the fruit of cultural institutions the notion that the institutions themselves were the creations of men of character. The "singular sagacity, integrity, and courage" that created not only the institutions, but the private wealth that had sustained them, was not the possession of everyone. It was the property of a few men, an elite, capable of mobilizing the "common intelligence and honesty" of the masses. By the third quarter of the nineteenth century, the traditional doctrine of cultural steward-ship, which had lost its grounding in public authority and divine sanc-tion, had finally reanchored itself in the indisputable authority of Dar-winian science and liberal political economy. The Federalist defenders of respectability, education, property, and religion had become social democrats.

Neither Eliot nor his allies at Harvard and elsewhere had any illusions about the ease with which they could proceed from their ideas about the resynthesis of authority to the reality of a national order. Thanks to the war and to their social reading of Darwin, they could redefine their ideas about the locus of authority, shifting it from politics and religion to science, the world of matter in which the voice of God ex-pressed itself far more authoritatively than through the voice of the people. In concrete social and political terms, this shift altered the public perception of the relation between wealth, ideas, and power. The war was a lesson. Darwinism was a text. But as Darwinists, Eliot and his allies could see that the historical process was open-ended. Redemption, even in secular terms, was never sure. And the most that one could do in seeking to be the instrument of higher principles was to institution-alize one's relation to them by creating situations in which people could study science—social science, economic science, political science, the whole realm of matter included both basic chemical and biological pro-cesses as well as human ones—and could translate what they found into organizational reality. Eliot and the men of his generation had succeeded in resynthesizing morality and matter. But the key to the resynthesis was the institutional context in which one studied matter. And as the first fifty years of the nineteenth century had shown, that institutional context would have to be extended out into the whole of American life if it was to become genuinely effective. The War, the text, and the private institution were only the starting points of the process of realizing the promise of American life.

CHAPTER ELEVEN

The Civil War and the Moral Revolution: The Emergence of a National Elite

I am therefore of the opinion that when a democratic people engages in a war after a long peace, it incurs much more risk of defeat than any other nation; but it ought not be cast down by its reverses, for the chances of success for such an army are increased by the duration of the war. When a war has at length by its long continuance, roused the whole community from their peaceful occupations and ruined their minor undertakings, the same passions that made them attach so much importance to the maintenance of peace will be turned to arms. War, after it had destroyed all modes of speculation, because itself the great and sole speculation, to which all the ardent and ambitious desires that equality engenders are exclusively directed. Hence it is that the selfsame democratic nations that are so reluctant to engage in hostilities sometimes perform prodigious achievements when once they have taken the field.

As the war attracts more and more of public attention and is seen to create high reputations and great fortunes in a short space of time, the choicest spirits of the nation enter the military profession; all the enterprising, proud, and martial minds, no longer drawn solely of the aristocracy, but of the whole country. A long war produces upon a democratic army the same effects that a revolution produces upon a people; it breaks through regulations and allows extraordinary men to rise above the common level.[1]

The Civil War was welcomed by those individuals and groups who saw in it an opportunity to bring about the moral revolution in American life, that final fulfillment of the covenant that Americans had made in undertaking the political revolution of the eighteenth century. Those who viewed the coming crisis in this way included not only the Boston institutionalists, who were frustrated by their inability to transform benevolence into public authority, and the young Brahmins, who languished in search of careers that would enable them to join morality and utility, but also the vast network of individuals who, directly or indirectly, had been influenced by the activities of the evangelical united front. This influence was both general, in that it induced people to view their behavior and their relation to society and nature in a distinctive way, and specific, in that the models of character they emulated and the goals towards which they directed their activities were associated with particular persons who were members of particular social groups. Because of the specificity of the role models and institutions that influenced those within New England's moral net, the redemption of the nation was viewed, even by those who were not yet a part of the elite, as being closely tied to the redemption of the elite and its ability to reconnect political, moral, and economic authority. The rehabilitation of the Standing Order, in other words, was identified with national redemption, not only in the eyes of the upper classes themselves, but also in the eyes of those who aspired to become part of them or who looked to them for leadership.

This interpretation of the war as an opportunity to complete the American Revolution through rehabilitating its class of natural leaders is clear in the writing of Thomas Wentworth Higginson, who compiled the biographies of Harvard men killed in the war:

> The work not being a history, but a collection of biographies, historic interest has been kept subordinate to the exhibition of personal character. . . .

> If there is any one inference to be fairly drawn from these memoirs, as a whole, it is this: that there is no class of men in this republic from whom the response of patriotism comes more promptly and surely than from its most highly educated class. All those delusions which pass current in Europe, dating back to De Tocqueville, in regard to some suppressed torpor or alienation prevailing among cultivated Americans, should be swept away forever by this one book. The lives here narrated undoubtedly represent on the whole those classes, favored in worldly fortune, which would elsewhere form an aristocracy—with only an admixture, such as all aristocracies now show, of what are called self-made men. It is surprising

to notice how large is the proportion of Puritan and Revolutionary descent. . . .[2]

And the war was not merely the testing-ground of individual character and of the upper class, but also of the institutions that class had created for the purpose of inculcating character.

> And if there is another inference that may justly be deduced from these pages, it is this: that our system of collegiate education must be on the whole healthy and sound, when it sends forth a race of young men who are prepared, at the most sudden summons, to transfer their energies to a new and alien sphere, and to prove the worth of their training in wholly unexpected applications. So readily have the Harvard graduates done this, and with such noble and unquestioned success, that I do not see how anyone can read these memoirs without being left with fresh confidence in our institutions, in the American people, and indeed in human nature itself. . . .s[3]

The Civil War, in Higginson's view, not only justified the Brahmins and their institutional activities; it also justified those who participated in and supported those institutions and their proprietors. The war enabled the Brahmins to broaden their interests beyond Boston and its surrounding territories and to exert claims to national leadership and authority; it also enabled the nation to look to Boston and its leaders as the true stewards of the public interest. The future, as Holmes had suggested, lay with those cities capable of extending their "suction range" outward to the nation. The future of the nation lay in its willingness to place itself within the range of the metropolis and to permit its capital, talent, and beauty to be drained to locations where they might serve the greatest good of the greatest number. Thus Higginson after the war, like Holmes and Eliot before its outbreak, linked the survival of his class to the success of its institutions, and the success of those institutions to their ability to reach out to the nation.

Because Harvard was a metropolitan institution, it tended to view the Civil War as a vindication of metropolitan institutions and a mandate for the extension of metropolitan influence into the nation. For institutions like Yale and Princeton, however, the war was viewed as a tragedy. While Harvard issued numerous publications of the service records of its graduates and non-graduates and constructed a memorial hall on the campus, Yale and Princeton, with their more national constituencies, responded in a much more subdued fashion. Neither published service records of its graduates or erected memorials until the first years of the twentieth century.[4] Just as they had devoted their efforts before the war to the creation of a national culture and the training of a national moral leadership, so, when the war was over, they welcomed southern alumni to their commencements and encouraged them to send their sons North for schooling.[5]

It would be a mistake to suppose, however, that because Yale did not exult over the northern cause that it was indifferent to it. The alumni of both Harvard and Yale colleges served in the northern armies in proportions higher than the general population: of the 14.8 million white males between 15 and 50 years of age in 1860, 2.6 million—17.6 percent—served in the northern armed forces; of the 1482 living Harvard College graduates of the classes of 1841–1861, 359—or 24.2 percent—served the Union cause; of the 1900 Yale College graduates of the classes 1841–61, 432—or 22.7 percent—fought for the North.[6] From the classes graduating between 1855 and 1861, both Harvard and Yale sent between a third and a half of their living graduates. The service records of the graduates of the colleges associated with Yale in the evangelical united front—Dartmouth, Brown, Williams, Amherst, Colby, Middlebury, and Bowdoin—show levels of participation in the war comparable to Yale's. Princeton alumni did not serve in great numbers in the Union armies, but if one adds in the number who served the Confederacy, the figures closely resemble those of the New England schools. Only Columbia, which had the least developed national outlook during the first half of the century and which seldom either attracted students or sent graduates beyond the boundaries of New York State, showed a military service record well below the national average. Moreover, the representation of the northeastern states in the federal armies was impressive: of 120 staff officers who were not West Point graduates, 93 were natives of the New England states, New York, and Pennsylvania; of 134 cavalry officers, 73 were natives of the northeast.[7] The graduates of the New England colleges were represented among the officers of the federal armies in proportions far exceeding their share of the general population.[8] And the significance of the graduates of New England colleges in states outside of New England is attested to by the extent to which they dominate the civilian appointments from non-New England states.[9] Certainly, as Higginson asserted, the educated classes had acquitted themselves admirably in the war, contributing more than their share to saving the Union.

But the cause meant different things to different groups. Because Harvard alumni overwhelmingly lived in eastern Massachusetts, men like Higginson viewed the war as a test of Boston and its Brahmin-dominated institutions. For institutions with more scattered alumni and students who had been more widely recruited, the war was seen as a national tragedy, a painful sundering of bonds of friendship and kin-

Figure 5

Percent of Graduates of Harvard, Yale, Dartmouth, Brown, Princeton, and Columbia, Classes of 1841–1861, living in 1862, who served in the Union Armies, 1861–1865.

Class year	Harvard	Yale	Dartmouth	Brown	Princeton	Columbia
1841	15%	4%	12%	32%	5%	6%
1842	6%	6%	10%	—	8%	4%
1843	13%	11%	14%	4%	—	—
1844	13%	14%	12%	5%	8%	—
1845	18%	10%	10%	13%	6%	—
1846	14%	7%	10%	14%	7%	—
1847	14%	18%	2%	18%	11%	4%
1848	15%	12%	9%	8%	9%	8%
1849	8%	13%	21%	8%	11%	3%
1850	15%	15%	14%	14%	9%	4%
1851	25%	18%	11%	11%	4%	14%
1852	26%	28%	15%	18%	6%	12%
1853	17%	28%	18%	17%	14%	—
1854	21%	22%	17%	16%	15%	13%
1855	25%	33%	18%	14%	12%	5%
1856	29%	25%	19%	13%	11%	5%
1857	34%	32%	30%	13%	16%	11%
1858	35%	35%	30%	28%	21%	12%
1859	41%	37%	30%	33%	20%	6%
1860	44%	49%	32%	34%	11%	23%
1861	56%	42%	35%	50%	8%	19%

ship. Typical of the response to the war at institutions like Yale and Princeton was the address of General Randall L. Gibson, a graduate of the Yale Class of 1853, on the occasion of his fifteenth reunion in 1868:

> General Gibson thanked the instructors in the college for the influences of their teaching. "There has never been a moment since I left Yale," he said, "in which my feelings toward my own classmates and the college were not warm and hearty. I look forward to the day when the old flag will wave in harmony over all the land. (Cheers.) Whatever I, for one, can do to inspire among people hopefulness in the future and a faith in the National Government, will be done.[10]

Again and again in class reports and reunion speeches through the late 1860s and early 1870s, when "waving the bloody shirt" was the nation's most popular political pastime and relations between North and South were at their most bitter, similar conciliatory and nationally-oriented sentiments were coiced by both northern and southern alumni:

> At alumni dinner [in 1876], after Swayne [a former Union general, Yale '56] had finished, Depew remarked to President Porter that the alumni would probably like to hear from Colonel Finlay who had fought on the other side. General Swayne seized his crutches, and meeting Finlay, escorted him to the stand. The house came down in thunders of applause, reminding one of a mammoth biennial jubilee with every hard feeling over and everybody glad of it.[11]

It would be a mistake to suppose, however, that Yale and Princeton men viewed the war merely as a regrettable interruption of friendships with old chums. They too viewed the war as a cause. But where Bostonians viewed it as a test of Boston, the graduates of the evangelical institutions viewed it as a test of the scattered national network of which they were a part, and as a test of virtue. Although some Bostonians had been prominently identified with abolitionism, with the Whigs, and with the rise of the Republican Party, the real core of organized nationalism—the lyceum movement, the temperance societies, and abolitionism—had been part of the evangelical network, the Congregationalist-Presbyterian constituency that, from the 1780s on, had spread westward through New York, Pennsylvania, Ohio, Indiana, Illinois, California, and into the southern states. The ministers who had set forth the moral framework in which the western settlers acted were either graduates of Yale, Princeton, and the other evangelical northeastern colleges, or graduates of such institutions as Oberlin, Kenyon, Western Reserve, Wabash, and others, whose faculties and governing boards were dominated by New Englanders. Similarly, the lawyers and politicians who had set up the governments of these states and who had either ensured, or struggled to ensure, that they remained free of slavery were, to a very considerable extent, either graduates of evangelical colleges, communicants of Congregational or Presbyterian churches, or strongly influenced, as Abraham Lincoln was, by those groups and their institutions. These people saw the cause of the union less as an opportunity for extending regional hegemony than as a matter of morality. While they were willing to join forces with Bostonians whose motives may have been less elevated, it would be a great mistake to identify them too closely with the Boston sensibility.

To say that one group viewed the conflict as a test of virility and another group viewed it as a moral contest is not to deny the possibility that there was a common social and ideological meeting ground between the two. In fact, their divergent needs appear to have dovetailed, the network supplying Bostonians with a moral activism to cloak their social anxieties, the Bostonians giving an aristocratic cast to a group that had, through migration westward, put itself off from sources of social legitimacy.[12] This combination of moral activism and social elitism seems to have been a major source of the efforts of organizations like the United States Sanitary Commission.[13] Dominated by graduates of the New England colleges, the Commission was, according to George M. Frederickson, seen as a means of redefining the claims of the old Standing Order to national specifications:

> If the commission was directed by a conservative elite, the question remains as to what these men hoped to gain from the creation of a gigantic philanthropic organization. It would of course be cynical to ignore Christian charity and *noblesse oblige* as motives of action. Yet there is evidence that the commission's work was regarded not only as a duty, but as a heaven-sent opportunity for educating the nation. In a book published in 1863 as a semi-official statement of goals and purposes, Katherine Prescott Wormeley described the commission as more than an instrument for doing a necessary job; it was "a great teacher . . . guiding the national instincts; showing the value of order, and the dignity of work. . . . It has within it the means for a national education of ideas as well as of instincts." Statements of this kind suggest that the work of the commission was as much an attempt to revise the American system of values as to relieve the suffering of the wounded.[14]

It was also, moreover, a primary vehicle for promoting the value of institutionally-oriented expertise. Its hostility to unpaid volunteers in preference to trained professionals, usually graduates of Ivy League medical schools, was well known, and meshed with its overall preoccupation with subordination, order, and discipline:

> Men like Bellows, Strong, and Stille, welcomed the sufferings and sacrifices of the hour because they served the cause of discipline in a broader sense than demanded by purely military requirements. An unruly society, devoted to individual freedom, might be in the process of learning that discipline and subordination were good in themselves, and the commissioners wanted to play their role in teaching this lesson.[15]

It was the old organicism of the Standing Order recast in bureaucratic terms. It showed the political possibilities that institutions offered, especially when the friends of institutions could gain a monopoly over some vital service.

1. The Army as a Model of Organization

While the Sanitary Commission was an important organization, it was on the whole, largely an affair of women and intellectuals. It was, by its very preoccupation with functional specificity and trained professionalism, exclusive. The organization that both absorbed the majority of elite energies and inspired the greatest popular loyalty, while at the same time teaching the lessons of subordination and discipline, was the army itself, with the support services that enabled it to fight.

We have all been taught to think of the Civil War as the "first modern war." We tend, nonetheless, to visualize the conflict as a rather quaint affair. The photographs of Mathew Brady and the writings of Stephen Crane and Ambrose Bierce have fixed a misleading image in our minds: funny little locomotives with their trains of wooden cars, frozen-faced politicians holding their poses for *cartes-de-visite*, officers clowning for photographers, dead soldiers with the muskets lying beside them, different from their Revolutionary predecessors only in their uniforms. But if one really wants to get a sense of what the war was, as a effort of massed-humanity, he should obtain a copy of F. H. Dyer's *Compendium of the War of the Rebellion*. In three fat volumes it attempts to provide an organizational and statistical summary of the Union forces during the conflict. Just flipping through it, attempting to reconstruct the organizational features of the armies during the period 1860–1865, communicates, far more than words can, the incredible scale of the war effort. It had no precedents.

Two and a half-million men served in the Union forces between 1860 and 1865—almost one in every five men of military age living in 1860. Imagine the magnitude of the task of recruiting, training, equipping, feeding, and transporting such numbers under the conditions of the period! The entire federal government in 1861 had contained only ten thousand civilian employees; the regular army was only sixteen thousand strong.[16] Yet within a period of four years, with no large-scale organizational experience, the government would be coordinating the activities of millions of men and handling an annual budget whose expenditures had risen from sixty-six million dollars in 1861 to 1.3 billion only four years later.[17] How did the government, given its small number of personnel, its lack of experience, and the primitive state of technology, manage to handle such vast masses of men, equipment and money? How, moreover, was it able to do so over so wide a geographical area, ranging from Pennsylvania and Ohio in the north to Kansas and New Mexico in the west?

The organizational precedent did not come from government. While governmental administration had evolved since 1800, growing *volens-nolens* with the geographical boundaries of the nation, it was, as Leonard

White notes, in a state of stagnation: "The administrative art was, in fact, obscured by the art of politics."[18] While a national civil service was off to a promising start during the first two decades of the nineteenth century, the election of Andrew Jackson, with his contempt for educated expertise and his distrust of large-scale organizations, curtailed the development of efficient administrative practices and a trained civil service.[19] The corruption, jobbery, and confusion that characterized the first years of the war effort were the legacy of the "Age of the Common Man."

There is no simple answer to the question of how the Union was able to organize the first modern "total war." Because the task was without precedent, many of the organizational elements of the war effort were developed by trial and error over a period of years, not assuming their final form until the conflict was nearly over. Because no one at the outset of the war had imagined that victory would take four years to achieve, the North proceeded at first along traditional lines to recruit, equip, and train its army. For manpower, the Union depended on its small regular army, state-raised volunteer regiments, and private military companies.[20] Leadership was politically recruited from the ranks of the state militia bodies and politically ambitious members of the legal and business communities (many of whom had no military experience).[21] Supplies were assembled through a corrupt and chaotic system of private contracting.[22] The first year of the war was an unmitigated military and organizational disaster. An army had been raised; but it consisted largely of untrained civilians on short-term, three to nine months enlistments; it was commanded by politically-appointed officers with little or no military experience; it had neither adequate uniforms nor standarized up-to-date weaponry with which to fight.[23] The Union army of 1861 was, as one observer at Bull Run remarked, "an armed mob."

Ironically, the South suffered none of these problems. Its civil administration was dominated from the outset by military professionals like Jefferson Davis (West Point, 1823) who recognized both the preeminence of the military task faced by the Confederacy and the value of expertise unhampered by politics. The ability of the South to come so close to victory in spite of its underdeveloped industrial base and its smaller population had much to do with its early settlement of fundamental issues of policy-making and military organization.[24]

As the war moved into its second year and as its scope, scale, and probable duration exceeded the surmises of even the most pessimistic, new modes of organization began to emerge, based neither on a heritage of government organization, nor on the arts of war as cultivated by the regular army. Rather, the development of centralized and coordinated civil and military administrative structures and the effective use of new technologies of communication, transportation, and armament depended on a body of men whose administrative experience included not only military and government service, but also experience in the most highly developed branches of the private sector.

2. War and the Culture of Organization

As the events of 1861 showed, superiority of numbers and industrial capacity were not enough. The ability to coordinate manpower and resources was the key to the Union's ability to prevail on the field of battle. The fact that the new organizational modes emerged through trial and error should not be taken to suggest that they were developed *ab novo*. For certain essential elements for the creation of large-scale organizations were already extant by 1860. The first and perhaps most important of these elements was the existence of a pool of men socialized to universalistic values of competence and generalized leadership ability. The second element required that this pool of men have some real experience in administering large-scale geographically extensive organizations. The third element involved the necessity that these men share an awareness of the utility of the new modes of transportation, communication, and administration that had developed since the 1820. As it happened, most of these men were in civilian life when the war broke out. But the war served as a catalyst, uniting their diverse experiences and bringing them forward to the highest positions in the civil and military administration of the war effort.

The first element, the pool of universalistically socialized leaders, was largely the product of the private colleges—Harvard, Yale, Princeton, and the network of lesser institutions founded and staffed by their graduates. West Point, the United States Military Academy, was also an important contributor to this pool. Founded and fostered by graduates of Yale, Harvard, and Dartmouth, both through the membership of its Board of Visitors (which included educational reformers like George Ticknor) and through networks of post-graduate friendships between the Academy's staff and their former classmates in the world of higher education, West Point had kept abreast of the reforms in the ante-bellum American colleges.[25]

Although its curriculum did not include the classics, it retained the prescriptive elements of early nineteenth-century college curricula—and had the same character-forming goal in mind. As the *Annual Report of the Board of Visitors for 1830* stated:

Inheriting from our varied ancestry the discordant characteristics of every people on the globe, it yet remains the form of a specific and all prevading character for the American nation; nor do we conceive of any surer method of stamping upon the yet glowing wax a yet more majestic form, than by sending into every district young men emphatically the children of our country, trained to the manly exercise of arms, and imbued with the tastes of science and literature; instructed in the principles and action of our political system, and the living exemplar from which sound education may rear the social edifice.[26]

Beyond sharing the character goals of Yale and Harvard, West Point, under the Dartmouth graduate Sylvanus Thayer, adopted the parental system of discipline, abolishing fagging, introducing the merit system, and controlling cadets by persuasion and example rather than by threats and punishment.[27] Like Yale, West Point drew a national constituency. And just as Yale's graduates were progressively less inclined to enter the ministry so, for the first fifty years of the Academy's existence, a third to a half of every graduating class went into civilian life within a short span after graduation. West Point, in other words, while providing its students with the rudiments of military training and discipline, was functioning like any other New England-oriented collegiate institution.

The postgraduate experience of this pool of men comprised the second element needed for mounting the war effort: direct or indirect experience in administering large-scale organizations. On leaving college, a substantial proportion of men went into two fields, law and business.[28] While the law did not usually provide direct managerial experience, it certainly brought a great many attorneys into close familiarity with the problems of corporate administration. Lawyers wrote the charters and by-laws of the new manufacturing, communications, and transportation companies; they defended the interests of their corporate clients before state and federal courts. In addition to their legal duties, many lawyers served as directors and administrators of corporate enterprises. Of the sixty leading railroad executives of the period 1845–1890 studied by Thomas Cochran, fourteen (23 percent) were lawyers.[29] This group included the officers of the most important early trunk lines, including the New York Central, the Boston and Albany, the New York, New Haven & Hartford, and the western railroads in which Boston entrepreneurs had interests.[30]

The significance of railroads as contributors to the administrative expertise of the ante-bellum period lies in the fact that they posed, from an organizational perspective, a unique problem.[31] Unlike mills, mines, and factories, railroads were not concentrated in a single location; by their very nature, their physical plants and personnel were spread out across considerable distances. Further, they employed far larger work forces: the largest textile mills of the 1850s hired no more than eight hundred hands at a time; the New York and Erie Railroad during the same decade had nearly four thousand workers. In addition, a railroad differed from other types of transportation enterprises in that it not only owned and maintained its right of way, but also operated the equipment that ran on it. As Arthur Twining Hadley, later president of Yale, wrote in the 1890s in an essay on "The Railway in Its Business Relations":

> People at first thought of the railroad as merely an improved high-way, which could charge tolls like a turnpike or canal, and on which the public should run cars of its own, independent of the railroad company itself. In many cases, especially in England, long sheets of tolls were published, based on the model of canal charters, and naming rates under which the use of the road-bed should be free to all. This plan soon proved inpracticable. If independent owners tried to run trains over the same line, it involved a danger of collision and loss of economy. The former evil could perhaps be avoided; the latter could not. The advantages of unity of management were so great that a road running its own trains could do a much larger business at lower rates than if ownership and carriage were kept separate. The old plan was as impracticable as it would be for a manufacturing company to own the buildings and engines, while each worker owned the particular piece of machinery which he handled. Almost all the technical advantages of the new methods would be lost for a lack of system.[32]

The combination of road-bed ownership with rolling stock and traffic management presented unique administrative problems:

> Their day-to-day operations required decisions that were far more numerous and far more complicated than those for the working of a mill, a canal, or a steamship line. Unlike a textile company, whose group of mills could be viewed within half an hour, a railroad was spread over hundreds of miles and included a wide variety of ac-tivities and facilities—such as shops, terminals, stations, ware-houses, office buildings, bridges, telegraph lines, and so forth. . . . Weeks would be required to view all its men and equipment. So every day, railroad managers had to make decisions controlling the activities of many men to whom they rarely talked or even ever saw.

> Moreover, these operational decisions had to be made much more quickly and involved more crucial responsibilities than did most decisions made in the management of a textile factory, canal, or steam riverboat. The condition of the freight and the safety and, indeed, the very lives of the passengers depended on continuous, effective decision-making. . . .[33]

The mills and factories might be able to tolerate a modicum of nepotism and incompetence in their management, as Ayer's pamphlet on the Massachusetts textile industry suggests. But railroads required not only a high level of competence, but also innovative managerial structures. By the 1850s, the railroads were, of necessity, at the forefront of administrative innovation.

Where did these innovations come from? Who devised solutions to the problems of long-range planning and coordination of manpower and resources over large geographical areas? While certain solutions were derived from the work of the British railway pioneers, the greater part of the problems appear to have been solved by men with collegiate and, most importantly, military training. As primitive as the military art may have been as practiced in America, it was the only body of knowledge that dealt with the control of masses of men, with large budgets, and with efficient allocation of resources. By the late 1820s, as West Point graduates faced ever dimmer chances of promotion in the peacetime army, ever larger numbers of them began seeking places in civilian life. With their engineering skills (West Point was the only school teaching civil engineering before 1828), many graduates found jobs surveying routes for and ultimately working in the administrations of the earliest railroads. Among the West Pointers between 1800 and 1830 who worked as railroad pioneers were the presidents of the Hudson River, Panama, Philadelphia & Baltimore, Burlington & Missouri River, and Central of Georgia lines. West Point men served as the superintendents (chief operating officers) of the Baltimore & Ohio, Pennsylvania, and other smaller lines. The number of graduates who served as chief engineers for the early railroads is also impressive. Compared to the colleges, West Point supplied the greatest number of early railroad managers, followed most closely by Yale.[34] While higher education was not essential for early railroad men, it certainly seems to have been an important characteristic, especially from a technical standpoint.

By the 1850s, the legal and technical experts in the corporate world were drawing steadily closer to the business community, especially to bankers and brokers with access to large amounts of capital. Railroad building and, by the decade preceding the Civil War, railroad consolidation were requiring ever greater amounts of capital and new means of raising it. The development of investment banking in Boston, New York, and Philadelphia stemmed directly from this need.[35] Not only did involvement in railroads stimulate new means of mobilizing capital and new centers of financial power; more importantly, it drew more and more members of the business community into familiarity with the new forms of corporate organization and management. Most important of all, it began to bring New York, Boston, and Philadelphia financiers into cooperation with one another, laying the foundations for a national financial community.

Taken together, the college-trained corporate lawyers, railroad engineers and managers, financiers, and their less formally educated brethren who were brought up through the corporate ranks, receiving in the process a thorough managerial training, constituted by 1860 an administrative cadre whose skills would prove invaluable in organizing the war effort. A culture of organization had been developing, almost unseen, under the apparent chaos of Jacksonian politics and economics. Like the Boston philanthropists and patricians described by Samuel Atkins Eliot and Oliver Wendell Holmes, these men would not find their true vocations in the national destiny until the war came.

3. Organizing the War

After a year of military disasters, administrative incompetence, and incredible corruption, President Lincoln, himself a lawyer with extensive experience in representing corporations, was forced to take matters in hand. Early in 1862 he brought forward two men who would place the war effort on a sound organizational basis: Edwin M. Stanton and Henry W. Halleck. Stanton was a Pittsburg lawyer who had served as Attorney General in the waning days of Buchanan administration.[36] Educated at Kenyon College and in private study in law offices, he had moved from small-town lawyering to the "Iron City" in the 1840s. By the mid-1850s, he was one of the best paid lawyers in the state, including among his clients the New York and Erie Railroad and the McCormick Reaper Company. Although Stanton was a vocal critic of the Lincoln administration and a member of the Democratic Party, the President, dismayed by the incompetence of Simon Cameron, appointed him Secretary of War in January of 1862. On taking office, he found a situation of almost total disorder:

In the development of the government's institutions before 1861 the war office had been either an insignificant clerical convenience for army officers to employ or else an annoying obstacle for them to circumvent or overcome. The few pre-war secretaries who had tried to improve on this pattern had been evaded or merely out-waited by the military galaxy.

. . . the head of the Army's bureaucracy plodded along in accus-tomed paths, binding up the growing regiments in rigid tentacles of bookkeepers' techniques, while spoilsmen fattened on the great profits available from the nation's emergency needs.

. . . the field commanders remained virtually independent of the civilian Secretary and the President. Generals such as Fremont and McClellan, enjoying strong political backing from their states and from congressional cliques, were taking matters of policy into their own hands.[37]

Stanton apparently recognized that more than armies were necessary to win the war, that high-level coordination and, most important, the establishment of clear lines of authority between the military and civilian bureaucracies were needed. He acted quickly to assemble a civilian and military staff to survey and make order out of the situation. His closest civilian aides included lawyers Peter H. Watson and Albert E. H. John-son, journalist Charles A. Dana (Harvard, 1839), and corporate execu-tives Thomas A. Scott, vice-president of the Pennsylvania Railroad, and Edward Sewell Sanford, President of the American Telegraph Com-pany.[38] In addition, he successfully sponsored the passage of a bill placing the nation's railroads and telegraph companies under federal control. And he formed a council of military advisors known as the "Aulic Council." In addition to the retired General Ethan A. Hitchcock, the council included the heads of the major branches of the army: or-dinance, quartermaster-general, commisary-general, surgeon-general, adjutant-general, paymaster-general and inspector-general. By March of 1862, the basic outlines of a centralized, civilian-dominated admin-istration for the war effort were beginning to emerge.

But the most difficult and important task, the coordination of civilian and military bureaucracies, remained. As the general-in-chief, Mc-Clellan became increasingly difficult to control, and as it became ap-parent that he, like most of the generals, was totally unaware of the necessity for cooperation, coordination, and sharing of resources— much less the possibilities offered by the railroad and the telegraph— Stanton began to cast about for someone somewhat capable of reorg-anizing the military. His eye fell upon Henry Halleck, whose command of the Department of Missouri had led to the most important Union victories of early 1862, the capture of Fort Donelson and the beginning of the northern push into Tennessee.

Henry Halleck, like Stanton himself, was very much a part of the culture of organization. Brought up in the New England-settled "burned over district" of western New York, he had attended West Point in the late 1830's, graduating in 1839, third in his class.[39] He stayed in the army until 1854, teaching engineering at West Point, repairing fortifications, serving in the Mexican War, and writing one of the first American contributions to military theory, *Elements of Military Art and Science*. Although appointed a Professor of Engineering in the Lawrence Scientific School at Harvard in 1848, he declined the offer, going instead to California where, in spite of his military responsibilities, he became actively involved in the territory's political and economic life. In 1850, he became director-general of the largest mercury mine in the United States, the New Almaden Quicksilver Mine. By 1853, he had established himself as a member of the California bar. By 1855, he was serving as President of the Pacific and Atlantic Railroad. His interest in corporate matters was more than practical. Through the fifties he continued to write and translate works bearing on military, legal and corporate subjects. These included a new edition of his *Elements of Military Science* (1858), *A Collection of Mining Law of Spain and Mexico* (1859), *De Fooz on the Law of Mines* (1860), and a textbook on international law. Halleck— or "old Brains" as he was known to his soldiers—was an extraordinary man. At the same time, his career was, in its broad outlines, typical of the West Point graduates who left the army, went into law and corporate activity, and then enlisted in the war effort, bringing their extensive administrative experiences to bear on a situation which military expertise on its own was unable to handle.

After his experience in the Missouri campaigns of 1861 and early 1862, Halleck had come to share with Stanton an awareness of the administrative problems besetting the war effort. In spite of the most urgent pleas during the campaign, neither McClellan nor the other generals, some of whom were nominally under his command, would contribute manpower or materiel to his efforts. That he was successful at all was a tribute to his extraordinary organizational ability—and to the work of his promising protege, U. S. Grant. When Halleck was summoned to Washington in the spring of 1862, he and Stanton finally introduced a workable organizational structure to the war effort. Clear lines of authority were established, with the Secretary of War in charge of overall policy and coordination, advised by boards of civilian and military advisors. Under him served Halleck, the General-in-Chief and Chief-of-Staff. He presided not over any single army, but over the whole field of military operations, coordinating men, material, and communications. A distinction was beginning to emerge between staff and field operations, mediated by a clear and uninterrupted flow of intelligence to decision makers through their centralization of communications at the top of the structure. The structure was far from perfect: Halleck, for example, was a far better organizer than military commander, but the gains in efficiency and morale were substantive. By 1863, Union Generals like Grant and Meade, their actions supported by staff coordination, were winning important victories at Vicksburg and Gettysburg.

But the command structure was still imperfect. Its primary defect was its failure to make a clear enough distinction between staff and field operations. Halleck was too intellectual, too conservative, and too preoccupied with organization to be an effective leader in the field. His greatest strength was also his greatest weakness. What the Union needed was to supplement the organizational expertise of Halleck and Stanton with the battlefield genius of U. S. Grant. Accordingly, when Grant came to Washington in March of 1864, it was not to replace a deposed Halleck, as Halleck had replaced McClelland. It was to supplement him. Grant became General-in-Chief, commander of the field forces, while Halleck remained as Chief-of-Staff, organizing the support services. A staff system had finally emerged, and through it the North was finally able to match the South as an organizational entity. By April of 1865, the war was over and the task of reconstruction lay ahead.

It is crucial to understand that the organization of the war effort was not solely a product of the men at the top. While the leaders certainly brought their legal, corporate, and military knowledge together to draw out the broad outlines of a workable command structure, their ability to implement those plans depended on having men below them able and willing to follow orders and act responsibly without constant supervision. Not surprisingly, these men were drawn extensively from the ranks of the culture of organization—the lawyers, the military, and the corporate business community—the group of men who had been trained in the professional schools and the colleges. While many, like the younger Holmeses, Higginsons, and Adamses, took their places on the front lines, as heroic leaders of men, a remarkable number occupied equally important, if less visible, positions as paymasters, quartermasters, clerks, and administrators, in charge of the logistical and financial underpinnings of the war effort.[40]

4. Embracing the Marketplace

If the decades preceding the war had been ones of loosely coordinated but remarkably effective resocialization of the nation's economic and cultural leadership, the war itself brought the leaders together, giving them not only a sense of the possibilities of national-scale organization, but also a new sense of their public role as an administrative elite. On the one hand, they had learned the value of large-scale bureaucratically organized enterprise. On the other, they had learned that the implementation of superior organization, like the winning of battles, was not an automatic process. If the avatars of the culture of organization wished to implement their ideas successfully, they would have to do so in the market place.

The war and the broad acceptance of Darwinism among the educated classes since 1859 had transformed attitudes about the marketplace. Before the war, the marketplace was viewed negatively. Oliver Wendell Holmes wrote of money and trade as inferior and rather ungenteel matters, making a clear distinction in his writings between social legitimacy and the "fugitive fact" of wealth. Young Henry Lee Higginson, writing to his banker-father from Germany in 1853, stated:

> Law seems to me a profession calculated to draw forth the disagreeable, disputations, quarrelsome features, which are more or less in every man's character. . . . As regards a merchant, you yourself are most strongly set against any of us following the profession, and I for myself am too—if anything better offers. In the first place money is *the* thing with a merchant. . . . . How often have both you and Grandfather Lee said to us all, "Don't be merchants; anything else is better!" . . . There is but one conclusion to be drawn of your opinion of wealth, which I know you have always had—that it is very dangerous. Moreover, what good *personally* does a man derive from money further than that always derived from *giving*?[41]

The war dramatically altered these attitudes. After mustering out, Henry Lee Higginson gave up his ambitions to become a musician and went into cotton farming and oil prospecting; by 1868, he was a partner in the family investment banking firm, Lee, Higginson & Company. As an entrepreneur, he became one of the most active and innovative organizers of national-scale enterprises, ranging from western railroads and copper mines through the American Telephone & Telegraph Company, General Electric, and General Motors.[42] He was also one of the major allies of Charles W. Eliot in his effort to transform Harvard into a national institution. Similarly, Higginson's cousin, Thomas Wentworth Higginson, wrote after the war:

> When I left the service, two years of army life, with small access to books, had so far checked the desire for active literary pursuits, on my part, that I should actually have been content not to return to them. I should have liked better to do something that involved

the charge and government of men, as for instance in the position of agent of a large mill or a railway enterprise. This mood of mind was really identical with that which led some volunteer officers to enter the regular army, and others to undertake cotton-raising at the South.[43]

The Higginsons were not isolated instances. Oliver Wendell Holmes, Jr., on mustering out, turned his energies to the legal profession, seeking not merely to become another successful corporate lawyer, but to become a great judge. The synthesis of his war experiences with his readings of Darwin and Spencer resulted in a legal philosophy that was evolutionary and activist, viewing the marketplace not only as a jungle but, more importantly, as the testing ground on which the practicability of ideas and men could be worked out. It was very much suited to the economic and social development of the post-war world.[44] Charles Francis Adams, Jr. had abandoned his legal and literary ambitions by 1869 and had embarked wholeheartedly on a career as a railroad reformer and executive. As George Frederickson has remarked, the "lost generation" of the 1850s had, by 1865, found itself:

> The military experience, which had taught the young patrician intellectuals to take pride in a life of service and to emphasize professional skills and professional objectives, had destroyed whatever respect they may have had for anti-institutional thinking, radical individualism, or transcendental hopes of self-fulfillment.[45]

And the experience was not confined to what Frederickson calls intellectuals. The career preferences of Harvard and Yale classes graduating after 1855 shifted dramatically towards business: between 1800 and 1855, only five to eighteen percent chose business careers; between 1856 and 1900, the percentage entering business ranged between twenty and fifty percent.[46] Interestingly, the trend towards business careers did not develop gradually, but began with a pronounced upward swing in the classes graduating in the mid-fifties, the same classes that would send between a third and a half of their members into the army.[47] This shift towards activism, towards commerce rather than contemplation, was not merely an individual matter. It involved a transformation of the legacy of the Standing Order from one that based its claims for leadership on past achievement to one that based them on ability and willingness to compete in the present, matching the virtues of the "man of family" against those of the "self-made men" in situations in which all other things really were equal. The patricians, moreover, were now able to transform their institutions from ones whose primary function was character-building to ones whose primary functions were the production of technicians, administrators and specialized knowledge.

This shift in Brahmin social thought and institutional ideology was matched by a transformation in general public attitudes towards wealth, power, and institutions. It is no coincidence that Horatio Alger's wildly popular series of boys' books began appearing in 1867, for their publication signalled the apotheosis of the man of wealth.[48] Alger's heroes, while struggling upward from humble beginnings, were invariably aided by kindly men of means and, through their patronage and through the heroes' own hard work, were able to become wealthy, kindly, and powerful themselves. While admiration for material success was nothing new to American popular culture, its association with institutions certainly was. In the post-war world, public and patrician were moving towards one another in a broad ideological consensus. This consensus, founded on popularized social Darwinism and the experience of total war, made credible Charles W. Eliot's assertion to the Massachusetts legislature that state owed its "mental and moral characteristics, and its wealth to eight generations of people who have loved and cherished Church, School, and College"—the Brahmin Caste of New England. And the Civil War, by bringing the evangelical and the metropolitan strands of the Standing Order together again, permitted Brahminism—in Holmes' original sense, as the common heritage of the educated classes—to include not only the urban wealth of Boston, but also the national networks of the evangelicals.

CHAPTER TWELVE

Towards a Meshing of Patterns: The Nationalization of Business and Culture

Free and democratic communities, then, will always contain a multitude of people enjoying opulence or a competency. The wealthy will not be so closely linked to one another as the members of the former aristocratic class of society; their inclinations will be different, and they will scarcely ever enjoy leisure as secure or complete; but they will be far more numerous than those who belonged to that class of society could ever be. These persons will not be strictly confined to the cares of practical life, and they will still be able, though in different degree, to indulge in the pursuits and pleasures of the intellect. In those pleasures they will indulge, for if it is true that the human mind leans on one side to the limited, the material, and the useful, it naturally rises on the other to the infinite, the spiritual, and the beautiful. . . .

As soon as the multitude begins to take an interest in the labors of the mind, it finds out that to excel in some of them is a powerful means of acquiring fame, power, or wealth. The restless ambition that equality begets instantly taken this direction, as it does all others. The number of those who cultivate science, letters, and the arts, becomes immense. The intellectual world starts into prodigious activity; everyone endeavors to open for himself a path there to draw the eyes of the public after him. . . .[1]

What the country needs is a steady supply of men well trained in recognized principles of science and art, and well informed about

established practice. We need engineers who thoroughly understand what is already known at home and abroad about mining,
road and bridge building, railways, canals, water-powers, and
steam machinery; architects who have thoroughly studied their art;
builders who can at least construct buildings which will not fall
down; chemists and metallurgists who know what the world has
done and is doing in the chemical arts, and in the extraction and
working of metals; manufacturers who appreciate what science and
technical skill can do for the works which they superintend.

. . . the question is, not how much our freedom can do for us
unaided, but how much we can help freedom by judicious
education.[2]

If the development of national-scale organizations was inevitable,
there was little evidence of any significant trends in that direction before
the war. In the industries in which national organization would have
been most rational and efficient, telegraphs and the railroads, the steps
towards nationality were very tentative. In the railroad industry, as of
1861, no more than half-a-dozen lines crossed state lines.[3] Gauges (the
distance between rails) and equiment were non-standarized. As a result,
uninterrupted transportation for more than a hundred miles was usually
impossible. Even the short run from New York to Philadelphia required
several changes of trains. Given the local origins of the railroads—almost
every town of any size was projecting a line in the 1830s and 1840s—
the fragmented situation of the industry is not surprising. But the situation of the telegraph industry, which had been organized in the 1840s
with a bold plan of national integration, was no less disorganized in the
decade before the war. The plan, dreamed up by the Yale graduate S.
F. B. Morse and the Dartmouth graduate Amos Kendall, was a remarkable anticipation of the scheme that the national telephone system
would follow sixty years later:

Kendall's experience as Postmaster-General had given him a thorough familiarity with the main commercial routes of the country.
He proposed, therefore, to interest private capital in the construction of trunk telegraph lines along these routes, and then to build
the numerous side or feeder lines necessary to serve the entire
country. After the money had been raised, lines built, and companies organized, stock was to be issued to those taking part in the
enterprise. In most instances fifty percent of all stock issued was
to be turned over to the patentees in return for conveyance of patent
rights to the respective companies. Through this controlling stock
interest Kendall expected to maintain that degree of unity among

individual companies which he believed to be essential to the efficient working of a nationwide system of telegraphs.[4]

Born before its time, the plan soon ran afoul of administrative inexperience, technical obstacles, and problems in raising capital.

By the 1850s, both the railroad and the telegraph industries had become battlegrounds for the contending interests of urban-based entrepreneurs, each struggling for control of national markets. These entrepreneurs, while projecting large ventures, were nationally-based only in their anticipated range of exploitation. Management and financing tended to be narrowly based in particular cities. In the railroad industry, entrepreneurs resisted rather than welcomed standardization of guages and equipment, fearing that cooperation would interfere with their imperial schemes. In the telegraph industry, though consolidation of smaller and financially unsound companies into a handful of regionally-dominant systems was underway, the leaders of the major companies still resisted full-scale integration. Curiously, investment bankers, who would be the major instruments of national integration in the post-war period, were of little importance during the fifties.[5] Before the war the primary activity of such firms as Winslow, Lanier & Company of New York, Lee, Higginson & Company of Boston, and other large suppliers of capital was the promotion of schemes sponsored by their own cities' entrepreneurs. The primary function of the new investment banking industry was less the mobilization of domestic capital than the channelling of European investment into the American market, usually along lines of sectional interest.

1. War and Economic Nationality

The war changed everything. Not only did its military and administrative structure require national coordination, which brought into being by Stanton, Halleck, and their staffs, but government's other needs, especially those for finance and transportation, had to be met by national coordination.

By the end of the first year of the war, it was apparent that traditional means of government financing would not be adequate to the demands of a protracted conflict. The Government of the United States had come to depend on the ability of eastern investment bankers to dispose of large amounts of their securities to European capitalists. But with the war's outcome in doubt and with influential groups favoring the southern cause, European investors were not eager to bet on the North. Faced with their reluctance, the Treasury was forced to consider means of mobilizing the nation's own capital resources.

Two basic steps were taken to mobilize the capital of the Union, to get it out from under mattresses and out of private investment into the yawning coffers of the state. First, through a series of acts passed between 1862 and 1864, the government created both a national banking system and a national paper currency.[6] Briefly, this program involved that chartering (or rechartering) of banks by the federal government. These "national" banks were to have a monopoly on the distribution and redemption of a new form of paper money called "national bank notes." These notes were to be legal tender for all debts public and private and were guaranteed to be redeemable at their face value, in general circulation notes called "greenbacks."[7] Unlike the banknotes issued by private banks before 1861, these banknotes were redeemable at any bank in the country, not only at the bank that had issued them. This was the first paper currency to circulate nationally. The issuance of "national bank notes" was more than a crude inflationary scheme. The amount of notes that any one bank could issue was limited by two things: one, the relation of the amount of notes outstanding to the bank's assets (i.e., the bank could not issue more notes than it could redeem); two, the amount of notes given to any one bank to distribute were required to be secured by bank investments in government bonds. Thus, rather than simply increasing the money supply without any guarantee that it would be invested in the war effort, the government greatly enlarged the market for its bonds and ensured a steady flow of investment in them.

But the Treasury was not content to rely on a captive market of federally chartered banks to increase its credit lines. It also wanted to increase direct sales of bonds to individuals. Accordingly, it encouraged the efforts of Philadelphia investment banker Jay Cooke to create a national market for bonds, encouraging especially the participation of small investors. Cooke

> organized a nationwide sales force and directed it from his enlarged Philadelphia headquarters. In February of 1862, he opened a Washington branch, both to make sales and keep him informed of potential developments that might affect the progress of the bond drive. In New York, Boston, and other cities, Cooke recruited private bankers and brokers to act as his subagents. In the western states, where there were few private bankers or brokers, Cooke selected local business, community leaders, or other volunteers. All in all, he gathered some 2500 salesmen, in every state and territory. He aided this huge organization by a nationwide publicity campaign, which included the press, as well as posters, handbills, and educational literature. These reminded every social and economic group of its duty to its country and itself.[8]

The organization of the drive, its national scope, and its use of local nabobs as subagents resembled more than anything else the structure of the Yale fund drive in 1832, the American Education Society, and many other evangelical fund-raising efforts of the ante-bellum period.[9] This is hardly surprising, given Cooke's having come of old Connecticut stock and having grown up in the "New Connecticut" region of Ohio.[10] Like the philanthropies, Cooke's activity not only took place on a national scale, but enlisted national cooperation among the participants. The bond drives were enormously successful, tapping not only the capital of large entrepreneurs, but also that of small investors. Through his efforts, the Treasury not only raised the funds necessary to fight the war, but also succeeded in doing so without causing the kind of catastrophic national inflation that had followed such emergency measures during the Revolution and the War of 1812.

Although eastern consumers of cargoes shipped by rail from the west had been agitating for years for greater integration among the nation's railroads, their petitions had tended to fall on deaf ears. As late as 1861, travellers and freight passing between such points as New York and Chicago, New York and St. Louis, or Boston and Washington had to change gauges, and hence trains, at least three times.[11] The military exigencies of the war, the need for uninterrupted movement of cargoes and troops, led the War Department to pressure non-standard railroads either to adopt standard gauge (4 feet, 8 1/2 inches) or to add a "straddle track," a third rail that would permit standard equipment to operate over non-standard trackage. This movement for standardization was given added impetus by the passage of the Pacific Railroad Act in 1863. This act, which provided for the construction of a transcontinental railroad, was accompanied by fervent debates over whether it should adopt standard gauge, which was used by most eastern lines. When the issue was finally decided in favor of "standard," a major technical obstacle to national railway integration was removed. Similarly, when open war between North and South began to threaten in 1860, Congress passed the Pacific Telegraph Act, providing for the construction of a transcontinental telegraph to be financed by land grants to private companies.[12] All the telegraph companies in the country except one, the American Telegraph Company, cooperated in the construction of this line, which was completed in October of 1861.

The outbreak of war in March of 1861 encouraged cooperation between former competitors. In the south, consolidation was imposed from above when Confederate Postmaster-General John H. Regan placed all telegraphs under military control.[13] In the North, consolidation, like other aspects of the mobilization, proceeded in piecemeal fashion. Although the Secretary of War, Simeon Cameron, had placed a brilliant administrator, Thomas Scott, General Manager of the Pennsylvania Railroad, in charge of all military railroads and telegraphs, Scott had his hands full in simply dealing with the chaotic state of northern railroads. He delegated the task of organizing an effective military telegraph system to his young assistant, a Scots immigrant named Andrew Carnegie. Carnegie turned to Edward S. Sanford, President of the American Telegraph Company, and to Anson Stager, Superintendent of Western Union, to coordinate the operations of the civilian and military telegraph systems.

As the nation, North and South, fought out a total war, engaging not only military skills, but also civilian populations, industrial capacity, technology, and organization, the previous century's assertions of nationhood were finally beginning to take on more than rhetorical significance. The large-scale integration of transportation, communications, and credit facilities and the reorganization of government agencies were—even if impelled by civil war—at last leading Americans towards the achievement of functional nationality.

2. Postwar Disorder: The Problem of "Methodless Enthusiasm"

The war demonstrated to Americans that high levels of coordinated and cooperative administration, production, and communications could be achieved and sustained. It also brought forward a pool of administrators "eager for the government of large bodies of men." But these accomplishments, even in the exultation of the victorious celebration of regained national unity, did not lead to a permanent state of integration. Demobilization and the withdrawal of the federal government from the task of coordinating the activities of the private sector removed from the scene the only force capable of imposing order on the ambitions, rivalries, and conflicting intentions of the marketplace. Although the virtues and feasibility of large-scale enterprise had been successfully demonstrated, the events of the postwar period suggest that such economic nationality was conceived of in terms of national domination of particular industries and regions by individual magantes and groups of big-city based entrepreneurs. The war, in many ways, merely raised the stakes in the game and provided traditional rivals with new weapons for waging the battle for regional control of markets and raw materials.

But the wartime lessons in the possibilities of cooperation and coordination were not entirely forgotten. In the telegraph industry, for example, the four major operating companies—Western Union, American, North American, and U.S. Telegraph—had, by 1866, merged into a single entity, creating the first successful monopoly in American history.[14] In railroading, the picture was more complex. In certain areas, such as the through-shipment of freight and the standardization of equipment, permanent gains were made. In other areas, however, developments were less encouraging. Fueled by government land grants, accumulated wartime profits, and postwar inflation, rival groups of eastern-based entrepreneurs continued their struggles for domination of western markets. Although the Transcontinental Railroad, completed in 1869, was a cooperative effort of New York, Boston, and California financiers, it was really exceptional. The new roads that fed into it, paralleled it, and competed with it were engaged in frantic efforts to gain returns on their investments, often an impossible task. In 1873, the railroad bubble, swollen by inflated capitalization, unprofitable routes, and redundancies, burst, sparking a national depression that lasted for nearly a decade. Only in the late seventies would private investment bankers, led by the young J. P. Morgan of Morgan, Drexel & Company and Henry Lee Higginson of Lee, Higginson and Company, begin to cooperate in reordering the capital structure and operations of the nation's railroads.[15]

Ironically, Jay Cooke, the man who underwrote the northern war effort, would fail spectacularly in his efforts to translate the economic lessons of the war into peacetime possibilities. Having succeeded in his efforts to market government securities to a national marketplace during the war, he was eager to tap that same vast source of capital in marketing the stocks and bonds of private corporations. In 1869, Cooke was making arrangements with another Philadelphia firm, E. W. Clarke & Company, to form a syndicate to "buy, advertise, and sell on joint account" the bonds of the Lake Superior & Michigan Railroad. Rather than simply selling the bonds to Philadelphia investors, Cooke and his associates planned to follow the marketing strategies that had proved so successful during the war.

> Working closely together, these two firms shared the Philadelphia market and assigned to each other exclusive rights to advertise and manage the distribution in New York and Boston. . . . Commissions and stock bonuses were divided equally, each house keeping one quarter and assigning half to a joint account to be divided later. The next year, again under Cooke's leadership, the syndicate was developed still further by the introduction of an underwriting commitment. If the issuer failed to sell its own securities, the syndicate guaranteed to buy and dispose of them.[16]

The profitable possibilities for cooperative national marketing suggested by Cooke's successful syndicate venture of 1869 were observed with interest by other investment bankers. In 1870, Cooke was able to enlist seven other firms in an underwriting syndicate to handle a two million dollar bond issue for the Pennsylvania railroad. By 1871, Cooke was no longer the only promoter of intercorporate and intercity cooperation in financing private ventures. In that year, Anthony J. Drexel, head of a Philadelphia investment banking firm, persuaded Junius Spencer Morgan (father of J. P.), a Connecticut and New York banker who had been a partner of the Boston-born but London-based banker, George Peabody, to join him in forming a new firm, Drexel, Morgan & Company, with offices in New York, Philadelphia, London, and Paris.[17] And this powerful firm was not alone. By the early seventies, Bostonians and Philadelphians in considerable numbers began purchasing seats on the New York Stock Exchange.[18] Although these developments were certainly encouraged by the financial turmoil and political agitations of the preceding decade, by the early eighties a distinct national financial community based on cooperation and coordination of resources was beginning to emerge, which traced its origins directly to the financing of the war.

But if economic nationalism was an overall and irresistible trend, it followed a very uncertain path. The Panic of 1873, brought about to a large extent by the unbridled rivalries of the entrepreneurs of large eastern cities, was sparked by the collapse of the premier economic nationalist of the era, Jay Cooke. Cooke had undertaken the sale of five million dollars worth of bonds of the Northern Pacific Railroad. He had hoped to sell them using the techniques that had served him so well during the war and that, on a smaller scale, seemed to be successful in the peacetime market. He found, however, that London investors, who in 1871 had bought $110,000,000 in American securities, were, in the wake of the Franco-Prussian War and fears about the stability of the American economy, unwilling to buy them.[19] Moreover, the patriotic impulses that had led small investors into national securities markets during the Civil War and the immediate postwar period were weakening as they confronted the spectacle of corrupt financial operators like Jay Gould, Jim Fiske, and Daniel Drew, the scandalous revelations of the Credit Moblier investigation, and the money panic of 1869:

The money market was tight, and revelations of speculation and corruption in other railroads combined to defeat Cooke's hope of selling a sufficient quantity of bonds in the United States.

By mid-August 1873 the Northern Pacific's indebtedness to Jay Cooke's firm stood at $5.1 million. The market for bonds was poor, business conditions were generally no better, and Cooke's depositors grew uneasy and started to withdraw their money. Unable to stand the pressure of withdrawals, Cooke & Company, the 'foremost American banking house,' was forced to close its doors on September 18, 1873, triggering a severe panic on Wall Street. That catastrophe brought down numerous other well-known firms, among them Fisk & Hatch, E. W. Clark, and Henry Clews.[20]

Although set back by the great crash of 1873, economic nationalism did not fail with the collapse of Jay Cooke & Company. Out of the wreckage of panic and depression came a renewed appreciation for the value of coordinated and centralized management. This appreciation took several forms. First, investment bankers began to buy up, refinance, and reorganize poorly managed railroads, creating coherent national systems. In doing so, they began to move beyond a simple banking role, becoming active in corporate management in which they played not only a watchdog role, but also began to engage in long-term corporate planning.[21] As the scale of industrial and transportation enterprises grew, they required ever greater amounts of capital, amounts that could no longer be supplied by reinvestment of earnings and other forms of self-financing. They turned to a small group of investment bankers, survivors of the calamitous seventies, whose strength lay in their connections to domestic financial institutions, especially those of New England, and to powerful groups of foreign investors. By the late eighties, these investment bankers, with their tight hold over major sources of capital, were in a position to occupy the role that government had played during the Civil War in fostering rational and efficient administrative and operating practices.

But integration was not simply imposed from above by the eastern investment bankers. Led by John D. Rockefeller, an Ohio oil refiner, entrepreneurs were beginning, in the late sixties, not only the vertical integration of production and marketing within particular fields of endeavor, eliminating competitors by fair means or foul, but the horizontal integration of enterprises through the creation of industrial trusts. With investment bankers relieving them of the burden of capitalizing their operations, their own earnings were freed for pursuing new strategies for gaining security in the unstable economy of the Gilded Age. The tapping of large new sources of capital

> . . . allowed Carnegie, for instance, to pour his savings back into steel with the assurance that he would have coal with which to make it and railroads to deliver it. It allowed Rockefeller to devote his energies to petroleum refining and Armour his capital to dressing and packaging beef and pork, certain as they were that others could furnish transportation for them.[22]

This certainty was not, however, based on blind confidence in the operation of the market system. Rather, it rested on a set of formal and informal arrangements—"gentlemen's agreements," pooling, rebates, mergers, and trusts—that sought, in many cases successfully to eliminate the dangers of over-production, the inefficiencies of unrestrained competition, and the other hazards of an unregulated laissez-faire marketplace. While there were unquestionably a variety of purposes being served by these arrangements, pooling, for example, serving those businessmen who resisted consolidation, trusts serving those who favored it, both courses of action were integrative in character. And both, in the long run, served the group most in favor of national integration, the investment bankers. As Thomas Cochran and William Miller wrote in *The Age of Enterprise*:

> Trusts could appear only in a society in which the corporation had become the dominant type of business organization, in which property rights were represented not by land or other physical assets, but by negotiable paper easily convertible into other types of negotiable power.[23]

Whether through trusts, pools, or other arrangements, the *Magistri Ludi* were coming to be groups of men whose power rested not on their ability to produce, but on their ability to organize and administer. Though their judgment was not, as the Panic of 1907 showed, infallible, and though as Gabriel Kolko has convincingly demonstrated, they never really succeeded in establishing a monopoly over the sources of capital, the direction of American economic development after 1880 was largely in the hands of the investment bankers of the northeast.[24] The establishment of the foundations of economic order, harnessing the "methodless enthusiasm" of the Jacksonian laissez-faire marketplace and restoring to a significant extent the concern with the common weal that had characterized the Federalist and Whig economic ideology, was the achievement on which the ultimate establishment, the partnership of government and the private sector in the twentieth century, would be built.

3. The Search for Order: The Civil War Generation Comes of Age

Thus far, this sketch of the development of economic organization in the post-Civil War period has dealt with the tendency to consolidation and rationalization between industrial sectors. This movement, however, rested neither soley on reactions to economic and social turbulence nor on war-derived notions of the profitability and feasibility of economic integration. Rather, the movement towards integration depended in the final analysis on the existence of administrative cadres capable of confronting immense organizational tasks, on sources of information from which intelligent practical decisions could be made, and on the development of ongoing efforts to improve the art of administration, to gather and digest economic and social information, and to comprehend and deal with the consequences of new economic, social, and political realities. While it has become a social historian's commonplace to characterize the transformation of occupational roles in the second half of the nineteenth century as a movement towards the professionalization and specialization of activity, it was not a mere concentration of the focus of intellectual and practical activity that give the modernization of post-bellum culture and commerce its most distinctive features. Had the channeling of occupations in the late nineteenth century been a simple matter of professional specialization, the overall social impact would have been fragmentation rather than integration. As important as specialization may have been, its most significant historical impact is derived from the institutional framework within which specialization developed. It was through this framework that the search for authority described by Thomas Haskell in *The Emergence of a Professional Social Science: The American Social Science Association and the Nineteenth Century Crisis of Authority* was transformed into a more comprehensive search for and establishment of social and economic order.[25]

The problems confronting American society as it entered the post-Civil War period were different from those that confronted it after the American Revolution only in degree and scale. To be sure, by 1870, the number of Americans living in the countryside and engaging in agriculture was vastly smaller. A transportation revolution had taken place, enmeshing almost all Americans in the market system. The scale of enterprises had vastly increased. But these quantitative changes did not of themselves suggest a resolution of the fundamental questions posed by the disintegration of traditional society in the late eighteenth century: the relation of the indvidual to society, the problem of defining and administering the common good, and the sources of moral, political, and intellectual authority remained moot. With the erosion of traditional institutions and sources of authority, the will of the majority and the operations of the marketplace became the ultimate arbiters of policy. While certain groups could insulate themselves from the majority through cultural and commercial corporations, using those organizations as bases for influencing the marketplace, the ultimate resolution of basic issues remained open-ended and beyond control. The professionalization of activity within those corporate enterprises, while certainly enhancing their effectiveness in their particular fields of endeavor, did not resolve the basic issues. Such a resolution could only occur through the development of a framework that could reintegrate economic, cultural, and political activity, a framework that would involve not only concrete linkages between sectors of activity, linkages among commercial enterprises among cultural enterprises, but also those *between* the commerical and cultural sectors. Further, such a framework would not only have to encompass the training and employment of the new professionals; also it would have to generate and synthesize the information that comprised the bases for professional activity and enlightened decision making. Finally, this framework would have to command a broadly acknowledged respect across occupational, economic, and political lines; like the colonial Standing Order, it would have to constitute an establishment whose authority transcended faction.

It has been asserted with varying degrees of boldness by recent historians of the second half of the nineteenth century that the renewed sense of confidence of the professional classes was derived from the transcendent authority of science, that Darwinism and other developments in the intellectual and technical worlds (including the concrete need for higher levels of expertise) not only provided the professional classes with a new assurance of the legitimacy and utility of their endeavors, but also persuaded the general public that the scientifically trained expert was the true guardian of the common good.[26] While the dramatic increase in the visible importance of science and technology— as well as that of trained expertise in all fields, old and new—was unquestionably an important feature of the post-bellum decades, it is significant that the adulation for science, expertise, and efficiency did not result in technocracy. Even when respect for the trained expert was at its peak during the Progressive Era, scientific professionalism, whether of the social or physical variety, was always conceived of as subordinate to a greater good.[27] And for all the elaboration of occupational specialization, the growth of professional organizations, and the rhetoric of scientifically trained expertise that occurred after 1870, in no instance did these developments occur outside the framework of lay-controlled institutions. The containment of the movement towards professionalism and occupational specialization within or subordinate to more comprehensive institutions suggests that the real source of authority of professionals lay not with science, but with an institutional context that invested assertions of scientific expertise with credibility.

While it might be argued that these lay-controlled institutions derived their authority from their proprietorship of the scientific enterprise, such an assertion ignores several important facts. First, at no time did a scientific or preprofessional bias become apparent in any major university curriculum.[28] Secondly, the scientific schools at Yale and Harvard and the technical schools such as MIT were at no time considered as prestigious as their liberal arts counterparts.[29] Third, for all the investment of money and personnel in the graduate and professional schools after 1870, the central preoccupation of most university administrators, trustees, and donors remained the undergraduate component.[30] The fact is that the balance of cultural power and authority after 1870 at no time resided with the specialists. G. Stanley Hall's attempt to operate Clark University as a center of pure research and graduate-professional training was a notable failure.[31] Even Johns Hopkins, with its notable graduate schools, justified its fundamental task in terms that were antithetical to any notion of scientific ascendancy. Its president, Daniel Coit Gilman, stated in 1886, in addressing the members of Phi Beta Kappa at Harvard, that he hoped the American university would never become

> merely a place for the advancement of knowledge or for the acquisition of learning; it will always be a place for the development of character. A society made up of specialists, of men who have cultivated to the extreme a single power, without simultaneously developing the various faculties of the mind, would be a miserable society of impractical pessimists, it would resemble a community made up of boys who can paint portraits with their toes, who can calculate like lightning, who can remember all the hats of all the guests at a fashionable hotel, or perform innumerable feats on the tight rope.[32]

In making this argument against mere specialization, Gilman was no more kowtowing to the spokesman for traditional liberal culture than Charles W. Eliot was in asserting that "the material prosperity of every improving community is a fruit of character," that it is "energetic, honest, and sensible men that make prosperous business, and not prosperous business that makes men." Eliot, Gilman, and the other academic and cultural leaders of the post-bellum period shared with business magnates like Henry Lee Higginson a conviction that the primary goal of the university was the formation of character, not the cultivation of specialized pursuits. That is not to say that they opposed science or specialization, but rather that they saw it as subordinate to other, broader, more compelling concerns.

These concerns can be summed up in a statement made by Charles W. Eliot to a journalist regarding the utility of universities. Fearing that the writer was construing the notion of utility too narrowly, Eliot suggested that such an approach overlooked the principal service which every university renders—namely the service which its graduates render to the community. What you call the extra-pedagogical activities of American universities are of course important; but their pedagogical activities are infinitely more important to the industrial and political life of the community. With regard to the contributions to science which universities make, it is a grave error to suppose that only those which contribute *immediately* to industrial progress are important from that point of view. The plain fact is that nobody can tell which of the contributions of to-day are to be most important for industrial or social progress fifty or one hundred years hence.[33]

Utility for Eliot did not mean vocationalism. He and his contemporaries well knew that narrow technical training could not fit men to face the rapidly changing world of the late nineteenth century, that politics, economics, and society would inevitably present challenges for which narrow training could not successfully provide specific solutions. Although reformers like Eliot differed sharply with academic conservatives like Yale's Noah Porter and Princeton's James McCosh on specific issues, such as the role of classics and the desirability of retaining compulsory chapel attendance for undergraduates, these differences were largely symbolic. They had more to do with the conservatives' anxieties about the declining role of the clergy (for McCosh and Porter were both men of the cloth) than with fundamental differences in outlook on the purposes of university education. As Lawrence Vesey remarked,

The minister, not the educational theory, became the common denominator of all these varied argumets. What the orthodox college president would not concede, in effect, was that a minister was simply one kind of careerist and an engineer another.[34]

But if there was fundamental agreement on the importance of character as the final product of higher education, there were at the same time significant differences among both educators and laymen as to the most effective strategies for developing character. These differences hinged on divergent interpretations of the nature and extent of the changes in American society since the founding of the Republic and varying understandings of what constituted the role of education and the educated in an industrialized democracy. As conceived of in the early nineteenth century, character education was seen as a means of preparing men to occupy leadership roles in undifferentiated social contexts in which the influence of the educated became manifest primarily through example, eloquence, and other face-to-face relations.[35] Whatever their particular callings, the leadership of the educated converged on a common influence; effective character stemmed not from particular professional pursuits, but from a broadly-based, commonly acknowledged, generalized leadership ability. Accordingly, the major reforms in the colleges between 1780 and 1830 did not involve major changes in curriculum. Rather, they embraced alterations in the system of collegiate discipline, in the composition of the teaching staff, and in the organization of student life.

While the colleges, as Henry Adams conceded, sent out into the world young men "with all they needed to make respectable citizens and something of what they needed to make useful ones," they also, as the social and economic context grew more complex, produced a pervasive sense of frustration among their graduates. The problem was not merely that students felt the classical curriculum irrelevant to their future occupational goals or that college delayed their entrance into the race for wealth. It was, rather, that the kind of undifferentiated leadership and occupational roles envisioned by the educators of the early Republic no longer existed. The world of Adams' father and grandfather, which permitted a practicing attorney be a statesman, an intellectual, and a paterfamilias as well, had been supplanted by a world in which face-to-face relations were segmented socially and occupationally, in which success was derived from specialized achievement, and in which ascent to positions of generalized leadership depended on successful accomplishments in particular fields of endeavor. The troubled college graduates of the 1850s were bewildered not by the absence of career opportunities after graduation, but by their plentitude and by the fact that these opportunities, because they were more specialized, did not offer the comprehensive possibilities for influence, reputation, and usefulness that had existed for earlier generations. The undergraduate curriculum in no way prepared them to reconcile the generalized ideal of service cultivated in college with the occupational and social realities that they confronted after graduation.

The war experience, however, brought to the generation of graduates of the late 1840s, the 1850s, and the early 1860s to a redefinition of character education in which the notion of the specialized vocation played a crucial role. As Eliot asserted in his inaugural address as President of Harvard:

As a people, we do not apply to mental activities the principle of division of labor; we have but a halting faith in special training for high professional employments. The vulgar conceit that a Yankee can turn his hand to anything we insensibly carry into high places where it is preposterous and criminal. We are accustomed to seeing men leap from farm or shop to courtroom or pulpit, and we half believe that common men can safely use the seven-league boots of genius. What amount of knowledge and experience do we habitually demand of our lawgivers? What special training do we ordinarily think necessary for our diplomatists?—although in great emergencies the nation has known where to turn. Only after years of the bitterest experience did we come to believe the professional training of a soldier to be of value in war. This lack of faith in the prophecy of a natural bent, and in the value of a discipline concentrated upon a single subject amounts to a national danger.

The civilization of a people may be inferred from the variety of its tools. . . . As tools multiply, each is more ingeniously adapted to its own exclusive purpose. So with the men that make the State. For the individual, concentration, and the highest development of his own peculiar faculty, is the only prudence. But for the State, it is variety, not uniformity, of the intellectual product, which is needful.[36]

But the emphasis on the importance of specialized training was only one side of the issue. The concrete experiences of ante-bellum corporate development and the organization of the war effort had taught their practical lessons about the context of effective specialized activity:

The principle of divided and subordinate responsibilities, which rules in government bureaus, in manufactories, and in all great companies, which makes the modern army a possibility, must be applied in the university.[37]

In making this assertion, Eliot was not merely speaking of the organization of university administration. For in the phrase "divided and subordinate responsibilities" lies the kernel of the philosophy of the elective system: although their tasks might be "divided and subordinate," individuals were no less responsible for their actions than if their tasks were comprehensive and ordinate. The key to training individuals to face specialized tasks responsibly, to develop character while, at the same time, confronting a specialized world, was a system of education which "gave students abundant practice in making wise free choices of the kind any man would have to go on making during the remainder of his days on earth."[38] Eliot and the other university reformers were not advocating vocational training in promoting the elective system. Rather, by presenting students with a vast range of possibilities, they were transforming the university into a model of the world. The difference for Eliot between a professional school and a university lay not in the degree of specialized courses offered, but in the purposes for which students pursued their studies:

> In the college the desire for the broadest culture, for the best formation and information of the mind, the enthusiastic study of subjects for the love of them without any ulterior objects, the love of learning and research for their own sake, should be the dominant ideas. . . . The student in a polytechnic school has a practical end constantly in view . . . he is studying the processes of nature, in order afterwards to turn them to human uses and his own profit.[39]

Just as President Quincy had prepared his charges for responsible manhood by allowing them to discover the real consequences of their actions in the realm of discipline, so President Eliot and the university reformers allowed their charges to discover the real consequences of their curricular choices, and through the possibilities offered by such freedom of choice, further to develop their capacities for responsibility. What prevented the elective system from degenerating into vocationalism, however, was more than the spirit that animated it. American society needed both specialists and generalists: like any real army, manufactury, or railway, it consisted of more than a set of subordinate tasks. The world's work was hierarchically organized according to degrees of responsibility. Just as an army required a general staff with a responsibility for coordinating the numerous specialized tasks necessary for military success, so society itself selected out, by virtue of their specialized achievements, leaders whose task it was to coordinate and take ultimate responsibility for the common good. The elective system, in other words, had in no way abandoned the Federalists' quest for training responsible leaders. Nor had it mindlessly embraced the notion of specialized professional training. Rather, it had extended into the curriculum the principles of individualism and self-discipline that had, a quarter century before, reorganized the extracurriculum. And in allowing students the freedom of responsible choice, it rendered intrinsic to particular studies the moral content that the classical curriculum had imposed extrinsically.

What saved the reformers' concept of society and the university's role in it from being anti-democratic was their liberal interpretation of social Darwinism, their conviction that leadership, character, and ability came not through inheritance and ascription, but through education and achievement. As Eliot remarked in his inaugural:

> The poorest and richest students are equally welcome here, provided that with their poverty or their wealth they bring capacity,

ambition, and purity. The poverty of scholars is of inestimable worth in this money-getting nation. It maintains the true standards of virtue and honor. The poor friars, not the bishops, saved the church. The poor scholars and preachers of duty defend the modern community against its own material prosperity. Luxury and learning are ill bedfellows. Nevertheless, this College owes much of its distinctive character to those who, bringing hither from refined homes good breeding, gentle tastes, and a manly delicacy, add to them openness and activity of mind, intellectual interests, and a sense of public duty. It is as high a privilege for a rich man's son as for a poor man's to resort to these academic halls, and so take his place among cultivated and intellectual men. To lose altogether the presence of those who early in life have enjoyed the domestic and social advantages of wealth would be as great a blow to the College as to lose the sons of the poor. The interests of the College and the country are identical in this regard. The country suffers when the rich are ignorant and unrefined. Inherited wealth is an unmitigated curse when divorced from culture.[40]

Eliot, like the senior Holmes, knew that "the millionocracy" was "but a perpetual fact of money with a variable human element."[41] He shared with Holmes a belief in "Nature's Republicanism" through which

... families . . . refine themselves into intellectual aptitude without having had much opportunity for intellectual acquirements. A series of felicitous crosses develops an improved strain of blood, and reaches its maximum perfection at last in the large uncombed youth who goes to college and startles the hereditary class-leaders by striding past them all.[42]

Eliot knew that the untapped reserves of talent and intelligence in the United States were as extensive as the nation's material resources, and that the future of Harvard, his class, and the nation itself depended on the ability of Harvard and other private institutions to recruit promising youth, regardless of social background. As his friend and ally Henry Lee Higginson crudely put it:

How else are we to save our country if not by education in all ways and on all sides? What can we do so useful to the human race in every aspect? . . .

Democracy has got fast hold of the world and *will* rule. Let us see that she does it more wisely and humanely than the kings and nobles have done! Our chance is *now*—before the country is bull and the struggle for bread becomes intense and bitter.

Educate, and save ourselves and our families and our money from mobs!

I would have the gentlemen of this country lead the new men, who are trying to become gentlemen, in their gifts and in their efforts to promote education.[43]

Eliot, Holmes, Higginson, and the other institution builders of the post-war period firmly believed in an aristocracy of talent:

. . . to which the sons of Harvard have belonged, and, let us hope, will ever aspire to belong—the aristocracy which excels in manly sports, carries off the honors and prizes of the learned professions, and bears itself with distinction in all fields of intellectual labor and combat; the aristocracy which in peace stands firmest for the public honor and renown, and in war rides first into the muderous thickets.[44]

But for all their insistence on the importance of democracy, freedom of choice, and the value of specialized accomplishment as a prerequisite for leadership, Eliot and his allies were no less concerned with the importance of continuity and social order, and with the special place of their class in providing guidelines and an overall framework for democratic inclusion and social development. Eliot did not see the Civil War as a conclusive event in the effort to establish nationality. In 1869, he wrote:

The American people are fighting the wilderness, physical and moral, on the one hand, and on the other are struggling to work out the awful problem of self-government. For this fight they must be trained and armed.[45]

Looking into the future, he foresaw a prolonged conflict in which the advantaged had a role of particular importance. He was willing to insist, as Holmes had a decade earlier, that the "cumulative humanities of at least four or five generations," which comprised the special Brahmin combination of wealth and culture, led not only to "good breeding, gentle tastes, and a manly delicacy . . . openness and activity of mind, intellectual interests, and a sense of duty," but also to the very real fulfillment of those duties both on the field of battle during the Civil War and in the broader struggles that would follow. Turning to the assembled graduates and friends of the College as he concluded his inaugural address, he asserted:

> Honored men, here present, illustrate before the world the public quality of the graduates of this College. Theirs is no mercenary service. Other fields attract them more and would reward them better; but they are filled with the noble ambition to deserve well of the republic. There have been doubts, in times yet recent, whether men of culture were not selfish; whether men of refined tastes and manners could really love Liberty, and be ready to endure hardness for her sake; whether, in short, gentlemen would in this country prove as loyal to noble ideas as in other times they had been to kings. In yonder old playground, fit spot whereon to commemorate the manliness which there was nurtured, shall soon rise a noble monument which for generations will give convincing answer to such shallow doubts; for over its gates will be written: 'In memory of the sons of Harvard who died for their country.' The future of the University will not be unworthy of its past.[46]

Clearly, in Eliot's view, neither wealth nor specialized ability would be sufficient in and of itself to meet the challenges of establishing a mature and responsible nationality. Mere aristocracy, "founded on wealth, and birth, and an affectation of European manner," and mere specialized application "which can, at best, produce but a fruit with a stone at its heart," were not the ingredients of nationhood.[47] Rather, by competing freely with one another, by discovering their own special abilities, by learning to take responsibility for their own lives, talented students, rich and poor, would be led towards vocations. Through their achievements in those vocation, they would be led either towards positions of more generalized leadership or towards a merely useful professional life. The successful would, on the basis of proven achievement, assume their positions on the general staff of the society and its economy and culture. The University would, Eliot hoped, in proving itself worthy of its past, train the officers in this army as it fought the coming battles for the achievement of nationhood.

Eliot's ideas were by no means as simple or consistent as this summary would suggest. They developed piecemeal over the space of a forty-year incumbency as Harvard's president. Nonetheless, their basic premises—a vision of the bureaucratic character of society and its endeavors, an emphasis on individual achievement, an insistence on the crucial role of educated character in the struggle for nationality—were all in place in the late 1860s. The most important aspect of Eliot's ideas, however, was not their clarity or their originality, but, rather, the extent to which they both represented a continuity with the past and expressed the consensus of his own class and generation.

As tempting as it is to see Eliot and the other institutional reformers as rebels, repudiating the outworn ideas and authorities of the past in order to forge new paths into the future, the facts suggest not only that Eliot appreciated and accepted the past, but also that he was sponsored in advancing his reforms by older men. His two most enthusiastic proponents among the Fellows of the Corporation were its two senior members, Francis B. Crowinshield and John Amory Lowell (Lowell had served as a Fellow since 1837).[48] Similarly, his strongest supporters among the Overseers included those who had served longest on the board. These included men like James Walker (who had served as an Overseer since 1825, as a Fellow between 1834 and 1853, and as President of the University 1845–46, 1853–60). As one of them, William Adams Richardson, would later write:

> When he was chosen President of the College I was one of the Board of Overseers, serving the last year of my first term by election of the legislature, under the old but not the oldest system. Having been reelected by the alumni under the new system, I continued to serve on the Board for six years thereafter while he was preparing the ground, planting the seed and developing his ideas, the steady growth of which I have ever since watched with deep interest and great pride for my Alma Mater.[49]

Eliot's proponents, whether senior or not, were already convinced of the need for wide-ranging university reform along the lines advanced by him on his assumption of the Presidency. A month before his name came before the Fellows as a candidate, a committee of Overseers headed by James Freeman Clarke had concluded that more instruction in the natural and social sciences and an elimination of the prescribed curriculum were essential to Harvard's future.[50] Interestingly, the major opposition to Eliot's election came from the faculty; "the classicists feared him, the scientists despised him." Both groups knew that Eliot, with his cosmopolitan outlook, his comitment to general education, and his strong ties to the non-academic world, would threaten their autonomy.

Ironically, the scientists had as much to lose as the clergy to the threat of lay control. The most influential, including Harvard's Josiah Cooke, Wolcott Gibbs, and Louis Agassiz, had been active promoters of academic structures following the lines of the German universities, institutions controlled by the professors and focused on advanced research.[51] It was hardly reassuring for them to read Eliot's 1869 essay, "The New Education," in which he asserted:

When the American university appears, it will not be a copy of foreign institutions, or a hot-bed plant, but the slow and natural outgrowth of American social and political habits, and an expression of the average aims and ambitions of the better educated classes. The American college is an institution without parallel; the American university will be equally original.[52]

Nor could they have been happy with Eliot's dismissal of the quality of their most strenuously promoted efforts, the scientific schools at Yale and Harvard:

The Lawrence Scientific School at Cambridge is, and always has been, what the Yale school also was at first—a group of independent professorships. . . . Each student is, as it were, the private pupil of some one of professors, and the other professors are no more to him than if they did not exist. . . . The range of study is inconceivably narrow; and it is quite possible for a young man to become a Bachelor of Science without a sound knowledge of any language, not even his own, and without any knowledge of philosophy, history, political science, or of any physical or natural science, except the single one to which he has devoted two or three years at the most.[53]

For Eliot, and for those who promoted his candidacy, neither the scientists nor the clergy were capable of fostering the foundation of the new social order, the education of the men who would administer and organize the national bureaucracy. Nor, in his view, should the responsibility for the task be surrendered to publicly controlled bodies: for the world of politics and government was too dominated by special interests to permit the kind of academic freedom essential to his vision of intellectual democracy.[54] Only a set of institutions privately controlled and supported by men whose worth had been demonstrated through their success in the world could define the priorities of the growing nation.

4. Towards a New Order: The Bureaucratization of American Life

Eliot and his fellow reformers knew that in reorganizing American education they were merely planting a seed; it would be many years before their work would bear fruit. And as they looked ahead from 1869, they had few illusions about the difficulties that lay ahead as the American people fought "the wilderness, moral and physical" and struggled "to work out the awful problem of self government." But against a turbulent background of class violence, massive immigration, and economic dislocation, the obstacles to order began to fall away. The "New Education" championed by Eliot and others finally gained control of Yale as reform's most vocal and influential opponent, Noah Porter, was replaced in 1886 by Timothy Dwight (grandson of the old president), a warm friend of the elective system.[55] The coalescence of interests between the reformed universities and big business was eloquently testified to by the growth of university endowments: Harvard's grew from $2.4 million in 1869 to $12.6 million in 1900; Yale's grew in the same period from $1.5 million to $4.6 million.[56] Perhaps most important of all, the number of leading businessmen who sent their sons to private national institutions, especially Harvard and Yale, increased dramatically. Wealth and culture were drawing together.

Alfred Chandler, the leading historian of American business, has written that, during the period 1870–1930, the

> major thrust of organization building centered about the creation and refinement of primary organizations which had the following characteristics: (1) they tended to be national in organization and scope of operations; (2) they were largely in the private, not the public sector of the economy; (3) they centralized authority along bureaucratic lines; and (4) they were constrained in their internal and external development by a particular set of boundaries which were traditionally or historically defined. . . .

> By traditional boundaries we mean the kind of constraint exerted by the idea that a business firm in the iron and steel industry should continue to focus almost exclusively on the production of iron and steel goods. Was this necessary? Obviously not. But that was the way things had always been done—or seemed to have been done. Thus, the historically defined industry functioned as a constraint upon the expectational horizon of the firm's managers. The same thing could be said for the idea of a craft or skill and its impact on trade union development. The concept of the profession—of engineering or social work—had similar effects upon professional organizations developing during these years.[57]

While Chandler's overall description of the development of organizations during the period 1870–1930 is correct, and is certainly consistent with the "methodless enthusiasm" with which many large scale enterprises were projected and implemented during the "Age of Enterprise," his failure to consider two factors, the rise of investment banking and the changing composition of corporate administrative personnel, leads him to minimize the significance of coordination and liaison between organizations in the period before 1930. While it may be true, as he asserts, that the relative weakness of secondary bureaucracies was due to the dominance of the idea that "relations between organizations would be determined, as they had been in the pre-bureaucratic age, by such natural forces as the gold standard or competition," it may also be that, in looking for "trade associations, union federations, and some government agencies" as sources of coordination during the late nineteenth century, he is looking in the wrong places.[58]

It is certainly the case that Eliot and his allies in the Boston business world shared an open-ended view of the form that national consolidation would finally take. As liberal social Darwinists, they believed that the free and unhampered play of market forces should determine the final shape of American business and culture. As the same time, however, both historical experience and inherited social ideology gave them the conviction that the ultimate shape that the nation should and would take was one in which coordination, rationality, and order were preeminent features. The conspicuous successes of Boston's entrepreneurs between 1800 and the outbreak of the Civil War had been based to a remarkable extent on cooperation and collectivization of resources. As early as 1824, the leading bankers of the city had combined to form the "Suffolk System," a central clearinghouse which prevented country banks from draining Boston's reserves of specie.[59] By the 1830s, trust companies like the Massachusetts Hospital Life Insurance Company and private trustees were controlling and coordinating a significant portion of the city's capital investment in corporations.[60] And during the decades after 1830, a complex but coherent web of relationships developed between endowed non-profit cultural and social welfare institutions and financial institutions that constituted, for all practical purposes, a coordinating economic hierarchy. Out of this consolidation of interests and capital grew Boston's early preeminence in investment banking. The experience of the Civil War, from an organizational standpoint, merely amplified the possibilities of such coordination. Given the role of non-profit organizations, especially Harvard, in the city's earlier economic experience, it is hardly surprising that the financiers should have looked to Harvard as a fundamental entity for promoting cultural and economic nationality.

This preoccupation with coordination in no way contradicted the Brahmins' commitment to the free play of market forces. Through the first half of the nineteenth century they were acutely aware of the twin perils of class power: the tendency of accumulated wealth to dissipate through partition or irresponsibility and the stultifying dead-hand of the past trying to control the present and future.[61] This awareness lay at the very base of the Bostonian's system of wealth transmission, the "Prudent Man Rule" set forth in *Harvard College versus Armory*, which asserted that there was no such thing as a completely secure investment, that the only guarantor of the security of property was the *character* of a fiduciary, which enabled him to act with flexibility and discretion. And President Eliot was no less forceful in simultaneously asserting the centrality of the university in furthering social progress and the uncertainty as to the final form that progress would take. Really, the most accurate metaphor for the financiers' and the educators' concept of the relation between competition and control was the army, an organization which, ideally, allowed men to rise and fall on their skills alone, while at the same time containing the play of individuals within a disciplined and ordered framework. Within such a structure, as Eliot readily acknowledged, training and ability played essential roles—hence the role of education as a crucial factor in successful warfare and its moral equivalent. At the same time, comradeship and a sense of common purpose, along with hierarchical subordination, gave overall shape and purpose to the enterprise.

Boston's attitudes towards and historical experiences of coordination did not point towards the creation of "secondary bureaucracies" as a basis for cultural and economic integration. Rather, they emphasized common training and values for a nationally recruited group of future leaders, the encouragement of ongoing relationships between members of that group, and convergences of responsibility only at the highest levels of economic and social action. Before Eliot, when Harvard's primary concern was the training of Boston's elite, the College could depend on most leading or ambitious families to send their sons to Cambridge; by the 1850s, over eighty percent of the sons of Brahmin families went to Harvard. So recruitment was not a matter of great concern.[62] Nor did the College have to worry about ongoing relationships among graduates; since most of them came from and remained within a fifty-mile radius of Boston, most had grown up together, and would see one another socially and in the world of business and the professions.[63] On the basis of these ongoing relationships, men could be judged and, if found fit, promoted beyond their specialized pursuits to generalized positions of leadership as trustees and directors.[64]

When Bostonians became concerned with promoting national integration after the Civil War, they appear to have favored the same informal and particularistic mechanisms that had proved effective in the past. To recruit a nationally-based student body at Harvard, they began administering standardized written admissions tests in western cities in the mid-seventies. By 1880, the examinations were being given in

Cambridge, Exeter, New Hampshire, New York, Philadelphia, Chicago, Cincinnati, and San Francisco.[65] They also encouraged the founding of private boarding schools that would draw together the sons of the best families of the nation, thus institutionalizing the common experiences and acquaintanceships that had once taken place by chance through residental contiguity, the Boston Latin School and playing together on Boston Common.[66] Ongoing relationships among the nationally recruited and nationally dispersed graduates were encouraged in a number of ways. Beginning in 1864, Harvard Clubs were formed in New York and Philadelphia; by 1870, one had been established in Chicago, and by 1880, one in Minneapolis.[67] Class organizations, which had operated informally and erratically, depending solely on the *esprit* of their members, were regularized. Their publications increased in quality and comprehensiveness. Reunions and class dinners became important events, occasions for gathering together the scattered alumni and renewing old ties. In 1893, the *Graduates Magazine*, which was sent to all Harvard degree-holders, began publication. Perhaps most important of all, in 1880, the Board of Overseers was opened to Harvard graduates living outside of Massachusetts.[68] These actions facilitated other, more concrete relationships among graduates, such as marriages and business enterprises.

By the 1880s the Bostonians had succeeded not only in making the Harvard degree the most universally recognized social and professional credential in America, but also had made Harvard itself a major, if not the major, instrument for recruiting a national business and cultural elite. Certain major investments banks and brokerage firms such as J. P. Morgan and Company in New York came to be known as "Harvard firms," due to the predominance of graduates of Cambridge among their partners and employees.[69] The organization of the national preparedness movement, which enlisted the energies of America's leading businessmen and cultural figures before our entry into the First World War, took place under the auspices of the Harvard Club of New York.[70] But it is essential to recognize that Harvard's role in the process of consolidating a national leadership group was not based on its, or Boston's, fostering the growth of "secondary bureaucracies." Indeed, Harvard and Boston tended to reject mechanisms of this type until the dawn of the Progressive Era. Although Harvard men favored the creation of the pioneering Massachusetts State Board of Charities in 1863 for the purpose of rationalizing the state's locally-based system of social welfare, the Board was in no sense a comprehensive secondary bureaucracy.[71] It merely sought to "publicize abuses and coordinate a decentralized system of almshouses, hospitals, and *ad hoc* relief."[72] The basic assumptions of the Board's promoters with regard to the problem of social welfare were identical to those of Harvard's reformers with regard to nationality: that the reform of society proceeded from the reform of individuals and not the other way around. (This identity of outlook is hardly surprising, as both groups contained many of the same individuals.) Similarly, although Eliot spearheaded the movement for the standardization of college admissions and was responsible for encouraging the upgrading of private and public secondary schools to meet Harvard's entrance requirements, he resisted the "certificate system" of admissions.[73] This scheme would have imposed a standardization of secondary school curricula through a system of university-controlled inspection. Graduates of conforming institutions would have then been eligible for admission to university on the issuance of a "certificate of fitness" by a principal or headmaster. Eliot rejected the certificate system, preferring examinations of individual applicants as the best means of stimulating competition among schools and students for excellence.

The attitudes of Boston's leading business figures paralleled exactly those of its reformers with regard to coordination through secondary bureaucracies. Henry Lee Higginson, although recognizing the problem of corporate abuses, based his resistance to government regulation of business on philosophical grounds:

> I also have certain views about corporate managements, which do not entirely agree with those of other people. I do think that the corporations have been rather too eager, just as certain rich men have. It is perfectly natural in the struggles to succeed, and stil more in the effort not to fail,—as we [General Electric] came near to doing in '93, in the desire to do good work, and to prevent others doing mischief,—that we should have become too eager, and have forgotten other people who are either stupid or inefficient; and we sometimes forget our workmen or our competitors. I do not believe that, because a man owns property, it belongs to him to do with as he pleases. The property belongs to the community, and he has charge of it, and can dispose of it or use it, if it is well done and not with the sole regard to himself or to his stockholders.[74]

Rather than depending on regulation to enforce this morality, Higginson preferred to depend on market forces, which would drive out badly-run enterprises, and on the character and good sense of the majority of businessmen:

> . . . As to the interlocking directorates, I have no doubt that there has been some trouble from them, and in many cases they should be avoided. May it not be more safely left to the businessmen, to

the business sense of the community, to correct that evil? And when we are considering, should not we consider all the great advantages that come from interlocking directorates? My trouble with Mr. Wilson and his Cabinet is that they do not understand how business should be done, and of course some of the methods of the past fifty years have not been sound.[75]

A corollary of his beliefs in the morality of the market, the stewardship of property, and the capacity of the business community to regulate itself was his conviction, identical to Eliot's, that progress was open-ended, depending on individual exertion and risk-taking of a kind that no public authority could promote:

In a discussion of prices for necessaries, and especially public-service corporations and their just reward or return, not a word is said of the fool who risks and loses money in sundry experiments, and who succeeds in a few. Hear my sad tale: I have been putting money into a well-studied experiment to make magnetic iron out of ore at a much lower cost than at present. With several friends, I have spent $60,000 or more. It is a failure. If it had been a success, it would have reduced the cost of pig-iron or magnetic steel four or five dollars a ton. . . .

A lot of us took up the Submarine Signal Company some twenty years ago, and have spent $1,750,000 of real money on it. The company is eminently successful, but never has made a penny of return; it saved lots of lives and property, and the whole joy of it is in that fact. . . .

Some idiots— . . . Bill Forbes, Cochrane, Vail, and I—risked our money on the Telephone in a dream of '76 or '78. . . . This time it was 'trumps'—and think of the blessing to the world!

If our country is to grow, through developments, the 'economists' and the 'regulators' must allow for the losses in risks, else we shall get behind countries which do allow for brains, character, and ability. . . . [76]

It is perfectly true that the general public too often wants to eat its cake and have it too; or, to put it in other words, wants to play the game, heads we win, tails you lose. When an enterprise is in its inception, the immense majority will have nothing to do with it; when that same enterprise happens to have carried through the period of risk and difficulty to the stage of success, that same majority wants a handsome share of the profits.[77]

Higginson's attitudes might be discussed as the usual free-market cant, the fulminations of an old plutocrat, were it not for the fact that he considered himself a Progressive, voting for Roosevelt in 1904, Taft in 1908, Wilson in 1912, and Hughes in 1916.[78] Moreover, he was unwavering in his support for Eliot in his reformation of Harvard, believing, as Eliot did, that the best solution to the problem of national order lay in the education of individuals to ideals of service, stewardship, and cooperation.

5. The Patrician as Social Democrat

As one reads the words of Higginson and Eliot, one sees social attitudes that seem to have more in common with the lost worlds of Winthrop's Boston and the Federalist Standing Order than with the brave new worlds of high technology, giant corporations, and mass society. At the same time, there are crucial differences: an optimistic faith in the possibilities of democracy, a rejection of regional chauvinism in favor of nationalism, and a whole-hearted embracing of the market place. These differences represented a fundamental shift in Boston attitudes away from the impasse mentality that prevailed before the war and that had limited Boston's influence to its own region. The war provided an illuminating experience for Brahmins, which was complemented by the social lessons drawn from Darwin's delineation of natural history and Spencer's interpretation of it. Experience and ideology taken together allowed them to formulate a new vision of American society, a vision in which democracy and the marketplace were compatible with order. At the base of this vision lay a special appreciation for the role of education, not as a crude instrument of cooptation and social control, but as a positive means of enlightenment and progress. But education served more than the general goals of progressive social evolution. It also suggested that the strategies for pursuing those goals lay not with creating rigid, inelastic, regulating "secondary bureaucracies," which imposed order from above, but, rather, with primary bureaucracies, the activities of which would be integrated and coordinated by particularistic relations among the individuals who comprised the upper administrative echelons. The relationship between the universities and the specialized learned professions and disciplines as they develop during the late nineteenth century is a good example of this model of subordination: individual professionals strove competitively for success within their fields; the criteria for success were defined externally, by a pecking order of universities whose relative prestige was determined, once again, by such enternalities as the power and influence of alumni and officers of governance, for the constituencies of the institution determined the quality of its facilities. The power and influence of alumni and officers was not an independent variable, for it, in turn, was a product—ideally, at least—of achievement in the real world. And such achievement was viewed as the ultimate product of training and character. The university was the hub of the system, the vehicle for creating the aristocracy of talent and virtue. But important as it was, the university was neither identical with nor the handmaiden of that aristocracy, for in the case of Harvard at least, the priorities of the institution were set not merely by th five Fellows and the President, but by a counterbalancing of interests:

> The real function of the Board of Overseers is to stimulate and watch the President and Fellows. Without the Overseers, the President and the Fellows would be a board of private trustees, self-perpetuated and self-controlled. Provided as it is with two governing boards, the University enjoys that principal safeguard of all American governments—the natural antagonism between two bodies of different constitution, privileges and powers. While having with the Corporation a common interest of the deepest kind in the welfare of the University and the advancement of learning, the Overseers should always hold toward the Corporation an attitude of suspicious vigilance. They ought always to be pushing and prying. It would be hard to overstate the importance of the public supervision exercised by the Board of Overseers. Experience proves that our main hope for the permanence and ever-widening usefulness of the University must rest upon this double-headed organization.[79]

The social vision of men like Eliot was astonishingly comprehensive and foresighted. Accepting the challenge of nationality posed for their generation, they recognized the need for policy elites in a mass society and sought to make those elites as democratic as possible. Aesthetes like John Jay Chapman might sneer that

> . . . Eliot goes about in a cab with Pierpont, hangs laurel wreaths on his nose, and gives him his papal kiss. Now . . . what has Eliot got to say to the young man entering business or politics who is about to be corrupted by Morgan and his class?[80]

And radical critics like Thorstein Veblen complain that

> Plato's classic scheme of folly, which would have the philosophers

take over the management of affairs, has been turned on its head; the men of affairs have taken over the direction of the pursuit of knowledge.[81]

But to portray the Brahmin reformer's model of a democratic nation and the role of the university in it as a mere slavish deference to business is inaccurate. Neither the attitudes of businessmen regarding education nor their patterns of benevolence, neither the statements of educators nor their conduct suggest that either wished to be narrowly useful to one another. Whether one approves of the final product of their labors or not, one must concede the complexity and open-endedness of their vision. And if they, as an economic and social elite, were self-serving, it was because they saw in their own collective past the special role that they had played in the nation's history. Having no other model for reconciling democracy and order, democracy and the common weal, they can hardly be blamed for attempting to project on the nation an enlarged image of themselves.

CONCLUSION

The Promise of American Life

What the individual can do is to make himself a better instrument for the practice of some serviceable art; and by so doing he can scarcely avoid becoming also a better instrument for the fulfillment of the American national Promise. To be sure, the American national Promise demands for its fulfillment something more than efficient and excellent individual instruments. It demands, or will eventually demand, that these individuals shall love and wish to serve their fellow-countrymen, and it will demand specifically that in the service of their fellow-countrymen, they shall reorganize their country's economic, political, and social institutions and ideas.[1]

In his peroration at the conclusion of *The Promise of American Life*, one of the central ideological statements of the Progressive Movement of the early twentieth century, Herbert Croly gave voice to a theme about the relation between the individual and society. The roots of that theme can be, and have been in this book, traced back through the post-Civil War educational reformers and businessmen, the ante-bellum philosophers of benevolence, the evangelicals, and the ideology of Federalism, to its foundations in the social philosophy of the seventeenth-century New England Puritans. If Croly's sentiments were idiosyncratic, they could be dismissed as unimportant. But they are not idiosyncratic. His ideas about the relation between "really edifying individual education" and the "gradual process of collective education by means of collective action and formative collective discipline" and his emphasis on "the selection of peculiarly competent, energetic, and responsible individuals to perform the peculiarly difficult and exacting parts in a socially constructive drama" are representative of the attitudes of Progressives from Jane

Addams and John Dewey through Theodore Roosevelt and Woodrow Wilson.[2] He expressed a set of ideas that characterized Progressivism in both its intellectual and its political manifestations.

What are we to make of the rhetoric of Progressivism? Was it mere opportunism that caused Croly, Dewey, Addams, Roosevelt, and hundreds of thousands of others who "yearned to socialize their democracy" and rejoin ideals and utility to use the formulas of earlier political and social movements? Or were the Progressives, like Abraham Lincoln and thousands of individuals in his generation, either affected by or agents of a set of concrete institutions and a particular social class, a class which sought for a century to impose its distinctive values and behavioral orientations on the masses? To put the question another way, was Progressivism merely the reform wing of the early twentieth-century Republican Party? Or was it a broader movement that underlay politics and other sectors of social action through which the educated professionals—men like Roosevelt, Taft, Hughes, and Wilson—came to dominate politics? And if it was, to what extent was this broader movement, a movement that penetrated into every aspect of American life, a product of the New Education, and the New Education, in turn, a product of the earlier movement of ministers, merchants, and magistrates of the nineteenth century who sought to redeem the promise of American life by joining to the political revolution of 1776 a moral revolution?

Henry Adams, who taught at Harvard between 1870 and 1877, had no doubts about the connection between the New Education and the triumph, in the nineties, of a unified capitalist order. He confessed his teaching a failure and abandoned it, not because he was bad at it or because his students were reluctant to learn. He gave it up because he was all too successful at it and because his students, men like Henry Cabot Lodge and Theodore Roosevelt, learned their lessons all too well. Surely Adams had these men in mind when he wrote, in 1905:

A parent gives life, but as a parent, gives no more. A murderer takes life, but his deed stops there. A teacher affects eternity; he can never tell where his influence stops. A teacher is expected to teach truth, and may perhaps flatter himself that he does so, if he stops with the alphabet or the multiplication table, as a mother teaches truth by making her child eat with a spoon; but morals are quite another truth and philosophy is more complex still. A teacher must either treat history as a catalogue, a record, a romance, or as an evolution; and whether he affirms or denies evolution, he falls into all the burning faggots of the pit. He makes of his scholars either priests or atheists, plutocrats or socialists, judges or anarchists, almost in spite of himself. In essence incoherent and immoral, history had either to be taught as such—or falsified.[3]

Adams could not bring himself to falsify history. And, as a result, his students learned its immoral lessons—immoral only in that, as they took their places in the world, they carried Adams and the world even further from the eighteenth century for which he yearned. Whether or not he liked it, his students identified with State Street, the immoral world of diversity and force, not with Quincy, which represented a moral principle, a morality that Adams identified with a colonial order that was irrecoverable. Adams, though he lamented the direction of history, did not condemn his students for choosing State Street over Quincy. He was not offended at a student's reply to the question of what he would do with his education: " 'The degree of Harvard College is worth money to me in Chicago.' "[4] He knew that they were trapped in their time, as he had been in his own, and that if the degree of Harvard College had been an impediment as he sought a career, it was no longer one. Education and ancestry were handicaps for Adams. He had been trained to live in the seventeenth or eighteenth century, but he had found himself required to play the game of the twentieth.[5] Looking back, he wondered about what he should have done:

> He could under no circumstances have guessed what the next fifty years held in store, and no one could teach him; but sometimes, in his old age, he wondered—and could never decide—whether the most clear and certain knowledge would have helped him. Supposing he had seen a New York stock-list of 1900, and had studied the statistics of railways, telegraphs, coke, and steel—would he have quitted his eighteenth century, his ancestral prejudices, his abstract ideals, his semi-clerical training, and the rest, in order to perform an expiatory pilgrimage to State Street, and ask for the fatted calf of grandfather Brooks and a clerkship in the Suffolk Bank?

> Sixty years afterwards he was still unable to make up his mind. Each course had its advantages, but the material advantages, looking back, seemed to lie wholly on State Street.[6]

Adams chose to be a "politician and priest" in the mold of his ancestors, men who, in their persons, combined wealth, learning, and respectability. And he found that the species had become extinct, though that did not stop him from aspiring towards it. He knew well that many of his contemporaries and classmates, including his two older brothers, had gone to State Street and asked for the fatted calf. He did not grudge his students for doing the same.

But as his students chose the material world over the spiritual, the future over the irrecoverable past, the outcome became inevitable. If Adams' own contemporaries—men who shared his background and experience like Phillips Brooks, H. H. Richardson, Charles W. Eliot, John Hay, and Henry Lee Higginson—had succeeded as counting "as a force in the mental inertia of sixty or eighty million people," the institutionalization of the ideas of these men would lead, as Adams saw that it did by the 1890s, to the "expression of American thought as a unity."[7] The Columbian Exposition, in Adams' mind, posed the question "whether the American people knew where they were driving."[8] The answer was affirmative, and disturbingly so, since it was his own class that had determined its direction:

> For a hundred years, between 1793 and 1893, the American people had hesitated, vacillated, swayed forward and back, between two forces, one simply industrial, the other capitalistic, centralizing, and mechanical. In 1893, the issue came on the single gold standard, and the majority at last declared itself, once for all, in favor of the capitalistic system with all its necessary machinery. All one's friends, all one's best citizens, reformers, churches, colleges, educated classes, had joined the banks to force submission to capitalism; a submission long foreseen by the mere law of mass. Of all forms of society or government, this was the one he liked least, but his likes or dislikes were as antiquated as the rebel doctrine of State rights. A capitalistic system had been adopted, and if it were to be run at all, it must be run by capital and by capitalistic methods; for nothing could surpass the nonsensity of trying to run so complex and so concentrated a machine by Southern and Western farmers in grotesque alliance with city day-laborers, as had been tried in 1800 and 1828, and had failed even under simple conditions.[9]

The answer offered by Chicago in 1893 was offered again after the turn of the century in a more unmistakable form, when Adams' students, Roosevelt and Lodge, became the most powerful men in America, and his best friend, John Hay, Roosevelt's Secretary of State. As Adams noted,

> The work of domestic progress is done by masses of mechanical power—steam, electric, furnace, or other—which have to be controlled by a score or two of individuals who have shown capacity to manage it. The work of internal government has become the task of controlling these men, who are socially as remote as heathen gods, alone worth knowing, but never known.[10]

Adams recognized and regretted their power, not only because "a friend in power is a friend lost," but because he doubted that they could really control the forces they had harnessed:

> Modern politics is, at bottom, a struggle not of men but of forces. The men become every year more and more creatures of force, massed about central power houses. The conflict is no longer between men, but between the motors that drive the men, and the men tend to succumb to their own motive forces.[11]

If Henry Adams questioned the success of the New Education and its product, Progressivism, he did so not because he thought that the men trained by Harvard and the other universities had failed to take control of America. They had unquestionably succeeded in that task. He wondered, however, whether control and morality were the same things, whether ideals and utility could ever really be joined outside of a pre-industrial world. The Progressives themselves did not share his doubts. They held power. Through the universities, the professions, and the bureaucratic structures of nationality, they had, by the beginning of the twentieth century, reintegrated political, economic, and intellectual authority. In so doing, they had reasserted the relation between wealth, learning, and respectability and the masses. And they believed that they had carried out a moral revolution that redeemed the political revolution.

Is it idle speculation to enquire into the meaning of Progressivism, its rhetorical and institutional origins? What does the present have to do with moral revolutions, Progressivism, the New Education, the Civil War, the evangelical united front, Federalism, or the decay of Puritan society? These phenomena have nothing to do with the present if one views them as discontinuous. But one can, as this book suggests, view them in another way. One can view Progressivism as the final product of the evolution of nationality, the reintegration of political, economic, and intellectual authority. And one can view this reintegration as the product of a set of regional elites which, as they struggled to regain the power they had lost at the end of the eighteenth century, were able to balance off the inclusivity necessary to sustain their effectiveness with the exclusivity (or myths of exclusivity) necessary for maintaining their identities and sense of mission. These elites, from 1800 on, identified themselves with nationality. They identified nationality with higher principles. Thus, even though they had come by the mid-nineteenth century to connect their morality with material success, they were able, by the 1880s, when they discovered that the material conditions out of which their power proceeded were undermining their moral claims and endangering the achievement of nationality, to alter those conditions, to make material success available to even larger numbers of people, and thus to maintain their claims to national leadership. With the Progressive movement, they made good those claims, and they have never relinquished them.

Progressivism as a political movement may have come to an end in the aftermath of the first World War. But the cultural dynamic, sustained by powerful social groups and institutional arrangements, is still very much with us. Richard Hofstadter's analyses notwithstanding, Progressivism was the parent of the modern liberal state in which we live today. The central institution of Progressivism, the university, is still the primary source of leadership and of the information on which social policy is based. And the bureaucratic organization of activity, Progressivism's most notable and permanent product, remains the dominant mode of organizing national activity, the primary means of articulating the relation between elites and the masses. Indeed, the very ethos by which Americans justify nationalism and the bureaucratic organization of activity in pursuit of national goals was brought into public life by the Progressives and their ancestors. Both rhetorically and in terms of concrete historical continuities, the distance between Croly's peroration and John Kennedy's urging Americans not to ask what their country could do for them, but what they could do for their country, is not a great one.

If the sources of nationality are what I take them to be, if the continuity between the events of the eighteenth century, the Progressive era, and the present is as strong as I suggest, then Henry Adams' doubts about the Progressives' success, particularly would their ability to resist becoming "creatures of force" who "tend to succumb to their own motive forces," have particular bearing on the present crisis in our national life. For eighty years, we have been able, on the whole, to sustain the uncomfortable linkage of principle and power, thinking that, because an historically designated group operated with an ethos of higher principle, the achievement of political power by that group necessarily meant the apotheosis of principle, the fulfillment of the promise of American life, the accomplishment of the moral revolution. We have been able to sustain that linkage because we, as a people, have been extraordinarily and continuously successful. Americans are, on the whole, the best educated, best fed, best clothed, and best sheltered people in the world. We are what we are because of a social and economic democracy brought into being by a particular group, the Progressives and their liberal descendants. But since the late 1960s, it has become apparent that something is not right. That "something" was evident to Henry Adams in 1905 and to a few literary intellectuals after the first World War. We were able to protect ourselves from it after the second World War by our enormous power, by our material successes, and by the fact that the only visible alternatives were fascism and communism. But, try as we may, we can no longer avoid the questions posed by Henry Adams.

The American crisis of the late twentieth century has many familiar features, though the actors are different and the scale is very much enlarged. We are undergoing a crisis of authority comparable to those of the late eighteenth and the late nineteenth centuries, crises which were, as ours is, characterized by the impotence of leadership and the failure of public policy. In the crisis of our time, however, the stakes are very much higher. When we refer to the disastrous consequences of political unwisdom and public ignorance, we do not merely fear, as Timothy Dwight and Lyman Beecher did, the rule of the mob and the excesses of revolution. The United States in the twentieth century is surrounded by enemies who would rejoice at our national extinction, and the price of our extinction could well be the extinction of life on earth. As persons of "higher principle" look to the very real possibilities of global conflagration and try to stave off that agony by dealing dispassionately with the very real problems of population, resources, and ordered relations among the world's peoples and their institutions, they look to them, much as they did during the nineteenth century, as outsiders. The collapse of liberalism in the 1960s brought into power the Jeffersons and Jacksons of our own time, men who regarded the scope of their actions as being limited only by the will of the electorate. And our own crisis of faith, a crisis which has permitted political authority to diverge again from higher principles, has developed out of our recognition that there is a difference between rationality as a method (which dream of reason produced the monsters of world war and the concentration camp) and a higher rationality that men once identified with God and, having lost God in the mid-nineteenth century, with science. But science, rather than revealing a transcedant order, has revealed the abyss. Our collective crisis is not unlike that personal experience of Adams when, after the agonizing death of his sister, he had his:

> first serious consciousness of nature's gesture—her attitude towards life.

It took form then

> as a phantasm, a nightmare, an insantity of force. For the first time, the stage scenery of the senses collapsed; the human mind felt itself stripped naked, vibrating in a void of shapeless energies, with resistless mass, colliding, crushing, wasting, and destroying what

these same energies had created and labored from eternity to perfect. Society became fantastic, a vision of pantomime with a mechanical motion; and its so-called thought merged in the mere sense of life, and pleasure in the sense.[12]

From an ebullient self-confidence in which we say everything is possible, all reasonable goals within reach through the application of organized intelligence, we find ourselves helpless, our public men willfully ignorant, and the earth itself an inconsequential speck of rock drifting through the void. And because of the peculiar circumstances of our time, the crisis we have entered is not merely a crisis of faith. It is a crisis of survival.

This book, in attempting to suggest the continuities of American development, is an effort to engage the task of survival. I see that task as predicated on an understanding of the fundamental mechanisms that have created the present crisis an understanding that can be translated into a new mastery of our fate. Henry Adams doubted the efficacy of Progressivism because he thought that the Progressives had confused power with mastery, and in so doing had become "forces as dumb as their dynamos, absorbed in the development or economy of power."[13] But we do not have to be the tools of our tools. We can, however, only establish mastery if we know what our tools are, what the range of tools available to us is, and to what purposes we want to put those tools. We can only do this by looking into the past, the arena in which the comparative utility and availability of instruments can be assessed.

The task of survival can be viewed in many ways. But in the end, it has to be cast not merely in individual or national terms, but, given the unquestionable interdependence of mankind, in terms of the survival of mankind in all of its variety. The past has taught us certain lessons. The lesson of our own society is that one can never tell where, from what location or what social or economic circumstance, talent will emerge. Triage is not a solution to the world's problems, for one cannot know, in writing off a people, a class, or a species, whether one is destroying an invaluable or irreplacable resource. Another lesson is that no social, political, or economic order can last long that is based on oppression, violence, or injustice. These lessons are, of course, hardly new. They are the very ones that the merchants and the evangelicals had to learn when they faced the intractable realities of unrestrained capitalism and popular democracy. They are the ones the intellectuals and administrators of the late nineteenth century had to learn when they contemplated the ultimate cost of coercive repression of the working classes. Justice and survival are inextricably linked. And if mankind is one's reference point, survival is not amoral.

But what do survival and morality have to do with Progressivism and its antecedents? In my opinion, everything. For the Progressive synthesis, in suggesting that individuals should perfect themselves as instruments whose moral purposes would be defined by their part in the reorganization of "their country's economic, political, and social institutions," and ideas, was assuming that the ultimate morality was defined in national terms. By subsuming themselves to the national purpose, they thought they were necessarily both redeeming themselves as individuals and collectively fulfilling the promise of American life. But they failed to realize the historical concreteness and specificity of that promise. They confused their success as a class with America's success as a nation. And in doing that, they confused the rationality of their methods with the rationality of their ultimate goals. What is more, this confusion became institutionalized not only in politics, but in the enterprise of knowledge itself. Objectivity and disinterestedness were defined by the extent to which knowledge served the national interest, which was, in turn, identified with historical progress. Men, by virtue of their knowledge and success, became part of the national elite, and the nation, led by that elite, saw itself as the hope of mankind, the delimiter of progress.

The events of the last twenty years have made it difficult to sustain that illusion. Our vanguard role is no longer clear. And our own actions, especially those in Viet Nam, brought home to us the confusion of means and ends, the horror of being led to genocide by the "best and the brightest." We have spent a century perfecting ourselves as instruments, but the moral revolution, so long hoped for and, for decades, thought accomplished, seems as remote as it must have to Timothy Dwight and George Cabot.

The ending of this long historical cycle should be viewed positively. Though the problems we face are very real, their reality, and our inability to deal with them by the usual means, releases us from the iron cage in which Max Weber feared we were trapped. This book has attempted to suggest the extent to which our view of the world and its possibilities, the enterprise of knowledge, has been a product of a particular set of institutions and social groups. The power of these groups and their institutions was culturally determined, the product of fundamental relationships between resources, human needs, and social groups which the persons who comprised them were not, for the most part, even aware of. The "light cloak" of Puritanism did indeed, as Weber suggested, become an iron cage. But our entrapment has only recently become obvious to us. In fact, we could only perceive our entrapment when the conditions that had formed it had begun to undergo fundamental change, and when we began to perceive our inability to respond effectively to that change. Our map of reality only became inadequate when it ceased to resemble the territory through which we were trying to navigate.

This book is not for those who will attempt to deal with crisis by denying the past or by finding fault with its actions and actors. The past is all we have, and it cannot be denied. For denial will not decrease its influence. Some may not like elites and bureaucracies, but their reality, even if their effectiveness is impaired, cannot be denied. Others may not like my suggestion that the pursuit of knowledge in America has been less than disinterested. But denying that fact will not make it go away. The reality is that the pursuit of knowledge is interested, and that the boundaries of its interestedness have been historically set by the character of the institutions in which we have pursued it. We cannot change that fact by doing away with those institutions. And it must be recognized that there are degrees of disinterestedness. By tying the pursuit of knowledge to national goals defined not politically, but by the social and economic interests of elite elements in the private sector who saw themselves as the stewards of nationality, those elements greatly broadened the possibilities of disinterestedness. We face a similar challenge as we look forward to internationality.

For the century and a half between the election of Thomas Jefferson and the end of the second World War, the fulfillment of the promise of American life meant the full achievement of nationality. Nationality was achieved through organizations based in the private sector that enabled Americans in all regions and in all social and economic circumstances to put aside their differences in pursuit of a common goal. We finally achieved that goal by the 1940s, through the coalescence of privately-based elites and elite institutions in the service of the state. But we were not able to reconcile our achievement of nationality with the international role that we had been called upon to play by the conditions of the post-war world. And the more active we became in the world, the more confused we became about the relation of our national goals to the interests of mankind.

We are far from extricating ourselves from that confusion, though we are beginning to understand the sources of it. Having identified those sources, as this book has attempted to do, one might be tempted to urge, as many radicals have, an end to policy elites, a dismantling of bureaucracies, and a placing of power in the hands of the people.[14] To do so would be disastrous, for the people are incapable of understanding the dimensions of the problems that the world faces or comprehending their solutions. Making the will of the people the delimiter of rationality would lead to outcomes very like those experienced by the American automobile industry in allowing the public to dictate that it should manufacture large fuel-wasting automobiles—even though the auto-mobile executives themselves knew that such vehicles would, in the near future, become too expensive for the average motorist to drive. Those who possess the specialized intelligence to comprehend the global crisis must exercise their independent judgement. And they must do so as elites in the service of the masses. That too is an undeniable part of our historical continuum. And to deny it, however attractive it may be for those of the right and of the left to do so, is to deny that mankind can take responsibility for its own survival.

We stand in circumstances very like those faced by the wealthy, learned, and respectable New Englanders in 1800. We can only hope that we will be as adequate to realizing internationality as they were to the task of fulfilling for us the promise of American life.

Notes

Introduction

1. A. L. Kroeber and Clyde Kluckhohn, *Culture: A Critical Review of Concepts and Definitions* (New York, 1952), pp. 118–19.

2. United States Department of Commerce, *Historical Statistics of the United States* (Washington, 1961), pp. 7, 236. According to Wood, Struthers & Company, *The Trusteeship of American Endowments*, the amount of property held by private philanthropies (churches, hospitals, foundations, universities, and organized charities) as of 1919 exceeded the annual receipts of the United States government by over eight billion dollars. Not until the 1940s did federal, state, and local governments become the largest source of income for institutions of higher education (*Historical Statistics*, p. 212). The number of students attending public universities did not exceed the number of attending private ones until the 1970s; see U.S. Department of Commerce, *Statistical Abstract of the United States, 1978* (Washington, 1978), p. 132. Even today the number of private hospitals exceeds the number operated by governments 23,000 to 4,002.

3. *Historical Statistics*, p. 14. As of 1850, only 3.5 million Americans lived in centers of 2,500 or more versus 19.7 million who lived in smaller communities. As of 1890, 22.1 million lived in places of over 2,500, but 40.8 million still lived in more rural areas. Urban population did not exceed rural population until 1920. On the consumption patterns of such places, see Robert and Helen Lynd, *Middletown* (New York, 1925).

4. *Historical Statistics*, p. 74.

5. Alfred D. Chandler, Jr., *The Visible Hand: The Managerial Revolution in American Business* (Cambridge, 1977), p. 3.

6. Lynd and Lynd, *Middletown*; and Steward Ewen, *Captains of Consciousness* (New York, 1978).

7. Chandler, p. 4; and Bernard Bailyn, *Education in the Forming of American Society* (New York, 1960), pp. 1–14.

8. On this point, see Carol F. Baird, "Albert Bushnell Hart: The Rise of the Professional Historian," in *The Social Sciences at Harvard, 1860–1920*, ed. Robert Church et al. (Cambridge, 1965), pp. 129ff.

9. Perhaps the most influential of these works was Theodore Adorno, et al., *The Authoritarian Personality* (New York, 1948), on which Hofstadter, Stanely Elkins, and other pluralist historians drew extensively for theoretical insight.

10. M. P. Rogin, *The Intellectuals and McCarthy: The Radical Specter* (Cambridge, 1969), p. 5.

11. In my opinion, the major post-pluralist syntheses are Robert Wiebe, *The Search for Order* (New York, 1967); Burton Bledstein, *The Culture of Professionalism* (New York, 1976); Lawrence Veysey, *The Emergency of the American University* (Chicago, 1965); and Alfred D. Chandler, *The Visible Hand*.

12. In my opinion, the major post-pluralist monographs are those of Philip Greven, *Four Generations: Population, Land, and Family in Colonial Andover, Massachusetts* (Ithaca, 1970); David Allmendinger, *Paupers and Scholars: The Transformation of Student Life in Nineteenth Century New England* (New York, 1973); Morton Horowitz, *The Transformation of American Law: 1780–1860* (Cambridge, 1977); Stephan Thernstrom, *Poverty and Progress:*

Social Mobility in a Nineteenth Century City (Cambridge, 1964); Ronald Storey, *The Forging of an Aristocracy: Harvard and the Boston Upper Class, 1800–1870* (Middletown, 1980); David Rothman, *The Discovery of the Asylum: Social Order and Disorder in the New Republic* (Boston, 1971); Edward Pessen, *Riches, Class, and Power Before the Civil War* (Lexington, 1973); George Frederickson *The Inner Civil War: Northern Intellectuals and the Crisis of the Union* (New York, 1965); Thomas Haskell, *The Emergence of a Professional Social Science: The American Social Science Association and the Nineteenth Century Crisis of Authority* (Urbana, 1977); John S. Whitehead, *The Separation of College and State: Columbia, Dartmouth, Harvard, and Yale* (New Haven, 1973); and James McLachlan, *American Boarding Schools* (New York, 1970). Most will be frequently cited below by short title.

13. On the integration of history and the social sciences, see Gerald Platt and Fred Weinstein, *The Wish to Be Free* (Berkeley, 1969); Arthur Stinchcombe, *Theoretical Methods in Social History* (New York, 1978); and Thomas Bender, *Community and Social Change in America* (New Brunswick, 1979).

14. See Talcott Parsons, "The Professions and the Social Structure," in *Essays in Sociological Theory* (New York, 1964).

15. On this point, see David McClelland, *The Achieving Society* (New York, 1969); Thomas Cochran, "The Role of the Entrepreneur in Capital Accumulation," in National Bureau of Economic Research, *Capital Accumulation and Economic Growth* (Princeton, 1955); and *Men in Business: Essays on the Role of the Entrepreneur*, ed. William Miller (New York, 1962). For more recent and more sophisticated statements of this problem, see *Men and Organizations*, ed. Edwin J. Perkins (New York, 1977), and Arthur Stinchcombe, "Social Structure and Organizations" in *Handbook of Organizations*, ed. J. G. March, Chicago, 1965), pp. 142ff.

16. "The Role of the Entrepreneur," p. 310.

17. Kroeber and Kluckhohn, *Culture*, pp. 267–68.

18. Kroeber and Kluckhohn, p. 290.

19. Kroeber and Kluckhohn, pp. 355ff.

20. Bailyn, pp. 4–5.

Chapter One

1. On the difference between the regions during the colonial period, I especially recommend Jackson Turner Main, *The Social Structure of Revolutionary America* (Princeton, 1965). Gary B. Nash, *Class and Society in Early America* (Englewood Cliffs, 1970) is also useful.

2. On the relation between religious ideology and institutions, see E. Digby Baltzell, *Puritan Boston and Quaker Philadelphia: Two Prostestant Ethics and the Spirit of Class Authority and Leadership* (New York, 1980).

3. On the significance of partible inheritance, see Greven, *Four Generations*. For especially insightful accounts of the impact of partible inheritance on rural society, see Kenneth Lockridge, *A New England Town, The First Hundred Years* (New York, 1970), and his article, "Land, Population, and Evolution of New England Society, 1630–1790," in Nash, *Class and Society*, pp. 149ff. See also John J. Waters, "Patrimony, Succession, and Social Stability: Guilford, Connecticut in the Eighteenth Century," in *Perspectives in American History* 10 (1976).

4. For an especially good account of the diversification of New England agriculture and the commercial entanglements of eighteenth-century New England farmers, see Richard Bushman, *From Puritan to Yankee: Character and the Social Order in Connecticut, 1690–1765* (New York, 1970).

5. On the outmigration of New Englanders, see Lois K. Mathews, *The Expansion of New England* (New York, 1909).

6. One of the few studies of the migration of landless young men to the cities in the late eighteenth and early nineteenth centuries is A. S. Horlick, *Country Boys and Merchant Princes: The Social Control of Young Men in New York* (Lewisburg, 1975). See also David F. Allmendinger, *Paupers and Scholars* (New York, 1973).

7. On the ascendancy of the merchants in New England, see Bernard Bailyn, *The New England Merchants of the Seventeenth Century* (Cambridge, 1955); Richard J. Purcell, *Connecticut in Transition, 1775–1818* (New Haven, 1918); Arthur M. Schlesinger, *Colonial Merchants and the American Revolution* (New York, 1918); and Richard Bushman, *From Puritan to Yankee*.

8. On the transformation of Harvard under mercantile auspices, see Ronald Story, *The Forging of an Aristocracy*; on the rise of lay influence in Connecticut, see Charles I. Foster, *An Errand of Mercy: The Evangelical United Front, 1790–1837* (Chapel Hill, 1960), pp. 132ff.

9. On the role of Boston in national economic development, see A. M. Johnson and B. E. Supple, *Boston Capitalists and Western Railroads: A Study in the Nineteenth Century Investment Process* (Cambridge, 1967); William B. Gates, *Michigan Copper and Boston Dollars* (Cambridge, 1951); and Gabriel Kolko, "Brahmins and Businessmen: A Hypothesis on the Social Basis of Success in America," in *The Critical Spirit: Essays in Honor of Herbert Marcuse*, ed. Barrington Moore and Kurt Wolfe (Boston, 1967).

10. On the intactness of the older social order in New England, see Stephan Thernstrom, *Poverty and Progress*, pp. 31ff. Richard Purcell, *Connecticut in Transition*, is excellent on the efforts of the new commercial order to preserve older modes of authority. I believe that Richard Bushman's account of the transformation of the corporatist Puritan into the individualist Yankee somewhat distorts the time frame. He attributes to the mid-eighteenth century changes that did not, in my opinion, become pervasive until the nineteenth.

11. See J. T. Main, *Social Structure*, pp. 44–67, 167–74; and Gary B. Nash, *Class and Society*, pp. 11–12. Gordon Wood has suggested that Virginia underwent a major social crisis in the course of the eighteenth century; see his article, "Rhetoric and Reality in the American Revolution," *William and Mary Quarterly*, 3rd Series, 23 (1966): 3–32. While Virginia agriculture certainly became more commercial and the position of small farmers was certainly compromised, I would argue that the crisis and its resolution were far less profound than New England's. There are, nevertheless, intriguing parallels.

12. The best source on this group is Frank Owsley, *Plain Folk of the Old South* (Chicago, 1949).

13. On the Great Awakening in the South, see Howard Miller's superb book, *The Revolutionary College: American Presbyterian Higher Education, 1707–1837* (New York, 1976).

14. One of the best accounts of the impact of cotton agriculture on southern literary and intellectual culture is Clement Eaton, *The Growth of Southern Civilization* (New York, 1961). See also William R. Taylor, *Cavalier and Yankee: The Old South and American National Character* (New York, 1961).

15. Eaton, pp. 221ff., 114–19.

16. Eaton, pp. 196–200.

17. On the comparative development of the major cities, see Carl Bridenbaugh, *Cities in the Wilderness* (New York, 1938). On Pennsylvania, see J. T. Main, *Social Structure*; Sam Bass Warner, *The Private City: Philadelphia in Three Periods of its Growth* (Philadelphia, 1968), pp. 3–48; J. T. Lemon, *The Best Poor Man's Country* (Baltimore, 1972); and J. T. Lemon and G. B. Nash, "The Distribution of Wealth in Eighteenth Century America: A Century of Change in Chester County, Pennsylvania," in *Class and Society*, ed. Nash, pp. 166ff. On New York, see P. U. Bonomi, *A Factious People* (New York, 1971) and Thomas Archdeacon, *New York City, 1664–1710* (New York, 1976).

18. On Philadelphia merchants, see E. Digby Baltzell, *Philadelphia Gentlemen* (New York,

1964); F. B. Tolles, *Meeting House and Counting House: The Quaker Merchants of Colonial Philadelphia* (New York, 1948). On New York merchants, see V. D. Harrington, *The New York Merchant on the Eve of the Revolution* (New York, 1935) and R. G. Albion, *The Rise of New York Port* (New York, 1939). For a comparative treatment of elites in all three cities, see Edward Pessen, *Riches, Class and Power*.

19. On the religious opposition to institutionalization, see E. Digby Baltzell, *Puritan Boston and Quaker Philadelphia*. On legal structures in New York and Pennsylvania, see H. S. Miller, *The Legal Foundations of American Philanthropy, 1776–1844* (Madison, 1961). On attitudes towards corporations in New York and Pennsylvania, see Joseph S. Davis, *Essays in the Earlier History of American Corporations* (Cambridge, 1918) and Louis Hartz, *Economic Policy and Democratic Thought* (New York, 1948). Edward Pessen's discussion of the participation of mercantile elites in voluntary organizations, because it is concerned with delineating the similarities between urban mercantile groups, misses some important differences. It is certainly true, as he suggests (and in contrast to Tocqueville), that the wealthy took the lead in all cities in underwriting and controlling the activities of a wide variety of artistic, literary, educational, and charitable organizations. But I am persuaded that such institutions were less central to the identities and function of New York and Philadelphia elites than to those of Boston. Especially telling as far as New York is concerned are not only differences in the legal status of charitable trusts and the ability of testators to make bequests to them, discussed by James Barr Ames in "The Failure of the Tilden Trust," in *Lectures on Legal History* (Cambridge, 1913), pp. 285ff., and by A. W. Scott, "Charitable Trusts in New York," *New York University Law Review* 26 (1951): 2, 251ff., but also the patterns of college attendance by families listed in Moses Yale Beach, *Wealth and Biography of the Wealthy Citizens of the City of New York* (New York, 1845). A study of the patterns of college attendance of thirty of the most prominent families listed by Beach through 1930 shows that, while Columbia is the institution most resorted to, a surprising number of sons were sent to other places, especially Harvard, Yale, and Princeton. The Livingstons, for example, sent thirty sons to Columbia, fourteen to Yale, twelve to Princeton, and eleven to Harvard. The Primes sent only three sons to Columbia, but five to Yale, five to Princeton and one to Harvard. The Roosevelts sent eight to Columbia, thirteen to Harvard, four to Princeton, and one to Yale. The basic pattern shows a number of interesting features: 1) that religion, at least before 1860, was an important determinant of college choice—Presbyterians attended Yale and Princeton, Episcopalians attended Columbia, and Dutch-Reformed split their choices between Harvard, Yale, Princeton, and Rutgers; 2) that after 1860, prominent New Yorkers abandoned Columbia in favor of Harvard and Yale; 3) that the overall attendance of prominent New Yorkers at any college is far lower than the attendance of Bostonians at Harvard.

20. On political conflicts over institutionalization in New York, see David Humphreys, *From King's College to Columbia* (New York, 1969) and John S. Whitehead, *The Separation of College and State*.

21. On the state in Pennsylvania enterprise, see Louis Hartz, *Economic Policy*. See also A. D. Chandler, *The Visible Hand*, pp. 34ff.

22. On Boston's economic importance, see G. T. White, *History of the Massachusetts Hospital Life Insurance Company* (Cambridge, 1964) and Vincent F. Carosso, *Investment Banking in America* (Cambridge, 1970).

23. On the origins of Princeton students, see *The Princetonians*, ed. James McLachlan (Princeton, 1979); on Yale, see F. B. Dexter, *Yale Annals and Biographies* (New York, 1896); on Harvard, see Ronald Story, *Forging of an Aristocracy*; on Columbia, see David Humphreys, *From King's College to Columbia*.

24. On opposition to the Constitution, see J. T. Main, *The AntiFederalists, 1781–1788* (Chapel Hill, 1961).

25. On the nationalization of political life, see J. M. Blum, *The Republican Roosevelt* (New York, 1954).

Chapter Two

1. Alexis de Tocqueville, *Democracy in America,* ed. Phillips Bradley (New York, 1945), vol. 1, p. 50.

2. John Winthrop, "The Model of Christian Charity," in *The Annals of America,* ed. Mortimer Adler et al. (Chicago, 1968), pp. 113ff. Winthrop's assertions of the corporate nature of society were more than rhetorical exercises. The two most significant early controversies in the Bay Colony, between Winthrop and the Antinomians and between Winthrop and merchant Robert Keayne, centered precisely on this issue. In the case of the Antinomians, the basic issue had to do with the credence to be granted individual religious revelations that conflicted with the interests of the corporate social order. See Emery Battis, *The Antinomian Controversy* (Chapel Hill, 1963). In the case of Keayne, the issue was whether a merchant's first obligation was to provide the community with needed goods at a reasonable price or to turn a profit. The medieval corporate nature of early Puritan economic legislation is discussed extensively by Bernard Bailyn in *The New England Merchants of the Seventeenth Century* (Cambridge, 1955).

3. The ideal type of division actually gave a third to the widow (which, if she failed to remarry, was usually divided among her children on her death), a double share to the eldest son, and equal shares among the later-born sons and daughters. There was, however, considerable variation in how partitions were carried out. Sometimes widows relinquished their shares in exchange for support during the remainder of their lifetimes. Sometimes daughters received only cash and personalty, while sons received land and farm implements. In spite of the richness of the sources, there have been few comprehensive studies of inheritance practice in early New England. Among the studies that have been done, the best are: George L. Haskins, "The Beginnings of Partible Inheritance in the American Colonies," *Yale Law Journal* 51 (1942): 1295ff.; Philip Greven, *Four Generations;* Bernard Farber, *Guardians of Virtue;* John J. Waters, "Patrimony, Succession, and Social Stability: Guilford, Connecticut in the Eighteenth Century," *Perspectives in American History* 10 (1976): 131–60; and "American Colonial Stem Families: Persisting European Patterns in the Old World" (unpublished paper presented to the History Department Faculty Seminar, Wesleyan University, 1978); Janice Cunningham, "From Fathers to Sons: The Emergence of the Modern Family in Rural Connecticut, 1700–1850" (unpublished M.A. thesis, Wesleyan University, 1979); and William Ritchie, "Inheritance Practice in Hartford County, Connecticut, 1650–1750" (unpublished seminary paper, Wesleyan University, 1977). My own dissertation, "Family Structure and Class Consolidation among the Boston Brahmins" (SUNY at Stony Brook, 1973), deals extensively with inheritance practices among the merchant families of Salem and Boston.

4. The absence of formal organizations and their halting development in colonial America is discussed in J. S. Davis, *American Corporations,* and in E. M. Dodd, *American Business Corporations until 1860 with Special Reference to Massachusetts* (Cambridge, 1960). The best general account of the dependence of the colonists on the family as a mediator of basic social, economic, and cultural functions is Edmund S. Morgan, *The Puritan Family* (New York, 1966).

5. There is a good deal of argument among historians as to the point at which individualism does become a significant factor in colonial New England. Some, like Darrett Rutman in *Winthrop's Boston* (Chapel Hill, 1965) place it as early as 1650. Others, like Richard Bushman in *From Puritan to Yankee,* place it almost a century later. This argument

is hardly unique to American historians—medievalists have been wrangling over the issue for some time. It is a rather fruitless controversy, the results depending largely on how one defines "individualism" and where one conducts one's investigations. Certain overall parameters of the problem are clear, however. To the extent that the individual does become significant in the seventeenth century, this occurs first in the large cities and among merchants. Like so many developments in the colonial period, individualism was slow to penetrate the countryside. And even where it did exist among urban merchants as a mode of economic behavior, it was constrained by the dependence of merchants on kin for capital and manpower.

6. On the cellular character of expanding settlements, see Lois Kimball Elkins , *The Expansion of New England* (Boston: Houghton Mifflin, 1909); Page Smith, *As a City Upon a Hill: The Town in American History* (Cambridge, 1973); and Michael Zuckerman, *Peaceable Kingdoms: New England Towns in the Eighteenth Century* (New York, 1970).

7. On the peculiar nature of American law during the colonial period, see *Law and Authority in Colonial Massachusetts*, ed. George A. Billias (Barre, 1965); William E. Nelson, *Americanization of Common Law: the Impact of Legal Change on Massachusetts Society, 1760–1830* (Cambridge, 1975); Morton Horowitz, *The Transformation of American Law*; Dwight Loomis and J. Gilbert Calhoun, *Civil and Judicial History of Connecticut* (Boston, 1895); and Charles Warren's invaluable history of the Harvard Law School, *Of Early Legal Conditions in America* (New York, 1908).

8. On the early medical profession, see Joseph Kett, *The Formation of the American Medical Profession* (New Haven, 1969); William G. Rothstein, *American Physicians in the Nineteenth Century* (Baltimore, 1972); and Richard Shryock, *Medical Licensing in America* (Baltimore, 1967). The general literature on the history of the medical profession in America is impoverished, especially for the colonial period. The best sources are still local histories, biographies, and proceedings of state medical societies.

9. The best account of the development of the New England clergy is David D. Hall, *The Faithful Shepherd: A History of the New England Ministry in the Seventeenth Century* (New York, 1972). Daniel H. Calhoun's *Professional Lives in America: Structure and Aspiration, 1750–1850* (Cambridge, 1965) is also useful.

10. On the nucleated character or early New England towns, see Bushman, *From Puritan to Yankee*; Sumner Chilton Powell, *Puritan Village* (Middletown, 1963); and John Reps, *The Making of Urban America* (Princeton, 1965). On the collective and anti-individualistic character of life in these settlements, see David H. Flaherty, *Privacy in Colonial New England* (Charlottesville, 1973).

11. One of the best studies of the familial character of the crafts is Bernard Farber, *Guardians of Virtue*, pp. 98ff. Alan Dawley, in *Class and Community: The Industrial Revolution in Lynn* (Cambridge, 1976), Edmund S. Morgan, in *The Puritan Family*, and Carl Bridenbaugh, in *The Colonial Craftsman* (New York, 1950), have written about their products and techniques, but little is known of their identities or patterns of organization.

12. On the failure to carry guild organization to New England, see Bernard Bailyn, *New England Merchants*, pp. 35–37. On town regulation of crafts, see Oscar and Mary Handlin, *Commonwealth: A Study of the Role of Government in the American Economy, Massachusetts, 1774–1861* (New York, 1947, p. 68.

13. On merchants, see W. T. Baxter, *The House of Hancock: Business in Boston, 1724–1775* (Cambridge, 1945); K. W. Porter, *The Jacksons and the Lees* (Cambridge, 1937); and my dissertation (cited above, n. 3).

14. On the clergy's problems in adjusting to New World conditions, see David D. Hall, *The Faithful Shepherd*. In understanding the situation of the ministry, it is essential to recognize that early seventeenth-century puritanism was not a monolithic, coherently organized set of doctrines but, rather, a general body of dissent from the English religious

establishment. There was fundamental disagreement and heated controversy on almost every major issue of theology and ecclesiastical organization. The New England experience was Puritanism's first real venture in institutionalization. And in attempting to make flesh of the word, issues like the nature of the covenant and the status of the clergy, which had seemed fairly unimportant—or at least largely theoretical—in character, became compelling problems in the distribution of social and political power. Similar conflicts developed in England during the Puritan Revolution of the 1640s and 50s between Congregationalists (Separatists) and Presbyterians.

15. On the impact of these "coping strategies" on the rural population, see James Henretta, "Families and Farms: *Mentalité* in Pre-Industrial America," *William and Mary Quarterly*, 3rd Series, XXXV (1978): 3–32.

16. Kenneth Lockridge, "Land, Population, and the Evolution of New England Society, 1630–1790," in G. B. Nash, *Class and Society*, p. 156.

17. Philip Greven, *Four Generations*, pp. 105, 183.

18. Greven, pp. 124ff.

19. John J. Waters, "Patrimony, Succession, and Social Stability," pp. 131–60.

20. Janice Cunningham, in "From Fathers to Sons," gives an especially interesting account of the role of fathers in underwriting the mobility of their sons from Middlefield, Connecticut to Granville, Massachusetts and to communities in the South.

21. Alan Dawley, *Class and Community*, pp. 16–20, 42ff.

22. Bernard Farber, *Guardians of Virtue*, pp. 66ff.; Janice Cunningham, "From Fathers to Sons," pp. 71–119.

23. Cunningham, pp. 66ff.

24. Dawley, pp. 42ff.

25. Richard Bushman, *From Puritan to Yankee*, pp. 196ff.

26. Lyman Beecher, *Autobiography* (New York, 1864), vol. I, p. 159.

27. Bushman, pp. 235–66. An excellent view of New and Old Light alliances can be found in Edmund S. Morgan's discussion of the "Wallingford Controversy" in his biography of Ezra Stiles, *The Gentle Puritan: A Life of Ezra Stiles, 1727–1795* (New Haven, 1962).

28. On the unspecialized character of the eighteenth-century mercantile firm, see K. W. Porter, *The Jacksons and the Lees*, and Alfred D. Chandler, *The Visible Hand*, pp. 17–49.

29. James Jackson, *Notes and Reminiscences of Hon. Jonathan Jackson* (Boston, 1866), p. 11.

30. Additional material on Jackson and his career can be found in Porter, *The Jacksons and the Lees*; in James Jackson Putnam, *A Memoir of Dr. James Jackson* (Boston, 1907); and in John P. Marquand, *Timothy Dexter Revisited* (Boston, 1960).

31. On postwar commercial instability in New England, see Porter, *The Jacksons and the Lees*; Samuel Eliot Morison, *Maritime History of Massachusetts, 1783–1860* (Boston, 1921); and numerous primary accounts of mercantile tribulations, the best of which are *Henry and Mary Lee: Letters and Journals*, ed. F. R. Morse (Boston, 1924), and John, Francis and Charles R. Codman, *An Exposition of the Pretended Claims of William Vans on the Estate of John Codman* (Boston, 1837).

32. Among the many sources on Loyalists in New England during the Revolution are Wallace Brown, *Good Americans: Loyalists in the American Revolution* (New York, 1969) and Richard D. Brown, "Confiscation and Disposition of Loyalists's Estates in Suffolk County, Massachusetts, "*William and Mary Quarterly*, 3rd Series, 21 (1964): 534ff. An especially interesting discussion of the identities, wealth, and activities of Boston Loyalists can be found in J. D. Prown, *John Singleton Copley* (Cambridge, 1966).

33. James Henretta, *The Evolution of American Society, 1700–1815* (Lexington, 1973) and E. P. Douglass, *Rebels and Democrats* (Chicago, 1955) give excellent accounts of the impact of the war and social change on politics.

34. For discussions of the postwar rise of poverty and deviance, see Handlin and Han-

dlin, *Commonwealth*, pp. 247ff.; David Rothman, *Discovery of the Asylum*, pp. 57ff. Some commentators suggest that the apparent increase in deviance was a function of changing definitions of the boundaries of acceptable behavior and an increasing sensitivity among the respectable to the social threat posed by unconventional behavior. While both points are certainly well taken, the *Selectmen's Records* and *Town Accounts* of cities like Middletown show an unmistakable and dramatic increase after 1780 in the number of persons requesting public assistance. Many were itinerants. But a remarkable number were local families who could no longer care for their aged parents and mentally defective siblings.

35. On British corporate traditions, see Lawrence Stone, *The Crisis of the Aristocarcy* (New York, 1965) and W. K. Jordan, *Philanthropy in England, 1480–1600: A Study of Changing Patterns of Social Aspiration* (London, 1959).

Chapter Three

1. Tocqueville, *Democracy*, vol. 1, pp. 198–99.

2. On the chartering of cities, see Handlin and Handlin, *Commonwealth*, p. 255. The Connecticut cities to receive charters immediately after the Revolution were New Haven, Hartford, Middletown, New London, and Norwich.

3. Dorothy Lipson, *Freemasonry in Federalist Connecticut* (Princeton, 1977). I am also grateful for insights into the social function of masonary to my student, Barry Wilder, who wrote a brilliant paper on Middletown Masons.

4. These organizations included Alexander Hamilton's New Jersey-based Society for Useful Manufactures, the Massachusetts Society for the Encouragement of Useful Inventions, and the Connecticut Society for the Encouragement of Manufactures.

5. These included the Philadelphia Agricultural Society (1785), the Massachusetts Society for the Promotion of Agriculture (1792), the New Haven County Agricultural Society (1803) and the Berkshire (Mass.) Agricultural Society (1811). As Purcell suggests, these organizations were founded "in order to educate the farmer." Basically, the merchants were attempting to encourage farmers to produce better crops more efficiently. An important feature of these societies was their promotion of fairs, both for the exchange of agricultural information and to regularize relations between agriculture and the marketplace. The significance of prize-giving at these affairs should not be overlooked as a mechanism for socializing the farmers to competitive modes of behavior. Richard Purcell, *Connecticut in Transition*, pp. 103–11.

6. The most comprehensive listing of denominationally-connected reform societies is contained in Charles I. Foster, *An Errand of Mercy*, pp. 275–80.

7. A great many individuals served in the Revolutionary armies. But, inasmuch as they served in particular units and had little contact with one another, the war for the average enlisted man did not enormously increase his circle of acquaintance. In any case, the rise of organizations like the Society of the Cincinnati—and the failure of comparable associations to develop among veterans at the lower levels of service—suggests that the role of military service in fostering broader patterns of trust was limited to the officer corps. The officers who formed the Cincinnati did so on a state-wide basis. As such, they comprised individuals who were already related to one another, who had attended college together, or who knew one another through earlier political, professional, or business contacts. The earlier contacts, when added to the intensive common experience of war, led to the formation of the formal organization.

8. Joseph Story, *Commentaries on the Law of Partnership* (Boston, 1841), vol. 4, pp. 94, 130–33.

9. Story, vol. 9, pp. 169, 261.

10. For good surveys of factors affecting marital choice, see Bernard Farber, *Kinship and Class: A Midwestern Study* (New York, 1971); *Readings in Kinship and Social Structure*, ed. Nelson Graeburn (New York, 1971); and Lynd and Lynd, *Middletown*, pp. 110ff.

11. Greven, *Four Generations*, pp. 79ff.

12. Studies of colonial marriage patterns include the work of Greven, Farber, Cunningham, and Hall, which I have already cited. See also Robert Gough, "Marriage Practices and Family Arrangements among the Wealthy in Late 18th Century Philadelphia" (a paper presented at the Annual Meeting of the Organization of American Historians, New York, 1978). This topic, though largely ignored by scholars of North American society, has been extensively studied by Latin Americanists.

13. Such patterns of consolidation would be of particular importance in older settlements that had been founded on the open-field system. This system nucleated families in village centers and scattered their holdings over different types of land, ensuring that each family obtained its share of meadows, woodlots, and so on. By the eighteenth century, according to Bushman, farmers were attempting to consolidate these scattered holdings. And the newer "outliver communities" began with consolidated holdings, the familiar homestead. See Bushman, *From Puritan to Yankee*, pp. 54ff., and Powell, *Puritan Village*.

14. My work—and that of the Greater Middletown Preservation Trust—in the Middletown *Proprietors' Records* and Probate material indicates that daughters and their husbands tended to receive both less land and land further from the center of the settlement after 1700.

15. On efforts to keep farms in the paternal line, see Waters, "Patrimony" and Henretta, "*Mentalité.*"

16. These patterns of marital exchange are enormously complex—so much so that they cannot be presented on a two-dimensional area. One such pattern can be seen in the interrelations of the Wetmore, Stow, Bacon, and Hubbard families of Middletown. One can get a sense of the intensity of these interconnections when one sees, for example, the marriages of the fourteen children of Thomas Wetmore (b. 1652) and Elizabeth Hubbard (1659–1725). Of the fourteen, four married Stows, five married Bacons, and one married a Hubbard. The children of Elizabeth (Hubbard) Wetmore's brothers, George and Nathaniel, favored marriages to Robbards, Johnsons, Wetmores, and Millers. As one traces out these patterns, one discovers an ebb and flow of connections between generations—regular patterns of exchange that include some families in the community, but exclude others.

17. By the second half of the eighteenth century, however, the pattern breaks down as different branches of the families pursue different occupations with varying degrees of success or become outwardly mobile. By the end of the century, marriages are along occupational lines—with scattered first-cousin marriages. I have reconstructed these patterns from the Middletown *Vital Records*.

18. Henretta, "Economic Development and Social Structure in Colonial Boston," in G. B. Nash, *Class and Society*, p. 139.

19. The literature on artisans is very scanty—though recent work, most notably Alan Dawley's *Class and Community* and H. B. Rock's *Artisans of the New Republic: The Tradesmen of New York in the Age of Jefferson* (New York, 1979), are important and promising contributions to the field. Also useful are Bernard Farber, *Guardians of Virtue*; Bridenbaugh, *Colonial Craftsmen*; and Edwin Tunis, *Colonial Craftsmen and the Beginnings of American Industry* (Cleveland, 1965). The latter is especially helpful in establishing a sense of the contexts in which the different crafts were carried on and the technological processes involved.

20. I have constructed this typology on the basis of my readings in Farber and Tunis.

21. Dawley, *Class and Community*, pp. 18–19.

22. On the Quaker potters of Essex County, Massachusetts—and on potting generally as a colonial craft—see Laura W. Watkins, *Early New England Potters and Their Wares* (Cambridge, 1950).

23. On the importance of the Philadelphia Conspiracy cases, see Rock, *Artisans*, pp. 249ff. and L. W. Levy, *The Law of the Commonwealth and Chief Justice Shaw* (New York, 1967), pp. 183ff. The conspiracy doctrine applied in the Philadelphia Shoemakers Case was first applied in England in 1721. According to Levy, it had an important effect through the eighteenth century on legal views of combination in both England and America.

24. Rock, *Artisans*, pp. 190ff.

25. On such alliances as a general matter, see Farber, *Guardians of Virtue*, pp. 104–07. On the shipbuilders of Middletown Upper Houses and Portland, see Greater Middletown Preservation Trust, *Cromwell* (Middletown, 1981) and *Portland* (forthcoming). For similar alliance patterns among tinsmiths, toolmakers, and peddlars, see S. S. DeVoe, *The Tinsmiths of Connecticut* (Middletown, 1969).

26. Farber, *Guardians of Virtue*, pp. 102–04.

27. An indispensable source on printing and its craftsmen is Isaiah Thomas, *The History of Printing in America* (New York, 1970). He gives a detailed account of the activities of the Greens and other early printing families.

28. Peter Bohan and Philip Hammerslough, *Early Connecticut Silver, 1700–1840* (Middletown, 1970), gives eloquent testimony to the breakdown of stability in this occupational group.

29. S. S. DeVoe, *Tinsmiths*, pp. 3–34.

30. Watkins, *Potters*, pp. 62–79.

31. Farber, *Guardians of Virtue*, pp. 98ff.

32. Thomas, Bohan, and DeVoe all discuss the arrival of new groups of English artisans after 1750. The Connecticut tinware industry was established by one such immigrant, Edward Pattison, an Ulsterman, who settled in Meriden in 1750.

33. Dawley and Thomas are excellent on the rise of entrepreneurs in printing and shoemaking.

34. Rock, *Artisans*, pp. 165–69: ". . . in their efforts to expand their operations in line with the growing markets, masters eagerly sought to obtain credit. The most suitable sources of capital were the cities' commercial banks. Unfortunately, bankers seldom made direct loans to independent artisan manufacturers; they preferred to invest in mercantile-controlled enterprises. Furthermore, merchant bankers, many of whom were Federalists, were disinclined to deal with the more predominantly Republican mechanics." In response, the artisans attempted to establish a "mechanic's bank." Though successful in obtaining a charter, it was so badly run that it was bankrupt in three years.

35. On the politics of artisans, see Dawley, Rock, and Charles S. Olton, *Artisans for Independence: Philadelphia Mechanics and the American Revolution* (Syracuse, 1975).

36. On the Hall alliances, see T. P. Hall, *Genealogical Notes* (Albany, 1886) and C. S. Hall, *Hall Ancestry* (New York, 1894).

37. These alliances are reconstructed from F. B. Dexter, *Yale Annals and Biographies* (New York, 1885–1912) and J. L. Sibley, *Biographical Sketches of Those Who Attended Harvard College* (Cambridge, 1893–1969). Also useful were genealogies of the Chauncey and Whittelsey families.

38. On the controversy between the New Lights and the Old Lights in Connecticut, see Bushman, *From Puritan to Yankee*. Also useful are Richard Warch, *School of the Prophets, Yale College 1701–1740* (New Haven, 1973); R. H. Gabriel, *Religion and Learning at Yale: The Church of Christ in the College and the University, 1757–1957* (New Haven, 1958); Louis Tucker, *Puritan Protagonist: President Thomas Clap of Yale College* (Chapel Hill, 1962); and Stephen Nissenbaum, *The Great Awakening at Yale College* (Belmont, California, 1972).

39. On the Wallingford Controversy, see Edmund S. Morgan, *The Gentle Puritan*.
40. J. B. Sears, *Philanthropy in the Shaping of Higher Education* (Washington, 1922), p. 23.
41. Sears, p. 24.
42. Sears, p. 23, and Ronald Story, *Forging of an Aristocracy*, pp. 25ff.
43. Sears, p. 24, and Ebenezer Baldwin, *Annals of Yale College* (New Haven, 1838), pp. 306ff.
44. Baldwin, pp. 316–17.

Chapter Four

1. Bailyn, *Merchants*, p. 87.
2. Bailyn, p. 190.
3. Porter, *The Jacksons and the Lees*, pp. 88–89.
4. Porter, p. 97. In stating that the merchant group in the late eighteenth century was "pretty much of a closed corporation" in which "one does not encounter barefooted farm boys," Porter somewhat overstates the exclusivity of the merchant families. He himself cites Patrick Tracy, who climbed from the fo'c'sle to the counting house. A better known example is Joseph Peabody, who began as a crewman during the Revolution for the Salem merchant and privateersman E. H. Derby and who, by the beginning of the nineteenth century, was the richest man in New England.
5. Bailyn, *Merchants*, pp. 41–44, 108ff., 134ff. See also Emory Battis, *The Antinomian Controversy*. Battis points to the mercantile constituency of the Bay Colony's first major religious struggles.
6. L. V. Briggs, *History and Genealogy of the Cabot Family* (Boston, 1927), p. 38; and S. E. Morison, *Three Centuries of Harvard* (Boston, 1936), pp. 104–05.
7. See pp. 134ff.
8. An invaluable source on early mercantile alliances is Edward Savage, *Genealogical Dictionary of the First Settlers of New England* (Boston, 1860–1862).
9. On Hull, see Savage, *Dictionary*, vol. 2, pp. 492–94, and Bailyn, *Merchants*, pp. 134ff. Hull's *Letter Book, 1670–1685* at the American Antiquarian Society is a major source on early mercantile activity. On Codman, see C. C. Wolcott, *The Codmans of Charlestown and Boston, 1637–1929* (Boston, 1930).
10. On the Leveretts and Dudleys, see Savage, *Dictionary*. On the Higginsons, see T. W. Higginson, *The Descendants of the Reverend Francis Higginson* (Boston, 1910).
11. Savage, *Dictionary*, vol. 3, pp. 500–01.
12. Bushman, *From Puritan to Yankee*, pp. 43–53.
13. Bailyn, *Merchants*, pp. 174–76.
14. Bailyn, pp. 126ff.
15. *The Jacksons and the Lees*, pp. 11–12.
16. See Porter, pp. 11ff.; Bailyn, pp. 78ff.
17. *Merchants*, p. 136. My insight into the significance of clerical connections came from checking Bailyn's chart against Savage's more complete reconstruction of the families.
18. Savage, *Dictionary*, vol. 3, pp. 513–14.
19. Bailyn, *Merchants*, p. 137.
20. Considering the significance recent social historians have placed on partible inheritance, there have been remarkably few studies of testamentary practice. Among the more useful are those contained in the discussions of agricultural families by Greven and Waters, and in a study by a student of mine, William Ritchie, "Inheritance Practice in Hartford County, Connecticut, 1650–1750" (unpublished seminar paper, Wesleyan University, 1976).
21. All studies show a shift away from "thirds" and away from favoring of the first-

born son towards the middle of the eighteenth century. In some communities, such as East Guilford, Connecticut, studied by Waters, partible division was largely replaced by ultimogeniture, in which the youngest son inherited the paternal farm in exchange for taking care of his parents in their old age. My own work on Massachusetts merchant families shows a distinct tendency of testators to abandon "thirds" by the middle of the eighteenth century. This concides with the first use of trust-like arrangements. See my dissertation, pp. 195ff.

22. See Ritchie, "Inheritance Practice."

23. Savage, *Dictionary*, vol. 3, pp. 500–01, and Edmund Quincy, *Life of Josiah Quincy* (Boston, 1867), pp. 1–18.

24. Briggs, *Cabot Family*, pp. 33ff., and T. W. Higginson, *Descendants*, pp. 15–17.

25. On the Orne connection, see Briggs, "Pedigree of Horne of Orne of Salem, Mass.," in the Library of the Essex Institute, Salem, and *The Letters and Journals of Henry and Mary Lee*, ed. F. R. Morse (Boston, 1924).

26. On the Essex Bridge, see Briggs, *Cabot Family*, pp. 167–68, and Robert S. Rantoul, "The Building of the Essex Bridge," in *Historical Collections of the Essex Institute* 3 (1893): 63ff. See also Porter, *The Jacksons and the Lees*, pp. 488ff.

27. On the Charles River Bridge, see Briggs, pp. 75ff., and Stanley I. Kutler, *Privilege and Creative Destruction: The Charles River Bridge Case* (Philadelphia, 1971).

28. N. S. B. Gras, *The Massachusetts-First National Bank of Boston* (Cambridge, 1937) is the first definitive work on this institution. I have reconstructed the interrelationships of the first board of directors from a variety of genealogical sources:

George Cabot	Brother-in-law and first cousin of Stephen Higginson.
Stephen Higginson	Cabot's brother-in-law and cousin; partner of the Newburyport merchant, Jonathan Jackson.
John Lowell	Widower of Cabot's cousin, Susannah Cabot, and Higginson's sister, Sarah; husband of Thomas Russell's cousin, Rebecca Russell.
Isaac Smith	Cousin to Oliver Wendell and Jonathan Jackson.
Oliver Wendell	Cousin to Jackson and Smith and brother-in-law to Jackson's cousin, Edmund Quincy.
Thomas Russell	Cousin by marriage to Edward Payne and John Lowell.
Edward Payne	Cousin by marriage to Russell and Lowell.
William Phillips	His daughter, Abigail, married Jonathan Jackson's cousin, Josiah Quincy.
Jonathan Mason	Partner and in-law of William Phillips.

Three of the directors, James Bowdoin, Samuel A. Otis, and Samuel Breck, were not related in any direct way to the other nine or to one another. Bowdoin and Otis were probably included for political reasons; Bowdoin was Governor of Massachusetts, and Otis was Speaker of the House of Representatives. All three were wealthy merchants.

29. On the movement of Connecticut merchants to New York, see Pessen, *Riches, Class, and Power*, pp. 100ff.; H. M. Morgan, *A Season in New York: The Letters of Harriet and Maria Trumbull, 1801* (Pittsburgh, 1969). Moses Yale Beach's compendium of the rich men of New York identifies many migrants from Connecticut. Louis Auchincloss's novel, *Portrait in Brown-stone* (New York, 1962) is a *roman à clef* about the Williams-Palmer-Dixon cluster, which came from Stonington, Connecticut to New York. See also Priscilla S. Auchincloss, *The Ancestors and Descendants of Courtlandt Palmer Dixon and Hannah Williams* (New York, 1958). I am grateful to C. D. B. Bryan, a descendant of these families, for bringing these matters to my attention.

30. See Briggs, *Cabot Family*, and the genealogical chart of Cabot-Lee-Higginson-Jackson alliances in Porter, *The Jacksons and the Lees*. For a more substantive account, see J. J. Putnam, *Memoir of Dr. James Jackson*.

31. On the reorganization and elaboration of partnership firms, see Carl Seaburg and Stanley Paterson, *Merchant Prince of Boston: Colonel Thomas H. Perkins* (Cambridge, 1971) and Morison, *Maritime History*, pp. 273ff. Briggs and A. D. Munkittrick, "Samuel Wadsworth Russell (1789–1862)" (unpublished honors thesis, Wesleyan University, 1973) give good accounts of the activities of subsidiary firms in China.

32. On the Perkins connections, see Seaburg and Paterson, *Merchant Prince*, pp. 431–34, and T. W. Higginson, *Descendants*.

33. The best sources on Jeffersonianism in New England are Purcell, *Connecticut in Transition*; Noble E. Cunningham, *The Jeffersonian Republicans in Power: Party Operations, 1801–1809* (Chapel Hill, 1963); Paul Goodman, *The Democratic-Republicans of Massachusetts* (Boston, 1964); and W. A. Robinson, *Jeffersonian Democracy in New England* (Boston, 1916). It is not easy to make generalizations about the social and economic origins of the Jeffersonians. In Middletown, Connecticut, for example, leading Jeffersonians included such scions of distinguished old political and clerical families as Alexander Wolcott and William B. Hall (great-grandson of Gov. Law), such rising entrepreneurs as Nathan Starr, Arthur McGill, and Joshua Stow, and a motley collection of religious dissidents of artisan and agricultural background. It was not purely a religious phenomenon; Hall and Wolcott were Congregationalists. Nor was it simply a matter of economics, for a comparison of known Jeffersonians against the Middletown *Grand List* shows them to occupy both high and low positions. What is clear about the movement is its coalitional nature; it was an alliance of a diverse body of dissidents. The instability of the coalition is generously documented in J. M. Morse, *The Neglected Period of Connecticut History, 1818–1850* (New Haven, 1933).

34. On the troubles of the Middlesex Canal, see Christopher Roberts, *The Middlesex Canal* (Cambridge, 1938).

35. On the introduction of limited liability, see Handlin and Handlin, *Commonwealth*, pp. 159ff.; E. M. Dodd, *American Business Corporations*; and J. S. Davis, *American Corporations*.

36. This table appears in P. D. Hall, "Three Generations: Strategy and Modernization in Massachusetts Merchant Families, 1740–1799" (a paper delivered at the Annual Meeting of the American Historical Association, Washington, D.C., December 1980).

37. See my dissertation, pp. 195ff.

38. On the nature of these interconnections, see Ronald Story, *Forging of an Aristocracy*, pp. 160ff., and my dissertation, pp. 388ff. By the early 1820s, the directors lists of corporations in the Boston city directories show a stable pattern of interlocks between the major for-profit and non-profit enterprises. These connections were not merely ornamental. To some extent, as in T. H. Perkins' promotion of the building of the Bunker Hill monument and his ownership of the major supplier of granite to the project, they were simply ways of stimulating profits. The survival and failure rate of Boston banks in the panic of 1837, however, suggests that these connections served more significant economic control functions. For interlocks made available to threatened institutions the liquidity necessary for survival in a panic situation (see my dissertation, pp. 389ff.). G. T. White, in his *History of the Massachusetts Hospital Life Insurance Company* (Cambridge, 1955), makes clear the role of this corporation and the interlocking roles of its directors in facilitating the movement of capital from families into selective industrial ventures. The Company was complemented in its control function by the Suffolk System, an alliance of leading Boston banks, which, by requiring that non-Boston banks deposit specie with them equivalent to the amount of their paper in circulation in the city, protected Boston institutions against specie drains. On the Suffolk System, see D. R. Whitney, *The Suffolk Bank* (Boston,

1878) and Henry P. Kidder and Francis H. Peabody, "Finance in Boston," in *The Memorial History of Boston*, ed. Justin Winsor (Boston, 1880–1881), pp. 160ff.

39. Story, *Forging of an Aristocracy*, pp. 89ff., gives an excellent account of the changing patterns of preparation of Harvard students in the early nineteenth century.

40. Quoted in Bliss Perry, *The Life and Letters of Henry Lee Higginson* (Boston, 1921), p. 15. For similar descriptions, see the Lee correspondence edited by F. R. Morse, pp. 51–52, and Briggs, *Cabot Family*, pp. 228ff.

41. On the expansion of Atheneum proprietorships, see Josiah Quincy, *History of the Boston Atheneum* (Boston, 1856). This volume lists the ownership and changes in ownership of every share in the Atheneum. By linking these lists to those of directors of known Jacksonian banks, it becomes possible to trace the accomodation of the older and the newer groups.

42. On Jeffersonian families, see Farber, *Guardians of Virtue*, pp. 111ff. On the membership of the Grays, Silsbees, Crowninshields, and others in the Porcellian Club by the 1820s, see *Catalogue of the Porcellian Club, 1791–1961* (Cambridge, 1961).

43. On Joseph Story's career, see G. T. Dunne, *Justice Joseph Story and the Rise of the Supreme Court* (Cambridge, 1971) and W. W. Story, *Life and Letters of Joseph Story* (Boston, 1851). Story was instrumental in creating the legal doctrines that underlay the Brahmin institutional system, most notably through his decision in the Girard Will case.

44. See Harold Bowditch, *The Bowditch Family of Salem, Massachusetts* (Boston, 1936) and W. M. Whitehall and W. C. Endicott, *Captain Joseph Peabody* (Salem, 1962). On the Lawrences, see R. M. Lawrence, *The Descendants of Samuel Lawrence of Groton, Massachusetts* (Cambridge, 1904).

45. Typical of this perception of the "decline" of the Brahmin elite are Frederick Cople Jaher, *Doubters and Dissenters* (New York, 1964) and Robert Lucid's introduction to *The Journal of Richard Henry Dana* (Cambridge, 1968). For a brilliant and intuitive critique of this approach, see Gabriel Kolko, "Brahmins and Businessmen," cited above, ch. 1, n. 9.

46. These accounts include Edward Pessen, *Riches, Class, and Power*, and Ronald Story, *Forging of an Aristocracy*.

47. Oliver Wendell Holmes, *Elsie Venner, A Romance of Destiny* (New York, 1961), pp. 16–17.

48. Oliver Wendell Holmes, *Autocrat of the Breakfast Table* (New York, 1957), pp. 119–20.

49. Holmes, p. 119.

Chapter Five

1. Tocqueville, *Democracy*, vol. 1, p. 203.

2. Vol. 1, p. 219.

3. For a particularly good discussion of this optimistic attitude and its transformation in the course of the career of one prominent Federalist, see Richard Rollins, *Noah Webster* (New York, 1980). See also Richard Buel, *Securing the Revolution: Ideology and American Politics, 1789–1815* (Ithaca, 1972) and William N. Chambers, *Political Parties in a New Nation* (New York, 1963).

4. "The Massachusetts Constitution of 1780," in *Massachusetts, from Colony to Commonwealth* (Boston, 1950), pp. 127ff.

5. *Massachusetts*, p. 133.

6. *Massachusetts*, p. 136.

7. See the table on wealth-holding in Boston in 1771 in Henretta, "Economic Development and Social Structure in Colonial Boston," in *Class and Society*, ed. Nash, p. 140.

8. Richard Purcell, *Connecticut in Transition*, pp. 113ff.

9. Purcell, pp. 140–41.

10. It is sometimes difficult to ascertain whether certain state constitutions were liberal or conservative documents. Elisha Douglass, for example, begins his discussion of the New York Constitution of 1777 by characterizing it as a conservative vehicle. But as he discusses the details of the document, it becomes clear that certain aspects of it, particularly the provisions for ballot voting, a minimal property qualification for voting, and direct election of the state senate, were significant departures from what the conservatives actually hoped to achieve. See Elisha Douglass, *Rebels and Democrats: The Struggle for Equal Political Rights and Majority Rule During the American Revolution* (Chicago, 1955), pp. 55ff.

11. J. S. Davis, *American Corporations*, vol. 2, p. 28.

12. For the best discussion of New York's restrictions on endowment trusts, see James Kent, *Commentaries on American Law* (New York, 1836), vol. 2, pp. 285ff. Kent states that the Elizabethan *Statute of Charitable Uses*, the act that enabled corporations to hold charitable trusts, had not been reenacted after the Revolution in New York, New Jersey, Pennsylvania, or Maryland. H. S. Miller, in *The Legal Foundations of American Philanthropy, 1776–1844* (Madison, 1961), argues that New York's laws took a liberal attitude towards charitable endowments. He overlooks, however, the significance of the Regents of the University of the State of New York in limiting the autonomy of privately supported and controlled institutions. For a discussion of the Regents, see John S. Whitehead, *The Separation of College and State*, pp. 21ff.

13. The best discussion of these ideological differences and their ultimate accomodation in a consensus about the role of parties in American government is Buel, *Securing the Revolution*.

14. On these struggles, see Douglass, *Rebels and Democrats*; Allan Nevins, *The American States During and After the Revolution* (New York, 1924); J. T. Main, *The Sovereign States, 1775–1783* (New York, 1973) and *The Anti-Federalists* (Chapel Hill, 1961).

15. On opposition to corporations, see J. S. Davis, *American Corporations*, vol. 2, pp. 66ff., 303–09, and Handlin and Handlin, *Commonwealth*, pp. 186, 229–35.

16. On the seventeenth-century origins of Puritan hostility to equity courts and their use by the Church of England, see Kent, *American Law*, vol. 4, pp. 289ff.; Zephaniah Swift, *A System of the Laws of the State of Connecticut* (Windham, 1795), pp. 411ff.; Joseph Story, *Commentaries on Equity Jurisprudence as Administered in England and America* (Boston, 1836); and A. W. Scott, *The Law of Trusts* (Boston, 1939).

17. Jefferson's efforts to impose public control on William and Mary are discussed in W. B. Shaw, *The University of Michigan: An Encyclopedic Survey* (Ann Arbor, 1942), pp. 7ff., and Sadie Bell, *Church, State, and Education in Virginia* (Philadelphia, 1930).

18. G. A. Calcott, *A History of the University of Maryland* (Baltimore, 1966), pp. 6–9 and E. F. Cordell, *History of the University of Maryland School of Medicine* (Baltimore, 1891).

19. W. B. Shaw, *Michigan*, p. 8.

20. D. H. Hollis, *South Carolina College* (Columbia, 1951), pp. 8ff.

21. A.F.C. Wallace gives an excellent account of Pestalozzi's theories of education and their connection to political radicalism in *Rockdale: The Growth of an American Village in the Early Industrial Revolution* (New York, 1978), pp. 259ff. The best and most complete discussion of politics and pedagogy is Paul Mattingly's *The Classless Profession: American Schoolmen in the Nineteenth Century* (New York, 1975). For an interesting, though overly simplified discussion of pedagogy and politics, see Michael B. Katz, *Class, Bureaucracy, and Schools: The Illusion of Educational Change in America* (New York, 1971). In my opinion, the two primary models, once paternalistic voluntarism becomes unworkable, are democratic localism—which I associate with Jeffersonianism—and corporate voluntarism—which I associate with Federalism. One must be careful, however, of overly associating

these organizational options with politics. In areas where Federalism remains strong, democratic localism can be associated with Federalism and corporate voluntarism with Jeffersonianism. Thus, for example, Episcopalians, who tended to be Jeffersonians in Connecticut, might be active promoters of private academies, while the Federalist-Congregationalists promoted the public schools. Further, I believe that Katz errs in associating bureaucracy too firmly with elite control. Bureaucracy, as Richard McCormick has shown in "New Perspectives on Jacksonian Politics," *AHR* 65 (1971): 288ff., is an instrument that can be used for radical purposes as well as conservative ones.

22. On the situation of corporations in New Jersey, see J. S. Davis, *American Corporations*, vol. 1, pp. 349ff., on the Society for the Establishment of Useful Manufactures. Although the leading promoters of the company, Alexander Hamilton and William Duer, were New Yorkers, and although the bulk of the capital came from Pennsylvania and New York, New Jersey was chosen as the location for the company's incorporation because "The State, having scarcely any external commerce, and no waste lands to be peopled, can feel the impulse of no *supposed* interest hostile to the advancement of manufactures. Its situation seems to insure a constant friendly disposition" (p. 375). On the New England influence on New Jersey and its institutions, see Howard Miller, *The Revolutionary College.*

23. On these organizations, see Foster, *An Errand of Mercy*; Carl Bode, *The American Lyceum* (New York, 1956); David Mead, *Yankee Eloquence in the Middle West: The Ohio Lyceum, 1850–1870*; Donald M. Scott, "The Popular Lecture and the Creation of a Public: Professionals and Their Audiences in Mid-Nineteenth Century America" (unpublished paper presented to the Davis Center Seminar at Princeton, February 1979); David F. Allmendinger, *Paupers and Scholars*, and "The Strangeness of the American Education Society," in *History of Education Quarterly* XI (1971):3–22. On the relation between religion, education, and institutions of this type, Paul Mattingly's *The Classless Profession* and Donald Scott's *From Office to Profession* (Philadelphia, 1978) are indispensible.

24. Lyman Beecher, *Address of the Charitable Society for the Education of Indigent Pious Young Men for the Ministry of the Gospel* (Concord, 1820), p. 20.

25. Quoted in Rev. Samuel J. Mills, *Memoirs* (New York, 1820), pp. 106–07.

26. For an insightful discussion of the problems of young men seeking employment in the cities and the related problems of employers in ascertaining the character of employees, see A. S. Horlick, *Country Boys and Merchant Princes.* On the general problem of the concept of character and the nineteenth century's perception of its meaning and importance, see Paul Mattingly, *The Classless Profession* and Wilson Smith, *Professor and Public Ethics: Northern Moral Philosophers before the Civil War* (Ithaca, 1956).

27. The following table, showing the number of positions in colleges and professional schools in four major sections of the country by graduates who received their degrees by 1840, gives a good general idea of the relative contributions of the major northeastern schools to the development of higher education in the United States before the Civil War. It does not include graduates with positions at their own alma maters.

College	New England	Middle States (NY, NJ, PA, MD, DEL, DC)	South (VA, NC, GA, TENN, LA, ALA, TEX)	West	Total
Harvard	29	23	3	6	61
Yale	39	62	28	53	182
Dartmouth	28	21	12	37	98
Brown	14	15	4	12	45

College	New England	Middle States (NY, NJ, PA, MD, DEL, DC)	South (VA, NC, GA, TENN, LA, ALA, TEX)	West	Total
Bowdoin	16	12	4	10	42
Williams	3	7	1	3	14
Amherst	3	2	2	11	18
Middlebury	3	14	19	35	68
Colby	1	3	2	3	9
Columbia	4	31	1	1	37
Princeton	4	62	54	28	148

Those schools most closely associated with Yale and with New Light theology were, as this table suggests, the most active in sending college instructors to far-flung regions of the United States.

28. On the New England influence at West Point, see Stephen E. Ambrose, *Duty, Honor, Country: A History of West Point* (Baltimore, 1966). Of particular influence is Ambrose's discussion of Sylvanus Thayer, the "Father of West Point." Thayer was a Dartmouth graduate in the class of 1807, a member there of one of the college's two student societies, and a classmate and life-long friend of George Ticknor, whose ideas about educational reform profoundly affected him. Because of the nature of the institution, West Point obviously could not follow the curricular pattern laid out in the Yale Report. Thayer's disciplinary methods, however, were very much along the lines of Dwight's and Quincy's. Reinforcing his pedagogical ideas was a faculty in which Yale and Dartmouth graduates predominated.

29. This tendency is suggested by Lee Soltow in *Men and Wealth in the United States, 1850–1870* (New Haven, 1975), pp. 148, 185.

30. Proportion of Adult Males Holding Total Estate Adjusted for Age and Occupational Differences (TEH adjusted), Classified by Region of Birth and Residence of Men in the United States in 1860

Region of Birth	Region of Residence		
	Northeast	Northwest	South
Northeast	.63	.70	.68
Northwest	.58	.65	.63
South	.61	.68	.67
Foreign-born	.50	.57	.55

Note: Values are obtained from a regression equation fitted to the spin-sample data of the form $TEH = .1651 + .4765 \log(age - 18) - .1362 \, nA - .0800 \, NE_{res} - .0154 \, So_{res} + .0477 \, NE_{bir} + .0360 \, So_{bir} - .8026 \, FB$, $R^2 = .19$, $N = 13,696$. Each of the three birth and two residence variables is a simple dichotomy with a value of 1 if an individual has the attribute and 0 if he does not.

Source: Soltow, p. 185. By permission of Yale University Press.

31. Tocqueville, *Democracy*, vol. 1, p. 304.

32. For figures on southerners at Harvard and Yale, see F. B. Dexter, *Yale Annals and*

Biographies, Yale Obituary Record, and the Harvard classbooks and necrologies. An interesting discussion of the social clout of southerners at Harvard can be found in Charles Francis Adams, *Diary* (Cambridge, 1964–68), in which he mentions the takeover of the Porcellian Club by southerners and the New Englanders' response.

33. L. A. Warner, *Lincoln's Youth: The Indiana Years, 1816–1830* (Indianapolis, 1939), pp. 198–99.

34. Warner, pp. 200ff.

35. Lincoln was surrounded by New Englanders and the New England influenced. His law partner, Herndon, was a graduate of Illinois College, the creation of Yale alumni and a hotbed of abolitionist sentiment. One of his best friends, James Cook Conkling, was a Princeton graduate in the Class of 1835; Cook was elected Mayor of Springfield on Lincoln's Whig ticket in 1845. In addition to being a member of the Washingtonian Temperance Society, Lincoln was, in 1836, a co-founder of the Springfield Young Men's Lyceum. In January of 1838 he delivered before this group an address entitled "The Perpetuation of Our Political Institutions," in which he spoke in terms tht would have sounded entirely familiar to any Federalist of the 1790s. In Lincolns' view, the primary danger to American institutions came not from foreign enemies, but from the increasing disregard for law, the growing disposition "to substitute the wild and furious passions in lieu of the sober judgement of courts." He concluded his address by stating: "They [the founding fathers] were the pillars of the temple of liberty; and now that they have crumbled away that temple must fall unless we, their descendants, supply their places with other pillars, hewm from the solid quarry of sober reason. Passion has helped us, but can do so no more. It will in future be our enemy. Reason—cold, calculating, unimpassioned reason—must furnish all the materials for our future support and defense. Let those materials be molded into general intelligence, sound morality, and, in particular, a reverence for the Constitution and laws; and that we improved to the last, that we remained free to the last, that we revered his name to the last, that during his long sleep we permitted no hostile foot to pass over or desecrate his resting place, shall be that which to learn the last trump shall awaken our Washington." (In *The Collected Works of Abraham Lincoln,* ed. John Hay and John Nicolay [New York, 1894], vol. 1, p. 50.)

36. Charles W. Eliot, "The New Education," *Atlantic Monthly* (1869): 214.

Chapter Six

1. James Kent, *American Law,* vol. 2, pp. 271–72.

2. J. S. Davis, *American Corporations,* vol. 1, pp. 3–110.

3. A good indication of the confusion on such basic issues as the life of corporate charters is the fact that James Sullivan, who drafted the charter of the Massachusetts Bank, was unable a decade later to determine whether he had assumed the charter to be a perpetual one or not. By the 1790s, Sullivan had become a Jeffersonian and was politically inclined to view charters as limited—but this was an issue that had not even occurred to him when drafting the charter. See T. C. Amory, *The Life of James Sullivan* (Boston, 1859), vol. 1, pp. 146–387. For good discussions of the clarification of such matters, see Handlin and Handlin, *Commonwealth,* pp. 144ff., and E. M. Dodd, *American Business Corporations.*

4. Swift, *Laws of Connecticut,* pp. 317ff.

5. In the 1780s and early 90s, newspapers were filled with letters protesting the danger of legislatures' chartering away the privileges and powers of the state to private bodies: "If the legislature may mortgage, or . . . charter away portions of either the privileges or powers of the state—if they may incorporate bodies for the sole purpose of gain, with the

power of making bye-laws, and of enjoying the emoluement of privilege, profit, influence, or power,—and cannot disannul their own deed, and restore to the citizens their right of equal protection, power, privilege, and influence,—the consequence is, that some follish and wanton assembly may parcel out the commonwealth into little aristocracies, and so overturn the nature of our government without remedy" (*Connecticut Courant*, 4 June 1787). By the turn of the century, the hostility towards corporations had moderated considerably, the Jeffersonians regarding their creation as regrettable, even if necessary. As Judge Spencer Roane stated in an opinion in the Virginia Supreme Court in 1809, "With respect to acts of incorporation, they ought never to be passed, but in consideration of the services rendered to the public. . . . It may often be convenient for a set of associated individuals to have the privileges of a corporation bestowed upon them; but if their object is merely private or selfish; if it is detrimental to, or not promotive of, the public good, they have no adequate claim upon the legislature for privileges." Currie's Admin. vs. Mut. Ass. Soc., *4H & M 315*, 347–8 (Virginia, 1809). For a good account of the transformation of the hostility from all-out defiance to reluctant acceptance, see the discussion of the debates over the creation of South Carolina College in H. H. Hollis, *South Carolina College* (Columbia, 1951), pp. 31ff.

6. The Handlins bring this point out in *Commonwealth*, p. 165. The truth of their suggestion that the Jeffersonians suffered ambivalent attitudes about corporations is borne out by the manufacturing interests of such prominent Middletown, Connecticut Republicans as the Starrs, the Magills, and the Wolcotts. See Howard Dickman, "The Middletown Manufacturing Company," in *Connecticut Historical Society Bulletin* 37 (1972): 52–58.

7. E. C. Elliot and M. M. Chambers, *Charters and Basic Laws of Selected American Universities and Colleges* (New York, 1934), pp. 514ff., and D. H. Hollis, *South Carolina College*, pp. 3ff. See also John Whitehead's discussion of the structure of accountability in New York in *The Separation of College and State*, pp. 21–23, and David Humphreys, *From King's College to Columbia*.

8. Davis, *American Corporations*, vol. 2, pp. 22–23.

9. Davis, vol. 1, p. 12. As Davis suggests, the southerners were so touchy about the use of incorporation by royal governors, that they opposed the granting of a charter to the city of Charleston (vol. 1, pp. 58–59).

10. Davis, vol. 2, p. 22.

11. Harvard University, *Quinquennial Catalogue* (Cambridge, 1936), p. 13.

12. D. D. Hall, *The Faithful Shepherd*, pp. 227ff., and S. E. Morison, *Three Centuries of Harvard*, pp. 46–75.

13. Davis, *American Corporations*, vol. 1, p. 84. As Governor Dudley is supposed to have remarked on the status of Harvard's charter after the suspension of the colony's own instrument of incorporation, "The Calf died in the Cow's Belly."

14. Davis, vol. 1, p. 75.

15. Elliot and Chambers, *Charters and Laws*, p. 508; Davis, vol. 1, p. 85.

16. For a detailed listing of Yale's property, see Ebenezer Baldwin, *Annals of Yale College*, pp. 327ff. and "Yale College Treasurer's Book, 1701–1828," Manuscripts and Archives, Yale University. The latter item is revealing about the extent of Yale's significance as a source of commercial capital to Connecticut merchants in the late eighteenth century. Mortgages and personal notes were the major *loci* of college investments.

17. For the struggles over Yale's location, see Richard Warch, *School of the Prophets*, pp. 129ff.

18. Warch, p. 129.

19. Bushman, *From Puritan to Yankee*, pp. 221ff.

20. Brooks Mather Kelley, *Yale—A History* (New Haven, 1974), pp. 67–68.

21. Ezra Stiles, *Literary Diary* (New York, 1901), vol. 3, pp. 457–58.

22. Handlin and Handlin, *Commonwealth*, p. 166; United States Constitution, Article IV.

23. Morton Horowitz, *The Transformation of American Law, 1780–1860* (Cambridge, 1977), pp. 160ff.; Handlin and Handlin, *Commonwealth*, pp. 166ff.

24. William Tudor, in "An Answer to a Pamphlet Entitled 'Considerations on the Public Expediency of a Bridge from One Part of Boston to the Other' "(Boston, 1806), and in the *Monthly Anthology* 7 (1809): 191ff., argued that corporate charters were private contracts and hence, beyond the control of the legislature.

25. *Quinquennial Catalogue*, p. 13.

26. Morison, *Three Centuries of Harvard*, p. 212.

27. John Whitehead, *The Separation of College and State*, pp. 16ff.; Morison, pp. 212–15; and Story, *Forging of an Aristocracy*, pp. 135ff.

28. Story, pp. 24ff. As Seymour Harris and M. S. Foster point out in their economic histories of Harvard, there has been considerable debate about the relative public/private contributions to Harvard before the beginning of the nineteenth century. Harris suggests that Samuel Eliot, the first individual to attempt an analysis of patterns of benevolence to Harvard, deliberately falsified his figures in favor of the private sector in order to legitimate the the merchants' takeover of Harvard and their redefinition of it as a private institution. See Seymour Harris, *The Economics of Harvard* (New York, 1970), pp. 240-43 and M. S. Foster, *Out of Smalle Beginnings . . . An Economic History of Harvard College in the Puritan Period* (Cambridge, 1962). The financial history of colleges and other non-profit institutions is *terra incognita*. Beyond Harris and Foster, the field lies barren. J. B. Sears, *Philanthropy and the History of American Higher Education* (Washington, 1922) is a useful but outdated attempt at comparative history. Merle Curti and Roderick Nash, *Philanthropy in the Shaping of American Higher Education* (New Brunswick, 1965), give the intellectual background to American philanthropy, but little quantitative insight.

29. On contributions to Yale, see Sears, *Philanthropy*, p. 24; Clarence Deming, "Early Gifts to Yale" and "Yale's Larger Gifts," in *Yale Alumni Weekly* (1910): 607–09, 634–37; Ebenezer Baldwin, *Annals of Yale College*; R. B. Dexter, *Documentary History of Yale College* (New Haven, 1916); and S. R. Betts, "Alumni Gifts to Yale," in *The Book of the Yale Pageant*, ed. G. H. Nettleton (New Haven, 1916).

30. Handlin and Handlin, *Commonwealth*, pp. 138–39. In Connecticut, the Federalist efforts to restrict medical practice did not fail by legislative enactment, but by erosion. By the 1870s, the situation had deteriorated to the point that the New Haven Medical Association was lamenting that "Connecticut is the happy hunting ground of the 'medical tramp.'"See C. J. Bartlett, "Medical Licensure in Connecticut," in *The Heritage of Connecticut Medicine*, ed. Herbert Thoms (New Haven, 1942), pp. 126–36.

31. Sears, *Philanthropy*, pp. 23–24; Harris, *The Economics of Harvard*, p. 293.

32. Samuel Atkins Eliot, "The Charities of Boston," in *North American Review* (July 1860): 149ff.

33. Story, *Forging of an Aristocracy*, pp. 26–27.

34. See records of the Centum Milia Fund in *Treasurer's Records*, Yale University Archives. A list of donors and amounts contributed to this effort can also be found in Baldwin, *Annals*, pp. 327–42.

35. Of the thirty Boston Brahmin family sons who became physicians during the nineteenth century, twenty served on the staffs of the Massachusetts General Hospital, the Harvard Medical School, or the Boston Dispensary. Harvard itself was dominated in the nineteenth century by such socially prominent faculty members as John Quincy Adams, John Collins Warren, Jacob Bigelow, James Jackson, James Russell Lowell, and Charles Eliot Norton. As Story points out in his chapter on the Harvard faculty, one of the functions of Harvard professors after 1840 was to serve as social models for their students.

Notes

Notes

36. Quoted in *American Higher Education, A Documentary History*, ed. Richard Hofstadter and Wilson Smith (Chicago, 1961), vol. 1, pp. 205, 210.

37. *American Higher Education*, p. 211.

38. The best account of the final supplantation of the political and religious Overseers at Harvard is in Story, *Forging of an Aristocracy*, pp. 135–59. As he makes clear, the legislature through the 1850s was still attempting to politicize Harvard. And it was only through the most adroit maneuvering between the state's political factions and the conscientious building of alumni organizations that the University was finally able to achieve complete autonomy. Legally, of course, the Dartmouth College Case remained the foundation of the University's claims. These were buttressed by half a century of private benevolence that enabled Harvard to downplay the importance of the state's financial contributions. But, in the end, the ability to modify the charter required the cooperation of the legislature which, in an atmosphere of post-Jacksonian hostility to private power, was not easily persuaded.

39. Kelley, *Yale—A History*, pp. 235–36.

40. James Kent, *American Law*, vol. 4, pp. 284–85.

41. Lawrence M. Friedman, *A History of American Law* (New York, 1973), pp. 47–48; Swift, *Laws of Connecticut*, pp. 411ff.; and A. W. Scott, *Select Cases and Other Authorities on the Law of Trusts* (Cambridge, 1940).

42. Friedman, p. 47; see also the discussion of equity in *Proposed Revision of the Statute Laws of the State of New York* (Albany, 1828), pp. 29–44.

43. *Laws of Connecticut*, p. 423.

44. Quoted in Horowitz, *Transformation of American Law*, pp. 160ff.

45. Friedman, *History of American Law*, pp. 130–31.

46. Swift, *Laws of Connecticut*, p. 321.

47. Swift, p. 321 on the case of Bacon vs. Taylor, 6 *Kirby* 368 (1788).

48. Ibid.

49. Prescott vs. Tarbell, 1 *Massachusetts Reports* 204 (1804).

50. Parsons et ux. vs. Winslow, 6 *Massachusetts Reports* 169 (1810).

51. Swift, *Laws of Connecticut*, p. 182.

52. A. W. Scott, *Cases*, pp. 526ff.

53. Harvard College and Massachusetts General Hospital vs. Amory, 9 *Pickering's Reports* 446 (1830).

54. S. P. Dresch, "The Endowment Trust: Positive Theory and Normative Implications" (unpublished paper, New Haven, 1973), p. 4.

55. Howard Miller, *Legal Foundations of American Philanthropy*, pp. 21ff.; Irvin G. Wylie, "The Search for an American Law of Charity, 1776–1844," in *Mississippi Valley Historical Review* 46 (1957): 230ff.; on this case, see The Trustees of the Philadelphia Baptist Association vs. Hart's Executors, *Wheaton* 1, 4 L. ed. 499 (1819).

56. On the situation in New York, see James Barr Ames, "The Failure of the Tilden Trust," in *Lectures on Legal History* (Cambridge, 1913), pp. 286ff,; and A. W. Scott, "Charitable Trusts in New York," in *New York University Review* 26 (April 1951): 251ff.

57. See *Proposed Revision*, pp. 29–44 and Kent, *American Law*, vol. 2, pp. 268ff.; vol. 4, pp. 289ff. That New York took these restriction on the establishment of charitable trusts and on the actions of testators seriously is attested to by the fact that the state's courts repeatedly upheld them before the famous Tilden Case—as in Williams vs. Williams, 8 *New York Reports* 525 (1853), in Bascom vs. Albertson, 34 *New York Reports* 584 (1866), and in Cornell University vs. Fiske, 136 *United States Reports* 152, 10 S. Ct. 75, 34 L. ed. 427 (1890). According to Scott, had the Tilden bequest been made in New York, Michigan, Minnesota, Maryland, Virginia, and West Virginia, it would have been held invalid. Both New York and Virginia had changed their laws by early 1890s.

58. Cornell University vs. Fiske (1890).

59. These restrictions stem from the Georgian Statute of Mortmain, *9 Geo. II. c 36* (1736). Unlike the English Statute, which applied only to the holding of real estate, the American versions also applied to personalty. Such statutes were passed in California, the District of Columbia, Georgia, Idaho, Montana, New York, Mississippi, Pennsylvania, and Ohio. See Scott, *Cases*, pp. 541–42.

60. J. B. Sears, *Philanthropy*, pp. 23, 24–25.

61. Sears, p. 26.

62. These figures are drawn from the catalogues of graduates of Harvard, Yale, Princeton, and Columbia.

63. The *Patients' Register* in the Medical Library of the Institute of Living (Hartford Retreat) shows that prominent New Yorkers seem to have preferred to treat mentally ill members of their families in Connecticut rather than at their own New York Hospital's Bloomingdale Asylum. Of the patients admitted to the retreat between 1822 and 1840, thirty-five percent came from out of state, the largest number of these from New York; *The Eighteenth Annual Report of the Officers of the Retreat for the Insane at Hartford* (Hartford, 1840), p. 27.

64. On treatment of the mentally ill in New York State, see David Rothman, *Discovery of the Asylum,* and Eric Larrabee, *The Benevolent and Necessary Institution: New York Hospital, 1771–1971* (Garden City, 1971). The best primary source for making comparisons between states and between the public and private sector is the *American Journal of Insanity,* which began publication in 1844. See also H. M. Hurd, *The Institutional Care of the Insane in the United States and Canada* (Baltimore, 1916).

65. By 1840, only a third of Yale's students were natives of Connecticut; see ch. 8, n. 22.

66. The situation of charitable trusts in Pennsylvania was far more complex than Miller suggests. He states that the courts and the legislature of the state were friendly to private benevolence. Scott, however, makes clear that this was not necessarily so. First, trusts were not enforceable under equity in Pennsylvania, which had no equity courts—though they were, by the 1820s, enforceable under limited circumstances in common law courts (thanks to a decision by Federal court Judge Henry Baldwin, a Connecticut native, in the case of Sarah Zane's will). Secondly, Pennsylvania had passed a version of the Mortmain Statute, limiting the ability of testators to leave bequests to charity. Third, the heterogeneity of the state militated against the effective concentration of charitable wealth. On equity in Pennsylvania, see Friedman, *History of American Law,* pp. 130–31; S. R. Liverant and W. H. Hitchler, "A History of Equity in Pennsylvania," *Dickinson Law Review* 32 (1933): 156ff.; and Scott, *Cases,* pp. 526ff.

67. Miller, *Legal Foundations of American Philanthropy,* p. 36; see also, *The Girard Will Case* (Philadelphia, 1854) and C. C. Binney, *The Life of Horace Binney* (Philadelphia, 1903), pp. 214ff.

68. Tilden vs. Green, 130 *New York Reports* 29 (1891).

69. Sears, *Philanthropy,* p. 26.

70. E. Digby Baltzell, *Puritan Boston and Quaker Philadelphia,* pp. 369ff.

Chapter Seven

1. Benjamin Rush to David Hosack, 12 June 1812, quoted in Eric Larrabee, *The Benevolent and Necessary Institution,* p. 174.

2. An examination of the account books of the Middletown physicians William Brenton Hall and Ebenezer Tracy makes clear the breadth of orthodox medicine's constituency by

the first decade of the nineteenth century. Especially interesting are the entries listing obstetrical services in Hall's accounts. He had studied at the University of Pennsylvania, where his teachers had been trained in obstetrics. He owned William Smellie's *Treatise on the Theory and Practice of Midwifery* (1764) and the obstetrical appliances recommended by Smellie. While one is not surprised to find women of the upper classes taking advantage of Hall's expertise as an *accoucheur*, it is remarkable to discover that his obstetrical patients included women from all classes. Clearly, in Middletown at least, the mass of people had abandoned traditional non-medical modes of childbirth. A xerox copy of the Hall account book can be found at the Wesleyan University Library. Ebenezer Tracy's papers and account books are at the Connecticut State Library. For an excellent account of changing obstetrical practices, see Catherine Scholten, "A Great Change in Customs and Manners: Childbirth in America, 1760–1820," a paper delivered at the Annual Meeting of the Organization of American Historians, St. Louis, 1976.

3. See Kenneth Lockridge, *The New England Town*, pp. 66–69; and Philip Greven, *Four Generations*, pp. 24–30, 186–97.

4. Greven, *Four Generations*, p. 191.

5. Greven, p. 189.

6. Greven, p. 107. For general works on the deterioration of public health in New England, see John B. Blake, *Public Health in the Town of Boston, 1630–1822* (Cambridge, 1959); John Duffy, *Epidemics in Colonial America* (Baton Rouge, 1953); and O. E. Winslow, *A Destroying Angel: The Conquest of Smallpox in Colonial Boston* (Boston, 1974).

7. On the Puritan ideology of family, see Morgan, *The Puritan Family*.

8. The most provocative account of the efforts of families to accomodate themselves to changes in the occupational structure is Bernard Farber, *Guardians of Virtue*.

9. On the effect of partible inheritance on merchants, see my dissertation (cited above).

10. The clearest discussion of this widespread phenomenon is contained in Herbert Thoms, *The Doctors Jared of Connecticut* (Hamden, 1957), an account of the medical dynasty found by the Reverend Jared Eliot of Guilford.

11. These tables are constructed from a number of sources: the accounting of early physicians comes from Rufus Mathewson, "Biographical Sketches of Early Members of the Middlesex County Medical Society," in Connecticut State Medical Society, *Proceedings*, vol. 85 (1877) and "The Medical Profession of Middlesex County," in J. B. Beers & Company, *History of Middlesex County* (New York, 1884); see also Henry Bronson, *Medical History and Biography* (New Haven, 1876); E. E. Atwater, *History of the City of New Haven* (New York, 1887). Population figures for the counties are drawn from the colonial censuses, reprinted in the *Connecticut Archives* for 1894, and from the federal population statistics quoted in Beers and Atwater.

12. United States Department of Commerce, *Historical Statistics of the United States* (Washington, 1961), p. 34.

13. The career lines of physicians in these places were reconstructed from the biograhies listed in note 11 and from biographies in Franklin B. Dexter, *Yale Annals and Biographies* (New York, 1895).

14. Dexter, IV:186.

15. "Titus Morgan, Cromwell, Connecticut, to Mason Fitch Cogswell of Hartford," in Cogswell Papers, Connecticut Historical Society, Hartford.

16. Walter L. Burrage, *A History of the Massachusetts Medical Society* (Boston, 1923), pp. 8–10. See also Richard Shryock, *Medical Licensing in America, 1650–1965* (Baltimore, 1965); Joseph Kett, *The Formation of the American Medical Profession: The Role of Institutions, 1780–1860* (New Haven, 1968); and S. A. Green, *History of Medicine in Massachusetts* (Boston, 1881).

17. See Hall, *The Faithful Shepherd*.

18. On the structure of authority in the legal profession, see Hollis Bailey, *Attorneys and*

Their Admission to the Bar in Massachusetts (Boston, 1907); W. T. Davis, *History of the Judiciary of Massachusetts* (Boston, 1900); Dwight Loomis, *The Judicial and Civil History of Connecticut* (Boston, 1895); *The Yale Law School, The Founders and Founder's Collection* (New Haven, 1935); and C. R. McKirdy, "Lawyers in Crisis: The Massachusetts Legal Profession, 1760–1790" (Ph.D. dissertation, Northwestern University, 1969). See also William R. Johnson's first-rate *Schooled Lawyers, A Study in the Clash of Professional Cultures* (New York, 1978).

19. On early efforts to organize medical societies, see Burrage, *Mass. Medical Society*, pp. 1–36; and Connecticut State Medical Society, *Proceedings*, vol. 1 (Hartford, 1884).

20. Burrage, pp. 4–8, 416–23; one Boston physician was quoted as stating that quacks in the city abounded "like the locusts in Egypt," in Rhoda Traux, *The Doctors Warren of Boston* (Boston, 1968).

21. S. H. P. Lee abandoned medicine for the more lucrative commerce in nostrums. His "New London Bilious Pills" were advertised in newspapers throughout New England. A founder of the Connecticut Medical Society, his colleagues gave him the choice of ceasing to manufacture his patent preparations or leaving the society. He chose the latter. (A biography of Lee is contained in Thoms, *Heritage.*) Elisha Perkins, another founder of the society, developed devices called "metallic tractors" to which he attributed a variety of curative virtues. He was expelled from the society in 1796. Connecticut State Medical Society, *Proceedings*, vol. 1, pp. 39–40.

22. Burrage, *Mass. Medical Society*, pp. 1–2.

23. Quoted in Burrage, pp. 3–8.

24. Burrage, p. 6.

25. Burrage, p. 13.

26. New Jersey Medical Society, *Minutes and Proceedings* (Newark, 1875); and Burrage, pp. 8–9.

27. Connecticut State Medical Society, *Proceedings*, vol. 1, pp. iii–iv.

28. The William Hall *Account Book* shows that some patients took up to ten years to settle up their bills.

29. On hostility to early corporations, see Davis, *American Corporations.*

30. On the Saybrook Platform, see Bushman, *From Puritan to Yankee*; Richard Warch, *School of the Prophets*; and Harold J. Bingham, *History of Connecticut* (New York, 1962), vol. 1, pp. 228–29.

31. On the Yale charter of 1745, see Elliot and Chambers, *Charters and Basic Laws*, pp. 588–94; Ebenezer Baldwin, *Annals of Yale College*; Thomas Clap, *Annals or History of Yale College*; and L. L. Tucker, *Puritan Protagonist, Thomas Clap of Yale College.*

32. On the revolution of Connecticut's legal system, see Dwight Loomis, *The Judicial and Civil History of Connecticut* (Boston, 1895).

33. Burrage, *Mass. Medical Society*, pp. 20–21, gives an account of the military and political activity of the founders of the Massachusetts Medical Society. Connecticut physicians were also politically active in the late eighteenth century: nearly a third of the fellows of the society served in the General Assembly or were known to be politically active—most notably Samuel Woodward, one of the organizers of the Middletown Convention. One early member of the society, John S. Peters, was later elected governor of Connecticut.

34. Burrage, p. 20; Massachusetts Historical Society, *Proceedings* 7 (1866): 177–84.

35. Massachusetts Medical Society, *Catalogue of Officers, Fellows, and Licentiates* (Boston, 1894), p. 317.

36. *Catalogue*, pp. 18–19.

37. Ibid., and Harvard University, *Quinquennial Catalogue of Officers and Graduates* (Cambridge, 1936).

38. Mass. Medical Scociety, *Catalogue*, pp. 19–21.

39. Burrage, *Mass. Medical Society*, pp. 44–46.

40. An examination of the backgrounds of the seventeen incorporators of the Massachusetts College of Physicians in Sibley and the Harvard *Necrologies* shows that seven of them can be identified as Jeffersonians. See also Charles Warren, *Jacobin and Junto, or Early American Politics as Revealed in the Diary of Dr. Nathaniel Ames, 1758–1822* (Boston, 1931).

41. S. E. Morison, *Three Centuries of Harvard*, pp. 222–23; see also L. E. Hawes, *Benjamin Waterhouse, M.D.* (Boston, 1974).

42. Burrage, *Mass. Medical Society*, p. 78.

43. Burrage, p. 81.

44. The best discussions of the changes in Harvard's charter are in J. S. Whitehead, *The Separation of College and State* and Ronald Story, *The Forging of an Aristocracy*.

45. Morison, *Three Centuries of Harvard*, p. 213.

46. Whitehead, *The Separation of College and State*, pp. 18–21; Morison, *Three Centuries of Harvard*, pp. 210–14.

47. Ezra Stiles, *Plan of a University* (New Haven, 1953); for a background of the writing of this document, see Stiles, *Literary Diary*, vol. 2, pp. 207–59 and P. D. Hall, "Politics, Medicine and Higher Education: A Pre-History of the Yale Medical School" (Working Paper #6 of the Higher Education Research Group, ISPS, Yale University, 1976). Contrary to what most historians of eighteenth-century higher education have stated, Stiles did not initiate this plan. Rather, the General Assembly, in the hope of broadening the nature of the college beyond its religious emphasis, had expressed a willingness to donate funds to Yale to establish additional professorships. It requested of Stiles—one of several candidates under consideration for the presidency of the college—a memorandum describing what form these professorships might take. The initiative for professional education at Yale was, in other words, political in its origins.

48. Connecticut Medical Society, *Proceedings*, vol. 1, pp. vi–viii.

49. *Proceedings*, vol. 1, p. 50 (May 1797).

50. *Proceedings*, vol. 1, p. 72 (October 1799).

51. *Proceedings*, vol. 1, p. 75 (May 1800).

52. Evidence for this Jeffersonian conspiracy is entirely circumstantial. It is, however, persuasive. The 1801 election of officers put known opponents of Yale and Federalism—Woodward, Potter, and Hall—into office in place of known Federalists like Cogswell and Munson. Munson's letter of resignation, quoted in Henry Bronson, *Medical History and Biography*, pp. 27–28, refers to a conspiracy without giving any details. Cogswell's bitter but undated poem rounds out the circumstantial picture.

53. Mason Fitch Cogswell, "From the Characteristics—An Unpublished Poem," *Cogswell Papers*, Connecticut Historical Society, Hartford.

54. Woodward was, in fact, one of New England's most distinguished physicians and progenitor of a remarkable medical dynasty. An excellent biography can be found in Samuel Orcutt, *History of Torrington, Connecticut* (Albany, 1878), pp. 623–26.

55. On Hall, see Dexter, *Yale Annals*, vol. 4, pp. 481–82; T. P. Hall, *Hall Family Records*; C. S. Hall, *Hall Ancestry*, pp. 376–85; and Rufus Mathewson, "Biographical Sketches," in the Connecticut Medical Society *Proceedings*, vol. 85 (1877).

56. A copy of this handbill is reprinted in Thoms, *Heritage*, p. 35. Evidence suggests that Hall, who was responsible for editing and publishing the Society's revised by-laws in 1802, inserted this handbill in each copy of the pamphlet (a copy of the original is pasted into the cover of the copy of the by-laws owned by the Historical Medical Library of the Yale University School of Medicine). It must have enraged the Federalists!

57. On Cogswell, see Dexter, *Yale Annals*, vol. 3, pp. 321–26; Grace Cogswell Root, *Father and Daughter: A Collection of Cogswell Family Letters and Diaries* (Hartford, 1924). *Re* Cogswell's connections to Timothy Dwight and Nathan Strong: Strong's father was a college classmate and close friend of Cogswell's father, James; they served life-long pas-

torates in adjoining parishes; young Cogswell entered the medical profession on Strong's advice; and Strong preached the funeral sermon over Cogswell's father. Cogswell's brother was married to Dwight's wife's first cousin; Dwight and Cogswell referred to one another as "cousin" in their correspondence; Dwight's younger brother, Theodore, was Cogswell's best friend; another brother, Nathaniel, studied medicine with Cogswell. Cogswell's organizational interests included not only the medical society, but also the Hartford Retreat and the American Asylum for the Deaf and Dumb.

58. Connecticut Medical Society, *Proceedings*, vol. 2, p. vii (January 1807).

59. *Proceedings*, vol. 1, p. 136 (May 1807).

60. *Proceedings*, vol. 1, p. 136; *re* Eli Ives, see Bronson, *Medical History and Biography*, p. 32; *re* Foot, see Bronson, pp. 96–97.

61. Benjamin Silliman, "Origins and Progress of Chemistry, Minerology, and Geology in Yale College," Silliman Family Papers, Yale University Archives, vol. 4, pp. 61–64; Connecticut Medical Society, *Proceedings*, vol. 1, p. 139.

62. H. S. Burr, "The Connecticut State Medical Society and the Medical Institution of Yale College," in Thoms, *Heritage of Connecticut Medicine*, pp. 24–30; Francis Bacon, "The Connecticut Medical Society, A Historical Sketch of Its First Century," in the Connecticut Medical Society, *Proceedings*, vol. 100, pp. 177–206 (1892).

63. S. A. Eliot, "Public and Private Charities of Boston," *North American Review* (July 1845): 141–47. The willingness of wealthy Bostonians to support medical institutions was undoubtedly connected to the number of merchant sons who intended to enter medicine; see my dissertation, pp. 112–94, 367–86. The original subscription to the hospital raised almost one hundred thousand dollars in two weeks!

64. "List of Original Subscribers to Retreat for the Insane," Medical Library, Institute of Living, Hartford. The Yale Endowment at this time amounted to approximately $40,000.

65. On battles over the control of the establishment of medical schools and the granting of degrees in New York and Pennsylvania, see John Shrady, *The College of Physicians and Surgeons* (New York, 1901) and Joseph Gayley, *A History of the Jefferson Medical College of Philadelphia* (Philadelphia, 1858). In New York, the failure of Columbia to maintain its authority resulted in a fragmentation of resources between Columbia, the College of Physicians and Surgeons (a creature of the New York Medical Society), Rutgers Medical School (founded by dissenters from P & S), and the hospitals. A comparable struggle took place in Philadelphia between the University of Pennsylvania and the Philadelphia Medical Society, members of which eventually founded the Jefferson Medical College. By the 1850s, there were over a dozen medical schools of various sorts operating in Philadelphia. The rhetoric in the battles between physicians in these places was explicitly political, the medical societies accusing the colleges of forming "learned aristocracies" and being sources of "exclusive privileges and immunities."

66. Shrady, p. 42; and *A History of Columbia University* (New York, 1904), pp. 318–19.

67. Gayley, *Jefferson Medical College*, pp. 14ff.

68. G. H. Callcott, *University of Maryland*, pp. 16–17; E. F. Cordell, *History of the University of Maryland School of Medicine* (Baltimore, 1891), pp. 23ff.

69. Callcott, p. 29.

70. Callcott, p. 47.

71. Sarah Stage's *Female Complaints* (New York, 1979) gives the best recent account of the extent and the ideology of the patent medicine business.

72. The best account of Connecticut physicians' resistance to medical reform is Wendy Jacobson, "American Medicine in Transition: The Case of the Yale Medical School, 1900–1920" (Honors Thesis, Wesleyan University, 1976). According to Jacobson, New Haven physicians fiercely resisted Yale's efforts to take over the New Haven Hospital and the replacement of local clinicians as medical school teachers by research professionals.

Chapter Eight

1. Lyman Beecher, *Plea for the West* (Cincinnati, 1835), pp. 43–46.

2. D. H. Fischer, "The Myth of the Essex Junto," in *William and Mary Quarterly* 21 (1964): 219.

3. Charles I. Foster, *Errand of Mercy*, p. 185.

4. Foster, pp. 61ff.

5. D. F. Allmendinger, *Paupers and Scholars*, and "The Strangeness of the American Education Society," in *History of Education Quarterly* 11 (1971): 3–22. See also David Potts, "American Colleges in the Nineteenth Century: From Localism to Denominationalism," in *HEQ* 11 (1971): 363ff. On the general issue of the significance of education and cultural networks, Mattingly's *Classless Profession* is definitive.

6. For a relatively complete listing of these organizations, see Foster, *Errand of Mercy*, pp. 275–80.

7. Paul E. Johnson, *A Shopkeeper's Millenium: Society and Revivals in Rochester, New York, 1815–1837* (New York, 1978), pp. 62ff. See also Leonard E. Richard's discussions of abolitionist and anti-abolitionist groups in Utica and Cincinnati in *Gentlemen of Property and Standing: Anti-Abolition Mobs in Jacksonian America* (New York, 1971).

9. Johnson, *Shopkeeper's Millenium*, pp. 128ff.

9. A. F. C. Wallace, *Rockdale*, p. 265.

10. Michael B. Katz, *Class, Bureaucracy, and the Schools*, p. 10. I disagree with Katz's association of the Lancastrian system with Federalist authoritarianism. Really, it was a mode of control much more appropriate to the new Jeffersonian middle classes who, in implementing the system, not only saved money, but also replicated on a larger and more rationalized scale traditional educational practices. The advent of the Lancastrian system in Middletown, Connecticut came under the aegis of a Republican city government, a government dominated by Jeffersonian manufacturers (see *Record Book of the First School Society, 1800–1854*, Town Clerk's Office, Middletown, Connecticut). The Lancastrian system was implemented in Boston by a similar group; see Peter D. Hall, "Essay Review of Stanley Schultz, The Culture Factory: Boston Public Schools, 1789–1860," in *Science and Society* 39 (1975): 3. Carl Kaestle's *Evolution of an Urban School System* (Cambridge, 1973) provides an illuminating discussion of this issue.

11. On the founding of academies, see James McLachlan, *American Boarding Schools*, pp. 19ff. and Katz, pp. 22ff. Once again, Katz errs in calling the academies "profoundly public institutions." They were public in the same way that Harvard and Yale were—that is, they had public purposes, but were privately governed and supported.

12. On Dwight, see Charles E. Cunningham, *Timothy Dwight, 1752–1817* (New York, 1942) and Benjamin W. Dwight, *History of the Descendants of John Dwight* (New York, 1874).

13. Cunningham, *Timothy Dwight*, pp. 148–49.

14. Timothy Dwight, "Greenfield Hill," following the text given in *Connecticut Wits* edited by V. L. Parrington (New York, 1969), pp. 183ff.

15. Foster, *Errand of Mercy*, pp. 128ff.

16. For a billliant discussion of eighteenth-century collegiate discipline, see Phyllis Vine, "Preparation for Republicanism: Honor and Shame in the Eighteenth Century College" (a paper presented at the Annual Meeting of American Historians, New York, 1978).

17. Kelley, *Yale—A History*, p. 121.

18. In 1790, the Yale faculty consisted of the President, three tutors, and Samuel Wales, the elderly and decrepit Professor of Divinity. The tutors were little older than the undergraduates. By 1805, the faculty consisted of the President, the tutors, and professors of divinity, mathematics and natural philosophy, chemistry, and law. By 1813, these were joined by three professors of medicine.

19. "The Yale Report of 1828," quoted in *American Higher Education*, ed. Hofstadter and Wilson, vol. 1, p. 278.

20. *American Higher Education*, vol. 1, p. 287.

21. On the changing composition of the student population in the early nineteenth century, see David Allmendinger, *Paupers and Scholars*, and Colin Burke's Ph.D. dissertation, "The Quiet Influence: The American Colleges and their Students, 1800–1860" (Washington University, 1973).

22. Nativity and residence of Yale graduates, 1760–1860 (calculated from Dexter, *Yale Annals*, and the *Yale Obituary Record*).

Year of Graduation	Yale Graduates Born in Connecticut	Yale Graduates Living in Connecticut After Graduation	N
1760	84%	65%	32
1770	79%	53%	19
1780	96%	62%	27
1790	76%	38%	29
1800	88%	41%	34
1810	72%	34%	53
1820	60%	26%	57
1830	44%	22%	68
1840	32%	19%	105
1850	30%	16%	77
1860	27%	13%	109

23. Occupational Choices of Yale College Graduates, 1760–1880 (calculated from Dexter, *Obituary Record*, and class books).

Year of Graduation	Clergy	Law	Medicine	Business	Other
1760	41%	16%	19%	3%	21%
1770	42%	16%	5%	11%	26%
1780	19%	39%	12%	12%	23%
1790	21%	35%	21%	10%	13%
1800	9%	53%	9%	12%	24%
1810	15%	49%	6%	11%	19%
1820	23%	35%	11%	12%	19%
1830	24%	28%	7%	16%	25%
1840	27%	31%	9%	9%	24%
1850	17%	35%	5%	8%	25%
1860	22%	29%	14%	18%	17%
1870	10%	39%	9%	22%	20%
1880	7%	34%	13%	27%	19%

The low proportion of graduates entering medicine is probably accounted for by the fact that Yale's Medial Institution did not require a first degree for entrance and by the fact that medical practice in Connecticut and points west was non-institutional in character. This is a pronounced contrast to the situation in Massachusetts. The "Other" category includes teachers, engineers, journalists and other miscellaneous occupations.

24. Mobility of Yale Graduates, classes of 1760, 1770, 1780, 1790, 1800, 1810, 1820, 1830, 1840, 1850 (reconstructed from Dexter, *Yale Annals, Obituary Record*, and classbooks).

Class Year	New England	Middle Atlantic	South	West
1760	−9%	+9%	—	—
1770	−15%	+15%	—	—
1780	−27%	+23%	+3%	+3%
1790	−42%	+34%	+2%	+4%
1800	−18%	—	+17%	+4%
1810	−44%	+27%	+9%	—
1820	−33%	+10%	+7%	+14%
1830	−29%	+1%	+13%	—
1840	−25%	—	+7%	+18%
1850	−30%	+10%	+2%	+18%

147 The residency patterns of Yale graduates for the same classes show the following pattern:

Class Year	New England	Middle Atlantic	South	West	Foreign
1760	84%	16%	—	—	—
1770	85%	5%	—	—	10%
1780	70%	24%	3%	3%	—
1790	55%	37%	3%	4%	—
1800	79%	—	17%	4%	—
1810	43%	32%	17%	8%	—
1820	37%	19%	21%	23%	—
1830	26%	32%	25%	17%	—
1840	36%	28%	16%	20%	—
1850	22%	39%	17%	22%	—

25. "The Funds of Yale College, 23 March 1818," *Treasurer's Papers*, Yale University Archives.

26. Kelley, *Yale—A History*, p. 146.

27. There is some disagreement on the amount collected by Yale between 1820 and 1825. Sears gives a figure of $21,000. Ebenezer Baldwin's *Annals of Yale College* is the source of the figure I have given here.

28. The tangled story of the Eagle Bank failure has been reconstructed from a number of sources. These include correspondence in the *Treasurer's Papers* at Yale; Rollin Oster-wiess, *Three Centuries of New Haven* (New Haven, 1949); W. S. Hasse, *Banking and Money in Connecticut* (New Haven, 1957); and biographies in Dexter, *Yale Annals*.

29. "Statement of the Amount of Principal of the Funds," (1820) *Treasurer's Paper*, Yale.

30. "An Addition to an Act Entitled 'An Act Relative to the Investment of Certain Corporations in the Banks of the State,'" manuscript copy, 2 June 1824, *Treasurer's Papers*, Yale.

31. "An Agreement made by Daniel Potter, et al. of Plymouth, Litchfield County and James Hillhouse," 23 June 1824, *Treasurer's Papers*, Yale.

32. *Potter, et al. versus James Hillhouse*, Connecticut Superior Court, March 1827; and

letters from Asa Bacon to Stephen Twining, 28 June 1828 and 12 February 1828, in *Treasurer's Papers*, Yale. Because of the bank failure, the College's endowment dropped from $56,635 in 1825 to $17,856 three years later.

33. For a brief biography of Warner, see *Obituary Record 1859–70*, pp. 348–49. He was typical of the hundreds of young farm boys who, struck by the Second Great Awakening, decided at the advanced age of 22 to attend college. He early found that he had a particular talent for fundraising, being active in the Dwight Professorship drive of 1828–29. His letter to Jeremiah Day is dated 7 February 1831.

34. Quoted in Kelley, *Yale—A History*, p. 151; "Circular Furnished by Professor Goodrich, July, 1831," *Treasurer's Papers*, Yale.

35. John T. Norton to Professor Denison Olmsted, Albany, 24 August 1831, *Treasurer's Papers*, Yale.

36. "The Case of Yale College," printed broadside, dated 1 December 1831, *Treasurer's Papers*, Yale.

37. Ibid.

38. Analysis of contributors Centum Milia Fund in Pledge Books in *Treasurer's Papers*, Yale.

39. Wyllys Warner to Jeremiah Day, New York, 21 December 1831, *Treasurer's Papers*, Yale.

40. Warner to Day, Washington City, 11 February 1832; Day to Warner, New Haven, 15 February 1832, *Treasurer's Papers*, Yale.

41. Rev. Calvin Durfee, *Williams Biographical Annals* (Boston, 1871), p. 50.

42. Princeton University, *General Catalogue, 1746–1906* (Princeton, 1908) and James McLachlan, *Princetonians*.

43. Allmendinger, "The Strangeness of the American Education Society," and Stanley King, *A History of the Endowment of Amherst College* (Amherst, 1950). Amherst grew out of an education society the endowment of which, the Charity Fund, became the basis of the college's endowment. King gives an excellent account of the significance of local entrepreneurs and laymen in the college's financial affairs.

44. On college literary societies, see James McLachlan, "The Choice of Hercules: American Student Societies in the Early Nineteenth Century," in *University and Society*, ed. Lawrence Stone (Princeton, 1974), vol. 2, pp. 449ff., and T. S. Harding, *College Literary Societies: Their Contribution to Higher Education in the United States, 1815–1876* (New York, 1971).

45. A survey of the members of Skull and Bones, Yale's most prestigious secret society, for example, shows that for the classes of 1840, 1850, 1860, and 1870, members are nearly evenly divided between New England, the Middle Atlantic States, the South, and the West in terms of nativity and between business and the professions occupationally.

46. Durfee, *Williams Annals*, pp. 223–24.

47. For an account of the society system at Yale, see Lyman Bagg, *Fours Years at Yale* (New York, 1871) and the catalogues of the student societies in Manuscripts and Archives, Yale University. See also Kelley, *Yale—A History*, pp. 107–08.

48. W. R. Baird, *Manual of American College Fraternities* (New York, 1912) is an invaluable source on the organization and development of student societies.

49. I have reconstructed Runk's activities from a variety of sources including the Yale Class of 1841 *Album* (New Haven, 1866), the Yale *Obituary Record, 1880–1890*, and his obituary in the Allentown *Chronicle and News*, 11 May 1885. I have reconstructed his tangled financial affairs from the *Deed, Mortgage,* and *Continuance Dockets* in the Lehigh County Prothonotary's Office in Allentown. Runk's real estate empire collapsed in the late 1870s.

50. For an account of Hall's career, see his biography in *History of Broome County, New York* (Binghamton, 1893). For an account of his Yale friendships and their significance, see "Charles S. Hall, *Class Album*," in Yale Manuscripts and Archives. The significance of

networks is difficult to reconstruct without referring to the most minute sorts of materials in the context of particular communities. When one looks at particular places, such as Rochester, New York, one finds collegiate clusters interacting with kinship clusters. Thus, for example, Elisha Strong, Yale 1809, and Heman Norton, Yale 1806, were friends at Yale. In 1807, Norton married Strong's sister. In 1816, Strong bought a tract of land near Rochester with Elisha Beach, Norton's brother-in-law, and moved to New York State. In 1819, Norton followed. In 1825, they moved into Rochester and went into business together. Rochester also possessed a remarkable number of members of the Yale Class of 1787, including James Wadsworth, Gideon Granger, William Kibbe, and Moses Atwater. Similar clusterings can be found in other western cities, including Troy, Utica, Buffalo, Cincinnati, and southern Indiana and Illinois.

51. On the collegiate preferences of firms, see Yale and Harvard classbooks, especially post-1870.

52. Durfee, *Williams Annals*, pp. 375–76.

53. Carl Bode, *The American Lyceum*, p. 19; David Mead, *Yankee Eloquence*, pp. 239ff., shows itineraries of prominent Yankees on their midwestern lecture tours.

54. On the origins of the YMCA, see Horlick *Country Boys and Merchant Princes*. Particularly influential in this effort was Joel Hawes, who also served as a Yale Fellow between 1846 and 1867. The founders of the YMCA in Binghamton were graduates of New England colleges, including Charles S. Hall, Yale 1848. The man who delivered the dedicatory address at the opening of the YMCA in New York in 1852 was Daniel Lord, Yale 1814. His speech would have delighted Dwight, for it embodied all of Dwight's ideas about character: "As he saw it, the success of the YMCA 'will raise up a body of active and influential men on the verge of middle life who shall be the supporters of every public enterprise and the creators of many a private charity. The principles of temperance, moderation, industry, and perseverance which flow from religion can turn your eyes to not a few among our merchants and men of wealth who are examples of social virtue and religion. Soon you will stand in their places and from you will be expected those devotions of wealth to purposes of usefulness which make wealth an honor.'" Quoted in Horlick, p. 236.

55. Dr. Burton, "To the Public: Priestcraft Exposed and Primitive Christianity Defined: A Religious Work" (Lockport, New York, 1828), as quoted in Foster, *Errand of Mercy*, p. 185.

Chapter Nine

1. Tocqueville, *Democracy*, vol. 1, pp. 169–70.

2. Oliver Wendell Holmes, *Elsie Venner*, p. 19.

3. On this point, see Cleveland Amory, *The Proper Bostonians* (New York, 1947).

4. See M. C. Crawford, *Famous Families of Massachusetts* (Boston, 1930). Jules David Prown's biography of John Singleton Copley gives a wonderfully detailed analysis of sitters for Copley portraits. They, like Copley himself, were of the Tory persuasion. It is remarkable how few of Boston's elite as depicted by Copley remained in the city by the end of the Revolution.

5. For wonderful descriptions of the proximity and imtimacy of the Boston clans, see James Jackson Putnam, *Memoir of Dr. James Jackson,* and the correspondence of Henry and Mary Lee, ed. F. R. Morse. See also Henry Adams' discussions of boyhood in ante-bellum Boston in the early chapters of *The Education of Henry Adams* (New York, 1931).

6. *The Oxford English Dictionary* shows that the earliest uses of the term "character" to connote "the groups of traits that have social significance and moral quality" date from

the late eighteenth century. Before that point, the word was used in connection with peculiarities and unique features of persons and objects.

7. Henry Adams, *Education*, pp. 54–55.

8. See the *Harvard Quinquennial Catalogue*.

9. On Harvard expenses, see Ronald Story, *Forging of an Aristocracy*, and Seymour Harris, *The Economics of Harvard*, p. xxiv. The upward shift in expenses at Harvard is in contrast to the situation both at Yale and at the Western colleges. Colin Burke, in "The Quiet Influence," pp. 110ff., shows that ante-bellum colleges did not, on the whole, become inaccessible on financial grounds during this period.

10. Morison, *Three Centuries of Harvard*, p. 174.

11. Morison, p. 196.

12. Morison, pp. 180–83, 202–03; see also T. S. Harding, *College Literary Societies*, pp. 55–86.

13. Morison, p. 232; Ronald Story, *Forging of an Aristocracy*, pp. 109–134. Essential to understanding reform at Harvard in this period is David Tyack's *George Ticknor and the Boston Brahmins* (Cambridge, 1967).

14. The best biography of Josiah Quincy is Edmund Quincy, *The Life of Josiah Quincy* (Boston, 1868).

15. Quincy, p. 438.

16. Ibid.

17. Morison, *Three Centuries of Harvard*, pp. 252–53.

18. Bailey B. Burritt, *Professional Distribution of College and University Graduates* (Washington, D.C., 1912), p. 14.

19. Ronald Story, "Cultural Institutions and Class Consolidation in Boston, 1800–1870" (unpublished Ph.D. dissertation, SUNY at Stony Brook, 1972), p. 43.

20. J. C. Ayer, "Some of the Uses and Abuses in the Management of Our Industrial Corporations" (Lowell, 1863), p. 3.

21. Ayer, p. 5.

22. Ayer, p. 9. An analogous controversy—in this case over the management of testamentary trusts—was publicly waged between the proper Bostonians John Amory Lowell and Edward Brooks. See Edward Brooks, *A Correspondence Between Edward Brooks and John A. Lowell* (Boston, 1847); Edward Brooks, *An Answer to the Pamphlet of Mr. John A. Lowell* (Boston, 1851); and John A. Lowell, *Reply to a Pamphlet Recently Circulated by Mr. Edward Brooks* (Boston, 1848). See also my dissertation, pp. 195–322.

23. On Samuel Atkins Eliot, see Henry James, *Charles William Eliot* (Boston, 1930), pp. 3–35.

24. See also S. A. Eliot, *A Sketch of the History of Harvard College and Its Present State* (Boston, 1848).

25. Harris, in *The Economics of Harvard*, pp. 240–41, is scathingly critical of Eliot's calculations: "Perhaps the most vigorous espousal of the view of greater gains from private than from public contributions is to be found in comments on a study by Samuel A. Eliot in the year 1845. Undoubtedly the emergence of a free enterprise system and its accompanying spawning of millionaires contributed to the increasing acceptance of this view. . . . For the period before 1780, the critic concluded that the government gave only one-third as much as individuals. But in arriving at these conclusions, he omitted the funds given by the government to replace Harvard Hall, which was destroyed by fire in 1764." Morison, on the other hand, uncritically accepts Eliot's assertions.

26. Samuel Atkins Eliot, "Public and Private Charities in Boston," in *North American Review* (July 1845): 156–57.

27. Ibid.

28. Eliot, "Charities": 163–64.

29. "Charities": 164–65.

30. Oliver Wendell Holmes, *Autocrat of the Breakfast Table*, pp. 21–23.

31. On Holmes, see Edwin P. Hoyt, *The Improper Bostonian: Dr. Oliver Wendell Holmes* (New York, 1979).

32. Holmes, *Autocrat*, pp. 119–20.

33. *Autocrat*, pp. 244–45.

34. Ibid.

35. Oliver Wendell Holmes, *Elsie Venner*, p. 15.

36. *Elsie Venner*, p. 16.

37. Tocqueville, *Democracy*, vol. 1, p. 51.

38. Vol. 1, p. 54.

39. Vol. 1, p. 48.

40. Holmes, *Elsie Venner*, pp. 17–18.

41. *Elsie Venner*, p. 28.

42. Ibid.

43. *Elsie Venner*, p. 356.

Chapter Ten

1. Abraham Lincoln, "Springfield Speech," 27 June 1857, in *Complete Works*, ed. Hay and Nicolay, vol. 2, pp. 333–34.

2. "Temperance Speech," 22 February 1842, in *Complete Works*, vol. 1, pp. 207–09.

3. Ibid.

4. "Speech on Subtreasury," 20 December 1839, in *Complete Works*, vol. 1, pp. 115–16.

5. 9 *Pickering's Reports*, 446 (1830).

6. 460–61.

7. "Report from the Majority of the House Committee on Finance, December 18, 1838, Mr. Lincoln Its Probable Author," in *Uncollected Works of Abraham Lincoln*, ed. R. R. Wilson (Elmira, 1947), vol. 1, p. 351.

8. "Fragment on Sectionalism," 1 October 1856, in *Uncollected Works*, vol. 2, p. 303.

9. "Speech at Peoria," 16 October 1854, in *Uncollected Works*, vol. 2, p. 205.

10. Edmund Wilson, *Patriotic Core: Studies in the Literature of the American Civil War* (New York, 1966), p. 38.

11. Charles W. Eliot, "Views Respecting the Present Exemption from Taxation of Property Used for Religious, Educational, and Charitable Purposes," in Harvard University, *Annual Report* (Cambridge, 1875), p. 369.

12. Eliot, *Annual Report*, p. 371.

13. *Annual Report*, pp. 271–72.

Chapter Eleven

1. Tocqueville, *Democracy*, vol. 2, pp. 292–93.

2. *Harvard Memorial Biographies*, ed. Thomas Wentworth Higginson (Cambridge, 1866), p. iv.

3. Higginson, *Harvard Biographies*, p. v.

4. Eliot Ellsworth, *Yale in the Civil War* (New Haven, 1932), p. vii; for the war service of graduates of other colleges, see catalogues of graduates. Princeton's attitudes towards the war are discussed in T. J. Wertenbaker, *Princeton, 1746–1896* (Princeton, 1946).

5. Ellsworth, *Yale in the Civil War*, pp. 60–61.

6. These estimates of service are low, since I have only counted college graduates. Had I counted non-graduates and degree holders from the professional schools, the figures would have come out very much higher, especially for the post-1855 classes. Had it been possible to count government service by matriculants of these institutions in non-military government service, the figures would have come out higher still. Thus, while one might quibble with my exact figures, particularly with my use of the whole white population between 15 and 50 as a source of potential military manpower, I doubt that any greater degree of statistical sophistication would dispute my basic finding—that college men were more likely to serve the Union than the population as a whole.

7. G. V. Henry, *Military Record of Civilian Appointments in the United States Army* (New York, 1869).

8. F. A. P. Barnard, in the "Declining Popularity of Collegiate Education" (New York, 1866), estimates that between one male in eighty-three and one man in sixty-four of the white population were college educated. The representation of college men in the civilian appointments to the United States Army was about two in ten.

9. The bulk of the civilian appointments was from New York and Pennsylvania. Of the college men among these, over half were graduates of New England colleges.

10. Ellsworth, *Yale in the Civil War*, p. 67.

11. Ellsworth, p. 72.

12. Although the early genealogical societies were first established in Boston and other cities in the northeast, the contents of their libraries were soon dominated by works penned by migrant branches of New England families. The lists of "Corresponding Members" of the New England Historic Genealogical Society before 1900 are revealing in this regard.

13. The original twenty-three members of the Sanitary Commission included four Yale graduates, four Columbia graduates, two Harvard graduates, one Brown graduate, one Middlebury graduate, and three West Pointers. I have been unable to ascertain the affiliation of the remaining eight members.

14. George Frederickson, *The Inner Civil War: Northern Intellectuals and the Crisis of the Union* (New York, 1965), p. 102.

15. Frederickson, p. 105.

16. *Historical Statistics of the United States, Colonial Times to 1957* (Washington, D.C., 1961), p. 710.

17. *Historical Statistics*, p. 711.

18.< Leonard D. White, *The Jacksonians: A Study in Administrative History, 1829–1861* (New York, 1954), pp. 550–51. One wonders why White omitted the Civil War period in his four-volume study of national administration. Curiously, we know next to nothing about either civil or military management during this period.

19. Stephen E. Ambrose, *Duty, Honor, Country*, pp. 106ff.

20. Fred Albert Shannon, *The Organization and Administration of the Union Army, 1861–5* (Gloucester, Mass., 1947), vol. 1, pp. 259ff.; Emory Upton, *The Military Policy of the United States* (New York, 1881), pp. 227ff.

21. Ambrose, *Duty, Honor, Country*, pp. 173ff.; Shannon, *Union Army*, vol. 1, pp. 159ff.

22. Shannon, vol. 1, pp. 53–150.

23. William A. Ganoe, *History of the United States Army* (New York, 1924).

24. Ganoe, pp. 248ff.; Upton pp. 444ff.

25. On the early history of West Point, see Ambrose, *Duty, Honor, Country*, and Joseph Ellis, *School for Soldiers: West Point and the Profession of Arms* (New York, 1974).

26. Ambrose, p. 120.

27. Ambrose, pp. 62–86. On the careers of West Point graduates, see G. W. Callum,

Biographical Register of Officers and Graduates of the United States Military Academy (New York, 1863).

28. Percentage of Yale and Harvard graduates entering law and business, classes of 1821–1870 (Source: Burritt, *Professional Distribution of College and University Graduates*, pp. 14, 22.

Years of Graduation	Law		Business	
	Harvard	Yale	Harvard	Yale
1821–25	18%	32%	5%	8%
1826–30	35%	25%	12%	9%
1831–35	32%	32%	13%	5%
1836–40	28%	28%	7%	11%
1841–45	36%	33%	9%	12%
1846–50	32%	34%	14%	15%
1851–55	33%	31%	15%	18%
1856–60	34%	26%	22%	20%
1861–65	24%	28%	29%	24%
1866–70	31%	35%	28%	22%

29. Thomas Cochran, *Railroad Leaders, 1845–1890: The Business Mind in Action* (Cambridge, 1953), pp. 250ff.

30. Thomas M. Johnson and Barry Supple, *Boston Capitalists and Western Railroads* (Cambridge, 1967) is a definitive account of the role of Bostonians in the development of the western transportation network.

31. *The Railroads*, ed. Alfred D. Chandler (New York, 1965), pp. 97–100.

32. Arthur Twining Hadley, "The Railroad in its Business Relations," in *The American Railway*, ed. Thomas M. Cooley (New York, 1893), p. 346. This book is one of the most interesting primary sources on American railroading. It contains articles by leading figures in all fields of management, operation, and finance.

33. Chandler, *Railroads*, pp. 97–98.

34. For sources on early railroad managers, see biographies in Callum, Dexter, the Harvard necrologies and classbooks, and the catalogues of Dartmouth, Princeton, Columbia, Bowdoin, and Williams.

35. Chandler, *Railroads*, pp. 43–47; Vincent Y. Carosso, *Investment Banking in America* (Cambridge, 1970), pp. 29ff. Carosso's book, though excellent, is only a first step—focusing primarily on the history of Kidder, Peabody. A thorough, social history-oriented account of investment banking (and of American business generally) is very much needed.

36. On Stanton, see B. P. Thomas and H. M. Hyman, *Stanton: The Life and Times of Lincoln's Secretary of War* (New York, 1962). Their description of the early relations between Lincoln and Stanton during their stints as corporate lawyers is a fascinating case study in the nature of the culture of organization.

37. Thomas and Hyman, *Stanton*, pp. 143ff.

38. *Stanton*, p. 153.

39. The best biography of Halleck is Stephen E. Ambrose, *Halleck: Lincoln's Chief of Staff* (Baton Rouge, 1962). See also Callum, *Officers and Graduates*, vol. 1, pp. 573–74. The best history of Halleck's administrative reforms is Emory Upton, *The Military Policy of the United States* (New York, 1881). Upton was a disciple of Halleck's and Upton's, whose writings would serve as the basis for a final and permanent creation of staff organization in the

army in the Progressive Era. (On this, see S. E. Ambrose, *Upton and the Army* (New York, 1964.)

40. The graduates of Middlebury, Dartmouth, Colby, Amherst, and Bowdoin appear to have been especially prominent in these administrative roles. The graduates of Harvard and Yale, on the other hand, seem to have preferred more visible positions as "leaders of men."

41. Bliss Perry, *Life and Letters of Henry Lee Higginson* (Boston, 1921), p. 64.

42. See Gabriel Kolko, "Brahmins and Business," pp. 349–52.

43. Thomas Wentworth Higginson, *Cheerful Yesterdays* (Boston, 1898), pp. 269–70.

44. Edmund Wilson, *Patriotic Gore*, pp. 743–96; Frederickson, *The Inner Civil War*, pp. 151–80; Merle Curti, *The Growth of American Thought* (New York, 1964), pp. 552–56.

45. *The Inner Civil War*, pp. 175–76.

46. See the chart from Burritt, *Professional Distribution of College and University Graduates*, reproduced above in note 28. Colin Burke does not find any great shifts in occupational choice among American college graduates during this period. He, of course, was counting a far larger population than the graduates of Harvard and Yale. The fact that the graduates from Cambridge and New Haven shift towards business as a major occupational choice thirty years before most other collegians do is highly significant. It may account in large part for their early dominance in the financial centers of the northeast.

47. For the classes graduating from Harvard and Yale between 1851 and 1855, the percentages entering business were fifteen and eighteen percent, respectively. By the classes graduating between 1856 and 1860, the proportion had increased to twenty-three and twenty percent; by 1861–65, twenty-nine and twenty-five percent.

48. I am well aware of the fact that the social setting into which Alger placed his heroes more closely resembled the personalized commercial world of the 1830s than the corporate world of the 70s. The significance of Alger and his popularity lies not in the accuracy of his portrayal of business institutions, but in his favorable attitudes towards business and earned wealth.

Chapter Twelve

1. Tocqueville, *Democracy*, vol. 2, p. 41.

2. Charles W. Eliot, "The New Education," in *Atlantic Monthly* (February 1869): 225.

3. George Rogers Taylor and Irene D. Neu, *The American Railroad Network, 1861–1890* (Cambridge, 1956), p. 32.

4. Robert L. Thompson, *Wiring a Continent: A History of the Telegraph Industry in the United States, 1832–1886* (Princeton, 1947), p. 39.

5. According to Thompson, the investment bankers of Boston, New York, and Philadelphia were uninterested in the telegraph industry until the 1860s. Major financing came from smaller groups of entrepreneurs, especially a group in upper New York State that included Ezra Cornell.

6. The clearest account of Civil War financing is contained in Paul B. Trescott, *Financing American Enterprise* (New York, 1963).

7. Trescott, p. 46.

8. Carosso, *Investment Banking*, p. 15.

9. On the national character of fundraising by charitable and educational organizations, see Allmendinger, *Paupers and Scholars*, pp. 64–78.

10. Ellis P. Oberholtzer, *Jay Cooke, Financier* (New York, 1907), pp. 1–50.

11. Taylor and Neu, *Railroad Notebook*, pp. 16ff.

12. Thompson, *Wiring a Continent*, p. 370.

13. Thompson, p. 374.

14. Thompson, p. 415.

15. Carosso, *Investment Banking*, pp. 29ff.

16. Carosso, p. 52.

17. Carosso, p. 21.

18. Francis L. Eames, *The New York Stock Exchange* (New York, 1894) gives the only published lists that I know of members of the exchange and the years that they joined. The lists, however, are incomplete—showing only those individuals still living in 1894. Strangely, there has been no modern history written of this organization.

19. Thomas Cochran and William Miller, *Age of Enterprise* (New York, 1961), p. 137.

20. Carosso, *Investment Banking*, p. 25.

21. Carosso, pp. 27ff.

22. Cochran and Miller, *Age of Enterprise*, p. 137.

23. Cochran and Miller, p. 142.

24. Gabriel Kolko, *The Triumph of Conservatism* (New York, 1963).

25. Thomas Haskell, *The Emergence of a Professional Social Science: The American Social Science Association and the Nineteenth Century Crisis of Authority* (Urbana, 1977).

26. For a useful discussion and a helpful bibliography on this point, see Burton J. Bledstein, *The Culture of Professionalism* (New York, 1976), pp. 80–128.

27. The consummate expression of this protofascistic notion of subordination to professionals is Herbert Croly's *The Promise of American Life*. In my opinion, John Dewey preached the same doctrines using a more libertarian rhetoric.

28. Hugh Hawkins, *Between Harvard and America* (New York, 1972), pp. 198–223.

29. On the attitudes of Harvard and Yale towards their own scientific schools, see Morison, *Three Centuries of Harvard*; and Kelley, *Yale—A History*, pp. 357ff.

30. This point, originally made by John Perry Miller, chief of the Campaign for Yale and Professor of Economics, is born out by figures in Sears and Harris. The fact is that the main source of alumni support for private universities is among the graduates of the colleges, not of the postgraduate schools. And the bulk of their money goes to the undergraduate components.

31. Lawrence Veysey, *The Emergence of the American University* (Chicago, 1965), pp. 165ff.

32. Quoted in Veysey, p. 161.

33. Quoted in Hawkins, *Between Harvard and America*, p. 201.

34. Veysey, *The Emergence of the American University*, p. 39; see also Hawkins, *Between Harvard and America*, p. 43.

35. *American Higher Education*, ed. Hofstadter and Smith, vol. 1, pp. 287–88.

36. Quoted in *American Higher Education*, vol. 2, pp. 608–09.

37. vol. 2, p. 621.

38. Veysey, *The Emergence of the American University*, p. 88.

39. Charles W. Eliot, "The New Education," in *Atlantic Monthly* (February 1869): 214.

40. Quoted in *American Higher Education*, vol. 2, p. 614.

41. Holmes, *Elsie Venner*, p. 18.

42. Ibid.

43. Bliss Perry, *Henry Lee Higginson*, p. 329.

44. Eliot, "Inaugural," quoted in *American Higher Education*, vol. 2, p. 614.

45. "The New Education," *Atlantic Monthly* (February 1869): 203.

46. "Inaugural," *American Higher Education*, vol. 2, pp. 623–24.

47. vol. 2, p. 614; see Hawkins, *Between Harvard and America*, p. 12.

48. W. A. Richardson, "How President Eliot Was Elected," *Harvard Graduates Magazine* 7 (1899): 535–37; Morison, *Three Centuries of Harvard*, pp. 323–27; and Hawkins, pp. 45–49.

49. Richardson, p. 536.

50. Thomas Haskell, *The Emergence of a Professional Social Science*, pp. 73–74; Hawkins, *Between Harvard and America*, p. 208.

51. Eliot, "The New Education," p. 216.

52. "The New Education," p. 210.

53. p. 208.

54. See also the quotations from Eliot in Hawkins, pp. 152–56.

55. Timothy Dwight, *Memories of Yale Life and Men* (New Haven, 1903) and Kelley, *Yale— A History*, pp. 273ff.

56. Harris, *The Economics of Harvard*, p. 358; "Statement of the Funds of Yale College, January 1, 1869," *Treasurer's Papers*, Yale; Kelley, p. 276.

57. Alfred D. Chandler and Louis Galambos, "The Development of Large-Scale Economic Enterprise in Modern America," in *Men and Organizations*, ed. Edwin J. Perkins (New York, 1977), p. 190.

58. On the strength of informal ties of coordination, see my dissertation, pp. 396–97.

59. Ibid.

60. Gerald T. White, *History of the Massachusetts Hospital Life Insurance Company* (Cambridge, 1957), p. 53.

61. Eliot, "Inaugural," in *American Higher Education*, vol. 2, p. 618.

62. See my dissertation, p. 167.

63. Harris, *The Economics of Harvard*, p. 3.

64. See my dissertation, p. 477.

65. Harvard University, *Report of the President 1880–81*, pp. 21–22.

66. Henry Adams, *Education*, p. 41. The definitive work on boarding schools is James McLachlan's *American Boarding Schools*.

67. Morison, *Three Centuries of Harvard*, p. 417.

68. Morison, p. 359.

69. This came especially to be the case after the graduation of the elder Morgan's son, J. P. Morgan, Jr., from Harvard in 1889.

70. On the Harvard origins of the preparedness movement, see John G. Clifford, *The Citizen Soldiers: The Plattsburg Training Camp Movement, 1913–1920* (Lexington, Ky., 1972), pp. 54–91.

71. Haskell, *The Emergence of a Professional Social Science*, pp. 92–97.

72. Haskell, p. 95.

73. Hawkins, *Between Harvard and America*, pp. 176–80.

74. Henry Lee Higginson to C. A. Coffin, 1911; in Perry, *Higginson*, pp. 446–47.

75. Higginson to C. W. Eliot, 19 December 1914; in Perry, pp. 444–45.

76. Higginson to F. W. Taussig, 16 March 1913; in Perry, pp. 447–48.

77. Higginson to Taussig, 20 March 1913; in Perry, p. 450.

78. See Perry, p. 433.

79. Eliot, "Inaugural," in *American Higher Education*, vol. 2, p. 618.

80. Quoted in Hawkins, *Between Harvard and America*, p. 216.

81. Thorstein Veblen, *The Higher Learning in America* (New York, 1957), p. 59.

Conclusion

1. Herbert Croly, *The Promise of American Life* (New York, 1909), pp. 438–39.

2. Croly, p. 428.

3. Henry Adams, *Education*, pp. 300–01.

4. Adams, pp. 20–21.

5. Adams, pp. 305–06.

6. Adams, p. 4.
7. Adams, p. 22.
8. Adams, pp. 315–41, 343.
9. Adams, p. 343.
10. Adams, p. 421.
11. Adams, pp. 421–22.
12. Adams, pp. 288–89.
13. Adams, p. 421.
14. For an example of this approach, see Richard Barnet, *The Roots of War* (New York, 1976).

Index